# EGYPT IN REVOLUTION

# EGYPT
# in Revolution

## An Economic Analysis

### CHARLES ISSAWI

*Professor of Near and Middle East Economics,*
*Columbia University*

*Issued under the auspices of the*
*Royal Institute of International Affairs*
OXFORD UNIVERSITY PRESS
LONDON NEW YORK TORONTO

*Oxford University Press, Amen House, London E.C.4*

GLASGOW   NEW YORK   TORONTO   MELBOURNE   WELLINGTON
BOMBAY   CALCUTTA   MADRAS   KARACHI   LAHORE   DACCA
CAPE TOWN   SALISBURY   NAIROBI   IBADAN   ACCRA
KUALA LUMPUR   HONG KONG

*First published* 1963
*Reprinted* 1965

*Printed in Great Britain*

*To*
*the memory of my father*
*and to my mother*

# Preface

This is my third attempt at presenting an economic study of Egypt; I can assure the reader that there will not be a fourth. The first study, *Egypt: an Economic and Social Analysis*, written in Cairo in 1942–3 and published in 1947, ran out of print and then was somewhat belatedly banned by the censor under the old régime. The second, *Egypt at Mid-Century*, an extensively revised edition, written in New York in 1952–3 and published in 1954, had a much smoother passage but eventually also ran out of print. The present work was prepared in Cairo, Beirut, and London in 1961–2. Except for the first chapter, which gives the indispensable historical background, this book has been completely rewritten. In some chapters, however, the previous framework has been retained, since it seemed the most logical one, and where things have not changed, either reference has been made to the earlier book or, where the argument needed it, the salient paragraphs have been reproduced.

The writing of a new book has been made necessary by the fact that, in the course of the last ten years, Egypt has undergone more radical changes than at any time in its long history, with the possible exception of the 1820's. Like so many underdeveloped countries, Egypt is passing through a number of superimposed revolutions: a nationalist upsurge, an internal shift in the balance of classes, a social awakening, a demographic explosion, an agricultural revolution and an industrial revolution, not to mention the ever-accelerating 'revolution of rising expectations'. But in addition, in the last year, it has embarked on a socialist experiment.

All this raises great difficulties for the student. In the first place, many institutions are in flux and it is almost impossible to keep up with the changes which are occurring daily. It seems likely that several of the statements made in this book will have become obsolete by the time it is published. But the outlines of the new order being forged are clear, and the experiment under way is important enough, and sufficiently advanced, to warrant description, analysis, and judgement.

The second obstacle is the lack of material; in the last few months it has become much more difficult to obtain information on most aspects of the Egyptian economy. Since the situation is unlikely to improve in the foreseeable future, it seemed pointless to hold up research in the hope of getting more material. But quite a few questions have had, perforce, to remain unanswered. For the same reason, however, a good deal of detailed information has been included, which cannot be easily found elsewhere and which is not likely to be made available in the next few years.

Several persons have helped me greatly in writing this book and I only wish I could thank them all in this preface. I cannot, however, fail to mention Dr Gabriel Saab, who allowed me to draw on his collection of material on Egyptian agriculture, Mr A. H. Hourani, Professor Bernard Lewis, and Miss Elizabeth Monroe who read the manuscript and made some very helpful comments, and Miss Hermia Oliver who edited it. I should also like to acknowledge the financial assistance I have received. Part of the research and writing was done during a sabbatical leave in which I held Guggenheim and Social Science Research Council Fellowships for the study of the recent economic history of the Arab countries. Needless to say, neither institution is in any way responsible for any of the statements made or views expressed in this book. The Royal Institute of International Affairs also assisted me with a research grant and showed great helpfulness and patience in rather difficult circumstances.

But above all I wish to express my deep gratitude to my wife who read every word (but not every figure), subjected the text to the severest criticism, made most valuable suggestions, and typed a far from clear manuscript.

C. I.

*July 1962*

# Contents

ix

# Tables

# Note on Sources

Each chapter in this book tends to rely on specialist sources; for this reason no general bibliography has been included but only a list of the principal UAR official periodical publications (p. 333). In regard to all other publications, with the exception of those included in the 'Abbreviations' below, each work is cited in full at the first mention but thereafter is given more briefly; for example, when only one work by an author is cited, his name only is given after the first reference. Unless otherwise indicated, and with the exception of publications by international bodies such as the United Nations, all English-language titles are published in London, all French in Paris, and all Arabic in Cairo. All official publications cited without the name of the issuing government are to be presumed to be UAR official publications.

# Abbreviations

| | |
|---|---|
| *Ann. stat.* | *Annuaire statistique.* |
| *Buhuth* | Société égyptienne d'économie politique, de statistique et de législation, *Buhuth al-id al-khamsini, 1909–59* (1960). |
| *Cadre du Plan* | National Planning Committee, *Cadre du Plan Quinquennal Général.* |
| CBE, *Econ. R.* | Central Bank of Egypt, *Economic Review.* |
| *Coll. Basic Statist. Data* | Dept. of Statistics, *Majmuat al-bayanat al-ihsa'a al-asasia* (Collection of Basic Statistical Data), 1961. |
| *Econ. Dev. & Cult. Change* | *Economic Development and Cultural Change.* |
| *Ég. contemp.* | *Égypte contemporaine.* |
| *Ég. indust.* | *Égypte industrielle.* |
| IMF | International Monetary Fund. |
| *Int. Aff.* | *International Affairs.* |
| INP | Institute of National Planning (UAR). |
| Issawi: *Egypt; EMC* | C. Issawi, *Egypt; an Economic and Social Analysis* (1947); *Egypt at Mid-Century: an Economic Survey* (1954). |
| *J. Econ. Hist.* | *Journal of Economic History.* |
| *M.E. Econ. Papers* | American Univ. of Beirut, *Middle East Economic Papers.* |
| NBE, *Econ. B.* | National Bank of Egypt, *Economic Bulletin.* |
| NPC | National Planning Committee (UAR). |
| *Pol. Sci. Q.* | *Political Science Quarterly.* |
| *R. écon. & financ.* | *Revue économique et financière.* |
| *Yb.* | *Yearbook.* |

# Units of Measurement and Symbols

One Egyptian pound (£E)=100 piastres (PT)=1,000 millièmes (m/m)=
£1 0s. 6d.=$2.87

| | |
|---|---|
| 1 feddan | =1·038 acres=4,201 sq. metres |
| 1 cantar of cotton (cr.) | =99 lb=45 kg |
| 1 metric cantar of cotton | =50 kg |
| 1 ardeb of cotton-seed | =2·70 cantars |
| 1 ardeb of wheat | =150 kg approx. |
| 1 ardeb of maize | =140 kg approx. |
| 1 dariba of rice | =935 kg approx. |
| 1 rotl | =0·99 lb=449 grammes |
| | |
| .. | =data not available |
| — | =nil or negligible |
| / between dates | =fiscal or financial year, e.g. 1956/7 |
| – between dates | =full period involved, including beginning and end years, e.g. 1954–6 |
| (  ) around a figure | =estimated figure, e.g. (20) |

# I

# The Background

---

*A capacity for conservation exceeding that of any other country in the world.*

S. R. K. GLANVILLE.

*Ce magnifique Delta, où il ne manque qu'un gouvernement libre et un peuple heureux.*

CHATEAUBRIAND.

### GEOGRAPHICAL

Egypt, or the United Arab Republic as it became after the union with Syria in February 1958 and as it is still officially designated in spite of the dissolution of that union in September 1961, lies in the desert belt which stretches across the northern hemisphere from the Atlantic Ocean through Arabia and Iran to the heart of China, and which forms the main habitat of the Islamic peoples. Apart from the narrow Mediterranean fringe, Egypt receives practically no rain during the whole of the year, and but for the Nile would have been as barren as the Sahara or the Libyan Desert.

The area of Egypt is 1 million square kilometres, or 386,000 square miles. Its topography is fairly simple. Along the Red Sea runs a mountain range with peaks of over 7,000 feet high which, after subsiding somewhat in the Sudan, rises again to considerable heights in Eritrea and Abyssinia.[1] The river valley itself offers some interesting peculiarities. From Aswan to Cairo it runs between two parallel ranges of hills, in certain places some miles apart, in others only a few hundred yards. North of Cairo stretches the Delta, formed by secular deposits of alluvial mud in what was once a broad estuary. The configuration of the Delta has been likened to the back of a leaf, the river and canal banks—which correspond to the veins of the leaf—being higher than the adjoining land. It is this fact which renders the danger of a Nile flood so terrible and makes it imperative to keep a careful watch over the river banks. To the west of the Nile

---

[1] For the physical and economic geography of Egypt see Raye R. Platt & Mohammed B. Hefny, *Egypt: a compendium* (NY, 1958); Jacques Besançon, *L'Homme et le Nil* (1957); L. Gordonov, *Yegipet* (Moscow, 1953).

lie the Libyan hills which gently subside into the Western Desert, a broad flat plain in some of the depressions of which are a series of scattered oases.

As regards climate, the year falls into two parts: a cool winter, from November to April, and a hot summer, from May to October, ushered in by the Khamsin, a scorching wind from the south. There is no rainfall in summer and very little in winter, except along the coast. Spring and autumn, as understood by Europeans, are un-known, not only because there is no climatic break between winter and summer, but also because practically no trees shed their leaves in winter while crops ripen not only in July and August but also in April and May. Except for the variations in temperature there is little difference between the seasons, and Egypt is deprived of the bracing effect of the sudden cyclonic changes which take place in Western Europe.

The vegetation faithfully reflects the regularity of the climate. The traveller passing through the country is struck by the monotony of the landscape, and is hardly conscious of any difference between the region just south of Alexandria and that immediately north of Aswan. He will be especially impressed by the contrast between Egypt and Palestine, where the sub-alpine regions of Mount Hermon are only a few miles away from the sub-tropical Jordan valley. The fact that Egypt's 6 million acres of cultivated land are strung out over eight degrees of latitude does, however, make for a certain diversity. In the north vines, apricots, and even apple-trees can be seen, while sugar-cane flourishes in the south. Yet maize, wheat, millet, and cotton, the principal crops, can be found all over the country.

No description of Egypt, however brief, can fail to mention the Nile. One of the most remarkable of rivers geographically, and historically perhaps the most important of them all, the Nile[1] has from time immemorial irrigated and fertilized Egypt's soil, served as its principal means of communication, and opened a gate into Central Africa. From the earliest times the main effort of the Egyptians has been directed towards the fullest possible utilization of the life-giving waters of their river. And today the much-quoted

[1] For a scholarly and readable account of the geography of the Nile valley and the utilization of Nile waters see H. E. Hurst, *The Nile* (1952). For a thorough study of the historical records relating to the Nile, which throws light on several aspects of Egyptian economic history, see William Popper, *The Cairo Nilometer* (Berkeley, Cal., 1951).

saying of Herodotus that Egypt is the gift of the Nile has lost none of its truth.

By the time it flows into Egypt, the waters of the Nile have been swollen from three main sources: the Atbara and Blue Nile originating in Abyssinia, and the White Nile whose source is just below the Equator. The White Nile, after issuing from Lake Victoria and passing through Lake Albert, flows northward to the Sudd or swamp region. Here it is joined by several tributaries of which the main ones are the Bahr al-Ghazal and Sobat. At Khartum the White Nile is met by the Blue Nile, flowing from Lake Tana, and at Atbara by the Atbara river, after which no further tributaries are received.

The most peculiar feature of the Nile is the seasonal flood between July and December, when an average rise in the level of the river of $7\frac{1}{2}$ metres is registered at Aswan and $4\frac{1}{2}$ metres at Cairo. The flood water is carried by the Blue Nile and Atbara, which in summer are turbulent torrents. The waters of the White Nile, regulated by their passage through the lakes and diminished by the enormous amount of evaporation over the Sudd, flow much more evenly and in winter supply the bulk of the discharge.[1]

It would seem that cultivation was first practised systematically in the Nile valley. At first snatch crops were probably grown on the moist soil after the recession of the flood waters. Later, in order to take the fullest possible advantage of the Nile water and alluvium, great banks of earth were raised, transversal to the river, dividing the land into basins. The banks served to retain the water a little longer during the flood and the basins were further irrigated by canals which brought them water from a slightly higher level upstream. This system of basin irrigation, still practised in certain parts of Upper Egypt, had, by ensuring a regular flow of water and an annual fertilization of the soil, made Egyptian agriculture one of the most stable in the world. Its abandonment for perennial irrigation, though it has increased the return of the land, has upset a centuries-old balance and raised several acute problems which will be described in later chapters.

## HISTORICAL

The national character and cultural background of a people are formed by its history as well as its environment, but not all the

---

[1] At its peak, around 8 September, the Nile discharges about 712 m. cubic metres per day, of which 70 m. are contributed by the White Nile, 485 m. by the Blue Nile and 157 m. by the Atbara. The minimum discharge, around 16 May, is about 45 m. cubic metres, of which 37·5 m. come from the White Nile and 7·5 m. from the Blue Nile (Hurst, p. 242).

events in its history contribute in an equal measure. Some are fleeting and leave a transient impression, others recur rhythmically or remain constant and deeply mark the nation. Egyptian history shows a remarkable series of constant features from the time of the Pharaohs to the nineteenth century.

## Unity

The first of these features is the unbroken unity of the country throughout its six or seven millennia of history. From the time that Menes unified Upper and Lower Egypt and founded the first dynasty up to the present day the land has always—except for brief periods during the Old and Middle Empires—had a single government. This unity may be explained in several ways. There is, first of all, the small size of the country and the fact that it is in effect a large oasis naturally bounded by sea and desert. There is also the flatness of the land, which makes it difficult for the inhabitants to resist an invader successfully once their sea or desert defences have been broken, and ensures a rapid conquest of the country by the enemy who has been able to obtain a secure foothold. (The only noteworthy exceptions are the Fatimid expedition of 935 which was driven out of Alexandria and the two invasions by the Crusaders, in 1163 and 1249, the first of which was beaten off near Cairo, the second at Mansura; neither the Turks, who reached the Suez Canal in 1915, nor the Germans, who were stopped at El Alamein in 1942, quite succeeded in breaking through Egypt's desert defences.) There is finally the vital fact that irrigation has to be planned and executed in terms of the country as a whole and cannot be safely left to independent authorities.

But whatever the cause, one effect of this long unity has been to blend the people of Egypt in a perhaps unparalleled degree of racial and temperamental homogeneity, sharply marking them off from their neighbours. The inhabitants of the Delta may be lighter in skin than those of Upper Egypt, but there is little difference in their build, their features, their psychological make-up or their ways of thought, while even the differences in idiom are negligible when compared with those prevailing in other countries—a striking contrast is provided by Jordan, Lebanon, and Syria, where almost every village has its own distinct mode of speech and where the swarthy, curly-haired beduin may be seen jostling blue-eyed, white-skinned high-landers. Foreign racial elements have of course often burst into Egypt, notably the Greeks, the Arabs, the Circassians, and Turks, but they have mostly been absorbed by the old national stock and can be distinguished only in the larger towns. To quote an Egyptian authority:

That the Egyptian people have more or less preserved the characteristics of their Pharaonic ancestors up to the present time is probably due to the fact that rural Egypt has always been the main reservoir which fed the cities with inhabitants. With the exception of the Arab conquerors, foreigners coming to Egypt settled in the cities. The Arab conquerors were not settlers at all, they were beduin tribes who lived and still live in tents on the outskirts of the valley. They had blood theories and noma-dic habits which kept them from intermarriage with the fellahin. Only the aristocracy—the army generals and the tribe leaders who came in the wake of the conquest—settled in the cities to trade.... With each invasion, the influx of foreign blood would alter the Egyptian physiognomy in the cities, but with succeeding generations of emigrants from rural districts, the foreign characteristics became submerged and the national type once more predominated.[1]

*Foreign Domination*

The second striking feature is the long period of foreign domina-tion, stretching unbroken from the Persian conquest in 525 B.C. to the nineteenth century. The Persians were ousted by the Mace-donians, who in turn had to make way for the Romans (in 30 B.C.). The Arabs wrested the country from the Byzantines in A.D. 640–2, and for about two centuries Egypt was successively governed from Madina, Damascus, and Baghdad. In 868 the Turk Ahmad Ibn Tulun felt strong enough to set up a dynasty of his own, which was supplanted by that of Muhammad al-Ikhshid, also a Turk. In 969 the heretical Fatimids overran the country from the west, founded Cairo, and inaugurated one of the most brilliant periods in the history of Egypt. In 1163 Egypt was saved from the Crusaders by the famous Kurd, Salah al-Din al-Ayyuby, who took over the government from the last of the Fatimids. The Ayyubid dynasty was supplanted by the Mamluks, a praetorian guard of Turkish and Circassian slaves,[2] who preserved their racial identity by

[1] M. M. Mosharrafa, *Cultural Survey of Modern Egypt* (1947), pt. 1, p. 17.
[2] Strictly speaking the word slave is a misnomer when applied to the Mamluks who enjoyed many rights normally not granted to slaves, such as property and inheritance. Both the wives and the children of Mamluks were free. If dissatisfied with their master, Mamluks could ask to be sold to another. Moreover many came to Egypt of their own free will, not as captives. In many ways the Mamluks were more like soldiers of fortune than slaves (Subhi Wihida, *Fi usul al-masala al-misriya* (1951), pp. 58–65).

continually importing fresh recruits.[1] After a temporary eclipse following the Turkish conquest of 1516, the Mamluks had by the eighteenth century regained their power, paying a perfunctory allegiance to the nominal authority of the Sultan and his representative, the Pasha.

For over twenty-five centuries, then, Egypt was never ruled by Egyptians. The seat of government might be in Persepolis, Rome, Constantinople, Damascus, Baghdad; or it might be in Alexandria or Cairo. But the rulers, the army, and the higher ranks of the bureaucracy were almost without exception foreigners whose one thought was to squeeze the utmost out of the fellahin, from whom they generally kept aloof. With the passage of time, the native population reasserted itself and would begin to occupy important positions in the state and to influence both policy and culture. This phenomenon may be clearly discerned under the later Ptolemies, during the last centuries of Byzantine rule, and under the Fatimids and Ayyubids. Each time, however, the newly emergent Egyptians were once more submerged by a fresh wave of conquerors and subjected to a new ruling class (the Romans, Arabs, Circassians, and Turks).

## Autocracy and Centralization

From the time of the Pharaohs, through the reigns of the Ptolemies, the Roman and Arab governors, and the Turkish kings and pashas, all administration was concentrated in the hands of the ruler and a few chosen ministers, and no initiative whatsoever was left to the provinces, except during the eighteenth century when Egypt was in effect partitioned into zones of influence among the beys and beduin shaikhs.[2] Unlike most countries, Egypt has not, during the last two millennia, had a hereditary landed aristocracy, with traditions of local autonomy. For, in the first place, the central government never broke down as completely as it did in Europe during the Dark and early Middle Ages. Secondly, the upper classes devoted their attention either to trade or to war, never to agriculture, and dwelt exclusively in the cities. Thus 'whereas the English aristocrat despised trade and settled in the country where the baron became the squire, the Arab aristocrat of the seventh century . . . eventually became the merchant prince of Cairo, Damascus or

[1] Many Mamluks married Egyptian women, but their offspring were not eligible for admission to the army or to military and political offices.

[2] H. A. R. Gibb and Harold Bowen, *Islamic Society and the West* (1950), i/1, p. 17.

Baghdad'.[1] Similarly the Mamluk warriors lived mostly in Cairo and the larger cities, and their children were excluded from the military caste. The only families which maintained their continuity over several generations were urban families of traders, men of law, and officials, who were too close to the central government to develop a spirit of independence. As was noted by a brilliant French scholar: 'Il n'y a pas de noblesse terrienne en Islam, il n'y a pas de Monsieur de. . . .'[2]

The result of all this has been greatly to weaken individualistic feeling and completely to suppress the spirit of municipal enterprise. Several millennia of centralized autocracy have accustomed Egyptians to look to the government to initiate any business whatsoever. At the same time the rapacity of the governors has led to a profound distrust of the government, the effects of which are still visible.

## Exploitation

In addition to political oppression, Egypt has always suffered from intensive economic exploitation. Some idea of the extent of this exploitation may be obtained by reckoning the amount of human labour which went to the erection of the Pyramids of Giza.[3] It is true that this monstrous sacrifice of the nation to its Pharaohs was more than even the docile Egyptians could stand and seems to have led to serious popular risings; but conditions under the later Pharaohs did not show any improvement, as is witnessed by the following letter written by a Middle Empire scribe to his son:

I have seen the blacksmith at work, at the mouth of the furnace. His fingers are as rough as a crocodile's skin. He stinks like the egg of a fish. Does any metal worker enjoy more rest than a labourer? His fields are in the woods, his tools are made of metal. At night, free in name, he goes on working. His arms work all day long and at night he has to watch over the fire.

The stonecutter plies away at all kinds of hard stone. When his work is over and his arms worn out he seeks some rest. Crouching from dawn, his knees and spine are broken down. . . .

I shall tell you of the bricklayer. Disease has its fill of him for he is exposed to downpours of rain, painfully laying his bricks, tied to the

---

[1] Mosharrafa, pt. I, p. 17.

[2] Jacques Weulersse, *Paysans de Syrie et du Proche-Orient* (1946), p. 71.

[3] It has been estimated by an American civil engineer that the labour cost of the 3 m. cubic yards of the Great Pyramid was about 400 man-hours per cubic yard. This compares with some 3 man-hours per cubic yard for a modern concrete structure such as the Grand Coulée dam (*New York Times*, 5 Oct. 1952).

lotus-shaped capital of the houses. Is it to gain his ends? His two arms are
worn out by work, his clothes are dishevelled. He gnaws at his own body;
his fingers are to him like bread. Once a day only does he wash himself.
He walks humbly, that he may not offend. He is a pawn moving from
square to square—squares ten cubits long and six wide—a pawn moving
from month to month on the beams of a scaffolding, hanging on to the
lotus-shaped capitals of the houses, doing odd jobs of work. When he has
earned his bread he goes home and beats his children.

The weaver within doors is more unhappy than a woman. His knees
reach up to the pit of his stomach. He does not know the taste of fresh air.
Should he one day fail to turn out the stipulated amount of cloth he is
seized and tied like a lotus in the marshes. It is only by winning over the
doorkeepers with gifts of bread that he contrives to see the light of day. . . .

The messenger, setting off for foreign lands, bequeathes his property
to his children for fear of wild beasts and Asiatics. What will happen to
him when he is back in Egypt? No sooner has he reached his field,
reached his home, than he must be off again. . . .

I have seen violence, I have seen violence.[1]

Under the Ptolemies the country was exploited if not more
intensively at least more systematically,[2] and the Romans faithfully
stepped into their shoes. Under the Arab Caliphate the tribute of
Egypt reached 14 million dinars, or about £6 million, but later
declined considerably from this figure. And the Patriarch Dionysius,
after his visit to Egypt in A.D. 815, when he passed through the textile
centre of Tinnis, wrote:

I have never seen a people so poor. On asking them, they said . . . 'our
wives spin the flax and we weave it all day long. The government buyers
and the merchant give us half a dirhem a day for wages. This is not
enough to feed our dogs. We pay a tax of five dinars (100 dirhems) a year
each. If we can't pay it, we are put in prison, and our wives and children
are held as hostages. For every dinar we cannot pay, we are made slaves
for two years.'[3]

Where the Arabs used whips the Turks and Mamluks used
scorpions. Cadalvène summed up the history of Egypt in his gloomy
statement: 'Étrange spectacle que celui de l'Égypte, de cette terre qui
semble ne devoir nourrir que des oppresseurs et des opprimés.' All
this may have been bearable in times of peace and abundance, but
when there was civil war or a failure of the Nile the most terrible

[1] Tr. from G. Maspero, *Hist. ancienne des peuples d'Orient* (1875).

[2] See P. Jouguet, *L'Impérialisme macédonien et l'hellénisation de l'Orient* (1926).

[3] Quoted in Mosharrafa, pt. 2, p. 44; recent papyrus studies suggest that the
picture painted by the Patriarch is somewhat too black.

famines were experienced, as in A.D. 42, 928, 967, 1064–72, 1201, 1262, and 1294. In some of these the people were forced to resort to cannibalism, as in 1069 when passers-by in the streets of Cairo were pulled up by hooks let down from house windows and eaten.

It is this unbroken record of misery which perhaps explains the Egyptian peasant's proverbial docility and, except for an occasional outbreak, his acceptance of the very hard conditions in which he lives. Unlike the peasants of many countries he has no golden past to which to look back, and the Egyptian countryside nurses few legends or traditions concerning the good old days.

*Frontiers*

The movements of Egypt's frontiers have been characterized by two main traits. In the first place, since the time of the Persian conquest, Egypt has always formed part of an empire, either as head or as dependant; secondly, Egypt's main line of expansion has always lain in a north-easterly direction, and it is from the north-east that it has most often been invaded.

In his *Philosophy of History* Hegel distinguishes three main zones in Africa: the regions south of the Sahara, which constitute Africa proper; north-western Africa, which he regards as forming part of Europe; and the Nile valley, which he classes with the great Asian river systems. In fact Egypt's historical and political ties have mostly been with south-western Asia. For to the west of the Nile valley lies the Libyan Desert, a formidable obstacle. To the north, the Mediterranean has constituted an effective barrier to Egyptian expansion, except for an occasional occupation of Cyprus. To the south stretches a vast indeterminate zone, in which Egypt's political influence has rarely reached farther than the second cataract (except in the nineteenth century when it extended to the Great Lakes), though its cultural influence has been felt well within Abyssinia.[1]

From the earliest times the Pharaohs established trading contacts with the Phoenician towns, mainly with the object of importing wood, of which Egypt has always been short. But no military expansion took place until the eighteenth dynasty when, following the expulsion of the Hyksos, the Egyptian armies reached the Upper Euphrates. Egypt soon, however, lost its Asian possessions and, after vainly trying to hold the balance of power against Assyria, was incorporated in the Assyrian Empire. Later, after brief spells of independence, it came under Persian and Macedonian rule.

[1] See Pres. of Council of Min., *The Unity of the Nile Valley* (1947).

No sooner were the Ptolemies established in Egypt than they turned their eyes towards Palestine, which they continued to dispute with the Seleucids until Rome stepped in and annexed both empires. Not until the time of Ibn Tulun did Egypt once more become independent, when it again annexed Syria as far as the Taurus. In the same way the Ikhshidids, the Fatimids, the Ayyubids, and the Mamluks always occupied a greater or smaller part of Syria, as well as most of the Arabian Red Sea coast, and Napoleon, Muhammad Ali, the British rulers of Egypt, and President Abdel Nasser felt the same *Drang nach Osten*.

## Indo-Mediterranean Trade

One of the chief causes of the persistent expansion outlined above is to be found in the desire of the rulers of Egypt to secure control over all the principal Indo-Mediterranean trade routes. From the beginning of the second millennium B.C. Egypt succeeded in establishing trade contacts with Southern Arabia and East Africa and was able to draw on the produce of India through the medium of the Southern Arabians, whose chief port, Aden, was a great entrepôt for international trade. Babylonia had been trading with India and Southern Arabia from even earlier times, and with the opening up of the Mediterranean by the Phoenicians, and the growing affluence of the Greeks, a strong current of trade began to flow from the Indian Ocean to the Mediterranean. This current could move through one of four main channels: the overland route across Persia to the Black Sea; the Persian Gulf and Euphrates and thence overland to Damascus or Aleppo and the Mediterranean ports; the sea route to Aden[1] and thence by caravan along the Red Sea coast to the caravan cities of Petra or Bosra and so to the Mediterranean; through an Egyptian Red Sea port, such as Qusair, across to the Nile valley, and thence down river to Alexandria. Very little traffic passed through Clyzma (Suez) owing to the dangerous nature of the coasts on either side as well as the prevalence of strong northerly winds which made navigation in the Red Sea very difficult until the use of steam.

This trade current has been of considerable importance to Egypt for, although the prosperity of the country always depended mainly on agriculture, the heavy tolls levied on the transit of goods and the trading profits made formed an important source of revenue. Hence almost from the beginning of the first millennium B.C. the rulers of

[1] George Hourani, *Arab Seafaring* (Princeton, 1950).

Egypt have constantly attempted, by peaceful or violent means, to attract as large a share as possible of the Indo-European trade to their country.

Thus, in the seventh century B.C., Necho cleared the twelfth-dynasty canal linking the Nile to the Red Sea. This canal was in more or less constant use until A.D. 776, though it often silted up owing to neglect. The Ptolemies founded the Red Sea port of Berenice, protected the caravan route between it and the Nile, and organized regular trading fleets to South Arabia and India. They also concluded commercial agreements with the Nabataeans of Petra, intended to divert the flow of goods from the Syrian ports to Egypt, and had to carry out this policy by force of arms in face of the vigorous opposition of the Seleucids.

The Romans cleared the Red Sea of pirates, possibly occupying Aden, and established trading colonies on the Indian coast. They were always anxious to develop the Syrian and Egyptian routes at the expense of the Mesopotamian, the upper reaches of which were controlled by the growing power of the Parthians and Sasanians. The latter, for their part, actively promoted trade between the Persian Gulf and India. Trade with India, through the Red Sea, seems to have remained active until the third century and to have declined thereafter.[1] From about the fourth century Arabia was involved in the play of power politics, the Persians backing the Arab kingdom of Himyar while the Romans used the Abyssinians of Axum for the promotion of their interests.

The Arab conquest filled in the thousand-year-old break caused by the Roman-Persian frontier,[2] and joined the Mediterranean and the Indian Ocean both politically and economically. Moreover Arab traders pushed vigorously to India and Malaya and even founded a commercial colony in Canton. But the Mediterranean was little used for trade, there being hardly any commercial demand and much military opposition from Europe,[3] and for such trade as there was the Egyptian route was overshadowed by the Syrian and Mesopotamian routes. It was not until the eleventh century, when the growing prosperity of Europe revived the demand for oriental products, that Egypt began to regain its former importance, as is

[1] G. F. Hourani, 'Did Roman Competition Ruin South Arabia?', *J. Near Eastern Studies*, Oct. 1952.

[2] A. J. Toynbee, *A Study of History*, 1, 75.

[3] Charles Issawi, 'The Christian–Muslim Frontier in the Mediterranean', *Pol. Sci. Q.*, Dec. 1961.

shown by the persistent attacks of the Crusaders on Damietta. Henceforth, and especially after the Tatar ravages in Iraq in the thirteenth century, Egypt became increasingly important as a channel for transit goods, and its Mamluk rulers gained a huge amount of wealth from their monopolistic position.[1]

The rounding of the Cape of Good Hope was a deadly blow to Egyptian trade. The Mamluks quickly realized its significance and, with the help of the Venetians and Arabs, attempted to destroy the Portuguese fleets in the Indian Ocean. These attempts were several times renewed by the Ottomans after the conquest of Egypt.[2] After several fierce battles, however, the Portuguese succeeded in establishing their mastery over the Indian Ocean, and henceforth the bulk of Indian goods came to Europe by way of Lisbon.[3]

## Stagnation under the Mamluks

Overshadowing all these factors has been the economic and cultural stagnation in which Egypt subsisted between the fourteenth and nineteenth centuries, and which almost completely deprived the Egyptian people of the fruits of their brilliant past. The achievements of Pharaonic Egypt need no emphasis and Ptolemaic Alexandria was the leading centre of science and scholarship. During the Christian era, Egypt played an important part in the elaboration of dogma and the evolution of ecclesiastical institutions. The Arab conquest cut Egypt off from the northern Mediterranean lands, with which it had been in close contact for several centuries, but this was more than compensated by the tightening of its ties with Mesopotamia, Persia, and India. The Fatimid period marks one of the peaks of Islamic civilization. Science and art flourished greatly under royal patronage, and industry reached a high level. As slavery played a very minor part in the Islamic economy, a stimulus was given to the utilization of inanimate sources of power. Windmills introduced from Persia in the tenth century, as well as waterwheels, multiplied in Egypt and in Mesopotamia. New industries

[1] Issawi, 'Crusades and Current Crises in the Near East', *Int. Aff.*, July 1957.
[2] See G. W. F. Stripling, *The Ottoman Turks and the Arabs* (Urbana, Ill., 1942).
[3] About the middle of the sixteenth century the spice trade through Syria and Egypt revived markedly, owing to the decline of Portuguese power in the east and to the excellent relations existing between the Ottomans and the French. The establishment of Dutch power in the Indian Ocean, at the end of the century, however, finally cut off the spice trade through the Levant. See F. C. Lane, 'Mediterranean Spice Trade', *Am. Hist. R.*, Apr. 1940 and Fernand Braudel, *La Méditerranée et le monde méditerranéen à l'époque de Philippe II* (1949).

were established such as paper-making, porcelain, sugar refining, and the distillation of gasoline; and old ones like linen and woollen textiles, leatherwork, and metal-work were perfected. Many of the processes worked out by the Arabs were transmitted to Europe, but as late as the thirteenth century the Arabs were still sufficiently creative to learn as well as to teach. Thus the distillation of alcohol and the use of the compass were taken over from Italy in the thirteenth century, and the early European church-tower clocks were adopted and perfected.[1]

But already in the eleventh century Islam was showing signs of fatigue and rigidity in many fields[2] and in the twelfth and thirteenth centuries it underwent a deep crisis. Assailed on all sides by the Crusaders and by the still more terrible Tatars, Islamic society succeeded in preserving itself, but only by paying an exorbitant price. On the one hand some of its most prosperous cities and provinces, such as Rayy and the whole of Mesopotamia, were ruined beyond repair. On the other hand Egypt, the main surviving Arab country, was transformed into a militarized state ruled by Turkish and Circassian Mamluks. The highly centralized administration it had enjoyed under the Fatimids and early Ayyubids was replaced by a military ruling class, supporting its troops from the revenues of its fiefs. Private ownership of land, once on a large scale, was greatly reduced. Insecurity and oppressive government led to a shrinkage of the cultivated area and to a fall in the population. Industry declined with the loss of many of its domestic and foreign markets. Only the trade in spices with India and Europe survived, being too profitable to be taxed out of existence by government cupidity.

Nevertheless, as late as the fourteenth century, visitors from Europe were still greatly impressed by the wealth of Egypt and the splendour of Cairo, a splendour reflected in the Arabian Nights, which took their present form towards the end of the Mamluk period.[3] In the fifteenth century, however, a further set of terrible blows struck the Mamluk empire. Timur Lenk sacked and burned Damascus, carrying off its most skilled inhabitants. A series of

[1] R. J. Forbes, *Man the Maker* (NY, 1950), p. 93.

[2] The best discussion of this topic is to be found in *Classicisme et déclin culturel dans l'histoire de l'Islam* (1957).

[3] Thus Frescobaldi, who visited Cairo in 1385, states that its inhabitants were more numerous than those of Tuscany and that the ships lying in its port were more than those in the ports of Venice, Genoa, and Ancona combined (quoted by Wihida, p. 84).

low-water Niles, for example, in 1398 and 1404, caused repeated famines. The debasing of the coinage led to a sharp rise in prices, which further disorganized the economy of the country,[1] as did the various measures taken by the Mamluk rulers to squeeze the spice trade.[2] Then came the rounding of the Cape of Good Hope and the diversion of the trade routes from the Mediterranean. Finally, there was the Ottoman conquest. The system of government set up by Sultan Selim might have given Egypt a respite, but it soon broke down, while the remaining crafts received a mortal blow from the deportation to Constantinople of thousands of artisans. Ottoman power, which was not sufficient to preserve order within Egypt, was, however, great enough to shield it from European infiltration, and the country spent the next three centuries in a stupor, unaware of the vast revolutions that were taking place across the Mediterranean and by-passed by the Renaissance and the Industrial Revolution.

### RELIGIOUS

Since the conversion to Islam of the mass of the population in the ninth century, that religion has played an important part in shaping Egypt's cultural background.

Theologically Islam is characterized by its transcendent theism, its ready and natural belief in predestination and its somewhat simplist outlook on the problems of sin and pain; it is rightly claimed by Moslems that 'Islam is a religion of ease, not of hardship'. Ethically, Islam is remarkable for its insistence on almsgiving and its relative freedom from racial prejudice, a freedom arising partly from the Prophet's precepts, partly from the conjugal liberty which enabled Moslems to have children from wives and slaves of many different races yet gave all these children much the same legal status. Politically, Islam differs from Christianity in that, from the very beginning, it took the form of a state as well as a religious movement; this is probably due both to the political as well as religious genius of Muhammad and to the fact that, unlike Jesus, who was a subject of Rome, he did not have an external governmental framework in which to work out his religion but had to create his own state and administrative organization.[3]

---

[1] A vivid account of some of these famines, together with a penetrating analysis of the effects of the inflation, is to be found in the work of the fifteenth-century historian al-Maqrizi, *Ighathat al-umma bi kashf al-ghumma* (1940).

[2] See Issawi in *Int. Aff.*, 1957.

[3] Issawi, 'The Historical Role of Muhammad', *Muslim World*, Apr. 1950.

All these facts have had a profound influence. The strict transcendentalism of Islam has prevented the emergence of a clergy acting as intermediaries between God and man, though it has not been proof against the infiltration of saint cults, or against the growth of a body of *ulama*, men learned in religion and canon law, who have the social function and influence associated with a clergy. Predestination, the rejection of the doctrine of the essential sinfulness of man, and the view that God cannot desire his elect to suffer, have combined to free Moslems from morbidity to a remarkable extent,[1] but, coupled with the doctrine of submission to God's will (*Islam*), have inclined them to accept too unquestioningly and apathetically the lot appointed them in this world and have at the same time deprived them of a powerful spiritual ferment.

This conservatism has been accentuated by the large-scale almsgiving and other forms of social charity, so strictly enjoined by Islam. It has also been greatly reinforced by the fusion of church and state and the wide range of personal and social activities regulated by Islamic canon law (the *Sharia*). This has meant that a much larger segment of the total body of law had a religious sanction than in Christendom, even when the power of the Papacy was at its height. This has, naturally, increased social rigidity, since reformers have to overcome not only men's usual resistance to social change but also their opposition to religious innovation. Thus, to take an example, an attempt to change inheritance laws in a Moslem state encounters much the same kind of opposition as an attempt to change divorce laws in a Catholic country.

The fusion of church and state in Islam has had another important consequence. In Europe, one of the mainsprings of liberalism has been the belief in the sinfulness of the state, a belief traceable to St Augustine and sharpened by centuries of struggle between the Papacy and Empire. For various reasons, the church supported

[1] In Egypt the suicide rate has, in recent years, averaged about 10 per million inhabitants. Corresponding rates were: Japan 240, Denmark and Austria 230, France 150, UK 110, USA 100. The huge difference between the Egyptian and the other rates is not to be explained solely in terms of youthful age composition and low degree of urbanization, industrialization and education, for in some agricultural underdeveloped countries high suicide rates are found, e.g. Taiwan 150, Puerto Rico 120, Burma 90 and Ceylon 80. Conversely, the only other Moslem countries for which figures are available also show very low rates, namely Aden, Iraq, Morocco and Turkey (UN, *Demographic Yb. 1957*). An analysis of the available data on suicides in Egypt for the years 1881–1918 is to be found in René Maunier, *Mélanges de sociologie Nord-Africaine* (1930). Another striking phenomenon is the extraordinarily small number of suicides recorded in Islamic history.

several movements which aimed at curtailing the power of the state, notably the revolt of the Italian cities against the emperors. In the struggle between church and state, individual liberty was born in Europe. But nothing of the kind happened in Islam. The fact that the state was not challenged by either an organized church, or independent cities, or a feudal nobility, or powerful corporations has led to a much more unquestioning acceptance of its power, much less awareness of its dangers, and much more pliant submission to its encroachments.[1]

Finally, the relative absence of race feeling, together with the fact that women are prohibited from marrying non-Moslems, has greatly increased the country's capacity to assimilate Moslems, while making extremely difficult any solution of the problems presented by its non-Moslem minorities. Lebanese and Syrian Christians, for instance, find themselves still unassimilated after five or six generations of unbroken residence in Egypt. Syrian Moslems, on the other hand, are often egyptianized a few years after arrival, and invariably after one generation. Similarly Negroes, Tunisians, Arabians, and even Indians have been quite easily assimilated.

Another important aspect is the Arabian origin of Islam. The twin roots of Christianity, Judaism and Hellenism have oriented the Christian world not only towards the Old Testament but equally towards the classics. Islam, on the other hand, is almost purely Arabian in origin, Greek influences on Islamic theology being relatively weak, and at least the Arab part of the Moslem world has never quite shaken off the grip of the desert and its beduins. It is significant that the Omayyad Caliphs sent their sons to be educated not at Antioch or Constantinople, but in the Syrian desert.[2]

It is true that, owing to the age-long hostility between fellahin and beduin,[3] the influence of the desert is much less perceptible in sedentary Egypt than in Syria or Iraq. Moreover, unlike its eastern neighbours, Egypt has always been exposed to African influences, a

[1] It has been often pointed out, among others by Louis Massignon, that one of the two basic political principles of Islam, along with *Jihad* or Holy War, is '*Taslim* or submission to legitimate authority'.

[2] One of the most extraordinary misreadings of history is Spengler's contention that whereas Hellenism never entered into the heart of Faustian (western) civilization, in spite of all appearances to the contrary, it dominated, formed, and distorted Magian (Arabian) civilization through the phenomenon of pseudo-morphosis. This view has been given wide currency in Arab countries by the able and prolific Egyptian philosopher Abd al-Rahman Badawi.

[3] 'For every shepherd is an abomination unto the Egyptians' (Genesis, xlvi. 34).

fact which may account for the wit and good humour of its inhabitants, as well as their keener sense of colour and form. Nevertheless the whole of Arab thought and literature is heavily charged with the atmosphere of pre-Islamic and Islamic Arabia, and in consequence tends to produce an archaic frame of mind in those subjected to its influence. This point emerges very clearly in the following statement, made by a distinguished professor of literature:

The literature which we read, study, memorize, enjoy and glory in; the literature in which we bring up our children, which we use to educate our emotions, character and imagination; whose virtues we take as examples and whose vices we use as terms of abuse. . . . The literature from which we take guidance in prosperity and adversity, which we quote, converse with and follow, whose persons we live with and whose events we witness—surely this is no other than Arabic literature.

The events related in Arabic literature, whether of pre-Islamic or Islamic times, are still the objects of our attention. . . . The verse of Zuhair, Antar, Labid, etc. . . . is still the sustenance and daily bread of the Egyptian poet and man of letters. . . . Egyptians still strive to attain the ideals and noble virtues which Arabic literature proclaimed. Courage, enterprise, self-respect, nobility, loyalty and generosity are still quickened by pre-Islamic poetry. . . .[1]

[1] Abd al-Wahhab Azzam, 'The Influence of Arabic Culture on Modern Egyptian Culture' (in Ar.), *al-Thaqafa*, no 235, quoted by Wihida, p. 40.

# II

# Integration in the World Economy
# 1798–1920

*Mon pays n'est plus en Afrique; nous faisons partie de l'Europe actuellement.*

ISMAIL PASHA.

*La colonisation et le capitalisme d'expansion auront joué dans le monde arabe, et plus largement dans le monde oriental, le rôle qu'a joué chez nous le péché originel.*

JACQUES BERQUE.

The economic history of Egypt in the last 160 years falls into three unequal periods. In the first, which is the subject of the present chapter and which ended with the First World War, the subsistence economy under which the country had lived for centuries was replaced by an export-oriented economy, the bulk of Egypt's available reserves of land, water and underemployed labour were brought into use and its total output and exports increased several times, with a consequent rise in real per-capita income and in the level of living.[1] The second period, which is discussed at greater length in the next chapter, covers the years 1920–52, and almost coincides with that of the independent monarchy. During these years several problems inherited from the past came to a head, the fall in cotton prices struck a heavy blow and there was a general stagnation in production and a fall in the level of living; however, in three important fields, industry, credit, and taxation, the groundwork for future development was laid. The third period was ushered in by the present military régime, in 1952; the difficulties faced and the results achieved by this régime form the main subject of this book.

[1] For an explanation of the terms 'subsistence economy', 'export-oriented economy', and 'complex economy' see Issawi, 'Egypt since 1800: a study in lopsided development', *J. Econ. Hist.*, Mar. 1961. In this chapter I have drawn heavily on this article. For further details on the period covered in this chapter see Issawi, *EMC*, chs. 2–3.

## GENERAL CHARACTERISTICS OF THE PERIOD

The French expedition of 1798 found Egypt a poor, isolated, and self-contained country, a neglected backwater of the Ottoman Empire, ruined by the diversion of trade from the Mediterranean to the Atlantic, and with a standard of living which was being forced still lower by the breakdown of government. Under Muhammad Ali an attempt was made to create an industrialized, closed, state-controlled economy, and to absorb part of the Ottoman dominions. This plan was defeated by the Powers in 1841, a date which marks the beginning of a process, consummated only after the British occupation, integrating Egypt as an agricultural colonial unit in the international politico-economic system. Its main features were: specialization in cotton; the expansion of the cultivated area by means of dams and canals; the freeing of agriculture from its legal and traditional shackles, thus giving growers an incentive to make the fullest possible use of the land; the opening up of the country by means of railways and canals; the immigration of foreign technicians and traders; the depression and eventual disappearance of most of the domestic industries owing to foreign competition; and the accumulation of a large foreign debt.

This process was not a local phenomenon. It extended over the whole colonial and semi-colonial world: South America, Africa, India, China. In most cases it led to a loss of independence and annexation by one or other of the European Powers.

Egypt had none of the advantages which enabled others to escape absorption: no Monroe doctrine, backed by power, to cover it as Latin America was covered; no immensity of territory or remoteness from Europe, as with China; not even, after the defeat of France in 1870 had removed the last check to British expansion, sufficient international rivalries to make it possible to play off one Power against another. Indeed, it had one positive disadvantage: the isthmus of Suez, which was bound, sooner or later, to be pierced by a canal, and which converted Britain's interest in Egypt from a negative to a positive one, from a desire to keep other Powers off Egypt to a desire to secure control over Egypt.

Even if the world-wide colonial tendencies be ignored and attention restricted to the chain of Moslem countries lying along the Mediterranean coast, it will be seen that in every case contact with the west led to financial indebtedness which in turn led to absorption: Tunis in 1881, Egypt in 1882, Morocco in 1910.[1]

[1] George Young, *Egypt* (1927), pp. xx-xxi.

Turkey, which alone contrived to combine the advantages of indebtedness with those of independence, is a striking example of the exception which proves the rule, since it did so only by making the fullest use of the rivalry between Britain and Russia and later between Britain, Germany, Russia, and the United States.

It may be said that Egypt lost its opportunity in the second half of the nineteenth century. If during that time it had had a government which was both national and enlightened and which could have laid the foundations of a modern educational system, carried out some measure of industrialization, and established the groundwork of a westernized administration without incurring such a large foreign debt as to jeopardize the country's independence, its economic and social structure might have been very different today. It is even possible that a rise in the standard of living and more widely diffused education might have checked the population growth. Egypt might have emerged into the twentieth century as a small-scale Japan. But it is only necessary to list all these conditions to realize how improbable it was that they should all appear in conjunction.

### MAMLUK EGYPT[1]

By the year 1798 the population, which had numbered about 6–7 million in Roman times, had shrunk to some $2\frac{1}{2}$ million, of whom perhaps 250,000 lived in Cairo and 8,000 in the ruins of Alexandria.[2]

The system of land tenure had hardly changed since the establishment of the Mamluk régime. The leading Mamluks parcelled out the country, each controlling a group of villages, whose taxes he often farmed, and holding tax-free land. Excluding *waqf* (mortmains in favour of religious institutions), the bulk of the land consisted of communal land subject to tax. Peasants enjoyed no property rights and were tied to the soil, but in practice they were left undisturbed and allowed to hand the plots to their children provided

---

[1] For conditions prevailing up to 1800 see Gibb & Bowen; France, Commiss. des Monuments d'Ég., *Descr. de l'Ég.* (1809–22); and Stanford J. Shaw, *The Financial and Administrative Organization and Development of Ottoman Egypt* (Princeton, 1962).

[2] Estimates of Egypt's population at this period are unreliable and show considerable variations. Volney put the total in the 1780's at 2,300,000. For the year 1800 Jomard gives the figure of 2,489,000 and Chabrol that of 2,400,000; Jomard's estimate is discussed in Mahmoud El-Darwish, 'Analysis of Some Estimates of the Population of Egypt before the XIX Century', *Ég. contemp.*, Mar. 1929; Chabrol's estimate is judged to be too low by Gibb and Bowen, who put the population in the fourteenth century at not over 4 m.

they met their taxes and supplied the requisite *corvée* labour on the tax-farmer's estate and irrigation works.[1]

The main crops were *shitwi* (winter), sown immediately after the recession of the flood waters, in November, and harvested in May; chief of these were wheat, barley, pulses, lucerne, tobacco, and flax. *Saifi* (summer) and *nili* (autumn) crops, sown in late spring or early summer, required first the raising of the low-river water to the level of the fields and then the keeping out of the flood waters. Maize, millet, rice, and sugar-cane constituted the principal *saifi* and *nili* crops. Cotton was grown on a small scale in Upper Egypt.

Industry was very rudimentary, having greatly declined from the high level reached under the Fatimids, and met only the simplest wants. It was carried on by guilds with apprenticeship rules similar to those prevailing in medieval Europe. Nile craft and camels provided the chief means of transport, there being no wheeled traffic. Both roads and river were highly insecure and convoys were generally formed for protection. The different regions were almost self-sufficing, the few towns serving as markets and centres of crafts. Foreign trade went chiefly to the Sudan, Arabia, Turkey, and southern Europe. Imports consisted mainly of European fine cloths, metal goods, and glassware; exports of wheat, rice, and onions; and re-exports of African gums, ivories, slaves, gold dust, and Arabian coffee and incense.[2]

## MUHAMMAD ALI

The 'Founder of Modern Egypt', Muhammad Ali (1805–49), attempted to effect a transition from the subsistence economy prevailing at the beginning of the nineteenth century to a 'modern' complex economy. In this he failed, but instead started Egypt on the road leading to an export-oriented economy. The methods pursued by him are very reminiscent of those used in the Soviet Union and elsewhere in the last forty years.[3]

[1] This brief account gives an over-simplified picture of the very complex and variable system of land tenure. For fuller details see Gibb & Bowen, i/1, 285–75, Helen A. Rivlin, *The Agricultural Policy of Muh. Ali* (Cambridge, Mass., 1961), chs 2 & 3, and Gabriel Baer, *Hist. of Landownership in Modern Egypt* (1962).

[2] Gibb & Bowen, i/1, ch. 6; see also A. E. Crouchley, *The Economic Development of Modern Egypt* (1937).

[3] Five studies have recently been made of Muh. Ali's economic policies: Muh. Fuad Shukri and others, *Bina dawlat Muh. Ali* (1948); Ahmad al-Hitta, *Tarikh al-ziraa al-misriyya fi ahd Muh. Ali al-Kabir* (1950); Ali al-Shafi, *al-Ashghal al-amma al-kubra fi ahd Muh. Ali* (n.d.); Ali al-Gritly, *Tarikh al-sinaa fi Misr* (n.d.); and Moustapha Fahmy, *La révolution de l'industrie en Ég. et ses conséquences sociales* (Leiden, 1954).

First, there was a revolution in the system of land tenure. Tax-farming was abolished and peasants paid their taxes directly to the government; large estates, often of uncultivated land, were granted to relatives or followers of Muhammad Ali; and the prevailing method of communal ownership was replaced by one in which peasants enjoyed *de facto*, though not yet legally recognized, rights of ownership.

Secondly, irrigation works were undertaken, which increased the land under cultivation and, what was more important, made it possible to replace basin irrigation by perennial irrigation and thus produce valuable crops that require summer water.[1]

Thirdly, the planting of long-staple cotton was started on a commercial scale in 1821, and it found ready markets in Europe. By 1824, over 200,000 cantars of cotton were being exported, and in 1845 the figure of 345,000 was reached.[2]

Fourthly, communications were developed, mainly in order to facilitate foreign trade; especially notable were the improvement of the port of Alexandria and its linking by canal to the Nile.

Fifthly, trade was conducted under a system of monopoly. Muhammad Ali bought crops from farmers at low fixed prices and resold them to foreign exporters at great profits. He also directly imported about two-fifths of the goods brought into Egypt.[3]

A similar monopoly was used in an attempt to build up a modern industry. Machinery was imported from Europe together with technicians, and by 1830 factories were turning out cotton, woollen, silk, and linen textiles, sugar, paper, glass, leather, sulphuric acid, and other chemicals. A well-run foundry met the needs of the

[1] It is difficult to determine the extent of the increase in cultivation. Al-Hitta (*Tarikh*, pp. 9 & 83) puts the cultivated area at 3,054,710 feddans in 1813, about 3,500,000 in 1835, 3,856,226 in 1840, and 4,160,169 in 1852. On the other hand Rivlin (p. 270), points out that during the French occupation (1798–1801) the cultivated area was 4,038,177 feddans and that by 1844 the area of village land, which probably included a small amount of uncultivated land, was 4,293,164 feddans, an increase of only 254,987; over the same period of time the amount of taxed land decreased by 400,862 feddans. Her conclusion is that 'any improvements made by Muhammad Ali were qualitative rather than quantitative'. Of course the two sets of figures can be reconciled on the very reasonable assumption that cultivation shrank greatly in the chaotic period following the withdrawal of the French troops.

[2] For fuller details see F. Charles-Roux, *Le Coton en Égypte* (1908) and Amin Sami, *Taqwim al-Nil* (1916–36).

[3] Crouchley, 'The Development of Commerce in the Reign of Moh. Ali', *Ég. contemp.*, Feb.–Mar. 1937.

government armament plants and arsenal, and simple machinery and spare parts were produced. Investments in industrial establishments up to 1838 amounted to about £12 million.[1] Some 30,000–40,000 persons worked in the factories,[2] an impressive figure in a total population of about 3 million, and the number engaged in handicrafts was considerably greater.[3]

The productive apparatus thus built up, with its very large bureaucracy, as well as the army and navy, required men trained in modern techniques. To meet this need, over 300 students were sent to Europe, and several times as many studied in the newly opened schools of medicine, engineering, chemistry, accountancy, and languages and in the military and naval colleges.[4]

In brief, Muhammad Ali was trying to carry out a programme of forced industrialization. His success was thanks primarily to the administrative protection that he gave to his infant industries, which did not, however, outlive that protection. The investment capital required was obtained from the profits of his monopoly of internal and export trade and from taxation and forced loans, and the losses of industrial enterprises were covered from the same sources.[5] The necessary unskilled labour was conscripted and paid low wages, while foreign technicians and skilled workers were attracted by high salaries. A market for the output of the factories was provided by the armed forces, by import substitution, and by displacing some handicrafts.

Other points of resemblance with recent programmes of rapid development should be mentioned. First, the level of living of the population certainly did not rise, and more probably declined, as a result of Muhammad Ali's intensive and often mismanaged investment and of the consequent inflation; the hardships entailed by this and by militarization caused thousands to flee the country in spite of his efforts to seal the frontiers. Nevertheless, a very good case can be made for Muhammad Ali; perhaps unwittingly, but judging from some of his remarks quite possibly consciously, he was trying

---

[1] Ahmad al-Hitta, *Tarikh misr al-iqtisadi* (1957), p. 174.  [2] Fahmy, pp. 84–85.

[3] Estimates of Egypt's population at this period also show considerable variations. For 1821 Mengin gave a figure of 2,536,000. For 1836 Caldavène gave one of 2,213,000; Duhamel one of 2½ m.; Clot one of 3 m.; and Muh. Ali one of 3½ m. In 1840 Bowring stated that the official estimate was 3,200,000 but that in 'the opinion of the best informed' the number was from 2 to 2½ million. In 1846 a census of houses showed a total of 4,543,000 but this figure is also not too reliable.

[4] J. Heyworth-Dunne, *An Introd. to the History of Modern Education in Egypt* (1938), pp. 104–287.  [5] Gritly, *Tarikh*, p. 97.

to lay the foundation for a balanced, diversified economy that in time would have greatly raised the level of living. However, his prime interest was in building up a modern army and navy to safeguard his position and extend his influence. Hence the compulsory reduction of his armed forces in 1841, following his defeat at the hands of the Great Powers, removed most of the incentive that had made him seek to industrialize Egypt. At the same time the enforcement of the Anglo-Turkish Convention of 1838 permitted foreign traders to buy and sell anywhere within the Ottoman dominions, including Egypt. Simultaneously deprived of Muhammad Ali's protection and encouragement and exposed to the competition of European industry, his factories began to decline and did not survive his death in 1849.

The collapse of Muhammad Ali's schemes points out one of the major obstacles to economic development in Egypt, an obstacle that was not removed until the 1930's: the lack of political autonomy. Economic development usually requires considerable aid in the form of tariff protection, tax exemptions, rebates on transport rates, cheap power, special credit facilities to certain sectors, educational policies, &c, which only a government enjoying a large measure of political and fiscal independence can provide. But except for a brief period when Muhammad Ali managed, by various subterfuges, to carry out his own economic policy, Egypt did not enjoy such independence until very recently. The tariff was fixed by conventions concluded between the Ottoman government and the Great Powers. No direct taxes could be imposed on foreigners without the consent of their governments, because of the Capitulations. And, more generally, until 1882 the Egyptian government was subject to great international economic and financial pressures,[1] and after that date it was under British control.

### AN EXPORT–ORIENTED ECONOMY

With the failure of Muhammad Ali's industrial plans and the abolition of his monopoly system, the first phase of Egypt's modern economic history came to an end. The attempted leap from a subsistence to a complex economy had failed, and instead the country had landed on the road leading to an export-oriented economy. Egypt could now be integrated, as an agricultural unit, in the world-wide economic system.

[1] See David S. Landes, *Bankers and Pashas: International Finance and Economic Imperialism in Egypt* (Cambridge, Mass., 1958).

The extent of this integration may perhaps best be gauged by measuring the growth of Egypt's foreign trade. The first reliable figures refer to 1823 and put imports at £E656,000 and exports at 1,455,000, giving a total of 2,111,000.[1] These figures probably represent an advance over the level attained at any time during the previous fifty years or more.[2] By 1838 the total value of trade had risen to £E3·5 million and by 1850 to 3·7 million. In 1860 the total stood at £E5·1 million, in 1880 at 21·8 million, and in 1913 at 60 million.[3] If one assumes that at the beginning of Muhammad Ali's reign the value of trade was about £E1·5 million, the expansion in the course of the hundred years preceding the First World War would be about fortyfold. Since Egyptian trade figures are officially stated to have been undervalued until 1911[4] and since the British price level in 1800–15 was about twice as high as in 1913,[5] an estimate of a fifty- or sixty-fold increase is not likely to err on the side of exaggeration.

The integration of Egypt into the world system necessitated a number of structural changes. First, the remaining restrictions on private ownership of land were gradually removed. By 1858 collective responsibility for land taxes had been abolished; the right of inheritance by both males and females had been fully affirmed and so had the right to sell or mortgage land; finally, foreigners were authorized to acquire any kind of land. This last provision was of particular importance, since it enabled foreign capital to enter Egyptian agriculture by means of mortgage and other loans.[6] During the following two decades various measures were taken removing remaining restrictions, improving the machinery of registration, and by the establishment of the Mixed Courts in 1875 setting up a legal framework that gave foreigners the widest measure of rights.

[1] John Bowring, 'Report on Egypt and Candia', in *Parliamentary Papers*, 1840, xxi. 63.

[2] For earlier estimates and a critical discussion thereof see Issawi, in *J. Econ. Hist.*, Mar. 1961.

[3] The 1838 figure is from John MacGregor, *Commercial Statistics* (1847), ii. 251; the others are from Crouchley, *Econ. Dev.*

[4] Crouchley, 'The Visible Balance of Trade since 1884', *Ég. contemp.*, Mar.–Apr. 1935.

[5] See Werner Schlote, *British Overseas Trade* (Oxford, 1952) for indices of British export, import, and wholesale prices.

[6] Between 1876 and 1883 the mortgage debt of farmers rose from £E500,000 to £E7 m. (Lord Dufferin, in a report to Lord Granville dated 6 Feb. 1883, quoted by I. G. Levi, 'La distribution du crédit en Égypte', *Ég. contemp.*, Feb. 1918). By 1914 mortgage debts stood at about £E60 m.

Land had become a commodity like any other, easily bought and sold. Concurrently labour was freed from all the ties binding it to the soil and also became a mobile, marketable commodity.[1]

Secondly, there was a vast expansion in the irrigated area. Under Ismail (1863–79) 13,500 km. of canals were dug, and under British rule (1882–1922) the Aswan dam (at the time the largest in the world) and other major irrigation works were built. Consequently the cultivated area increased from 4,160,000 feddans in 1862 to 4,743,000 in 1877 and 5,283,000 in 1913.[2] This made it possible not only to grow more crops, but also to concentrate more fully on such cash crops as cotton and sugar-cane, in which Egypt has a comparative advantage because of soil and climate.

Thirdly, there was a great improvement in transport. The first railway was opened as early as 1853, and by 1858 Cairo was linked to both Alexandria and Suez. In 1877 there were 1,519 km. of standard-gauge railways and by 1913 this figure had risen to 2,953; at the latter date there were also 1,376 km. of light railways.[3] Moreover not only the Nile but also many of the irrigation canals were navigable the whole year round. A network of telegraph lines, some 5,200 km. long, covered the country. Thus Egypt, whose total inhabited area is only 35,000 square km., had built up an internal system of transport and communications comparable to that of many European countries at a much higher level of development.

Nor did external communications lag behind. The port of Alexandria was repeatedly enlarged and improved, to become one of the two or three best in the Mediterranean, and the new ports of Suez and Port Said were built on the Suez Canal. The opening of the canal in 1869 served to channel a vast flow of international traffic through Egypt and to multiply the links binding it to the outside world.

The strengthening of the financial link binding Egypt with the international community constituted a fourth development. The currency reform of 1835 placed Egypt on a bimetallic standard, and in 1885 this was replaced by the gold standard. At the outbreak of the First World War a shift to a sterling-exchange standard occurred

[1] For these ties see Gibb & Bowen, i/1.260; and for their dissolution G. Baer, 'The Dissolution of the Egyptian Village Community', *Welt des Islams*, n.s., vi (1959), nos. 1–2.

[2] Crouchley, *Econ. Dev.*, pp. 132, 152–3.

[3] *L'Égypte: aperçu historique et géographique* (Cairo, 1926), pp. 312–15; L. Wiener, *L'Égypte et ses chemins de fer* (Brussels, 1932), pp. 71–88, and several articles in *Ég. contemp.*, Jan. 1933.

so that, to all intents and purposes, Egypt became an extension of the London money market, with large movements of funds to and from London each year. A spectacular growth of banking activity started in the 1850's; by 1877 eight banks were providing telegraphic exchange on Paris and London.[1] In 1880 two foreign mortgage banks were opened, and expansion continued during the next thirty years.

The fifth development, which cast a dark shadow over the progress achieved, was the accumulation of a huge public debt beginning in 1858. Part of the capital expenditure mentioned above was financed out of government revenue, but the greater part came from foreign loans. Other factors contributing to swell the debt were the fantastic extravagance of some of the monarchs, the corruption of their subordinates, and the usurious terms on which most of the loans were contracted. The Law of Liquidation of 1880 fixed Egypt's public debt at £98,377,000, and during the next twenty years a further £18,210,000 was borrowed. In addition, foreign private capital investment rose rapidly after 1900, reaching £E92 million in 1914.[2] The debt service and tribute to Constantinople absorbed just under £E5 million per annum, or over half the budget. The addition of interest on private capital raised Egypt's liabilities to foreigners to £E8·5 million per annum by 1914. Clearly, this could be met only if the country succeeded in building up a large export surplus.

This surplus was obtained by greatly developing the production and export of cotton (partly at the expense of wheat, which suffered from American and Australian competition), thus converting the economy into a highly specialized one-crop economy. Stimulated by the high prices prevailing during the 'cotton famine' provoked by the American Civil War, output of cotton rose from 501,000 cantars in 1860 to 2,140,000 in 1865. Thereafter progress was swift, output rising to 3,124,000 cantars in 1879 and 7,664,000 in 1913. Table 1 (p. 28) shows the corresponding increase in cotton shipments, and their overwhelming share in the country's total exports.[3]

---

[1] Crouchley, *The Investment of Foreign Capital in Egyptian Companies and Public Debt* (1936), pp. 29–37. For a detailed history of banking in Egypt see Ali al-Gritly, 'Tatawwur al-nizam al-masrafi fi misr', in *Buhuth*, pp. 197–302.

[2] Crouchley, *Investment*, p. 74.

[3] During Muh. Ali's reign Britain became Egypt's most important supplier and client, replacing France and Turkey; by 1885 it took 63 per cent of Egypt's exports and supplied 38 per cent of its imports.

TABLE I

## Foreign Trade, 1848–1956
### (Yearly averages)

| Year | Volume of cotton exports (m. cantars)[1] | Ave. price of cotton (talaris per cantar)[1] | Value of cotton exports incl. seed (£E m.)[1] | Value of all exports (£E m.) | Index of import prices (1938= 100)[2] | Buying power of exports (£E m. at 1938 prices)[3] |
|---|---|---|---|---|---|---|
| 1848–52 | 0·36 | 9·6 | .. | 2·2[4] | 58·8 | 3·7 |
| 1853–57 | 0·50 | 9·4 | .. | 2·8 | 66·5 | 4·2 |
| 1858–62 | 0·57 | 13·2 | .. | 3·1 | 66·5 | 4·7 |
| 1863–67 | 1·69 | 32·2 | .. | 10·9 | 84·7 | 12·9 |
| 1868–72 | 1·59 | 19·9 | .. | 9·9 | 75·6 | 13·1 |
| 1873–77 | 2·49 | 17·4 | .. | 13·5 | 74·2 | 18·2 |
| 1878–82 | 2·52 | 14·2 | 9·3[5] | 12·1 | 60·2 | 20·1 |
| 1883–87 | 2·78 | 12·9 | 8·7 | 11·7 | 54·6 | 21·4 |
| 1888–92 | 3·89 | 11·9 | 9·6 | 12·6 | 56·0 | 22·5 |
| 1893–97 | 5·20 | 9·0 | 10·7 | 12·9 | 51·8 | 24·9 |
| 1898–1902 | 5·89 | 9·3 | 12·9 | 16·1 | 56·7 | 28·4 |
| 1903–07 | 6·28 | 14·4 | 19·5 | 23·1 | 60·2 | 38·4 |
| 1908–12 | 6·72 | 16·8 | 24·9 | 28·1 | 64·4 | 43·6 |
| 1913–17 | 6·28 | 21·3 | 28·0 | 32·0 | 84·8 | 37·7 |
| 1918–22 | 5·10 | 46·5 | 50·8 | 58·3 | 198·4 | 29·4 |
| 1923–27 | 7·24 | 32·4 | 50·1 | 54·5 | 130·1 | 41·9 |
| 1928–32 | 7·06 | 19·6 | 33·4 | 37·6 | 105·4 | 35·7 |
| 1933–37 | 8·02 | 12·7 | 25·9 | 33·0 | 90·8 | 36·3 |
| 1938–42 | 6·72 | 15·3 | 20·5 | 26·0 | 171·2 | 15·2 |
| 1943–47 | 4·27 | 37·4 | 32·4 | 48·6 | 296·0 | 16·4 |
| 1948–52 | 7·36 | 81·4 | 147·5 | 158·6 | 339·0 | 46·8 |
| 1953–56 | 6·58 | 69·7 | 106·8 | 137·6 | 397·8 | 34·6 |

[1] Cotton season ending in year specified. A talari is one-fifth of an Egyptian pound.

[2] Until 1938, index of price of exports of manufactured goods from the United Kingdom; 1938–56, index of price of all imports into Egypt.

[3] Value of all Egyptian exports divided by price index of imports.

[4] Average of 1850–2.       [5] Average of 1880–2.

*Sources: Ann. stat.*; Crouchley, *Econ. Dev.*; Schlote; *The Economist*; NBE, *Econ. B.*

Cotton was the main beneficiary of the government's investment on public works and the magnet drawing private foreign capital to Egypt. All the other sectors of the economy, such as transport, commerce, and finance, had as their main function the moving of the cotton crop. Most of the capital investment that did not directly serve cotton was used for providing amenities, such as tramways, gas, electricity, and water, suitable to the level of income generated by the increase in cotton. And the greater part of the imports paid for by cotton exports consisted of consumer goods demanded by the beneficiaries of this rise in incomes. In other words, the large increase in production and exports achieved during this period was absorbed, partly by the population growth, to over 5 million by 1870 and 11,287,000 by 1907, and partly by a sharp rise in the level of living of the upper and middle classes and a distinct rise in that of the mass of the population;[1] little of it was reinvested.

The question that comes to the mind of any student of this period is why this vast influx of capital, the large-scale immigration of foreigners,[2] and the less spectacular but none the less real rise in the cultural level of the Egyptians did not lead to the development of other sectors of the economy. Granted that the government was unable or unwilling to help actively and directly beyond providing certain overhead facilities,[3] why is it that a group of foreign or native entrepreneurs did not emerge?

In the absence of research on this subject, any answer can only be highly tentative. As to the foreigners, it may be surmised that during the cotton and financial booms under Ismail the opportunities for making enormous and rapid gains in speculation, in banking, or at best in trade were so great that more prosaic occupations were, with few exceptions, neglected. Under the British, the hostile attitude of

[1] For sidelights on this, see G. Douin, *Hist. du règne du Khedive Ismail* (Rome, 1933–8), i. 239; and M. Rifaat, *The Awakening of Modern Egypt* (1947), p. 102. As an indication of the rise in mass consumption during the latter half of the period, it may be noted that imports of coffee increased from an average of 3,600 tons in 1885–9 to 6,900 in 1910–12, of tobacco from 3,100 to 8,700 tons, of cotton textiles reckoned by weight from 13,000 to 21,000 tons, and of cotton textiles reckoned by length from 4·3 to 61·2 m. metres (*Ann. stat.*, *1913*). None of these imports displaced domestic production. There is also good evidence that consumption of wheat increased considerably.

[2] The total number of foreigners rose from about 3,000 in 1836 to over 68,000 in 1878 (Heyworth-Dunne, p. 343) and to 221,000 in 1907. For a vivid picture of the immigrants, see Landes, ch. 3, entitled 'Klondike on the Nile'.

[3] In addition to the public works mentioned above, Ismail set up some sugar and textile units and a few other factories, enlarged, with private capital, a shipping company founded by his predecessor and sponsored a mixed trading company. All these enterprises were eventually liquidated or disposed of to private interests. See Abd al-Rahman al-Rafi, *Asr Ismail* (1948), i. 188–90, & ii. 12–13, and Landes, *passim*. For the fiscal and economic policy of the British Administration see Issawi, *EMC*, pp. 32–38.

the government to industrialization may have inhibited foreign enterprise in that field. As for the Egyptians, it is a strange fact, but one which had its counterpart in Turkey and other countries, that they left business almost entirely to foreigners or minority groups, who not only controlled finance and large-scale commerce but even dominated petty trade. As Lord Cromer put it, 'Bootmending, as well as bootmaking, is almost entirely in the hands of Greeks and Armenians. The drapery trade is controlled by Jews, Syrians, and Europeans, the tailoring trade by Jews.'[1] And the same holds true for the professions—practically all physicians, pharmacists and engineers were non-Egyptian, as were a very large number of lawyers.

Wealthy Egyptians bought land, and a few enterprising members of the royal family or aristocracy experimented with agricultural machinery, better varieties of seed, and new methods of culture. Educated Egyptians flocked to the rapidly expanding civil service, those with technical skills finding ready employment in the irrigation and railway services.[2] But practically none showed any interest in industry, trade, or finance, beyond the occasional purchase of stock in existing companies, and it was not until the 1920's and 1930's that an Egyptian business and professional class even began to emerge.[3]

A partial explanation of this lag may be found in the fact that, under the Capitulations, foreigners enjoyed a fiscal and judicial immunity that gave them a great advantage over Egyptian competitors. Another advantage was provided by their financial and commercial links with European markets. But other causes must also be sought, probably in the historical and cultural fields.

THE ECONOMIC EFFECTS OF THE FIRST WORLD WAR, 1914–20

Although Egypt was not a belligerent it could not escape some effects of the war, particularly in view of the presence of British troops on its soil.

After an initial drop, cotton prices rose very sharply to an average of $38 in 1916 and $90 in 1919, and exports jumped correspondingly

[1] *Ann. Rep. 1905*, Cd. 2817.
[2] A high proportion of civil servants were Copts—45 per cent in 1910 (ibid. *1910*).
[3] See Issawi, 'The Entrepreneur Class', in S. N. Fisher, ed., *Social Forces in the Middle East* (Ithaca, NY, 1955).

to £E88 million in 1920. Although the value of imports also rose their expansion was limited by shipping shortage until 1920, when the record figure of £E101,150,000 was attained. Hence a large export surplus was built up. At the same time British troops were disbursing sums estimated at £E83,946,000.[1]

Owing to a shortage of gold, the notes of the National Bank were, in 1914, declared legal tender. In 1916, in view of the difficulty of obtaining gold for the cover, the Bank was authorized to use British treasury bonds and bills as backing. The note issue rose to £E64 million at the end of 1919. Silver coins to the value of £E1,869,000 were minted,[2] but this proved inadequate and government currency notes totalling £E1,622,000 were issued.

The war also saw the development of deposit banking. After an initial crisis, allayed by a moratorium, deposits began to accumulate fast, those of the National Bank and Anglo-Egyptian Bank rising to £E35·5 million in 1920. At the same time mortgage debts were repaid, falling to £E29·3 million in 1920.[3]

The total favourable balance built up by Egypt during the war and immediate post-war years, after deduction of interest on foreign capital, was £E139 million. Of this some £E50 million was spent in the immediate post-war years on imports, travel, and unsuccessful speculation in foreign exchange. The bulk of the remainder went to repay mortgage loans, purchase foreign securities, and repatriate Egyptian securities held abroad. The war thus enabled Egypt considerably to reduce its foreign indebtedness.

But if the Egyptian economy as a whole profited, the war meant great hardship for the masses. The influx of money, the shortage of shipping, the presence of troops, and the cupidity of the landowners, who sacrificed wheat for cotton and evaded the government's restrictions on cotton acreage, forced up the wholesale price index from 100 in 1914 to 211 in 1918 and 312 in 1920. The great sufferers were naturally the urban proletariat and employees. The number of deaths, which had been in the neighbourhood of 300,000 before the war, rose to 375,000 after 1916; and in 1918 deaths, at 510,000, actually exceeded births.

[1] Crouchley, *Investment*, p. 174.         [2] Min. of Fin. Archives.
[3] Crouchley, *Investment*, p. 74.

# III

# Accumulating Difficulties, 1920–52

*The acuteness of the problem of backwardness at this stage is frequently proportional to the success and rapidity of 'economic development' at the second stage.*　HLA MYINT.

*Independence comes after all this, because it has no value unless there is also an internal liberation.*　SAAD ZAGHLUL.

During the period between the two world wars the underlying weaknesses in Egypt's economy began to make themselves increasingly felt, and the Second World War brought further difficulties and disruptions.[1] The rapid expansion in agricultural output through extension of the cultivated area, which had characterized the previous hundred years, came to an abrupt end with the First World War and henceforth production rose more slowly and only thanks to costly irrigation works and intensification. The sharp fall in world prices of primary products in general, and cotton in particular, in the 1920's and 1930's led to a deterioration in Egypt's terms of trade and a decline in the real value of its exports. Since agriculture accounted for the greater part of gross national product, and since the ratio of foreign trade to gross national product was high, it seems very probable that there was no significant increase in real national income during the inter-war period, and the Second World War caused a definite decline in it. At the same time the rapid population growth meant that per-capita incomes decreased sharply, and the level of living fell significantly during both the inter-war and the war years.

A few achievements of this period may be noted, though they fell short of outweighing the effects of the above-mentioned factors. First, Egypt's already adequate transport system was improved by the building of roads and airports and the modernization of railways. Secondly, some of the gaps in the credit system were

[1] For further details on this period see the relevant chapters in Issawi, *Egypt* and *EMC*.

filled by the creation of specialized, government-sponsored, banks and some control was established over financial institutions. Similarly the introduction of income and other direct taxes removed some of the defects in the fiscal system. Egypt's foreign indebtedness had already been much reduced during the First World War, and the Second World War saw the accumulation of huge sterling balances and the emergence of Egypt as a creditor. Lastly, and most important, the nucleus of a factory industry was formed during the 1930's and greatly expanded during the 1940's, and along with this a small body of technicians and skilled workers came into being.

## POPULATION, NATIONAL INCOME, AND LEVEL OF LIVING

In the inter-war period population continued to grow, at an average annual rate of about 1 per cent; the total rose from 12,751,000 in 1917 to 15,933,000 in 1937 (see Table 3, p. 77). Neither birth-rates nor death-rates seem to have changed significantly in these years, except during and immediately after the First World War when there was a sharp rise in mortality, but the figures are not sufficiently accurate to warrant a definitive judgement. In the late 1930's and 1940's, however, improved hygiene resulted in a distinct drop in death-rates, especially infant-mortality rates, and the growth in population accelerated; the 1947 census put the total population at 19,022,000.

Until close to the end of the last century Egypt had suffered from a shortage of labour and as late as the 1860's plans for large-scale immigration of Italians, Chinese, and other labourers were seriously considered. By the turn of the century, however, the labour supply was fully adequate and after that there were increasing signs of population pressure. The first warning was sounded in 1917:

If the rate of increase elicited at last census is maintained, it is not difficult to show that, in 50 years time, the population will be about 29 millions. The cultivable land will then be 7·7 millions of feddans cropped twice a year and so equivalent to 15·4 million feddans of land. . . . Now 4·4 million feddans at present barely support 13·1 million of people; will 8·7 [*sic*] million feddans support the 29 million of 1967? Yes if the yield of crops is improved; no if it is not.[1]

But it was not until the 1930's that population problems began to receive serious consideration and the first study pointing out the

---

[1] J. I. Craig, 'The Census of Egypt', *Ég. contemp.*, 1917.

existence and consequences of population pressure was published in 1936, by an American.[1]

Various estimates of national income were made during this period, but those dealing with the inter-war years are extremely tentative. The first attempt, in 1922, put the total at £E301 million, but this figure has been criticized as too high and alternative figures of 270 million and 200 million were suggested.[2] Another rough estimate gave a figure of £E265 million for 1925.[3] For the 1930's the following figures are available (£E):[4] 185 million in 1935; 180–200 million in 1938–9; 220 million in 1939; and 168 million in 1939. Post-war estimates range from 504 million and 600 million in 1945 to 860 million in 1950. A series prepared by the National Planning Committee put gross domestic product at market prices at £E193 million in 1938, 660 million in 1945 and 858 million in 1950; at 1950 prices, the figures were £E634 million, 688 million and 858 million respectively.[5]

The general trend indicated by these data is confirmed by estimates made by two Egyptian economists who put annual per-capita income, in 1913 prices, as follows (£E): 7·6 in 1880–97, 12·4 in 1913, 12·2 in 1921–8, 8·2 in 1930–3, 9·6 in 1935–9 and 9·4 in 1940–9[6] and a French economist whose figures (also in 1913 prices) were 12·4 for 1913, 8 in 1937, 7·5 in 1945 and 8·2 in 1948.[7]

There is also some evidence of an increasing maldistribution of income, as rents and profits rose while wages remained stagnant or declined. This is confirmed by the fact that consumption on luxury goods increased while that of staples, per capita, declined (see below, pp. 121–2).

## AGRICULTURE

The First World War marks the end of the period of rapid agricultural expansion. Owing to the fact that all readily available land had by then been reclaimed, the cost of extending cultivation began to rise sharply. In the inter-war period several large-scale

[1] Wendell Cleland, *The Population Problem in Egypt* (Lancaster, Pa., 1936).

[2] See the articles by I. G. Levi, J. I. Craig, and J. Baxter in *Ég. contemp.*, 1922.

[3] GB., Dept. Overseas Trade, *Rep. of U.K. Trade Mission to Egypt, Feb.–Mar. 1931* (1931).        [4] See sources in Issawi, *EMC*, p. 83.

[5] UN, Dept. of Econ. & Soc. Aff., *The Development of Manufacturing in Egypt, Israel and Turkey* (NY, 1958), p. 94.

[6] A. El Sherbini & A. P. Sherif, 'Marketing Problems in an Underdeveloped Country—Egypt', *Ég. contemp.*, 1956.

[7] H. Meunier, 'Comment a évolué le revenu national en Égypte', *R. d'Ég. écon. et financ.*, 1 Dec. 1951–9, Feb. 1952. See also the series in Besançon, p. 348.

irrigation works were built, total expenditure on capital irrigation works alone from 1927 to 1937 inclusive amounting to £E32·5 million.[1] The resulting increase in the total cultivated area was slight, from 5,280,000 feddans in 1912 to 5,845,000 in 1952, but dams, barrages, and canals made it possible to extend perennial irrigation to almost the whole country; consequently, in most places, three crops were grown in a two-year cycle on a given patch of land and the total *crop* area rose from 7·7 million feddans in 1912 to 9·3 million in 1952.

Simultaneously, an effort was made to intensify production. Already before the First World War cotton yields had begun to decline, dropping from a peak of 5·8 cantars per feddan in 1897 to as little as 3·13 in 1909. Among the causes of the decline were attacks by insect pests, overcropping and soil exhaustion, and a rise in the water-table because of inadequate drainage and of the fact that farmers tended and still tend to use too much water owing to the absence of irrigation charges. In the 1920's attempts were made to remedy these deficiencies. Drains were provided at considerable cost and the water-table, which was choking the deep roots of the cotton plants, was lowered in most areas. Cotton research and control were intensified; several new varieties, with higher yields, greater resistance to disease and longer, glossier, or tougher fibres, were produced by the Ministry of Agriculture and the Royal Agricultural Society and propagated all over the country and regulations regarding purity and standardization of seed were rigidly enforced. Methods of cultivation were improved, for example by closer spacing and earlier sowing, and after 1945 farm mechanization made some noteworthy progress. Still more important, pesticides and chemical fertilizers, introduced shortly before the First World War, began to be used on a very wide scale and by the late 1930's nearly 600,000 tons of fertilizers were applied each year, giving a higher figure per cultivated area than in any other country in the world.

These measures raised cotton yields again, from a low of 3·06 cantar per feddan in 1916 to a high of 5·52 in 1937, but naturally increased costs of cultivation. Similarly between 1921 and 1939 the yield of cereals, which had also dropped, was raised appreciably: wheat by 29 per cent, maize by 16, rice by 46, millet by 15 and barley by 32 per cent. This rise in yields, together with the extension of

[1] M. M. Hamdy, 'A Statistical Survey of the Development of Capital Investment in Egypt since 1880' (London Univ. Ph.D. thesis, 1943).

cultivation, increased output appreciably; between 1924–8 and 1935–9 a weighted index of the fourteen main crops showed a rise of 15 per cent. During the Second World War the sharp fall in imports of fertilizers and the disruption of the normal cycle of rotations by the need to increase output of grains and reduce that of cotton caused a fall of 25 per cent in total agricultural production by 1943. Thereafter conditions improved and by 1952 agricultural production was some 10 per cent above the 1934–8 level.

At the same time as it was attempting to increase total agricultural output, the government was trying to change its composition. In the belief that cotton prices could be raised by curtailing supply, the government restricted cotton acreage in 1921–3, 1926–9, and 1931–3; it also bought up and stored cotton in 1921, 1926, and 1929. These measures were signal failures; they cost £E9 million and stimulated the production of rival countries, notably the Sudan. After that there was no attempt, until the outbreak of war, to in-fluence cotton prices, but the landlords sought to recoup the decline in their cotton income by raising the price of cereals. A prohibitive tariff, imposed in 1930, cut off foreign imports and raised local prices, and in 1937 and 1939 there was a small-scale subsidization of wheat exports. The burden of this policy was of course borne by the urban working class and landless rural workers, whose consumption of wheat and maize was appreciably reduced and whose annual expenditure on cereals was increased by some £E5 million.

Following the poor 1941–2 grain crop it was, rightly if somewhat belatedly, decided to restrict cotton acreage and expand that of wheat, since the shortage of shipping impeded both the export of cotton and the import of wheat. Such restrictions have remained in force since then, but the proportions have varied from year to year, and various price-support schemes have been tried (see below, pp. 144 and 148). As Egypt is, however, no longer self-sufficient in bread grains, import duties on wheat and maize were abolished in 1950, a step which has the same symbolic importance as did the repeal of the Corn Laws in Britain.

Taking the period 1920–52 as a whole, there was little change in the proportion of the total area planted to major crops. At its close as at its beginning, cotton occupied one-fifth of the total area and the leading grains (maize, wheat, millet, barley, and rice) one-half. A few indications of a trend towards more rational use of the land may, however, be noted. First, the area planted to cereals showed a relative decline, which was most marked in those crops—barley and wheat—in which Egypt has the least comparative advantage. On the other hand the area under rice, a labour-intensive crop, rose from 200,000 feddans in 1915–24 to 500,000 in the late 1930's and over 700,000 in the post-war years; this expansion was made possible by greater availability of water. Secondly, the area under *berseem* (Egyptian clover), expanded appreciably, reflecting both the increasing need for restoration to the soil of the nitrogen taken out by other plants and the greater demand for fodder for the growing livestock herds. Thirdly, there was a large proportionate increase in the cultivation of fruit and vegetables; between 1913 and 1951 fruit acreage tripled and between 1929 and 1951 that of vegetables increased by 40 per cent; however, in 1951 their combined acreage was still under 300,000 feddans, or about 3 per cent of the crop area.

The relative value of the main crops fluctuated violently, the most variable element being cotton (see below, p. 139). But over the period there was a rise in the proportion of agricultural income derived from fruit, vegetables, and livestock products and a decline in that of the traditional field crops.

Owing to the rapid population increase, the relatively slow growth of the urban sector and the consequent land hunger, the distribution of agricultural income between landlords, tenants, and wage-labourers evolved on the lines predicted in the Ricardian analysis: rents rose considerably while real wages remained constant or declined (see below, p. 155). Thus the benefits of the increase in agricultural production went primarily to the owners of the scarce factor, land.

## FOREIGN TRADE AND BALANCE OF PAYMENTS

The First World War also marks the end of the rapid expansion of Egypt's foreign trade. The slowing down in the growth of agricultural production adversely affected exports; not until the mid-1930's did exports of cotton reach a level substantially above that of 1912–13 and after the Second World War increasing consumption by the local textile industry caused a further drop. At the same time the rapidly growing population ate into cereals exports. This decline was not offset by the small increase in exports of minerals and a few manufactured goods, such as textiles.

At the same time that the volume of its exports was stagnating, Egypt's terms of trade were deteriorating. A comparison of the price of cotton (which throughout this period accounted for 80 per cent or more of total exports) with a representative index such as that of exports of manufactured goods from the United Kingdom shows that Egypt's terms of trade improved from 1895 to 1913, fluctuated sharply during the First World War and immediate post-war years, and deteriorated markedly from 1925 to 1938. A further deterioration during the Second World War was followed by a sharp rise in 1948 and an equally sharp drop after 1951.

The last column of Table 1 (p. 28) shows Egypt's import capacity or the buying power of its exports. It will be seen that there was a very sharp rise until the First World War, a decline during the war and immediate post-war years, another rise in the middle and late 1920's, a sharp fall in the early 1930's, a gentler rise in the middle and late 1930's, a sharp drop during the Second World War, a sharp rise in the late 1940's and an equally sharp drop in 1952, followed by a levelling off at the pre-war level. It will also be seen that the curve seems to bump against a ceiling, represented by the figure of £E50 million in 1938 prices; only during the Korean War did it succeed in momentarily surpassing that figure.

The fact that the buying power of exports failed to increase after 1914 may be explained by both supply and demand factors. On the supply side was the small rise in output and the sharp increase in domestic consumption of cotton and cereals. On the demand side was the competition of other producers and of synthetics, which prevented cotton prices in terms of other goods from rising. In other words, three assumptions on which arguments for strict international specialization implicitly rest have proved dubious. First, in the last fifty years, in spite of the great rise in world industrial production, demand for agricultural raw materials has not increased as much as the spectacular growth of British imports in the nineteenth century would have led one to expect. Secondly, and largely because of the amazing increase in agricultural productivity in some of the larger and newer countries, such as the United States, Canada, and Australia, world agricultural output has greatly expanded. These two factors explain why, taking the world as a whole, the effect of diminishing returns has been repeatedly staved off and why the terms of trade did not move in favour of agriculture, as the earlier economists had expected. Thirdly, some countries, such as Egypt, have approached the limits of their agricultural productive capacity sooner than had been anticipated; this has meant that they have simultaneously suffered from the inelasticity of their supply and the unfavourable terms of trade for their exports.

Until the Second World War Egypt had few sources of foreign

exchange to supplement its export proceeds, the main ones being the local expenditures of the Suez Canal Company (£E2 million per year) and of the British army (a little under £E2 million), and disbursements by tourists. On the debit side were interest payments, as well as insurance premiums, remittances, and pilgrim and tourist expenditures of about £E1 million. Over the period 1920–38 there was a small import surplus and it is probable that the current account also showed a very small deficit, which was covered by net exports of specie.

During the Second World War two contrary tendencies dominated the balance-of-payments position. In 1940–5 inclusive there was an import surplus of £E98 million, because of the sharp decline in exports of cotton, which exceeded the reduction in imports. This, however, was more than compensated by Allied military expenditure, which aggregated £E314 million in 1940–5. By the end of the war Egypt had accumulated sterling balances of about £E400 million.[1] In the post-war period these balances were heavily drawn on and sterling releases, together with British army expenditure and local expenditure by the Suez Canal Company, filled the large import surplus which now emerged.

Some important changes took place in the direction and composition of foreign trade during this period. As regards direction, the most important trend was the continued decrease in the share of the United Kingdom in Egypt's trade. On the one hand the decline of the Lancashire cotton textile industry led to smaller purchases of Egyptian cotton, and the United Kingdom's share of Egypt's exports fell from 63 per cent in 1885–9 and 43 per cent in 1913 to 32 per cent in 1938 and 21 per cent in 1950. And on the other, growing competition from Germany, Japan, and during and after the Second World War the United States, caused a decline in the United Kingdom's share of Egypt's imports from 38 per cent in 1885–9 and 31 per cent in 1913 to 23 per cent in 1938 and 19 per cent in 1950.

As noted before, there was little change in the composition of Egypt's exports; cotton, with until the Second World War cotton seed, accounted for 80 per cent or more of exports. However, the composition of imports changed significantly. Owing to the rapid population growth Egypt, which had formerly been self-sufficient in cereals, came to import increasing quantities of wheat, though this was partly offset by greater exports of rice; imports of tobacco, tea,

[1] *Banker*, May 1950; also NBE, *Econ. B.*, i/1, 1948.

coffee, and sugar also rose. The imposition of heavy duties and the growth of local production caused a sharp fall in imports of textiles and other manufactured consumer goods. By the same token, there was a sharp rise in imports of machinery, spare parts, and raw materials. There was also an increase in imports of petroleum, in spite of greater local production, but this was more than offset by the disappearance of imported coal, which had previously been Egypt's leading source of energy.

FINANCE AND PUBLIC FINANCE

During 1920–52 no structural transformation of Egypt's money and credit system took place, but there were some important developments. As regards currency, during the First World War Egypt shifted from a gold to a sterling-exchange standard, on which it remained until 1948 (see below, p. 247). As for banking, development continued essentially on the lines laid down before the First World War. A large number of foreign banks continued to meet Egypt's seasonal credit needs by moving funds from and to their head offices in London, Paris, and other European capitals; these banks concentrated on internal and foreign trade while other foreign banks, mainly French, supplied mortgage credit. During the inter-war period other European banks, notably Italian and Belgian, opened branches in Egypt, as did some Middle Eastern banks during and after the Second World War. But the most important event was the establishment, in 1920, of Misr Bank, the first purely Egyptian owned and managed institution, which constituted one of the main nuclei around which the new Egyptian bourgeoisie was formed and which did important pioneering work in credit and industry.[1]

Attempts were made by the government to fill the gaps in the credit system existing in three important fields, agricultural, mortgage, and industrial credit, and to subject the banking and financial system to some measure of central control. In 1902 the Agricultural Bank was founded to grant short-term and mortgage loans to small farmers but after a prosperous start it was hit by the Five-Feddan Law in 1913, which exempted small properties from seizure, and eventually went into liquidation in 1937. In 1931 the Agricultural Credit Bank was founded and its activities expanded very rapidly (see below, p. 260).

[1] See below, p. 264, and L. Fridman, 'Kontsern Misr', in V. Lutskii, ed., *Ocherki po istorii Arabskikh stran* (Moscow, 1959).

As for mortgage credit, during the Depression the burden of indebtedness greatly increased and the government concluded agreements with the main mortgage banks in 1933, and again in subsequent years, by which the latter spread out the annuities payable by debtors while the government took over responsibility for the greater part of the overdue interest.[1] The rise in agricultural prices during the Second World War naturally lessened the burden of indebtedness. The government also intervened more directly by founding, in 1932, the Crédit Hypothécaire Agricole to provide mortgage loans to small farmers (see below, p. 264). Industrial credit was first provided by Misr Bank to its affiliated companies and, on a small scale, through that Bank by the government. In 1949 an Industrial Bank was founded; its activities are discussed on p. 265 below.

Government control was first extended to insurance companies—which until the end of the period covered in this chapter remained predominantly foreign—in 1939 when they were compelled to keep in Egypt a certain proportion of their reserves; this proportion was raised considerably in 1950. In banking the main feature of the inter-war period was the growth in the leadership of the National Bank of Egypt, a privately, and predominantly foreign, owned body which fulfilled certain functions of a central bank such as having a monopoly of the note issue, being the custodian of the government's funds and acting as financial adviser to and agent for the government. On the outbreak of war, in 1939, an exchange-control system was established and its operation entrusted to the National Bank. In 1940 the Bank's charter was extended, and in 1951 its powers (see below, p. 267).

One of the factors which had made it possible for Britain to occupy Egypt was the failure of the Egyptian government to meet its financial obligations, and the British knew that another bankruptcy would be used by the other Great Powers, notably France, to intervene once more in Egypt. Hence the overriding necessity for them to balance the budget and their subordination of all other considerations to fiscal ones. By the turn of the century, the 'race against bankruptcy' had been definitely won and a series of budget surpluses was used to build up a sizeable Reserve Fund.

In the inter-war period fiscal problems receded to the background. The general rise in money incomes in the 1920's and the

[1] For full details see J. Economides, 'Le Problème de l'endettement rural en Égypte', *Ég. contemp.*, 1952.

reduction in government debt reduced the burden of the budget, and except in 1920 and 1930 small surpluses continued to appear in it. During the Second World War expenditure shot up rapidly owing to the rise in prices, but on the whole revenue kept pace with expenditure and it was only in the post-war period that substantial deficits were recorded.

In the meanwhile important changes had taken place in the structure of Egypt's public debt. Up to 1939 a steady, if small, reduction was effected, interrupted only by a £E2·5 million loan in 1933. During the war two small loans were issued to finance government purchases of the cotton crop. In 1943 a vast refunding operation took place, as a result of which the old sterling 3½–4 per cent loans were replaced by Egyptian 3¼ and 2¾ per cent bonds; in other words, Egypt's foreign public debt was converted into a domestic one. In 1948 two loans of £E15 million each, at 3 and 2½ per cent, were floated to cover the costs of the Palestine war. In addition, during the war the government started to issue treasury bills, and by 1952 a total of £E85 million was outstanding.

More important still were the changes that took place in the structure of government revenue and expenditure. On the revenue side, until the 1930's the government was shackled by various international agreements concluded in the nineteenth century. Thus the land-tax assessment of 1899, which put the average rental value at £E3·595 per feddan and fixed the tax rate at 28·64 per cent, could not be modified before 1939, although the net revenue and rental value of land had considerably increased in the meanwhile. Similarly customs duties could not be modified before 1930 owing to international conventions. Finally, and most important, the Capitulations stood in the way of any direct taxation, as foreigners could not be taxed without the consent of their governments.

Beginning with 1930, the hands of the Egyptian government have been completely freed. Customs duties were modified in 1930, most of them being made specific instead of *ad valorem*, and ever since duties have been constantly rising, in response to the twofold impulsion of fiscal authorities in search of revenue, and landowners and industrialists seeking protection.

Land-tax was readjusted in 1939, and remissions and reductions were introduced in the following ten years. In 1939 the first income-tax law was passed, fixing varying rates on specified categories of income, and in 1949 a general income-tax on aggregate income from all sources was introduced. Death duties were levied as from 1944, and the rates were subsequently raised (see below, p. 283). In 1941 a tax on excess profits in industry, trade, and finance was introduced. Designed solely as a war measure, it was repealed in 1950.

Equally important changes occurred on the expenditure side. The most spectacular was the decrease in the proportion absorbed by the servicing of the public debt, from around 50 per cent at the turn of the century to 10 per cent at the outbreak of the Second World War and 3 per cent in 1950. Conversely defence, which absorbed only 6 per cent before the First World War, rose in the 1930's to 12 per cent and by 1950 stood at 21 per cent. There was also a sharp rise in expenditure on education, which rose from 1 per cent to 11 and 12 per cent respectively, and in that on health and social welfare.

### INDUSTRY

After the liquidation of Muhammad Ali's factories, no interest had been shown by either foreign or local capital in the unprotected Egyptian market. Muhammad Ali's monopoly system had borne very hard on the handicrafts and killed whatever spirit of enterprise may have survived in them.[1] For their part, subsequent governments were precluded from offering tariff protection, because of international conventions fixing the level of customs duties. Moreover the British administration had no desire to industrialize Egypt.[2] Hence, although a few food-processing, textile, and building-materials industries were established, a list of manufacturing enterprises operating in 1916 put the total number at 15 and employment at 30,000–35,000, of whom the bulk worked in the sugar industry.[3]

The need for industrialization began to be realized during the First World War, owing to the shortage of imported manufactured goods. The same shortage brought into being several minor industries, some of which survived the war, and gave the older ones a new lease of life.

After the war there was a desire to increase the country's political and economic independence by industrialization. Already in 1917 a government Commission on Trade and Industry, including among its members both Ismail Sidqi, the future Prime Minister and President of the Federation of Industries, and Talat Harb, who later founded and presided over Misr Bank, had urged much greater

[1] Gritly, *Tarikh*, p. 78.
[2] For details, see Issawi, *EMC*, p. 37 and Gritly, 'The Structure of Modern Industry in Egypt', *Ég. contemp.*, 1947.
[3] René Maunier, 'L'exposition des industries égyptiennes', ibid. 1916.

government help for industry. In 1920 Misr Bank was founded; one of its main objects was the fostering of Egyptian industry. A third landmark was the creation of the Egyptian Federation of Industries in 1922, representing employers.

Little more was done, however, in the 1920's. For one thing, high cotton prices seemed to promise continued prosperity for all. For another, capitalists preferred to invest in land, which was described as a 'bottomless sink' for Egyptian capital. Lastly, the government, bound by international conventions, could not modify customs duties, which were fixed at 8 per cent *ad valorem*. Hence by 1927 total employment in manufacturing plants employing ten persons or over was only 95,000 and manufacturing and mining probably accounted for less than 5 per cent of the GNP.

The catastrophic fall in cotton prices during the depression, the regaining of fiscal autonomy in 1930, the realization that Egypt's population was outrunning the absorptive capacity of agriculture, and the fact that certain branches of industry promised worth-while profits, however, combined to renew the urge for industrialization. This was reinforced by the social and political attractions it offered to backward countries.

The tariff reform of 1930, increasing duties on imported goods, marks the beginning of large-scale industrialization. In the absence of statistics on output, or of accurate figures on employment, it is difficult to judge the extent of the industrial advance. Of the established industries sugar increased its output from 79,000 tons in 1917 to 109,000 tons in 1928 and 159,000 in 1939; cement from 24,000 tons to 61,000 and 353,000; and mechanically woven cotton cloth from 9 million square yards to 20 million in 1931 and 159 million in 1939.[1] Some indirect light is also provided by trade statistics, which show a sharp increase in imports of producers and capital goods and a great decline in imports of manufactured consumer goods between 1913 and 1938 and by other figures, showing the percentage of local demand that was met by the most developed branches of industry in 1939.[2] The rise in industrial employment is indicated by the fact that in 1937 155,000 persons worked in manufacturing establishments engaging ten persons or over. But at the outbreak of war the share of manufacturing, mining, gas, water and electricity was still only about 8 per cent of the GNP.

The Second World War greatly stimulated Egyptian industry. Not only were imports reduced drastically, but the large-scale

[1] Gritly, in *Ég. contemp.*, 1947.          [2] See Issawi, *EMC*, p. 141.

expenditure of Allied troops stationed in Egypt, which at its peak represented some 25 per cent of the national income, greatly increased the demand for industrial products. Some 200,000 Egyptians, of whom 80,000 were skilled or semi-skilled workmen, were employed in British army workshops or camps. The Middle East Supply Centre also started a few essential industries, and assisted others by giving them technical advice and helping them to obtain spare parts and scarce raw materials.[1] Some Egyptian products found their way to neighbouring countries, where manufactured goods were even more scarce. Several industries expanded considerably, especially textiles, preserved foods, chemicals, glass, leather, cement and other building materials, petroleum and mechanical industries, while new industries were established such as the dehydration and canning of vegetables, rubber goods, jute processing, the making of spare parts and tools, and, above all, a wide variety of chemicals and pharmaceuticals.[2]

It is difficult to estimate the exact extent of the growth of industry during the war and immediate post-war years. The Industrial Production Censuses of 1947 and 1950, which had a different coverage from those of the Censuses of Industry used earlier, put total employment in establishments with ten or more persons at 278,000 and 244,000 respectively, but this would seem to exaggerate the extent of the rise in employment during the war years. The capital of industrial joint-stock companies rose from £E16·3 million in 1938 to 28·5 million in 1945 and 65·8 million in 1950.[3] As for output, an official quantum index of manufacturing production showed a rise of 138 per cent between 1938 and 1951[4] and another a rise of 50 per cent between 1945 and 1952.[5] By the latter date industry, in the broader sense, accounted for some 10 per cent of GNP.

[1] For the activities of the MESC, see George Kirk, *The Middle East in the War* (1953), pp. 169–93.
[2] Govt. Cttee on Industry, *Taqrir lajnat al-sinaa* (1948).
[3] NBE, *Econ. B.*, no. 4, 1951.      [4] NPC, Memo. no. 34.
[5] UN, *Dev. of Manufacturing*, p. 98.

# IV

# Arab Socialism

*Neither the law of justice nor divine law allows that wealth should be hereditary and that poverty should be hereditary, that health should be hereditary, that illness should be hereditary, that learning should be hereditary, that illiteracy should be hereditary, that human dignity should be hereditary and human degradation should be hereditary.*

GAMAL ABDEL NASSER.

*But what can we do if we don't resemble democracy, we don't resemble socialism, we don't resemble anything? Gentlemen, we should be proud of defying comparison! Because, Gentlemen, we resemble ourselves.*   ATATÜRK.

*Pour mieux gouverner il faudrait gouverner moins.*   D'ARGENSON.

In the ten years that have passed since the Revolution of 23 July 1952 the economic and social structure of Egypt has changed more fundamentally than at any previous period in the long history of the country, with the possible exception of the Muhammad Ali era. Moreover the changes have not been spread evenly over the whole decade but crowded into the period since July 1956.

In 1951 Egypt was an overwhelmingly agrarian country, in which industry accounted for under 10 per cent of GNP. It had a predominantly free-enterprise economy, with direct state activity restricted to such fields as irrigation and railways, although state supervision extended to other branches as well. Its fiscal system was characterized by the low level of taxes, by the predominance of indirect taxation, and by the moderate share—little over 20 per cent —of national income absorbed by the government. Its income structure showed a very marked degree of inequality. The part played by foreigners in the national economy, although appreciably reduced from its previous level, was still very important and in certain branches dominant. Lastly, Egyptian society was a civilian one, in which the army had a very minor role and in which a considerable amount of political and intellectual liberty prevailed.

By 1962 the picture was very different. Egypt had become a totalitarian socialistic state.[1] A series of nationalizations and sequestrations had transferred the ownership of the main branches of the economy—industry, transport, finance, and foreign trade—to the government; the main form of wealth remaining in private hands was rural and urban real estate, and even here state control was tight. The government budgets accounted for some 60 per cent of GNP, partly because direct taxation had risen very sharply but mainly because of the revenue yielded by the ever-increasing number of state enterprises. Inequality of wealth and income had been greatly reduced, first by the agrarian reform, higher taxation, and the extension of social services and then, much more drastically, by a series of nationalizations, sequestrations, and other measures, including the fixing of a maximum salary in government or company employment. Foreign ownership had been practically eliminated and the number of foreigners had fallen very sharply. Industry had made rapid progress, accounted for well over 20 per cent of GNP and was expected to contribute a larger share than agriculture by 1964.[2] Lastly, the army was in full control of both political and economic activity, and both political and intellectual freedom had been suppressed.

The successes registered by the military régime in its first ten years have undoubtedly been considerable—although they have hardly made a dent in Egypt's formidable economic problems[3]—

[1] With the important qualification that Egypt does not have a party organization extending to the lower levels of political, economic, and social activity. The absence of such a transmission belt makes it much more difficult for the government to carry out its plans, but also makes life easier for Egyptians than for the citizens of other totalitarian states. The nearest approach to such a party is the officer corps.

[2] It should, however, be noted that the value of industrial production is swollen by the heavy protection granted to it, a factor which appreciably raises its share in the GNP relatively to other sectors such as agriculture, which receive far less protection and produce at world prices. A still more important factor inflating the share of industry is the high and rising level of indirect taxation on manufactured goods (see below, p. 115).

[3] Moreover, another point of great importance should be borne in mind when judging the progress of Egypt, or indeed of any other country. The period 1952–62 has been one of rapid economic and social advance all over the world—not only in the developed regions but in most parts of the Middle East, Asia and Africa, and large parts of Latin America. The appreciable progress achieved by Egypt should be compared with that registered elsewhere if a fair assessment is to be made, and it should be noted that the per capita rate of growth since 1952 has been slightly below the world average.

and range over such distant fields as the evacuation of foreign troops, the nationalization of the Canal, the launching of an industrialization programme, the beginning of work on the High Dam, the reduction of social inequality, and the extension of education. Moreover, they have cost little blood and, considering the magnitude of the changes involved, not much suffering. But an observer writing in 1962 cannot help wondering whether they have not been partly achieved by laying heavy mortgages on the future. In the first place, the confiscation of foreign property has greatly undermined Egypt's credit-worthiness, and barred the flow of private capital to it; however, a cynical but realistic appraisal of conditions prevailing in the world today might lead to the conclusion that private capital, which had not flowed into Egypt in large quantities, was unlikely to do so anyhow and that, for various political and economic reasons, the flow of public funds would not be impaired (see ch. x). More serious is the fact that much of the development has been achieved by contracting large foreign debts, the servicing of which will constitute an increasing burden in the next few years. Thirdly, and still more important, is the effect of the massive and ill-conceived nationalizations of 1961, and the subsequent sequestrations, which have resulted in a fall in the efficiency of many nationalized enterprises,[1] in a widespread sense of insecurity, and in the discouragement of initiative and saving in the few sectors remaining in private hands. Fourthly, the sequestrations, arrests, and spy trials, and the wave of fear which swept through the country at the end of 1961 and the beginning of 1962, cannot but fill with foreboding anyone who has followed the progress of events in totalitarian countries. Lastly, one cannot avoid misgivings about the ultimate consequences of the stirring up of the masses by promises of better conditions and the raising in them of expectations which will almost certainly outrun the country's capacity to satisfy them.

### THE CONTEXT

Of course the Egyptian, like other revolutions, was not just an accident. On the one hand it can be fairly easily placed in its context

[1] Figures published on the industrial companies attached to the various Organizations show that the value of their overall gross output rose slightly after nationalization, although that of many declined; but value of gross output is only one index of efficiency and, in the absence of further information on prices, and costs and investments, the present writer does not believe that this rise, by itself, should cause him to modify the judgement made in the text, which is based on reliable information and personal observation (see details in *al-Ahram*, 1 June 1962).

of contemporary events and on the other its roots run deep in the previous Egyptian society.

Egypt's 'Arab Socialism' is only an extreme example of a fairly widespread and rapidly multiplying genus, the 'Socialist National-ism' of backward countries, which includes lands as far apart as Cuba and Indonesia, Iraq and Guinea. The prevailing social philosophy in these countries is a strange and amorphous amalgam of nationalism, militarism, and socialism. It is based essentially on resentment of western political and economic domination and a determination to assert national sovereignty and power. To this has been added a socialism consisting of an urge for greater social equality; an anti-capitalism based on the conviction that private gain is immoral and can be achieved only at the expense of the public interest; and a touching belief that socialist planning is the gimmick that will infallibly, painlessly, and simultaneously bring about national power, rapid economic development, and social welfare. A further factor, which may have operated in certain countries such as Egypt, is the conviction that international non-alignment cannot be achieved unless the economy is transformed into a pattern which is basically neither capitalist nor communist, since otherwise the economic structure is bound to tie the country up with one of the rival systems and blocs.

Inspiration for this philosophy has come from such varied sources as Soviet Russia and communist China—whose achievements have received full recognition, and more, while the appalling human costs involved and the political factors which made success possible have remained unperceived—Tito's Yugoslavia, and western and Indian theoretical socialism. This ideology has manifested itself in a series of improvised, haphazard measures which, were it not for their comprehensiveness and unmistakable twentieth-century grimness, might be described by the following judgement passed on Bis-marck's legislation:

Such measures were not really Socialism, properly defined, at all—the Social Democrats saw that from the first—except in the sense that every act of a State is 'socialistic'. It was the renaissance of the Mercantilism of the seventeenth century adapted to the benevolent and illuminated despotism of the eighteenth century and the conditions of a militarist State, remoulded by the phenomena of modern industrialism.[1]

As for the Egyptian roots of state intervention, some of them spring from the distant and others from the more recent past. At

[1] C. Grant Robertson, *Bismarck* (1918), p. 369.

the same time it should be emphatically stated that, although many of the roots are strong, the tree would not have flourished as luxuriantly as it is doing had it not been carefully tended and nurtured. In other words, there was nothing inevitable about the recent upheavals; a trend towards greater state control, social justice, and economic independence was evident in Egypt as elsewhere, but the pace, direction, and particular character of the changes was largely determined by a series of external political and economic factors.

The first long-term historical factor arises from the fusion of church and state in Islam (see above, p. 15). The idea that there is anything sinful, or even dangerous, about the state has always been, and still is, alien to Islamic thought. And secondly, private property has been more precarious than in Europe. From Abbasid times onward, the annals of the Middle East are replete with stories of sequestrations and dispossessions.

A third factor goes even farther into the past. In Egypt, as in other 'hydraulic' societies,[1] the power of the state developed to great proportions at a very early date, since the irrigation system could only be controlled by a central organism. The large-scale works carried out under Muhammad Ali and his successors, and the huge dams built by the British and Egyptian administrations necessitated further state control over this vital sector of the economy, a control extending to the distribution of water to individual fields.

Another important field in which the state established its control from the start was that of modern transport and communications. Not only the telegraphs but also the ports and the main railways were built and operated by the government. Judging from the experience of Syria, North Africa, and to a lesser extent Turkey, where private foreign capital did an expensive and inefficient job and left the country with an ill-planned and unco-ordinated network, Egypt has had no cause to regret this particular government initiative. Similarly, in education the government has since the early nineteenth century provided the bulk of the services and absorbed the bulk of the output (see below, p. 99).

It is true that after this vigorous start, to which should of course be added Muhammad Ali's abortive industrial and other schemes, government activity shrank to a minimum and remained negligible

[1] See the illuminating book by Karl Wittfogel, *Oriental Despotism* (New Haven, 1957); it is rightly pointed out, on p. 166, that Egypt is the most compact of the major hydraulic societies in world history.

until the 1930's. During this period the state provided the framework for private, and especially foreign, enterprise and adhered to a strict interpretation of *laissez-faire*. This was, after all, the dominant view in Europe and therefore, as so often since, tended to be accepted uncritically, but with a time-lag, in Egypt. It was also the only realistic philosophy, given the impotence of the government whose hands were tied by the Capitulations, commercial conventions, and foreign pressures, not to mention occupation.

In the 1930's government activity once more manifested itself in the form of protective tariffs, the beginnings of progressive taxation, some labour legislation, and various measures in the field of credit (see ch. iii); an attempt was also made to egyptianize business, which was still overwhelmingly foreign. During the Second World War government activity greatly increased, in Egypt as elsewhere. Exchange control was imposed in 1939, and was soon followed by import licensing. Growing shortages and inflation led to price controls, rationing, and rent controls. The rise in prices necessitated the levying of further progressive taxation, and the growing discontent of the working classes resulted in the passing of more social legislation. Lastly, the increasing weakness of the Europeans in Egypt facilitated a substantial shift of economic power from foreign to national interests.

This process was accelerated after the war. Exchange control was retained and with Egypt's departure from the sterling area, in July 1947, was made applicable to all foreign, and not only to non-sterling, countries. Import licensing was also kept, being tightened or relaxed according to the state of foreign-exchange reserves, and was increasingly supplemented by bilateral agreements. The promulgation of Law No. 119, of July 1948, meant a break with the hitherto prevailing sterling-exchange standard and its replacement by a managed currency (see below, p. 247). Other wartime measures, such as rent and price control, acreage allocation and the purchase and resale of grains, were also retained and further steps were taken in the direction of progressive taxation, social legislation, and egyptianization.

## FROM 1952 TO 1956

It seems most unlikely that any of the officers who carried out the coup d'état of 1952 had a clearly thought-out economic philosophy, much less that there was a doctrine shared by the whole group. A study of the government's actions in the economic and social field between 1952 and 1956, when civilian influence was predominant in that field, shows that it proceeded with great caution, and along highly orthodox lines, to restore economic stability, develop production, and bring about some measure of social welfare. In this it registered solid and appreciable, if not spectacular, progress which may be gauged by the rise in the agricultural production index (1935–9=100) from an average of 108 in 1950–2 to one of 121 in 1954–6, in the industrial production index (1954=100) from 91 in 1951 to 110 in 1955, and in the school population from 1,900,000 in 1951–2 to 2,573,000 in 1955–6.[1]

The new régime had inherited from its predecessor a chaotic situation in three vitally important fields: cotton, the budget, and the balance of payments, and one of its first tasks was to set them in order. In cotton, government manipulation and private speculation during the Korean boom had priced Egypt out of the world market. To prevent utter collapse following the break in world prices, the new government closed the cotton exchange in November 1952 and gradually reduced its purchase prices; later, helped by the slow recovery in world prices, it reopened the exchange in September 1955. As regards the budget, the 1951–2 fiscal year closed with the huge deficit of £E38·8 million. The military régime's immediate reaction was to reduce expenditure and to raise, to a slight extent, direct taxes on income, death duties, and customs and excise duties; as a result, the budget deficit was replaced by a surplus, which was then followed by much smaller deficits. Similarly, the huge deficit in the 1952 balance of payments was sharply reduced, by raising customs duties and applying much stricter import controls, and in 1954 there was actually a small surplus on current account, the only one recorded in the post-war period except for 1949. The government also continued the policy begun by its predecessor of trying to expand Egypt's export markets by means of bilateral agreements and attempted to stimulate re-export and transit trade by a system of drawbacks and by establishing free zones.

But the government aimed at much more than restoring stability. One of its first acts, on 9 September 1952, was to pass an Agrarian Reform Law, over the objections of both old-line politicians and the more conservative army elements, which limited maximum holdings

---

[1] For a review of this period see J. Economides, 'L'action du nouveau régime égyptien dans les domaines économique et social', *Ég. contemp.*, Oct. 1956; Keith Wheelock, *Nasser's New Egypt* (NY, 1960); Heinz Pentzlin, *Aegypten, eine Analyse der Entwicklungsprojekte* (Berlin, 1957); and P. J. Vatikiotis, *The Egyptian Army in Politics* (Bloomington, 1961).

to 200 feddans, plus another 100 if the owner had children (see below, p. 159). In this it pursued several objectives: to break the economic and political power of the landowning class; to bring about a greater measure of social justice and equality; to increase agricultural production; and to divert the flow of investment from agriculture to industry. On the whole, the first three objectives were achieved, but the capital diverted from agriculture went mainly into apartment building, a fact which led to the passing, in 1956, of Law No. 344, requiring permission for new building or repairs costing over £E5,000.

Another fundamental change was the more liberal attitude towards foreign capital, as exemplified in Law No. 156 of 1953 and Laws Nos. 26 and 475 of 1954.[1] Under these laws foreign capital was allowed to have a majority control of companies operating in Egypt, instead of only 49 per cent of the shares as stipulated in the law of 1947, and provisions regarding the transfer of profits and original capital abroad were considerably eased. No less important was the Mining and Quarrying Law of 1953, which was distinctly more liberal than that of 1948 in that it permitted the granting of new concessions to foreign as well as domestic petroleum companies and allowed longer extensions. Under this law, which was welcomed by foreign interests, petroleum concessions were granted to four companies in 1954. It may be added that arrangements were made for greatly increasing the amount of aid received from the United States; the original Point Four agreement had been signed in 1951, but the necessary Egyptian services were not organized until 1952; moreover, in November 1954, an agreement for the provision of an additional $40 million was concluded.

Attempts were also made to encourage domestic capital investment, especially in industry. Several changes were made in the tariff, raising duties on competing manufactured goods and abolishing or reducing them on raw materials and equipment. And in 1953 Law No. 430 exempted from taxes on profits, for seven years, new companies which were judged to promote economic development and, for five years, existing companies which increased their capital; further provisions were made for reducing taxation on undistributed profits by 50 per cent.[2] A few measures were also passed affecting industrial organization, for example the creation of a fund to promote the marketing of cotton textiles at home and abroad; making membership in industrial chambers compulsory for all

[1] NBE, *Econ. B.*, no. 1, 1953; nos. 2 & 3, 1954.     [2] Ibid. no. 3, 1953.

establishments with a capital of £E10,000 or over; slightly restricting eligibility to company directorships; and giving the government the right to appoint not less than two directors in any company whose profits it guaranteed.

Lastly, the government sought to promote economic development more directly. In 1953 the Permanent Council for Production was founded, to study and promote new projects, and it was soon followed by a Permanent Council for Social Services. In 1954 various government organizations, members of the Misr group, and a German firm combined to found a large iron and steel company and the following year the government also participated in the capital of a new commercial bank and a company for making railway wagons. A General Petroleum Authority was founded in 1954 and · a High Dam Organization in 1955. And a Development Budget was added to the ordinary budget, mainly financed by loans; among its most important projects were the installation of turbines on the Aswan dam, the building of thermic electric stations, petroleum refining, and land reclamation.

### FROM 1956 TO 1962

Since 1956 the Egyptian government has pursued a course which differs sharply from the one described in the previous section. This course has been characterized by the egyptianization of foreign establishments; by closer state control of business; by nationalization and sequestration first of foreign and then of Egyptian property; by intensified industrialization; and by sharply increased taxation on the higher incomes. These changes were accompanied by a swift break-away from the west in both political alignment and ideological approach and by an increasing use, in public pronouncements and the press, of pseudo-Marxist socialist and class-warfare slogans.

Many causes have contributed to this shift. First, there is the world-wide trend towards socialism and planning which has been already noted. Secondly, there may have been a slow realization that Egypt's economic and social problems were far more intractable than had been realized in the first flush of revolutionary enthusiasm, and the conclusion may have been drawn that much more drastic methods were required for their solution. Thirdly, there has been, in recent years, the desire to increase President Abdel Nasser's popularity among the masses in Egypt, and still more in other Arab countries, by representing him not only as the promoter of Arab unity but also as the champion of the people and the enemy of the ruling groups and classes.

But perhaps more important than all these trends has been a series of external political events which led, by a complex process of reaction and interaction, to the most unforeseen results. It began with the signing of the Baghdad Pact and the Israeli attack on Gaza in February 1955, which revealed the weakness of the Egyptian army. There followed a frantic search for arms and, upon the refusal of the United States to provide them except for cash or as part of an agreement which Egypt was not prepared to accept, came the conclusion of the arms deal with Czechoslovakia in September 1955. This was followed by a hasty United States offer of aid to finance the construction of the High Dam and Egypt's attempt to use this offer to secure better terms from the Soviet Union. By July 1956 the United States, having received no reply to its offer and judging that the Soviet Union was not seriously considering giving aid to Egypt at that moment, abruptly cancelled the proffered aid, whereupon President Abdel Nasser reacted by nationalizing the Suez Canal with both compensation to the sharcholders and guarantees to the users. There followed three months of tortuous international negotiations and the sudden Anglo-French-Israeli attack on Egypt on 31 October 1956. This led to the sequestration of British and French property, the seizure of much Jewish property, and the subsequent expulsion of British and French citizens and of many Jews. The government thus found itself with large assets, including some of the most important banks and insurance companies, and this both formed a nucleus for further expansion of state ownership and whetted the appetite for more. Thus the crisis in the Congo and the ensuing assassination of Patrice Lumumba was seized on as an opportunity to nationalize the considerable Belgian property in the United Arab Republic in December 1960. At the same time increasing Soviet aid, itself largely a consequence of the previous developments, together with United States, German, and other assistance, further helped to enlarge the public sector since such funds are naturally channelled through the government. Another factor operating in the same direction was growing militarization since, in Egypt as in other countries, the growth of a modern military establishment has led to rapidly increasing absorption by the state of the economic and technical resources of the community.

The main landmarks in this process of transformation may be noted under the following headings: increased taxation; social legislation; egyptianization; closer control of business; and the expansion of the public sector and transference of ownership to the government.

As regards taxation, there was no drastic change until 1961. The general income tax introduced in 1949 had a maximum rate of 50 per cent on incomes over £E100,000. In 1950 the maximum was raised to 70 per cent on incomes above £E50,000 and in 1952 to 80 per cent. By the end of 1960 the rate of 80 per cent was levied on incomes above £E30,000. And on 19 July 1961 Law No. 115 raised the rates on all incomes, one of 90 per cent being applicable to incomes above £E10,000; this was followed, on 25 July, by Law No. 129 which replaced the former flat tax of 10 per cent of annual rental value on buildings by a progressive tax rising from 10 to 40 per cent (see below, p. 281). Earlier, under Law No. 153 of 1957, an additional tax had been imposed on earnings of directors of joint-stock companies, ranging from 10 per cent for incomes above £E2,000 to 80 per cent on those above 10,000.

In the field of social legislation, some important measures had been taken, in 1952, after the Revolution, liberalizing previous laws governing labour relations and extending their coverage. Further action was taken in subsequent years and codified in Law No. 91 of 1959, which covered both regions of the UAR and, among other provisions, fixed the maximum working day at 8 hours and working week at 48 hours. Similarly, important social insurance legislation was passed in 1955 and 1958 and was followed by Law No. 92 in 1959 (see below, p. 198). In July 1961 five important measures were passed, applicable to both regions of the UAR.[1] Law No. 111, of 19 July, provided that, after certain obligatory deductions had been set aside (see below), 25 per cent of the profits made by a company should be allocated to its employees, of which 10 should be directly distributed to them, 5 used for social services and housing, and the remaining 10 appropriated for central social services.[2] Law No. 113, also of 19 July, prohibits any director or employee of a company from earning more than £E5,000 per annum. Law No. 114, of the

[1] See CBE, *Econ. R.*, no. 2, 1961. The full English text of some of these laws, together with an explanatory statement, is given in *New Laws to Implement and Consolidate the Socialist, Democratic, Cooperative Society in the UAR.*

[2] In May 1962 provision was made for the distribution of sums to workmen of firms that have made no profits, from the general allocations for central services (*al-Ahram*, 17 May 1962). This measure was designed to allay the discontent of workmen whose firms, for various reasons, did not show profits. Naturally it weakens the incentive provided by the original law (see also p. 194 below).

same date, decrees that the board of directors of every company shall include a representative of its employees and another of its workers among its seven members. Law No. 125, of 21 July, prohibits the holding of more than one post in government or company employment. And, finally, Law No. 133, of 28 July, fixes the maximum working week in industrial establishments at 42 hours (with no loss of pay for the shortening of the working week) and prohibits both overtime and employment in more than one establishment; this measure was not well received by workmen and was followed in November by a decree incorporating previous overtime pay in basic pay scales. It has been estimated that as a result of this decree employment will be provided in the Cairo area for 29,000 additional workers.[1]

As for egyptianization, the first and longest steps were taken on 14 January 1957. Law No. 22 decreed that banking business could be carried on only by Egyptian joint-stock companies, with nominative shares owned by Egyptians and with Egyptian directors and managers; banks were given one year, later extended to five, in which to effect the necessary changes. Law No. 23 applied the same provisions to insurance companies and Law No. 24 stipulated that export and import agencies and commercial representatives should be Egyptian citizens; both were allowed a delay of five years. On 12 August 1958 Law No. 114, discussed more fully below, decreed that a majority of company directors, instead of at least 40 per cent, should be UAR citizens and Law No. 115 made the use of the Arabic language compulsory in business establishments; hitherto the majority had used French or English.

Several measures were also taken to subject the private sector to closer government control. In 1957 Law No. 153 prohibited the founding of any insurance company without government authorization and decreed that a certain percentage of all reinsurance had to be done with Egyptian reinsurance companies. On 28 April 1958 Law No. 21 made it necessary to obtain a government permit for the setting up or expansion of an industrial establishment or for any change in its location or production line; establishments in a basic industry or enjoying a monopoly were prohibited from stopping production or reducing it beyond certain limits without authorization; the same law made provisions for standards and specifications. On 14 August 1958 Law No. 114 specified that the number of directors of any company should not be below three or above seven;

[1] *al-Ahram*, 6 Nov. 1961.

no one was allowed to accumulate more than two directorships, instead of six as previously, an exception being made for persons owning not less than 10 per cent of the shares of the companies in question; managing directors were ordered to confine their activities to one company; and the maximum remuneration derivable by directors from any one company was fixed at £E2,500. Early in 1959 Law No. 7 was passed, amending the Companies Law of 1954. It decreed that companies must set aside 5 per cent of their net profits for the purchase of government securities, after the distribution of a dividend equal to at least 5 per cent of their capital. Future distributions of profits, whether in cash or shares, were not to be more than 10 per cent above the 1958 level, a figure subsequently raised to 20 per cent. For new companies, whose 1958 profits were not more than 10 per cent of nominal capital, future dividends were to be limited to 10 per cent. Finally, two more measures taken may be noted: Presidential Decree No. 258, of 7 February 1959, subjected thirteen public utility companies to the control of the State Audit Department and Law No. 134, of 27 July 1961, authorized the Minister of Industry to determine the volume of production of industrial establishments as well as the number of their working shifts.

Minor measures to extend the public sector in this period include the setting up of the Petroleum Organization in March 1956 and the formation of the General Petroleum Company in July 1957, and government participation in companies for the exploitation of minerals in 1956, and marine transport and oil refining and trade in 1957. More important was the founding of the Economic Organization, in January 1957, to take over British and French property and participate in the formation of new companies and organizations (see below).

As for the transference of private ownership to the government, there were the nationalization of the Cairo Water Company on 1 July 1957 and of the National Bank of Egypt and Misr Bank on 11 February 1960, under Law No. 40; in all three cases compensation was paid in government bonds to shareholders on the basis of the stock-exchange prices quoted the day before nationalization. But the main measures taken during the period under review were the laws promulgated on 19 and 20 July 1961.[1] Law No. 117 nationalized all banks and insurance companies in both regions of the UAR, as well as 42 large industrial, transport, commercial, financial and land

[1] CBE, *Econ. R.*, no. 2, 1961 and *New Laws Issued*; the latter lists the companies affected.

reclamation companies in Egypt and 51 in Syria. Law No. 118 decreed the partial nationalization of 82 companies and establishments in Egypt and 11 in Syria; these enterprises were to be converted into Arab joint-stock companies at least 50 per cent of the shares of which were to be owned by a public organization. Law No. 119 prohibited any person or corporate entity from owning shares with a market value of more than £E10,000 in 148 companies in Egypt and 11 in Syria. The three laws provided for compensation in the form of fifteen-year negotiable government bonds, bearing 4 per cent interest and redeemable after ten years.

These general measures were accompanied by others of more limited application. Under Law No. 109 of 9 July ownership of the Khedivial Mail Line, the leading navigation company, was taken over by the government; compensation was to be paid in twelve-year bonds at a rate to be subsequently determined. Law No. 110, also of 9 July, amended by Law No. 120 (see below), nationalized cotton-pressing establishments; here compensation was payable in fifteen-year 4 per cent bonds. And Law No. 122 of 20 July terminated the concessions of the Lebon Gas and Electricity Company of Alexandria and the Cairo Tramway Company.

Another connected measure was Law No. 120 of 20 July, amending Law No. 71, passed shortly before on 22 June, which had decreed that cotton exports and purchases by local mills should take place through the Egyptian Cotton Commission. The new law decreed that all establishments engaged in cotton-export trade in Egypt must take the form of an Arab (i.e. belonging to the UAR) joint-stock company, at least 50 per cent of the capital of which must be owned by a public organization. On 22 June the Alexandria Futures Cotton Market was closed indefinitely and on 19 July the Cairo and Alexandria Stock Exchanges were closed for two months.

Three other measures further extended government ownership and control in the commercial and industrial sectors. Law No. 107, of 9 July 1961, decreed that only government-owned companies, or companies affiliated to public organizations and at least 25 per cent of the capital of which belonged to the government, could act as commercial agencies. Law No. 108, of the same date, decreed that all imports should be made by government-owned companies; this completed a process, begun several years earlier, by which government agencies had successively monopolized the importation of such commodities as tea, wheat, fertilizers, and pharmaceuticals. Lastly, under Presidential Decree No. 1203 of 20 July, all public works on behalf of government departments or organizations must be undertaken by companies at least 50 per cent of the capital of which is government-owned; this does not apply to contracts of less than £E30,000.

It has been stated by President Abdel Nasser[1] that property worth £E500 million was taken from 7,300 persons by the agrarian reforms of 1952 and 1961 and the July 1961 nationalizations. The latter figure is puzzling, since the number of shareholders in companies affected by Laws 117–19 was many times as great and a total of 40,000 has been mentioned in the Egyptian press. The value of the land taken over by the first agrarian reform may be put at £E77 million and that subject to the second has been estimated at 24 million (see below, p. 161).

The market value of the shares of companies affected by Laws 117–19 has been officially put at £E258 million, of which 33 million belonged to foreigners. Law 117 covered £E52 million, Law 118 33 million and Law 119 173 million, the shares of foreigners being 12·5, 28·2, and 10·7 per cent respectively.[2] Of the 132 companies affected by Law 119, 77 had shares with a market value of £E166 million, of which 54 million has been surrendered to the government by persons owning more than 10,000 apiece.[3] Under Law 118 some £E18 million worth of shares were taken by the government[4] and under Law 117 the whole of the 52 million. In other words the government took over, in all, £E124 million of shares, and acquired control of over 70 per cent of Egyptian company capital. The amount of shares remaining in private hands was put at £E194 million, consisting of the above total plus £E66 million of securities of companies not affected by the nationalization decrees.[5]

At the same time that the industrial, commercial, and financial classes were thus being dispossessed, the landowners received one more crippling blow. Earlier, in September 1958, the bonds issued in compensation for the land expropriated under the 1952 law had been changed from thirty to forty years and the interest on them reduced from 3 to 1½ per cent, while the maximum that could be owned by a man, his wife, and minor children was fixed at 300 feddans; and in September 1959 any such family owning 300 feddans was prohibited from leasing additional land. On 25 July 1961 two further laws were passed. Law No. 127 reduced the maximum size of individual ownership to 100 feddans, the maximum family

---

[1] Speech reported in *al-Ahram* 24 Dec. 1961.    [2] Ibid. 9 Feb. 1962.
[3] Ibid. 28 Feb. 1962.    [4] Ibid. 3 Mar. 1962.    [5] Ibid.

holding remaining at 300 feddans; unlike the law of 1952, this one also covered uncultivated desert land; compensation was payable in fifteen-year 4 per cent bonds; the leasing out of over 50 feddans was also prohibited, as was the renting of land by anyone owning 50 feddans or more. Simultaneously, under Law No. 128, instalments due to the government by beneficiaries of the previous land reform were reduced by half.

It will be seen from this brief account that whereas the previous measures had marked merely a gradual extension of state control or had applied only to foreigners, the laws of July 1961, following the nationalizations of 1960, constituted a revolutionary change in economic structure and power and spelled the liquidation of the Egyptian, as well as the foreign, bourgeoisie as a producing and active class and the final impoverishment of the landowners.[1] Once more Egypt seems to be moving towards a social order to which the following description concerning the first half of the nineteenth century seems applicable: 'Ce système centralisé, égalitaire, sans intermédiaire entre le prince et le paysan, semble bien avoir été l'idéal du monde égyptien, idéal réalisé plusieurs fois au cours de son histoire millénaire.'[2]

The application of most of these laws to Syria, where the landlord class was still powerful and the native bourgeoisie traditionally much more vigorous; where state intervention was a much more recent and restricted phenomenon; and where a remarkable rate of growth between 1945 and 1957 had been succeeded by a depression—partly owing to poor rainfall—following the union with Egypt in 1958 had dramatic consequences. Discontent, which had been smouldering for some time, flared up into the September revolt which dissolved the union.

This blow to Egyptian aspirations and ambitions in the Arab world, the most painful yet suffered, caused a still more violent reaction by the Egyptian government. Attributing the Syrian revolt exclusively to reactionary elements, and facing a difficult internal economic situation because of Nile floods and extensive damage to the cotton crop inflicted by the boll weevil, it decided to take harsher and more drastic measures against its own bourgeoisie, to

---

[1] The present official line is that the Egyptian Revolution was due to pass in 1958 from the purely political stage, devoted to fighting external enemies, to the social stage, in which the economy would be reshaped, but that the transition was put off in an attempt, which proved vain, to conciliate the Syrian upper classes.

[2] L'Inst. d'ét. du dév. éc. et soc. de l'Univ. de Paris, 'Pression démographique et stratification sociale dans les campagnes égyptiennes', *Tiers-Monde*, July–Sept. 1960.

sound the new note of class warfare and to seek support among the Egyptian masses by a mixture of socialist slogans and a small dose of social welfare measures such as price and rent reduction. In successive moves, in October to January, the property of about 850 persons was sequestrated.[1] A vigorous press campaign was launched against 'reactionary, feudalist, and capitalist elements', who were accused of plotting with foreign imperialists against their compatriots and over 7,000 persons, who had been affected by the two agrarian reforms or by some of the nationalization laws or by sequestration, or who had formerly played an active part in Egyptian politics, were deprived of their political rights and subjected to certain social penalties.[2] At the same time an unspecified number of army officers were arrested. Clearly, the Egyptian social revolution is by no means at an end.

### THE FRAMEWORK OF PRODUCTION

Egypt's economic structure is in flux, and the changes are so comprehensive and so rapid that any analysis must necessarily be highly tentative. An attempt will, however, be made to describe, as of the beginning of 1962, first the extent of government ownership and secondly the pattern of government organization of economic activity; the distribution between the public and private sectors in the main branches of activity are given in Table 11 (p. 117).

The bulk of the cultivated land continues to be privately owned, though about one-sixth is under the direct control and supervision of the Ministry of Agrarian Reform, and a third of that area is farmed by producers' co-operatives (see below, pp. 159 & 164). Agricultural production is still predominantly under private enterprise,[3] supplemented by credit and marketing co-operatives, but government policy is aiming at greatly extending the scope of these co-operatives and introducing producers' co-operatives in the

[1] Of the 641 persons whose names could be identified, 25 per cent were Muslims, 3 Copts, 18 Lebanese or Syrians, 50 Jews, 1 Armenians, 3 Greeks, and 1 other Europeans. These figures should be compared with those given on p. 89 below.

[2] According to a press announcement, owners of sequestrated property will receive an allowance from the government which is to be proportionate to their previous income but is not to exceed £E5,000 a year (*al-Ahram*, 2 Nov. 1961); in at least some cases, payment had started by the end of 1961.

[3] The agrarian reform of 1961 has fixed a ceiling of 100 feddans for individual holdings. According to President Abdel Nasser, this is to be interpreted as covering the total holdings of each family (*Draft of the Charter*, 21 May 1962, p. 66).

private sector; eventually, it is hoped to have 4,000 co-operatives, each covering about 1,500 feddans.[1] Irrigation and drainage and the bulk of land reclamation are being carried out by the government, which is also responsible for agricultural credit, the sale to farmers of chemical fertilizers and seed, and the purchase of cotton and other crops.

Manufacturing and mining are overwhelmingly under government ownership or control.[2] Sizeable private firms are to be found only in petroleum, but numerous small ones survive in various branches of manufacturing. Several of these have, however, asked the government to acquire a controlling interest in them, since they believe that only in this way can they do business with the public sector and get the necessary credit from banks.

For the same reason, in this case formalized by Decree No. 1203 (see p. 59 above), major construction firms have surrendered 50 per cent or more of their capital to the government. Many small private building firms are, however, still active.

Public transport is almost entirely owned and operated by the government, the standard-gauge railways having been, in recent years, joined by the light railways, country and city bus lines, tramways, river navigation, shipping, and airlines. Communications have always been owned by the government.

Foreign trade is also under the control of the government, which operates through the firms that previously imported or exported.[3] Internal trade, on the other hand, is still predominantly in private hands, but a large number of leading department stores have been sequestrated and are run by the Ministry of Supply.[4] The official aim is to raise the share of the government in internal trade to 25 per cent.

With the nationalization of banking and insurance, financial activity has passed completely into the hands of the government. Henceforth almost all securities traded on the stock exchanges will be either state bonds or bonds or shares of companies wholly or partly owned by the state.

Residential buildings are still almost entirely privately owned,

[1] *al-Ahram*, 16 Dec. 1961.

[2] According to President Abdel Nasser, the proportion is 95 per cent (ibid. 20 Jan. 1962).

[3] The private firms participate in 25 per cent of total exports (ibid. 23 May 1962).

[4] The prices of most goods are controlled; recently it has been decided that profit margins shall range from 11 to 25 per cent (ibid. 22 May 1962).

though rents are strictly controlled and a few buildings have been sequestrated. Large hotels have been nationalized, but small ones are privately owned and operated, as are cafés and other places of entertainment. No attempt has, so far, been made to nationalize the professions, but the bulk of engineers, doctors, and lawyers either already work in government enterprises or will soon do so.

As this brief summary shows, the sectors remaining in private ownership are agriculture, internal trade, residential buildings, the professions and, to a certain extent, construction and the various branches of entertainment. The government by now is responsible for some four-fifths of investment and other major economic decisions.[1]

As for government organization, Egypt's traditional structure consisted of ministries, of which by far the most powerful used to be that of finance; the number of ministries rose rapidly, to 23 in 1961. Since 1952, however, this has been supplemented by two other sets of organs. First, there were the planning bodies. In 1952 the Permanent Council of National Production was established and in 1953 the Permanent Council of Public Services; in 1956 both were absorbed by the National Planning Committee, founded in 1955. In 1960 an Institute for National Planning was founded, to carry out training and research.[2]

The other set of organs are the Public Organizations, bodies set up outside the ministerial framework and enjoying more autonomy than government departments. Early examples were the Petroleum Authority, the High Dam Organization, and the Suez Canal Authority. But the most important step was the founding of the Economic Development Organization, on 14 January 1957, to administer sequestrated businesses, holdings in joint-stock companies, and certain publicly owned corporations. In the following years it expanded considerably, by reinvestment and by the acquisition of more nationalized companies,[3] and its total investments rose from £E51 million in 1957 to 80 million in 1960 in banking,

---

[1] 'The investments of the public sector amount to more than 75 per cent of all investment in the plan' (I. H. Abdel-Rahman & M. Ramzi, *The Organizational and Administrative Aspects of Development Planning* (INP, Memo. no. 87).

[2] INP, Memo. no. 59; see also no. 63.

[3] In some of the nationalized or sequestrated companies the former owners or directors have been kept and are now running the business, while others have been dismissed. In both cases, however, ultimate authority is vested in a supervisor, often an army officer, appointed by the government.

insurance, mining, petroleum, manufacturing, commerce, and transport.[1] On 2 March 1961 two similar bodies were created: Misr Organization, which took over the assets of Misr Bank and its holdings in Misr and other companies, a total of £E331 million at the end of 1960; and Al-Nasr Organization, which controlled twenty-four companies (with a combined capital of about £E40 million) established by the General Organization for the Execution of the Five-Year Plan.[2] By the autumn of 1961 these three bodies, each of which was headed by a Cabinet Minister, controlled the bulk of Egypt's economic activity.

This situation naturally caused friction with the government departments and on 16 December 1961 Decree No. 1899 was issued establishing the Supreme Council for Public Organizations under the chairmanship of the President of the Republic and with the vice-presidents and certain ministers as members. The Council's functions are to define the production objectives of the Organizations, approve their budgets, co-ordinate their activities, and supervise the implementation of their programmes. An annexed list (see Appendix I, p. 316) shows that thirty-nine organizations, grouping 438 companies,[3] have been put under thirteen ministries. At the time of writing the Misr, Nasr, and Economic Development Organizations had not been abolished, but their powers seem to have been drastically reduced.

In conclusion a brief description, from the most authoritative source, may be given of the machinery of planning. The Higher Council of Planning consists of the President of the Republic and all the ministers; it

gives general directives and approves the plan in its final form. The plan is prepared by the Central Planning Staff, under the Ministry of National Planning . . . which receive proposals and programmes of development

---

[1] CBE, *Econ. R.*, no. 2, 1961; for further details see *al-Ahram al-iqtisadi*, 15 Jan. 1961.

[2] Min. of Treasury & Econ., *Exposé on Budget Project for FY July 1961–June 1962*, pp. 77 & 80–84.

[3] For detailed list see *al-Ahram al-iqtisadi*, 15 Apr. 1961, spec. suppl. on Public Organizations. The scale of salaries in these Organizations is to be as follows: President of the Board, not more than £E2,000 p.a. plus a representation allowance not exceeding 2,000; Director of the Organization, 1,800 plus 1,500; initial salary for holders of higher degrees, 240 plus 'job allowance' not exceeding 50 per cent of salary. Special 'encouragement allowances', not exceeding the equivalent of three months' salary, may be granted by the Board to outstanding employees and workers (*al-Ahram*, 27 Sept. 1961 & 19 Apr. 1962).

from all ministries and public agencies. . . . The development proposals are discussed, analysed, and co-ordinated by the Central Planning Staff to fit a general balanced plan, according to the directives set. . . . Each Ministry has its planning committee, which prepares the plan of development and follows up the progress of implementation through quarterly progress reports. . . . The Central Planning Staff have no executive responsibility. Ministries, departments and public enterprises are responsible, each in its field of work, for executing the projects and realizing the targets of the plan.[1]

### THE FIVE-YEAR PLAN

Egypt's economic activity is at present regulated by the Five-Year Plan, covering the period July 1960–June 1965. The French version of this plan consists of 414 pages of foolscap size, divided into twelve sections and seven appendices.[2] The aim of the Plan is to double Egypt's national income by 1970 and to increase it by 40 per cent by 1965 and at the same time to reduce the prevailing inequality of incomes. The social framework envisaged in the Plan was one in which the greater part of the means of production would continue to be privately owned but in which the state would provide the bulk of new investment and thus extend the public sector; this however has been drastically changed by the nationalizations and sequestrations of 1960 and 1961. The investment, employment, and income targets for the main sectors are shown in Table 2.

Employment is to rise by 1,026,000 jobs by 1965 and by another 1,937,000 by 1970.[3] Investment in the first five-year period is to consist of £E930·9 million of local currency and 646 million of foreign exchange, to which should be added £E120 million for working capital; for the second period the figures are 1,168 million

[1] Abdel-Rahman & Ramzi, *Organizational and Administrative Aspects*, p. 17.

[2] The sections cover the following topics: investments; national product; availabilities and uses of goods; imports and exports; final consumption; division of income between wages and property holders; employment and wages; public finance; economic activity of the state; national accounts; list of projects in plan; and classification index of commodities. (*Cadre du Plan*. Reference is made throughout to the French version since it is much fuller than the English one and more accessible to foreign readers than the Arabic.)

[3] Ibid. pp. 21 & 109–15. In 1962 the estimated increase by 1965 was put at 1,037,000 (*al-Ahram*, 17 Feb. 1962). A somewhat different estimate, in 1960, put labour requirements during the first five-year period at: higher degrees, 18,600 new jobs plus 25,000 for replacement; intermediate technical, 102,000 and 9,000; intermediate non-technical, 21,400 and 28,000; other, 645,000 and 365,000; giving a total of 787,000 new jobs and 427,000 replacements (NPC, Memo. no. 440).

TABLE 2

*Investment, Value Added, and Employment in Five-Year Plan*

(*£E million, in 1959/60 prices & '000 workers*)

| | 1959/60 | | | 1964/5 | | |
|---|---|---|---|---|---|---|
| | Invest-ment[1] | Value added | Employ-ment | Invest-ment[1] | Value added | Employ-ment |
| Agriculture | 392[2] | 400 | 3,245[3] | 412 | 512 | 3,800[3] |
| Industry & electricity | 579 | 273 | 632 | 555 | 540 | 847 |
| Construction | .. | 52 | 170 | .. | 51 | 159 |
| Transport & communi-cations | 272[4] | 97 | 219 | 255 | 117 | 226 |
| Housing | 175 | 73 | 16 | 275 | 84 | 20 |
| Commerce & finance | .. | 127 | 633 | .. | 162 | 730 |
| Security & defence | .. | 51 | 175[5] | .. | 61 | 186[5] |
| Govt. admin. & public services[6] | 49 | 40 | 92 | 60 | 54 | 119 |
| Personal services | .. | 89 | 511 | .. | 108 | 553 |
| Other services | 110 | 80 | 282 | 160 | 106 | 361 |
| Total | 1,697[7] | 1,282 | 5,975 | 1,717 | 1,795 | 7,001 |

[1] In 1960–5 and 1965–70 respectively.    [2] Of which 47 m. for High Dam.
[3] Nos. required to do work provided for in Plan; actual employment in agriculture was 4,220,000 in 1959/60 and was estimated at 4,660,000 in 1964/5.
[4] Of which 35 m. for Suez Canal.    [5] Excl. armed forces.
[6] Education, health, social and religious, and cultural and recreational services.
[7] Incl. 120 m. for working capital.

*Source: Cadre du Plan.*

and 549 million respectively.[1] Imports are expected to decline from £E229·2 million in 1959/60 to 214·9 million in 1964/5, owing mainly to greater domestic production of minerals and consumer goods which is to more than offset the rise in machinery, equipment and metal products; exports on the other hand are to rise from £E168·8 million to 229·3 million, the increase covering the traditional export crops, minerals, and certain manufactured goods.[2]

[1] *Cadre du Plan*, pp. 22–24. Investment during the first year of the Plan 1960/1, was put at about £E295 m.; of this 239 m. was to come from the public sector and 56 m. from the private; 170 m. was to consist of local exchange and 125 m. of foreign exchange (*Exposé on Budget Project for July 1961–June 1962*, p. 55). Estimates for the second year of the Plan, 1961/2, were £E366 m., of which the share of the public sector was 304·5 m. and of the private 61·5 m.; local exchange was to absorb 234 m. and foreign exchange 132 m. (*al-Ahram*, 11 Nov. 1961).
[2] *Cadre du Plan*, pp. 85–88.

As regards the distribution of the national product, the share of salaries and wages in total 'value added' is expected to decline from 45 to 42 per cent.[1] And as regards its final use, household consumption is expected to rise from £E975 million to 1,236·3 million and consumption by the government administration from 57·9 to 72·1 million; fixed capital formation in the government administrative sector is to rise from 80·1 to 96·8 million, and in the business sector (which of course includes government-owned enterprises)[2] from 103·7 to 127·8 million; inventory investment is expected to rise from 11·1 to 17·6 million and investment by the family sector in dwellings is expected to remain unchanged at £E9 million.[3] But of course both the distribution of income and its allocation have been drastically altered by the socialization measures of 1961.

Before proceeding to criticism, it is necessary to say a few words about the nature of the Plan. No detailed information has been released on the method or procedure adopted by the planners[4] but the following tentative propositions seem to be warranted. The Plan is not based on a comprehensive econometric model, in which the exact relations between a number of variables have been determined and which makes it possible to trace the impact of changes in, for example, investment or exports on the various branches of the economy. Nor is it based on an up-to-date input-output table,[5] which reveals the interdependence of the various sectors and industries and shows what are, for example, the additional inputs required if the output of steel is to be increased. But it does, to a limited extent, use the Soviet techniques of 'material balances' and 'labour balances', which seek to equate needs and availabilities in a selected number of 'leading branches' and which are supplemented by 'synthetic balances', which seek to equilibrate income and expenditure, &c.[6] Thus it has been stated that material balances were computed for some 200 commodities, covering five years and

[1] *Cadre du Plan*, p. 102.

[2] In 1959/60 income generated in the private business sector was put at £E1,126 m. and in the government-owned business sector at 98·2 m.; for 1964/5 the figures were expected to be 1,419·4 and 197·5 m. respectively.          [3] Ibid. p. 169.

[4] A very brief account is contained in INP, Memo. no. 63, pp. 34–38.

[5] A table with 83 sectors was made for 1954. But the changes that have taken place in the economy since must have altered the parameters on which it was based. References have been made to a 33-sector table for 1959.

[6] A. Kursky, *The Planning of the National Economy of the USSR* (Moscow, 1949); I. Yevenko, *Planning in the USSR* (Moscow, n.d.); Bela Balassa, *The Hungarian Experience in Economic Planning* (New Haven, 1959), pp. 63–91; for a brief criticism see Alec Nove, *The Soviet Economy* (1961), pp. 206–9.

showing sources of production and uses, in both physical and monetary terms.[1]

The Plan seems to have been drawn up as follows. The target of doubling national income first in twenty and then in ten years was set by the highest authorities; the various departments and armed forces put forward the different projects they had examined and wished to see implemented; and the planners put these projects together and, on various assumptions, calculated their investment needs and anticipated output and tried to work them into a consistent whole compatible with the targets. The relation between the physical and financial aspects of the Plan seems to be very tenuous.

This is not to impugn the quality of the staff of the National Planning Committee, which is ably led and contains a number of very well trained economists and statisticians. Moreover assistance has been sought from several very distinguished foreign experts, such as Ragnar Frisch, Oscar Lange, Jan Tinbergen, John Hilliard, and others, who helped in various aspects of planning, econometric models, and linear programming.[2] But the planners are operating under formidable handicaps and pressures. First, the overall objectives set are often unrealistic. Secondly, there is a dearth of the basic data without which no reasonable programme, much less an overall plan, can be constructed: capital-output ratios, propensities to save, consume, and import, income and price elasticities of demand and supply, technical coefficients &c, not to mention even simpler and more fundamental data on income distribution, savings, investments, and manpower resources. Lastly there is the fact that the parameters are constantly being altered: partly because of unforeseen changes in the social framework caused by such factors as the sudden nationalizations of 1961, the dissolution of the union with Syria and the constant changes in political and economic relations with other countries; and partly because of the transformations brought about by rapid industrialization and other technical and economic developments.

More detailed criticism of the Plan can be grouped under four headings: internal consistency; inter-sectoral relations; allocation of resources; and efficiency of the bureaucracy.[3] Before this is done,

[1] Lecture by I. H. Abdel-Rahman on 'National Planning Organization and Activities in UAR', delivered at Addis Ababa in November 1959 and reproduced as NPC, Memo. no. 417.

[2] It is interesting to note that Operations Research is being used to solve problems raised by Suez Canal traffic and other purposes (NPC, Memo. no. 404).

[3] The employment targets are discussed on p. 300 below.

however, one more general remark is in place: the Plan proposes to raise the annual compound rate of growth of GNP from approximately 4–4½ per cent, achieved in recent years, to 7·2 per cent; this, though not impossible, is certainly a very ambitious goal for a country with as few untapped natural resources as Egypt, and the targets for some sectors seem unrealistic. Population growth has also been underestimated, and hence the rise in per-capita income exaggerated.

As regards consistency, there is first the low capital-output ratios assumed: the overall implicit ratio is 3·1, the one for agriculture 3·5, for industry and electricity 2·2, for transport and communications 9·1, for housing 14·6 and for services 1·8.[1] Some of these figures seem low compared with those prevailing in other countries with similar conditions. Moreover the transfer of the productive sectors from private ownership to the government which has taken place since the Plan was formulated may be expected to have two adverse effects: a rise in the capital-output ratio, owing to less efficient operation, causing a slackening in the rate of growth of the GNP; and a rise in the rate of depreciation of capital, owing to less efficient maintenance, leading to a further fall in the rate of growth of the net national product. Like most backward countries, Egypt has been more impressed by the possibilities offered by new investment than by what can be achieved by more effective use of existing capital.

Secondly, there is the relation between available resources and the demands made upon them. Since no figures are given for production, imports, consumption, investment, and exports for each year of the Plan, the question of whether available resources will equal planned use $(Y+M=C+I+E)$ cannot be judged. But it may be pointed out that the investment ratio is put at 16 per cent in 1959/60 and is expected to rise to 20 per cent by 1964/5; allowing for foreign aid, at the beginning of the Plan, the corresponding savings ratios are put at 14 and 20 per cent. In order to achieve this very high rate of saving[2]—as well as to destroy all possible centres of opposition and to promote social equality—the government has seized the organized business sector[3] and is attempting to mobilize its surplus and at the

---

[1] *Cadre du Plan*, pp. 19–22.

[2] For purposes of comparison, the average savings rate in India is at present only 10 per cent and even the marginal rate only 16 per cent (*Internat. Development R.* (Washington), June 1962).

[3] In November 1961 the net retained profits of the organized sector were put at £E36·5 m. and its depreciation allowances at 44·1 m. If to this be added the profits accruing to the government under Laws 117, 118, and 119—8·1, 3·3, and 1·5 m. respectively—a total of £E93·5 m. is reached (NPC, Memo. no. 554).

same time to reduce the consumption of the upper and middle classes. But, as against that, mass consumption is increasing appreciably (see below, p. 122) and is being stimulated by the government's policy of subsidies, which are running at £E30 million a year and are due to rise to £E40 million,[1] of lower prices of goods,[2] and of reduced rates for public utilities; more important still, consumption by the government sector—officers, army, and bureaucracy—is rising rapidly and cutting farther into the surplus available for investment.

Similarly, doubts may be raised regarding the availability of the foreign exchange needed to meet the requirements of the first Five-Year Plan, £E646 million.[3] This is to be covered, presumably, by the credits or grants given to Egypt by various countries, which amount to nearly £E450 million (see Table 32, p. 240) *plus* that part of export proceeds and invisible receipts which is not spent on imports of consumer and producer goods, on services, and on payment of interest and principal.[4] In order to secure the necessary foreign exchange, exports are to increase by 36 per cent by 1964/5 and imports are to fall by 6 per cent, and the proportion of investment goods is to rise from 33·7 to 43·1 per cent of total imports. But the anticipated increase in exports is highly optimistic and the expected reduction in imports is unrealistic. For one thing the project descriptions on which the Plan is based may give an adequate estimate of the direct requirements of foreign exchange, but not of the indirect ones arising through increased needs for imports on the part of other sectors, which have to supply the given project with inputs. Nor is due account taken of increased needs for imports of consumer goods, or of increased production of domestic consumer goods needing imported inputs, or of decreased supply of exportable goods, because of the greater domestic consumption generated by the rise in incomes. And the experience of other countries suggests

---

[1] *al-Ahram*, 4 Mar. 1962.

[2] Price reductions have by no means been confined to necessities. Thus in February 1962 considerable cuts were made in the price of locally manufactured frigidaires, air-conditioners, and metal furniture, with the promise of more to follow (ibid. 28 Feb. 1962).

[3] The foreign-exchange component in investment in agriculture and irrigation is put at 20 per cent, in industry at 65, in transport and communications at 41, in housing at 17, and in services at 31.

[4] The deficit on current account was expected to rise from £E31 m. in 1959/60 to 57 m. in 1964/5 and that on capital account from 6 to 39 m. (NPC, Memo. no. 432).

that the 'recuperation period' of a project, i.e. the time that elapses before it begins to pay back the foreign indebtedness incurred because of it, is generally seriously underestimated. Lastly the question may be raised as to whether sufficient consideration has been paid to the rise in foreign indebtedness, which a distinguished economist guessed might reach a peak of £E1,000–1,500 million.[1]

Finally, doubts may be expressed regarding the availability of trained manpower. It is true that attempts have been made to assess the needs of the various sectors for qualified personnel and to provide them with it. But it is safe to say that many bottlenecks will be created by shortage of skills. And it is highly probable that overall efficiency will decline drastically because of reduced initiative and incentive due to bureaucratization—indeed there are many signs that this has already occurred.

The second subdivision, intersectoral relations, may be briefly dealt with. Given the almost complete lack of information on income and price elasticity of demand and supply and on consumption and production functions, and in the absence of detailed and up-to-date input-output tables, the allocation of investment and manpower between the various sectors must be based largely on guesswork and the probability of a balance being achieved is extremely low. The most striking aspect of the Plan in this matter is the large proportion allocated to industry—33·7 per cent of total investment in the first five-year period—and the consequent antici-pated increase of 97·8 per cent in net industrial output.[2] In so far as this includes electricity (8·2 per cent of *total* investment) and mining, it carries with it the hope that the necessary power and mineral raw materials will be forthcoming. And transport may not constitute a serious obstacle since the appreciable amount of excess capacity existing at present is to be supplemented by sizeable new investment. But, as in almost all countries which are implementing large-scale plans, agriculture is likely to prove the weak link. Agricultural out-put is expected to rise by 28 per cent by 1965, or at a compound

[1] Ragnar Frisch, 'Why National Planning?', NPC, *Current Notes*, no. 17; also reproduced in *Ég. contemp.*, Oct. 1960.

[2] Within the industrial sector, priority has been given to capital and producers goods, which are to absorb the bulk of new investment. Industries specifically designated as producing consumer goods are allotted only £E80·3 m. out of a total of 578·7 m. (ibid. p. 22). This disproportion is not necessarily unreasonable, given Egypt's circumstances and industrial aims, but may create difficulties since, with higher incomes, demand for manufactured consumer goods may be expected to rise sharply.

rate of 5 per cent per annum, which is much higher than the average of 2½ per cent achieved in recent years. The disasters which reduced the cotton crop of 1961 by one-third (see below, p. 137) and seriously damaged the maize, rice, and other food crops, have given the programme a very bad start. Moreover, even if the projected rate were attained, it is very doubtful whether agriculture will be able to meet all the demands made on it by other sectors for food, raw materials, and export products.

The third subdivision, the allocation of resources, may be studied under two headings: pricing of goods and factors of production, and investment criteria. As regards the first, Egypt faces all the difficulties encountered by countries with a mixed economy, in which a public and a private sector coexist and in which one sector operates on targets and the other on prices. These difficulties are greatly increased by the fact that whereas in such countries as the United Kingdom and Sweden private enterprise accounts for over 70 per cent of investment and other economic decisions, and in India for not much less, in Egypt the proportion is probably below 20 per cent.[1] This means that while in the other countries the government can leave the function of price-setting to the market, in Egypt it must perform this task itself, a matter which raises intricate problems. So far, no great difficulties have been encountered because economic activity is still predominantly guided by the price structure inherited from the pre-nationalization period. But as the government proceeds to control and change one price after another, it undermines the basis of rationality on which the economy has rested. The same applies to rents and interest, and it is an evil omen that interest on loans by the Agricultural Credit Bank to farmers was abolished in 1961.

As regards investment criteria, very little is known. Since the profit motive, and the consequent maximization of returns on capital invested, has been explicitly rejected, and in view of Egypt's shortage of capital and land, the use of any of the following criteria could be justified in any given case: maximization of the output-input ratio; minimization of the capital-output ratio; maximization of the present, i.e. discounted, value of anticipated income streams; maximum saving of foreign exchange per unit of imported capital; maximum absorption of unskilled or semi-skilled labour per unit of capital or land; economization of what is Egypt's scarcest resource,

---

[1] A similar problem arises in Yugoslavia, but the solution given to it is very different (see C. Dupont and F. A. G. Keesing, in IMF, *Staff Papers*, viii/1, Nov. 1960), and A. Waterston, *Planning in Yugoslavia* (Balt., 1962).

entrepreneurship and management, by reducing as far as possible the need for decision-making; and the choice of sequences which give the tightest backward and forward linkages, i.e. which induce further projects, though this is a criterion more applicable to predominantly private enterprise than to socialist economies.[1] All that can be said is that the last three criteria do not seem to have had any influence on the choice of projects. And, from the little information available, in very many cases there seems to have been a lack of 'good planning' defined as

to have ascertained whether it corresponds to a real need, whether proper engineering and market studies have been made, whether full financing has been assured so that it will not remain half completed for years, and whether alternative ways of filling *the same need* have been explored and rejected for good reasons.[2]

Another query which can only be raised, not answered, concerns provision for shortfalls. If shortages develop owing to the failure of other branches of the economy to supply the necessary inputs, or if balance-of-payments difficulties make it impossible to fulfil import plans, will many plants in all industries be allowed to operate well below capacity, as in Turkey in 1958? Or will priority be given to certain key sectors at the expense of others—usually consumer-goods industries—as is the Soviet practice?

Finally, there is the question of the efficiency of the bureaucracy, a matter of supreme importance in any modern state and one which is absolutely vital for a country embarking on socialism and planning. From the 1920's on, the level of the Egyptian civil service has been steadily declining, a process stimulated by the growth in its number, the constant increase in its functions, and the relative deterioration in its social and economic status due to inflation.[3] In the last few years the decline in efficiency seems to have been arrested, and perhaps even reversed, but the growth in numbers has been accelerated and there is no sign that Parkinson's law is about to be disproved in Egypt. One example may suffice: 'In 1952, it was thought that within five years hence, there will be no need to keep the staff [of the Agrarian Reform Committee] after the land distribution is completed. As it was found later, the staff has to be kept permanently and enlarged.'[4]

[1] For a discussion of some of these criteria see Mass. Inst. of Technology, Centre for Internat. Studies, *Investment Criteria and Economic Growth* (1961).

[2] A. O. Hirschman in ibid. p. 30.

[3] The best study of the Egyptian civil service is Morroe Berger, *Bureaucracy and Society in Modern Egypt* (Princeton, 1957).      [4] INP, Memo. no. 63, p. 12.

As anyone who has had dealings with it can testify, the Egyptian bureaucracy surrounds its business with an immense amount of formalities and red tape. An example was recently given in the press: officials have found it prudent to start action on their pension a full year before retirement; for one single form of the many in their file requires the signature of forty-seven different officials.[1] The difficulties arising from this are compounded by the tradition of rigid centralization, which requires the submission of the most trifling matters to Directors or even Under-Secretaries of State. In Egypt, as other parts of the Middle East, one may say that 'delegation of authority is a sign of inferiority'.

This situation was bad enough when the bulk of the country's economy was run by private enterprise, and when government officials could at most slow down and impede the momentum of the private sector. But socialization and planning have resulted in a replacement of the former dispersal of decision-making power by concentration in the hands of government bodies. This makes it even more important both to simplify procedure and to have much delegation, leaving only essentials for the men at the top. As a British socialist put it, 'local initiative must be preserved, and even increased, in an economy increasingly subject to central direction'.[2] But the prevailing political atmosphere is hardly conducive to such changes. Nor are they likely to be promoted by the recent attempt, similar to the ones undertaken in many socialist states, to cope with bureaucratic inefficiency and corruption by imposing much more stringent penalties, running up to eighteen years' imprisonment, for neglect of duty, bribery, and damage to state property, often defined in such a way as to include trifling and even absurd cases.[3] For a long time to come, the bureaucracy is likely to absorb a very large amount of the energy generated by the plans.

[1] *al-Ahram*, 13 Nov. 1961. Other examples recently mentioned in the press include a fourteen-month delay in obtaining a permit for a single-storey building, a seven-month delay in granting a bedridden official the right to retire, and a year's delay in paying to a widow a monthly pension of £E11 (ibid. 22 Oct. 1961).

[2] E. M. Durbin, *Problems of Economic Planning* (1949), p. 81.

[3] *al-Ahram*, 8 May 1962. Recently many examples of costly bureaucratic neglect have been revealed in the press—see, for example, ibid. 19–22 May 1962. It is true that an attempt to decentralize local services has been made by concentrating power in the Governors of the 21 provinces, and making each responsible for the execution of the plan in his province. But this may well result in merely adding one more link to the already long chain of authority.

# V

# Human Resources

*When goods increase, they are increased that eat them.*          ECCLESIASTES.

*They judge greatness in numerical terms, by the size of the population, but it is capacity, rather than size, which should properly be the criterion.*          ARISTOTLE.

*The human mind is our fundamental resource.*          JOHN F. KENNEDY.

*Après le pain, l'éducation est le premier besoin du peuple.*          DANTON.

## GROWTH OF POPULATION

Egypt is one of the many countries which, in the nineteenth century, entered a period of demographic transition, i.e. their populations are growing rapidly because the former balance between births and deaths has been upset. For when, as a result of the spreading of industrial civilization to traditional societies, order and security prevail, health conditions improve, and more food becomes available, the first effect is a decline in the death-rate. The birth-rate, however, which is determined mainly by social and religious factors, remains for a long time at its previous high level. It is only when an industrial civilization has had sufficient time to change the whole customs and outlook of the population that birth-rates begin to decline, as they have been doing in Western Europe, North America, and Japan.[1] Egypt is at present in the first stage, that of declining death-rates unaccompanied by falling birth-rates.[2]

The growth of the population since the first reliable census[3] is illustrated in Table 3 which shows clearly the acceleration in the

[1] It should, however, be noted that even before the Industrial Revolution the average age at marriage in Western Europe was distinctly higher than it is in the backward countries today, and the birth-rate somewhat lower.

[2] For a more refined analysis see UN, Dept. of Econ. & Soc. Aff., *The Future Growth of World Population* (NY, 1958).

[3] It may be noted that a census was taken in 1957 and put the total population, excluding a few districts, at 22,997,000 but, owing to the fact that the count was made shortly after the Suez attack, the results were regarded as unreliable and another was taken in 1960.

**TABLE 3**

*Growth of Population, 1897–1960*

| Year | Population (incl. nomads) | Ann. % rate of increase during interval |
|------|--------------------------|------------------------------------------|
| 1897 | 9,715,000 | — |
| 1907 | 11,287,000 | 1·51 |
| 1917 | 12,751,000 | 1·23 |
| 1927 | 14,218,000 | 1·09 |
| 1937 | 15,933,000 | 1·15 |
| 1947 | 19,022,000 | 1·78 |
| 1960 | 26,059,000 | 2·45 |

*Source:* Population Censuses.

rate of growth that took place in Egypt, as in so many under-developed countries, during the 1940's and 1950's. This acceleration may be expected to continue for some time to come, owing to a further decline in the death-rate unaccompanied by any appreciable fall in the birth-rate, and the annual rate of increase may well rise to over 3 per cent. Official extrapolations of 31,883,000–34,762,000 in 1972 and 38,473,000–44,682,000 in 1982 are distinctly too low. No calculation of reproduction rates has been made since 1937, when the gross reproduction rate was put at 3·11 and the net reproduction rate at 1·44 according to one estimate, and 2·8 and 1·6 according to another;[1] since then the net reproduction rate must have risen appreciably.

## BIRTHS AND DEATHS

Both birth- and death-rates are among the highest in the world. Published birth-rates have, in both the pre-war and post-war years, averaged about 42 per thousand, while death-rates averaged 27 in the pre-war, 23 in the early post-war period, and about 18 in the mid-1950's; the infant-mortality rate has declined from about 160 to 140 and 136 respectively per thousand live births and was put at 109 for 1959. Comparison of national averages with those of

[1] Clyde V. Kiser, 'The Demographic Position of Egypt', in F. W. Notestein, ed., *Demographic Studies of Selected Areas of Rapid Growth* (NY, 1944) and El Sayed El Daly, 'The Birth Rate and Fertility Trends in Egypt', *Ég. contemp.*, Oct. 1953.

localities having health bureaus, where health conditions are better and registration is more complete, 'suggest that the birth-rates for the former for 1939 should be 11 per cent higher, the death-rates about 14 per cent higher, and the infant mortality rates about 23 per cent higher'.[1] Similarly, it has been stated that 'the actual infant mortality rates are possibly almost twice the recorded rates, however, and may reach 300 to 400 per thousand live births in the rural areas. The infant mortality rate for Cairo was 248 in 1942 and for Alexandria 204,'[2] and recently it has been calculated that 'one-fifth of births die under one year'.[3]

Many causes contribute to the high birth-rate. First, the poverty, ignorance, and general wretchedness of the fellah make procreation one of the few pleasures left to him, and give rise to a slum psychology in the congested villages. Secondly, there is the influence of cotton cultivation, which provides employment for children and turns the child into a financial asset at the early age of four or five. A cotton expert declared that 'cotton requires not only a dense population but one with a birth-rate above the average'.[4] Thirdly, there are such social factors as the almost obligatory nature of marriage and the early age at which it is concluded, the limited opportunities for earning a livelihood open to women and also the prestige and legal advantages enjoyed by married women and the security against divorce which a child provides to its mother.

This is illustrated by the very high nuptiality rate prevailing in Egypt. Thus in 1947 less than 1 per cent of the women in the age-group 45–49 had never been married; the figure was naturally higher among younger women, but even for the 30–34 group it was under 3 per cent, for the 25–29 group 6 per cent, and for the 20–24 group 20 per cent; among women aged 15 to 19, as many as 36 per cent were already married, divorced, or widowed. Another

[1] Kiser, loc. cit.

[2] J. S. Simmons, ed., *Global Epidemiology* (Philadelphia, 1951), vii. 5.

[3] El Daly, loc. cit. A study of health conditions in five villages near Cairo, made by the Rockefeller Foundation in 1948–51, showed that the reporting of both death-rates and birth-rates was very inaccurate. Thus the true infant-mortality rate in one village, Sindbis, was 326 per thousand, against reported rates of 80–161 in the four other villages, while the real crude death-rate was 32 per thousand, against reported rates of 12–23. Similarly, the true birth-rates ranged from 56 to 61 per thousand, against reported rates of 44–50. It should, however, be remembered that Sindbis was chosen because of its exceptionally bad conditions, and therefore cannot be regarded as a sample (see J. M. Weir, 'An Evaluation of Health and Sanitation in Egyptian Villages', *J. Eg. Pub. Health Ass.* (1952)).

[4] Muhlberg, *B. de l'Union des agriculteurs*, 1940.

illustration of the early age of marriage is the fact that no less than 47 per cent of the total number of women who got married in 1950 were under twenty years of age and 73 per cent were under twenty-five.[1]

It is commonly believed that polygamy and divorce are largely responsible for Egypt's high birth-rate. But polygamous households among Moslems in 1937 represented only 3·1 per cent of the total and in 1947 3·8 per cent. Divorce is much more widespread, the ratio of divorces to marriages in recent years being 30 per cent for the country as a whole and 50 per cent for Cairo;[2] it is probable that frequent divorces and remarriages tend to increase the chances of child-bearing. The birth-rate among Moslems is higher than among Christians, and the fact that the rate of increase among Copts is very slightly higher than among Moslems is attributable to their lower death-rate.

The causes of high death-rates may be summed up in two words: malnutrition and, more important, endemic disease. Both are discussed more fully in subsequent sections.

No clear trend in birth-rates can be observed. Crude birth-rates have fluctuated, but fertility ratios, i.e. the ratio of children under five to women of child-bearing age, seemed to indicate a very slight decline until 1947, but then rose sharply. Similarly, the average family size, which had fallen from 5·8 in 1907 and 1917 to 4·7 in 1947, rose again to 4·9 in 1957 and 5·0 in 1960. Published birth-rates for 1955–7 show a drop, but it is not clear whether any significance should be attached to this change.

Some very interesting information on the subject of fecundity in Egypt has been gathered by the Committee on Population Studies of the Statistical Department.[3] In 1956–8 a questionnaire was circulated, with the help of social workers, to 6,067 women divided into an urban group (Cairo and Alexandria), a semi-urban group (the working-class quarter of Mahalla al-Kubra), and a rural group (two villages in Upper and one in Lower Egypt). A further classification was made on the basis of the degree of education of the

[1] For a very thorough analysis see NPC, Memo. no. 448. The author concludes that 'Marriage rates for females during the reproductive age groups, irrespective of their premarital status, show a tendency for rising in 1947 [compared to 1937] except at the youngest age group and at 40–44. The effect of these rises on reproduction are obvious.'

[2] 'The magnitude of the divorce rate shows that half the women get divorced sometime in their married lives, assuming no multiple divorces.' (ibid.)

[3] See a forthcoming study by Dr Hanna Rizk, who analysed the data.

husband. The investigation showed that, in urban areas, there was a
high inverse correlation between the fecundity of the wife and the
husband's degree of education at the upper levels; however, there
was no significant difference in fecundity between wives of men with
elementary education and those of illiterate men.[1] In the semi-
urban and rural areas, where few husbands had obtained secondary
or higher education, there was no significant difference between
fecundity among the wives of those with elementary education and
those of illiterate men. The differences in fecundity were partly
caused by later marriage; thus in urban areas the age at marriage of
women whose husbands had higher education was on average three
years higher than that of wives of illiterate men. But the differences
were also partly caused by the use of birth-control, as shown in
Table 4.

TABLE 4

*Percentage of Wives Practising Birth-Control, according to Locality and
Degree of Education of Husband, 1956–8*

|  | Urban | Semi-urban | Rural |
|---|---|---|---|
| Higher | 51–60 | — | — |
| Secondary | 28–46 | } 28 | — |
| Primary | } 19–25 | | } 3 |
| Elementary | | 15 | |
| Illiterate | 9–11 | 10 | 1 |

*Source:* Committee on Population Studies.

Another interesting finding is that not only did the desired size of
the family decrease with the degree of education but that at all
levels the desired size was distinctly lower than the actual size.[2]
This may mean that eventually, as knowledge about birth-control
methods spreads, family sizes may drop sharply. On the other hand
the fact that there are no significant differences between the semi-
urban and rural areas shows that even in an industrial centre such as
Mahalla values have not yet changed and that a much longer period

[1] The percentage of families with two children or less was 35 among those with
higher education, 22 among those with secondary education, and 8 among
illiterates.

[2] At all levels more boys were desired than girls, but whereas in rural areas the
ratio of desired boys to girls was 285 per cent, among those with higher or secondary education it was only 135 per cent.

of industrialization and urbanization may be required before birth-rates begin to decline appreciably.[1]

A considerable increase in life expectancy is shown by the following figures, taken from life tables constructed by R. al-Shanawany,[2] Clyde Kiser,[3] Ahmed Gad Abdel Rahman,[4] and Hanna Rizk[5] for 1917–27, 1927–37, 1936–7, and 1947 respectively.

TABLE 5

*Life Expectancy at Specified Ages, 1917–47*

(*Expectation of life in years*)

| Age | 1917–27 | | 1927–37 | | 1936–8 | | 1947 |
|---|---|---|---|---|---|---|---|
| | *Male* | *Female* | *Male* | *Female* | *Male* | *Female* | *Male* |
| 0 | .. | .. | 30·2 | 31·5 | 35·7 | 41·5 | 41·6 |
| 10 | 38·1 | 41·6 | 38·2 | 37·2 | 47·4 | 54·5 | 49·5 |
| 20 | 32·9 | 35·8 | 33·5 | 32·8 | 39·8 | 46·1 | 41·7 |
| 30 | 27·8 | 30·0 | 28·6 | 28·3 | 33·0 | 38·2 | 34·3 |
| 40 | 22·8 | 24·5 | 23·7 | 23·9 | 26·1 | 30·8 | 27·2 |
| 50 | 18·1 | 19·4 | 18·8 | 19·6 | 19·4 | 23·4 | 20·3 |
| 60 | 13·7 | 15·6 | 14·2 | 15·4 | 13·4 | 16·2 | 13·8 |

## AGE AND SEX DISTRIBUTION

Egypt's population is about equally divided between the sexes. In 1927 there were 7,058,000 males and 7,120,000 females, and in 1937 there were 7,967,000 males and 7,954,000 females. The 1947 returns show a slight preponderance of females, with 9,603,000 against 9,419,000 males, while the 1960 census puts the number of males at 13,113,000 and that of females at 12,946,000. In view of the margin of error in the censuses, however, little significance can be attributed to these changes.

[1] A study based on the 1947 census showed that fertility in Cairo and Alexandria is slightly lower than in the rest of Egypt; this may be partly attributable to the relatively large proportion of foreigners and minority groups in those cities, but it may also reflect a genuine decline in fertility in the very large cities (see Girgis Abdo Marzouk, 'Fertility of the Urban and Rural Population in Egypt', *Ég. contemp.*, Jan. 1957).

[2] 'The First National Life Tables for Egypt', ibid. 1936.      [3] In Notestein.

[4] 'Mortality Tables in Egypt and England', *Ég. contemp.*, 1950.

[5] Int. Statist. Ed. Centre, Beirut, *Muqaddima fi'l-ihsa al-tatbiqi*, based on mortality tables prepared by Rauf Maqqar.

The percentage age distribution at the last census years is shown in Table 6.

TABLE 6

*Population by Age-Groups, 1907–60*

(*percentages*)

| Age-groups | 1907 | 1917 | 1927 | 1937 | 1947 | 1960 |
|---|---|---|---|---|---|---|
| 0–9 | 30·1 | 28·0 | 27·5 | 27·2 | 26·4 | 36·0[1] |
| 10–19 | 18·5 | 20·3 | 20·3 | 20·5 | 21·7 | 15·7[2] |
| 20–29 | 18·0 | 15·5 | 16·4 | 15·2 | 15·1 | 12·8 |
| 30–39 | 14·7 | 13·5 | 14·1 | 14·7 | 13·8 | 12·6 |
| 40–49 | 9·0 | 9·0 | 9·2 | 10·1 | 10·4 | 9·6 |
| 50 & over | 9·7 | 13·7 | 12·5 | 12·3 | 12·7 | 13·6 |
|  | 100·0 | 100·0 | 100·0 | 100·0 | 100·0 | 100·0 |

[1] 0–11 age-group.      [2] 12–19 age-group.

*Sources:* Population Censuses, *Sample Survey of Labour Force, May 1961* (in Ar.).

The picture is that of a broad-based pyramid. Psychologically and historically the Egyptians are an old people, but biologically they are very young, nearly two-thirds of the population being under thirty.

MIGRATION

Throughout their history the Egyptians, one of the most sedentary and longest settled people in the world, have shown a marked reluctance to emigrate. This trait was no doubt reinforced by the fact that they have never been great seafarers and that the countries surrounding them, Cyrenaica, Palestine, Arabia, and the Northern Sudan, contained large nomadic populations. Hence, except for the few thousands of peasants who fled to Palestine in the early nineteenth century to escape Muhammad Ali's conscription, and the few hundreds of traders and officials who settled later in the Sudan, there has been practically no recorded emigration from Egypt. It is significant that during the short-lived union with Syria no attempt was made to transfer any Egyptian peasants to the sparsely populated Jezireh and Euphrates regions.[1]

[1] On 17 January 1962 it was announced by the Syrian Minister of Agrarian Reform that during the union of the two countries plans had been made by the

On the other hand Egypt has received, at various times, waves of immigrants such as the Greeks, Jews, and Romans before the Christian era and the Arabs, Circassians, and Turks after the Arab conquest; all these foreigners were, sooner or later, assimilated by the local population. The last such wave was that of the Europeans and Levantines who flocked to the country during the period 1830–1914 (see ch. ii). Like their predecessors, these immigrants occupied a very high position in the economic scale (see below, p. 88), but unlike them they were not assimilated partly because of the fact that Moslem women are prohibited from marrying non-Moslems and partly because of the difference in cultural and social levels. The number of foreign citizens reached its peak in 1907 when, excluding the Sudanese, they totalled 221,000 or 2 per cent of the population; foreigners concentrated in the main cities of Lower Egypt, where they formed 16 per cent of the population in Cairo, 25 per cent in Alexandria, and 28 per cent in Port Said. After that, there was a sharp decline, first proportionate and then absolute; first because of the cessation of immigration after the First World War, then because of the naturalization of many former Ottoman subjects in the 1920's and 1930's, and lastly because of the emigration, starting in the late 1930's and accelerated during the 1940's and 1950's, of both foreign citizens and many naturalized foreigners. By 1947 the number of foreign citizens had fallen to 146,000, or less than 0·8 per cent of the total population,[1] and by 1960 to probably under 100,000, or 0·4 per cent. A further exodus has taken place since then.

As regards internal migration, two main streams may be observed: from Upper to Lower Egypt, and from the country to the towns.

With a population of 9,229,000 in 1960 and an average crop area of 0·42 feddan per inhabitant, Upper Egypt is much more densely populated than Lower Egypt, for which (excluding Cairo, Alexandria, and the frontier districts) the corresponding figures were 10,934,000 and 0·59. In 1955/6 gross agricultural income was put at £E52 per person in agriculture in Upper Egypt, and in Lower Egypt £E75 per person; a breakdown by province shows a marked inverse correlation, —0·78, between population density per

central government to settle 4 m. Egyptian peasants in the Ghab and Jezireh regions (*L'Orient* (Beirut), 18 Jan. 1962). The presence of a large number of landless peasants in Syria clearly made it politically very difficult to take in Egyptian immigrants.

[1] Of these 57,000 were Greeks, 28,000 Italians, 28,000 British subjects, and 10,000 French subjects. Foreigners formed 7 per cent of the population of Alexandria and less than 3 per cent of that of Cairo.

cultivated feddan and agricultural per-capita income.[1] If it be re-membered, moreover, that Egyptian industry is concentrated in the Delta, which also contains practically all the big cities, it will be seen that there are strong economic inducements to emigration from south to north. In addition, there is the fact that the men of Upper Egypt, who suffer very much less from bilharzia and ankylostoma, are stronger than those of the Delta and are often employed on work for which the latter are unfitted. Furthermore, the people of Lower Egypt seem to be more attached to the soil than those of Upper Egypt.

In these circumstances, it is not surprising that during the decade 1937–47 population increased appreciably more rapidly in Lower than in Upper Egypt. Excluding the two border provinces of Menufia and Giza, the percentage growth in Lower Egypt ranged from 13·7 for Qaliubia to 20·1 for Sharqia, while in Upper Egypt it ranged from 14·8 in Asiut to −4·7 in Aswan. Moreover, again excluding the two border provinces, the percentage of the inhabi-tants of each province born outside its borders is distinctly higher in the Delta than in Upper Egypt; it ranges from 2·4 in Daqahlia to 9·6 in Sharqia whereas in Upper Egypt the range is from 0·8 in Qena to 3·1 in Bani Suef, though it should be added that the figure for Aswan was as high as 11·4, probably because of the influx of Nubians.[2]

The current migration to the towns is very much more important. Between 1917 and 1937 the population of Cairo rose from 791,000 to 1,312,000 and that of Alexandria from 445,000 to 686,000, representing an increase of 66 and 55 per cent respectively, com-pared with 25 per cent for the country as a whole. In the same period the population of the twenty largest towns rose from 1,883,000 to 2,944,000, an increase of 54 per cent. During the war migration to the towns was greatly accelerated by the opportunities for employ-ment provided by the Allied armies. The population of the five governorates (Cairo, Alexandria, the Canal zone, Damietta, and Suez) rose from 2,249,000 in 1937 to 3,416,000 in 1947. This move-ment continued after the war, owing to the 'pull' effect of greater industrialization and construction in the towns and the 'push' effect of increasing population pressure in the countryside,[3] and by 1960

[1] NBE, *Econ. B.*, no. 3, 1955.    [2] Ibid.

[3] In 1961, a sample study of 6,000 immigrant families in Cairo showed that only 53 per cent of the population of Cairo was born in that city; that 98 per cent of migrants came from rural areas; that 94 per cent of them were under 45 years of age; and that 40 per cent were illiterate while another 39 per cent had a rudimentary knowledge of reading and writing (*al-Ahram*, 17 Jan. 1962).

the population of the governorates (from which Damietta has been dropped) was 5,582,000 or 21·4 per cent of the total population. A further 4,048,000 persons, or 15·5 per cent of the population, lived in other towns (62 in Lower and 57 in Upper Egypt), while the remainder, excluding a few tens of thousands of nomads, dwelt in 2,339 villages in Lower Egypt and 1,682 villages in Upper Egypt.[1] The ratio of urban to total population has risen at an accelerating rate, from 21 per cent in 1917 to 24 in 1937, 30 in 1947, and 37 in 1960.[2]

It is now possible to inquire whether Egypt is overpopulated. The first fact to bear in mind is the phenomenal rise in the population during the last 150 years—from 2·5-3 million to 26 million. This tenfold increase is probably unparalleled in any other agricultural country. The second fact is that Egypt, in terms of cultivated area, is perhaps the most densely populated country in the world.

The increase in Egypt's population was made possible by two sets of circumstances: the order and security introduced by Muhammad Ali; and the growth of Egypt's wealth arising out of the extension of the cultivated area, the replacement of basin by perennial irrigation, the improvement in the yield of crops, and the extension of cotton cultivation.[3] No indices of production are available but the following sets of figures are illustrative.[4] In 1820–30 the cultivated area was 3 million feddans; in 1960 it was over 5,900,000 and the crop area nearly 10,300,000. During the same period the yield of

[1] According to the 1960 census, the largest towns were: Cairo, 3,346,000; Alexandria, 1,513,000; Ismailia, 276,000; Port Said, 244,000; Suez, 203,000; Tanta, Mahalla al-Kubra, Mansura, and Asiut.

[2] It has been pointed out that, compared with other countries, Egypt has a higher 'proportion of its population in large cities than can be explained on the basis of the proportion of her economically active males in agriculture'. This is traceable to the fact that the age and sex distribution in cities are, in contrast with other countries, strikingly similar to those of Egypt as a whole, which in turn is 'attributable to the fact that birth rates and infant mortality rates differ little between cities and all of Egypt. . . . This lack of age selectivity suggests that the cityward migration does not so much consist of individual adults, as is the case in Puerto Rico, as it does of entire families.' (Robert Parke, Jr, 'Urbanization and Cityward Migration in Egypt: Contrast with Puerto Rico', unpubl. paper, Columbia Univ., 1953.) But in fact migration from Upper Egypt consists mainly of adult males but from Lower Egypt of adult females or entire families as well (see tables compiled by Gene and Karen Petersen, of Columbia University, from 1947 census).

[3] To this should be added better public health and medical conditions, especially in recent years.

[4] Crouchley, 'A Century of Economic Development', *Ég. contemp.*, 1939; Rivlin, *Agricultural Policy.*

wheat rose from about 4 to 6·5 ardebs per feddan, that of cotton from 1 or 2 to nearly 6 cantars, and cotton exports from about 200,000 to 7 million cantars. Finally, industrial production has increased several fold in the last thirty years.

Over the whole period, Egypt's population may not have outrun its income. Nevertheless, during the last few decades the volume of agricultural production has failed to keep pace with the population, in spite of much technical research and improvements of methods of cultivation (see below, p. 135); while industrial production, though growing very rapidly, still plays a secondary part in the country's economy. Moreover the combination of high birth-rates and high death-rates has another adverse effect, namely that an appreciable proportion of the national income is invested in children who, because they die young, make little or no contribution to the economy of their country. This is aggravated by the fact that in Egypt, as in other underdeveloped areas, the excess of mortality-rates over those prevailing in more developed regions is much higher in the younger and more productive age-groups than in the older and unproductive groups. This factor is only partially offset by the tendency to start working at an early age. As a result, in 1947 the ratio of 'dependent' persons (under 15 and over 64 years of age) to 'productive' persons was 70 per cent, whereas in the United States it was 55, in Britain 50, and in West Germany 49 per cent.[1]

This subject will be discussed in detail in the following chapters. Here it is sufficient to say that Egypt may just hope to maintain its growing population but that, short of a technical break-through which will make it possible to utilize sea water for the cultivation of deserts, there is no prospect of an advance from the very depressed standard of living of today except through rapid industrialization and the immediate and energetic application of a birth-control programme.

### OCCUPATIONAL DISTRIBUTION: EGYPTIANS AND FOREIGNERS

The occupational distribution of the Egyptian population, as given in the last four censuses, is shown in Table 7. The census returns are not comparable, owing to differences in classification. In particular, the large numbers listed as unoccupied in 1927 and 1937 are misleading, since they obviously exclude women working on family farms, whereas these persons are included in

[1] UN, Dept. of Econ. & Soc. Aff., *The Ageing of Populations and its Economic and Social Implications* (NY, 1956), p. 8.

TABLE 7

*Number of Persons Occupied in Different Industries, 1927–60*

*('ooo, excl. children under 5 years)*

| | 1927 | 1937 | 1947 | 1959/60 |
|---|---|---|---|---|
| Agriculture . . . | 3,486 | 4,265 ⎫ | 7,555 | 4,200 |
| Fishing . . . . | 40 | 43 ⎭ | | (60) |
| Mining . . . . | 10 | 11 | 13 | (25) |
| Manufacturing & handicraft . | 483 | 478 | 709 | 607 |
| Construction . . . | 125 | 121 | 113 | 170 |
| Transport & communications . | 196 | 139 | 203 | 219 |
| Commerce & finance . . | 460 | 460 | 620 | 633 |
| Personal service (hotels, restaurants, bars, cleaning establishments, mortuaries, domestic servants, &c) . | 284 | 256 | 2,856 | 536 |
| Professions . . . . | 132 | 151 | 515 ⎫ | 540 ⎫ |
| Non-industrial public services . | 152 | 171 | | |
| Ill-defined & unproductive . | 596 | 1,327 | 1,570 | 1,572 |
| Unoccupied persons . . | 6,184 | 6,391 | 2,227 | .. |
| Total . | 12,148 | 13,813 | 16,381 | .. |

*Sources:* Population Censuses, *Cadre du Plan*, p. 112.

1947. More comparable estimates of the working force in agriculture put the total at 4,284,000 in 1937, 4,215,000 in 1947, and 4,220,000 in 1959.[1] Similarly, the figures on industrial employment have a different coverage and are not strictly comparable. A more accurate indication of its increase is given by the following estimate of employment in manufacturing: 248,300 in 1927; 323,200 in 1937; and 405,100 in 1947. After that, there was little change in employment until 1954, but the upward trend was then resumed and, in recent years, accelerated (see below, p. 174).[2] Tertiary activities have also increased. But the bulk of the population continues to draw its livelihood from agriculture.

In the last twenty years there has been a large growth in the professional class. Thus the number of physicians rose from 3,300 in 1937 to 5,700 in 1947 and about 10,000 in 1960, and that of teachers from 35,000 to 52,000 and 111,000. For other groups the 1947 figures

[1] CBE, *Econ. R.*, no. 2, 1961.
[2] UN, *Dev. of Manufacturing*, p. 103; *Statist. Pocket Yb, 1959*; *Census of Indust. Prod., 1st qr. 1961* (in Ar.).

were as follows: engineers 16,000, lawyers 5,000, and chemists and pharmacists 1,600.

Table 7 (p. 87) may be supplemented by the information derived from the sample surveys on the labour force carried out since 1957. In August 1960 Egypt's manpower (persons aged 6–65) was put at 18,789,000 out of an estimated population of 24,171,000, the latter being a considerable underestimate.[1] The labour force consisted of 6,038,000, of whom only 253,000 were women; this evidently excludes farmers' wives and daughters who help in various agricultural activities. The number of unemployed was put at 255,000 or 4·2 per cent of the labour force aged 12 or over, while the employed were broken down as follows: owners and managers, 14·7 per cent of the labour force; self-employed, 21·1 per cent; working for family, 15·5 per cent; and employees 44·4 per cent. The breakdown by branch of activity was as follows: agriculture, 55·2 per cent; mining and quarrying, 0·5 per cent; gas and electricity, 0·3 per cent; transformation industries, 8·7 per cent; building and construction, 1·7 per cent; commerce, 10·1 per cent; transport and communications, 3·6 per cent; government, 7·3 per cent; and services, 12·5 per cent. In other words, industrial activities at present employ some 10 per cent of the Egyptian population. As in other countries, the proportion of persons employed in agriculture has steadily declined, from an estimated 70 per cent in 1907 to 61, though their absolute number has shown little change.[2] Needless to say, the proportion employed by the government has risen greatly since the nationalizations of 1960 and 1961.

The occupational distribution of the foreign residents of Egypt differs sharply from that of the Egyptian population. In 1937 only 1 per cent of foreigners were engaged in agriculture against 50 per cent of Egyptians; 24 per cent worked in industry and transport against 10 per cent; 22 per cent in commerce and finance against 6 per cent; and 20 per cent in services against 5 per cent. The full import of these proportions can be grasped only if it be remembered that in Egypt the divergence between the remuneration of 'primary' and 'tertiary' industry is determined not only by local economic factors, as in other countries, but by the fact that two different societies, with very different standards of living, still coexist side by side. In the 1950's a rural labourer earned under £E4 per month,

---

[1] *Coll. Basic Statist. Data.*

[2] For slightly different figures, based on the 1958 sample survey, see NBE, *Econ. B.*, no. 2, 1960.

while a bank clerk started his career at nearly £E25 per month. The difference between the two salaries reflects the divergence in the standards of living of east and west.[1]

The predominance of foreigners was most marked in the higher levels of finance, trade, and, to a lesser extent, industry. As was pointed out in Chapter II, before the First World War all branches of the economy except agriculture and some sectors of internal trade were almost entirely controlled by foreigners. In the 1920's, how-ever, thanks to the pioneering efforts of the Misr group, Egyptian participation in industry and trade began to increase. This movement was stimulated by the tariff of 1930 and by various measures taken by the government in the 1930's to egyptianize business. Neverthe-less foreign control remained widespread. A classification of the list of company directors given in *L'Annuaire des Societés Anonymes, 1951*, showed that, of 1,406 names identifiable with any degree of centainty, 31 per cent were Egyptian Moslems, 4 per cent Copts, 18 Jews, 11 Syrians or Lebanese, 8 Greeks or Armenians, and 30 per cent Europeans.

This situation was drastically changed after 1956. Already at the outbreak of the Second World War the property of Italian and German nationals had been sequestrated and during the Arab–Israeli war of 1948 that of Jews suffered heavily. The attack of 1956 led to the sequestration of British and French assets, in addition to the Suez Canal which had already been nationalized, and to the expulsion of British and French citizens, while Belgian property was seques-trated in 1960 and various enterprises were egyptianized after 1957. A classification of the company directors listed in the *Egyptian Stock Exchange Yearbook, 1960* showed that of 1,399 names identifiable, 66 per cent were Moslems, 4 per cent Copts, 3 Jews, 13 Syrians or Lebanese, 6 Greeks or Armenians, and 8 per cent Europeans. The same analysis may be applied to the persons who owned over £E10,000 of shares in the 148 companies designated by Law No. 119 of 20 July 1961 (see ch. iv above). Of the 1,007 names of individuals figuring in the lists published in *al-Ahram* of 18 and 24 October 1961, and identifiable with any degree of certainty, 55 per

---

[1] At the same time it should be pointed out that in Egypt, as in several other underdeveloped countries, the gap between earning in 'primary' and 'tertiary' industries seems to be narrowing. Thus the post-war ratio of 6:1 compares with a pre-war ratio of 8:1. This seems to be attributable both to wartime inflation, which cut the real income of the middle class more than that of manual workers, and to the spread of education, which has increased the supply and reduced the scarcity value of white-collar workers.

cent were Egyptian Moslems, 6 per cent Copts, 5 Jews, 22 Syrians or Lebanese, 9 Greeks or Armenians and 4 per cent Europeans. In agriculture, which still represents the main form of wealth, foreign participation has always been very small and in 1961 foreigners owned only 2 per cent of the land. Naturally, foreign and minority group participation in the economic life of Egypt fell sharply below the level indicated by these figures after the nationalizations and sequestrations of 1961, which hit particularly hard the Swiss and Greeks among foreigners and the Lebanese and Syrians among minority groups, and the exodus of non-Egyptians has been accelerated. Hence, although the present occupational structure of foreigners and minority groups is still markedly different from that of Egyptians, their influence over the economy is now negligible.

### SOCIAL CONDITIONS

Egypt is rightly regarded as an underdeveloped country; but although it exhibits all the symptoms associated with underdevelopment, the disease manifests itself in a peculiar form. As the following chapters show, most of the known natural resources are intensively exploited and in many branches of activity a high technical level has been attained.[1] On the other hand Egypt's human resources have been hardly tapped relatively to those not only of advanced but even of comparatively backward countries.

A vivid illustration of this fact is provided by comparing conditions in Egypt with those prevailing in the poorer parts of Eastern Europe before the Second World War. Many economic criteria showed those regions to be not much ahead of Egypt, especially if differences of climate be taken into account. The social criteria, however, revealed an immense divergence.[2] Indeed in certain respects, notably literacy, some Asian countries, such as Ceylon, Burma, Korea, and Malaya, which are well behind Egypt economically, have a distinctly higher social level.[3]

[1] The main exception to this statement is Egypt's deserts, which are still almost completely unutilized.

[2] For statistical indicators, cf. the figures for Egypt and Greece in Table VII of Issawi, *EMC*, which refers to 1950. The enormous progress registered by Greece since that date has raised its economy to a much higher level than that of Egypt, and one which is more in line with its social development, as may be seen in Table 8 below; the same is true of the other East European countries.

[3] This is borne out by comparing the extremely low position occupied by Egypt on the 'demographic indicator' scale, which includes various indices of fertility and mortality, with its somewhat higher position on the income or

The reason for Egypt's cultural lag is to be found in the history of the last 400 years. At the risk of over-simplification, it may be said that whereas Eastern Europe was affected, although belatedly, by the Renaissance and Enlightenment, Egypt, like other parts of the Islamic world, was influenced only by the Industrial Revolution. By the eighteenth century Western European ideas were radiating all over Eastern Europe, books were being published in appreciable numbers, and schools were being opened. A striking proof of the penetration of western ideas is provided by the repercussions of the French Revolution; to take only two examples, in 1791 the Poles promulgated a constitution based on the French model, while in 1797 delegates from most parts of Greece met in secret conclave and planned a national uprising conditional upon French revolutionary help. It was only later, in the nineteenth century, that the Industrial Revolution impinged on Eastern Europe and that western capital began to pour in on a large scale.

Egypt, on the other hand, was entirely untouched by social and cultural developments in Europe until first Muhammad Ali and then European capital opened up its resources. As a result, Egypt's economic resources were developed relatively early while the social side was neglected. The consequences may be seen in all aspects of Egyptian social life, but perhaps most clearly in education and health.

Education may be dealt with briefly. According to the 1937 census, 82 per cent of the Egyptian population over 5 was illiterate, the percentages being 74 for men and 91 for women; by 1947 these figures had declined to 77, 67, and 87 respectively. In 1957–8 a sample survey showed that in the towns 41 per cent of men and 69 per cent of women over 5 were illiterate and in the countryside 71 per cent and 92 per cent respectively; the national totals were 60 and 84, giving an overall illiteracy rate of 72 per cent.[1] Nor is the supply of schools satisfactory since the great expansion during the last forty years has been, to a large extent, neutralized by the growth in population. But since the revolution significant progress has been made; in 1952 only 45 per cent of children of primary school age attended school but by 1960 the proportion had risen to 65 per cent —80 per cent for boys and 50 for girls. At present some 75 per cent

consumption scale (see E. Stockwell, 'The Measurement of Economic Development', *Econ. Dev. & Cult. Change*, July 1960).

[1] For an analysis of historical statistics on literacy in Egypt see Unesco, *Progress of Literacy in Various Countries* (1953), pp. 83–86.

of children reaching the age of 6 are admitted to school and it is anticipated that by 1969 facilities will be provided for all children attaining that age.[1]

Health conditions continue to be very poor, in spite of the progress achieved during the last thirty or forty years. It is true that large-scale epidemics, which were both frequent and devastating, have been eliminated or are localized and speedily stamped out.[2] It is also true that eye diseases are less widespread than they were, but Egypt still has a higher proportion of blindness than almost any country in the world. And the comparison of the Nile valley to a gigantic hospital has lost none of its validity. In 1950 it was estimated that 55 per cent of the population suffered from bilharzia, 30 from ankylostoma, and 15 from malaria. These diseases, which are brought about by perennial irrigation and inadequate drainage, affect mainly the villagers;[3] thus it was estimated that 75 per cent of the rural population was stricken with bilharzia. The urban population has its own diseases, namely pellagra which affected 6 per cent of the total population and tuberculosis which accounted for some 30,000 deaths each year.[4]

More recently, it has been claimed that malaria has been brought under control, and that would seem to be true of the epidemic but not of the endemic form of this disease. However, the percentage of those suffering from bilharzia was put at close on 60. This debilitating disease is estimated to reduce the productivity of patients by 25–50 per cent.[5] Similarly there has been no decline in the incidence of ankylostoma, which also reduces productivity by an estimated 33 per cent.[6] The peasants at first attempted to remedy the loss of vitality, and above all of sexual virility, caused by the diseases by taking hashish. When this was cut off, they replaced it by tea, total

---

[1] *al-Ahram*, 20 Oct. 1961. In 1955 the government had announced a ten-year programme designed to accommodate all children aged 6–12 by 1964; this has since been abandoned.

[2] The last major epidemics were outbreaks of malignant malaria and typhus during the war years and a small-scale cholera epidemic in 1947.

[3] In three districts of Qina and Aswan provinces the incidence of bilharzia and ankylostoma rose from 0 to 2 per cent under basin irrigation, which allows the soil to dry and thus causes the death of the snails carrying the disease, to 43–75 per cent three years after the introduction of perennial irrigation (Mosharrafa, pt. 2).

[4] Mahmud Abd al-Azim, 'Health Aspects of Social Welfare', in *Halaqat al-dirasat al-ijtimaia* (2nd Soc. Welfare Seminar for Arab States, 1950).

[5] *UAR Yb. 1961* (in Ar.), p. 909.

[6] Est. by Dr Abd al-Khaliq, quoted in Mosharrafa, pt 2.

consumption of which has increased severalfold since 1914—a condition reminiscent of England during the Hungry Thirties and Forties. As for eye diseases, the following statement by two sympathetic and observant journalists is worth quoting: 'In none of the numerous villages which we have visited, from Damietta to the Sudanese frontier, have we seen a single child whose eyes were perfectly intact.'[1]

## SOCIAL PROGRESS

Perhaps precisely because the need was so great, social progress has proceeded much faster than economic development during the last thirty years. In the main it has been the result of governmental actions but private efforts,[2] and to a greater extent external events, have also made their contribution. Here attention will be confined to four important tendencies; the growth of an intellectual élite; the spread of education; the improvement in the status of women; and the attempt to ameliorate the lot of the masses.

### Intellectual Élite

In the inter-war period Egypt produced some good jurists, a few competent irrigation engineers, a handful of historians, and some excellent physicians. For the rest, its intellectual leaders consisted mainly of the kind aptly described by the Turkish expression *hazarfen*, men of a thousand crafts. Some of the Egyptian men of letters, notably Taha Husain, Tawfiq al-Hakim, and Mahmud Taymur, achieved distinction but the vast majority consisted of jacks of all trades who cheerfully undertook to popularize all aspects of western culture. Of serious thought on social and economic problems the country was innocent.

By the early 1950's this picture had been modified in some important respects. Thanks to increasing contact with the west, expanding laboratory and research facilities, the diffusion of knowledge within the country, and a greater degree of national consciousness and self-confidence, Egypt had greatly raised the level of its élite. It could boast of many first-class physicians, some of whom

[1] Simone and Jean Lacouture, *L'Égypte en mouvement* (1956), p. 309.
[2] The main private agencies have been the foreign and private Egyptian schools and the numerous private organizations. At the end of 1959 there were 3,330 such organizations registered and engaged in charitable aid or working in such fields as religion, education, health, sports, &c. For details see Min. Soc. Aff., *National Social Activity* (1960, in Ar.), and Isis Istiphan, *Directory of Social Agencies in Cairo* (Cairo, 1956).

were making minor contributions to science. Its irrigation engineers had maintained their standards and were being joined by able geologists and agronomists, while competent researchers were beginning to appear in chemistry, biology, and other natural sciences as well as in some branches of mathematics. A group of talented painters had developed. In literature the social and intellectual conditions which had made possible the emergence of some interesting writers in French, such as Ahmad Rassim, Élian Finbert, Albert Cosséri, Andrée Chédid, and others—and stimulated such writers as Cafavis, Durrell, and Newby—had passed away; but the same process was contributing to the formation of a school of powerful, deeply integrated Egyptian novelists, short-story writers, and playwrights such as Nagib Mahfuz, Yusif al-Sibai, and Yusif Idris, and a promising Egyptian theatre was developing.[1] Some good work was being done on Islamic philosophy. But the most striking progress had been recorded in the social sciences where a group of first-class men, all under fifty, were working in the fields of anthropology, economics, geography, sociology, social work, and statistics. And parallel with this growth of an intellectual élite there was developing a no less important Egyptian administrative and managerial élite in the larger foreign owned enterprises, in the government industrial and transport enterprises, and, particularly, in such purely Egyptian concerns as the Misr and Abboud groups.[2] It was this combination of social scientists, many of whom took up cabinet or high administrative posts during the early years of the Revolution, with entrepreneurs, managers, and administrators which was to sustain the new régime during its first decade.

Since then there has been a further great change which has its counterpart in the communist countries and which may be summed up as a marked progress in technology, the natural sciences, and the applied social sciences, and an equally marked retrogression in history and the more theoretical aspects of the social sciences.[3] On

[1] It is encouraging to note that, very recently, several works by Egyptian authors have been translated into English, French, Russian, Hebrew, and other languages.

[2] For an excellent account of this élite see Frederick Harbison and Ibrahim Abdelkader Ibrahim, *Human Resources for Egyptian Enterprise* (NY, 1958), ch. iii.

[3] As for literature, no clear trend can be discerned. Several works by the above-mentioned authors are striking and vividly portray local conditions, but there is some truth in the remark recently made by a critic: 'Arabic literature is completely cut off from the currents of world culture' (Saad al-din Mursi, 'Arabic Literature between Nationalism and Universalism', *al-Ahram*, 18 Jan. 1962). Moreover the depressing effect of the censorship is making itself felt.

the one hand the revolutionary government has set up, with foreign or international aid, an atomic reactor, an isotope centre, an electronics laboratory, and numerous other facilities for scientific and technical research.[1] It has also helped to expand further the number of men trained in statistics, economics, accountancy, and public administration.[2] This is helping to bring about a most important and overdue change, the scientific approach; as a distinguished scholar put it: 'en somme, il aura fallu attendre le second après-guerre pour que se développe en Orient la quête de l'exact'. [3]

The increase in the number of natural scientists and technicians may be illustrated by a few figures from a report drawn up by the Higher Council for the Sciences.[4] The number of persons who have so far graduated from Egyptian faculties dealing with natural science or technology is 38,000;[5] to this should be added several thousands of graduates of foreign universities. But, as the report points out, of this number only 1,326 had their Master's degree and 639 their doctorates—the latter figure presumably excludes M.D.'s. The number of persons carrying out research in the natural sciences was

[1] The extent of scientific research in one field may be gauged by the list of publications by Egyptians given as an appendix to Ibrahim Hilmi Abd al-Rahman, 'Atomic Energy Programmes in the United Arab Republic', *al-Abhath* (Beirut), March 1961; the article is in Arabic and the appendix in English. Another index is the large number of Egyptian papers accepted for discussion by the UN in the conference on the use of science and technology for developing countries to be held in the spring of 1963 (*al-Ahram*, 23 June 1962).

[2] Two examples of the increase in trained personnel may be given. The first fully trained Egyptian statistician returned from England in 1933 and during the next ten or twelve years a course in statistics was successively introduced in the faculties of agriculture, law, arts, medicine, science, and education. In 1946 an Institute of Statistics was formed and attached to the School of Commerce; by 1959 nearly 150 students had graduated from it (see Hasan Husein, 'Tatawwur al-ihsa', in *Buhuth*, p. 487). The author was also informed that when, recently, the FAO announced a vacancy for a hydraulic engineer, no less than eighteen Egyptians with high qualifications applied for the post; while this reflects the eagerness of Egyptian intellectuals to leave the country—a completely new phenomenon, due to the recent changes—it also demonstrates the increase in the supply of technicians.

[3] Jacques Berque, *Les Arabes d'hier à demain* (1960), p. 253. In this connexion mention may be made of the gradual replacement, since 1959, of the Arabic and avoirdupois weights and measures by the metric system. One other development may be noted, an increased appreciation of classical western music; as in other totalitarian countries, music may be expected to provide an emotional outlet for an increasing number of people in the next few years.

[4] *al-Ahram*, 24 Nov. 1961.

[5] Of these 10,000 were engineers, 9,700 agronomists, 9,000 physicians, 5,000 scientists, 1,800 pharmacists, 1,100 veterinarians, and 800 dentists.

put at 148 in research centres, 663 in universities, 1,007 in government departments and 97 in private enterprises, a total of 1,915. Among the many handicaps under which these men are working is the great shortage of trained assistants. This is being remedied by sending Egyptians abroad and inviting foreign researchers to Egypt: during the next five years 1,859 Egyptians are to complete their advanced training in the natural sciences abroad and nearly 150 foreign scientists are to be invited. An attempt is also being made, by the Higher Council for Sciences which was founded in 1956,[1] to plan and co-ordinate scientific research; for this purpose a congress including 2,473 scientists, divided into 75 sections, was convened in November 1961 to discuss a five-year plan of research involving an expenditure of £E15 million.[2]

On the other hand the intensity of nationalism prevailing is leading to the most fantastic and inaccurate statements on topics ranging from the remotest past to the latest events. As regards the past the following quotation, from the official textbook used in the last year of secondary school and written by an otherwise distinguished historian, may suffice: 'Until the time of Moses the Jews worshipped stones and cattle; they learned from their Arab neighbours of the existence of the Supreme Being, Jehovah.'[3] And as regards the present, the perusal of the news on Britain, France, or the United States in any of the Egyptian papers provides more than sufficient examples.

## Education [4]

No aspect of British policy in Egypt has been so severely criticized as its attitude to education. As soon, therefore, as the struggle for independence was over, Egypt embarked on a vast educational programme, initiated by a law passed in 1923, making education free and compulsory between the ages of 7 and 12. The intensity of the effort made may be gauged from the fact that the total school population rose from 324,000 in 1913 to 942,000 in 1933, and, in spite of an interruption caused by the Second World War, to 1,900,000 in 1951. The budget of the Ministry of Education rose from £E1,600,000 in 1920, representing 4 per cent of the national

---

[1] For details see *UAR Yb. 1961*, pp. 600–17.     [2] *al-Ahram*, 3 & 6 Nov. 1961.
[3] Muh. Mustafa Ziadah, *al-Mufid fi tarikh al-arab* (1962), p. 22.
[4] For details on the evolution of Egypt's educational system see Roderic D. Matthews and Matta Akrawi, *Education in Arab Countries of the Near East* (Wash., 1949); for an appraisal of aims, tendencies, and results, see Abu al-Futuh Radwan, *Old and New Forces in Eg. Education* (NY, 1951).

budget, to £E29 million in 1951, representing 13 per cent. An even more striking index of growth is provided by enrolment in government secondary schools, which increased from 2,500 (all of whom were boys) in 1913 to 15,000 (of whom 1,500 were girls) in 1933, and 122,000 (of whom 19,000 were girls) in 1951. University students rose from a negligible number in 1913 to 41,000 in 1951 when there were also 1,400 Egyptians studying abroad.

This advance was accelerated under the revolutionary régime. By 1959 the school population had risen to 3,067,000, estimates for the 1961/2 school year were nearly 3½ million,[1] and a figure of 4 million is planned for 1964/5. Enrolment in all types of secondary schools, including technical secondary, was 207,000 in 1959 and in the universities 83,000. The number of students sent annually abroad on government missions, which averaged 185 in 1949–51, dropped sharply after the Revolution but more recently started rising again; it averaged 414 in 1957–9, and for 1962 a total of 680 was envisaged; in all there were 5,109 Egyptians studying abroad in 1960, of whom 3,456 were paying their own expenses.[2]

Some important changes in the structure of the educational system have also occurred. Until 1949 Egypt had a dual system: primary, secondary, and higher schools for the well-to-do and elementary schools for the masses.[3] The elementary schools were poor and pupils who finished the course could go no further. After 1949 an attempt was made to raise the level of these schools by lengthening the term of study and adopting a curriculum very close to that of primary schools. In 1956 the school attendance age was lowered to 6 and the first stage of schooling was unified and made co-educational.[4] After four years of primary schooling children who

[1] *Coll. Basic Statist. Data & al-Ahram*, 20 Oct. 1961.

[2] *UAR Yb. 1961*, p. 565 & *al-Ahram*, 9 Jan. 1962. Much confusion was caused in Egyptian educational missions by the violent changes in Egypt's international relations after 1956. Several hundred students were sent to the Soviet bloc but most of them were subsequently withdrawn and missions to the west were expanded as these countries offered special facilities for Egyptians. In 1960 the countries with the largest number of Egyptian students were W. Germany, Austria, the USA and UK, Switzerland, France, and the Soviet Union, in that order.

[3] These were of different types; they had in common, however, an emphasis on the four Rs (religion being the fourth) and the omission of foreign languages. A third set of schools, the religious schools feeding al-Azhar and other theological institutions, still exists.

[4] For a chart of the educational system see Harbison & Ibrahim, p. 109. For more details see ibid. pp. 105–28; Perm. Council for Pub. Services, *The Atlas of Services* (Cairo, 1955) (in Ar.); and *UAR Yb. 1961*, pp. 546–99.

pass their examinations go on to a four-year preparatory school, from which the more successful move on to three-year secondary schools. About half of those who attend secondary schools later enter universities, one of the highest ratios in the world.[1]

The number of universities has increased: Cairo University, organized in 1925, was followed by Alexandria in 1942, Ain Shams (Cairo) in 1950, and Asiut in 1957; in 1961 the 1,000-year-old al-Azhar, which had been somewhat modernized in the last seventy years but confined itself exclusively to theology, jurisprudence, and Arabic language and literature, was suddenly endowed with faculties of medicine, engineering, agriculture, public administration, and accountancy.[2]

Another important, and welcome, structural change has been the expansion of vocational education in the last ten years. Attendance at agricultural, industrial, and commercial schools, at both the primary and secondary levels, has considerably increased and much more is being spent on this type of education than before the Revolution. But it is still true that the student body of these schools consists mostly of those who have failed to qualify for preparatory secondary education and that employers are very reluctant to hire such students.[3]

Government expenditure on education has continued to increase, and in 1961 amounted to £E55 million or 16·5 per cent of the ordinary budget. At the same time an attempt has been made to encourage school attendance by supplying free meals in schools and reducing fees at the secondary and higher levels to negligible amounts; in addition over a quarter of university students are

[1] In 1957 it was estimated that the percentage of children of primary school age attending school was 60 (76 for boys and 44 for girls) compared with 69 for Syria in 1955, 48 for India in 1954, and 96 to 99 for W. Europe and the USA. For general and technical secondary education the corresponding Egyptian figure was 10 (25 for boys and 5 for girls), the Syrian 4, the Indian 11, and the W. European and American 45 to 60. For higher education Egypt had the rate of 3·5 (6·1 for boys and 0·9 for girls); this was much higher than the Syrian and Indian rates of 1·1 and approached the 4·8 figure for the UK and 6·7 for France, but in this field variations in quality make comparison very hazardous. The goal of the government at that time was to raise the primary figure to 70 (90 for boys and 50 for girls) by 1963, the preparatory to 22 (30 and 15), the secondary to 11 (16 and 6) and the higher to 4·0 (6·5 and 1·5); it was estimated that this would involve an extra initial cost of £E10·4 m. and additional running expenses of £E8·2 m. per annum by 1963 (NPC, Memo. no. 31).                                      [2] *al-Ahram*, 13 Nov. 1961.

[3] Ibid. 15 Nov. 1961. For a brief but able criticism of Egyptian vocational education see Harbison & Ibrahim, pp. 120–4.

exempt from fees. The expansion in the school population, although equalled or surpassed in several other Arab countries such as Iraq, Jordan, Morocco, Syria, and Tunisia, must be counted as a real achievement of the Egyptian government.

But, as in other countries in similar circumstances, quality has by no means matched quantity, and Egyptian educators have not been sparing in their criticisms. The accusations most frequently levelled were that Egyptian graduates lacked initiative and the spirit of adventure, preferring a job in the already overcrowded government service to any others;[1] that the government schools did not develop independent thinking and an understanding of social problems; and that the information acquired in them by painful memorization did not amount to really useful knowledge.[2]

This disappointing result is not surprising in view of the magnitude of the task undertaken—the education of an entire nation in one generation. It could be explained by: (1) the hot weather, which reduces the working capacity of pupils, most of whom have poor health and are undernourished; (2) the frequent changes of educational policy with the change of ministers; (3) the deadening effect of a rigid centralization which prescribes exactly the same curriculum and textbooks for every single school; (4) the overcrowding of the curriculum; (5) the disproportionately large place allotted to Arabic and foreign-language study, and it should not be forgotten that classical Arabic is so different from colloquial Egyptian as almost to constitute a foreign language;[3] (6) the importance given to examinations and their rigidity—failure in one subject means failure in the whole examination—and the consequent reliance on cramming; (7) the bad effects on discipline of the numerous student incursions into politics.

To these factors must be added two far more important social

[1] In the early 1950's it was estimated that 38·4 per cent of men and women holding a school certificate or a university degree were employed by the government; if doctors and lawyers outside government service be excluded, 'the overwhelming majority of degree holders has turned to government employment' (Mahmoud Kamel, *Tomorrow's Egypt* (Cairo, 1953), p. 77).    [2] Radwan, pp. 116–21.

[3] It is an interesting fact that, in spite of the far-reaching revolution which Egypt is undergoing, no suggestion for a simplification of the Arabic language or script has, to the knowledge of this author, recently been made. The nearest to this is the use of colloquial Arabic by the President in his speeches. His example has been followed by many, and accounts of debates and discussions in the colloquial are now often reproduced by the press. It may be added that recently foreign-language study has been drastically reduced, probably too drastically.

ones: the poor quality of teachers and the heavy burden put on their shoulders, and the absence of intellectual stimulus at home.

In the last ten years there have been both favourable and unfavourable developments affecting the quality of education. On the positive side must be set the ending of school and university strikes, more continuity in educational policy and, above all, the greater emphasis put on the natural sciences. But the negative aspects are still larger. First there is the suppression or subjection to stifling control of the 300 foreign schools which had trained such a large proportion of the Egyptian élite. Secondly, there seems to have been a marked drop in the level of teachers, due partly to rapid expansion and partly to the depressing effects of the prevailing political climate; this is particularly noticeable at the university level, where purges have also taken their toll.[1] Lastly, and most important, there is the systematic indoctrination to which students at all levels are at present subjected and which cannot but do them incalculable harm.

## Status of Women

One of the most encouraging features of the last forty years, in Egypt as in other Middle Eastern countries, has been the very marked improvement in the condition of women and their increasing participation in various fields of social activity. The emancipation of Egyptian women has come gradually and does not show such landmarks as Atatürk's abolition of polygamy, but the progress achieved has been none the less real. Egyptian women, a few years after the Syrian and Lebanese, have been given the vote and the various legislative bodies elected after 1956 have included a few women members; and in 1962 Egypt, following the example of Iraq, appointed a woman to its Cabinet as Minister of Social Affairs. The veil, never widespread among peasants, has almost disappeared in the towns and is now worn only by some working-class women.[2] Polygamy, statistically speaking never very great, was in the past confined to the upper classes; the social changes

[1] Another factor lowering the level has been the sending of teachers, whom Egypt can ill spare, to Arab or Moslem countries; in 1960 there were 3,032 such teachers in twenty countries, compared to 458 in 1952; the largest numbers were in Saudi Arabia, Sudan, Kuwait, Libya, Gaza strip, Morocco, Lebanon, and Somalia (*UAR Yb. 1961*, p. 584).

[2] A parallel change is taking place among men. The fez, also an urban article of clothing, has almost disappeared and is now worn by well under 10 per cent of townsmen. Another trend, which is however much less marked, is the replacement in towns of the traditional *gallabia* by trousers.

of the last fifty years have made it go out of fashion among these classes and it is now to be found almost only among the uneducated. It is being condemned by many Moslem theologians, who declare that it was frowned upon by the Koran. Divorce, however, is very common, Egypt's rate of over 30 per 100 marriages being among the very highest in the world. But although divorce and polygamy are recognized as major social ills and are increasingly condemned by enlightened public opinion, no laws have yet been passed to limit them, as has been done in Syria, Iraq, and Tunisia.[1]

In other respects, the legal status of Egyptian women has not changed, and there is no very great demand for changing it. Under Islamic law women have always been entitled to own property and transact business. Their share in the paternal estate is only half that of their brothers, but this is mitigated by the fact that the dowry is paid by the husband, not the wife. A more serious question is the share of wives and mothers in inheritance, since they receive only a small fraction of the estate of their husband or son. This arrangement, which was well suited to a society characterized by large patriarchal households, is causing increasing hardship with the spread of the western form of family life.

It is, however, in the social field that progress has been most marked. Education furnishes an outstanding example. In 1960 the number of girls attending school was 1,063,000, against 255,000 in 1934 and 31,000 in 1913 and since the Second World War girls have constituted 35 per cent of the school population, against 10 per cent in 1913. At the secondary level the proportion is 21 per cent and at the university level 14 per cent; these figures, although below those of some other Middle Eastern countries such as Lebanon, Syria, and Turkey, are far above those to be found among the Moslems of Soviet Central Asia for whom, according to Bennigsen, the overall proportion is only 2–3 per cent.[2] Qualitatively, too, results have

[1] The following passage illustrates the religious and social difficulties confronting reformers in this field: 'Recently, in 1955, the Rector of al-Azhar discussed the question of polygamy, praising and recommending it. A few weeks later the press published a strange news item. A rich young man had married 42 wives, divorcing 40 and retaining 2. He happened to be engaged in a lawsuit which brought this matter to the attention of the Public Prosecutor. When the latter asked why he had married such a large number of women he replied, simply and clearly, that he did not see what stopped him from doing so and that it was his right.' (Salama Musa, *al-Mara laisat libat al-rajul* (1956,) p. 26.) For a restatement of the fundamentalist position see the recent book by the Rector of al-Azhar, Mahmud Shaltut, *al-Islam aqida wa sharia* (1959).

[2] Vincent Monteil, *Les Musulmans soviétiques* (1957), p. 112.

been most satisfactory, all observers agreeing that the work of the Egyptian schoolgirl compares very favourably with that of the schoolboy. Girls are also fully participating in extra-curricular activities such as athletics. In 1949 there were 30,000 Egyptian Girl Guides and by 1960 the figure had risen to 40,000, compared with 35,000 Boy Scouts.

Except in agriculture, where they perform a vital function both in the fields, during harvest time, and in such activities as dairying and poultry raising, women continue to play a minor, though rapidly growing, part in Egypt's economic life. The prevalence of underemployment, and the consequent lowness of men's wages, as well as the general conservative social outlook, prevented them until very recently from entering in force such fields as industry and clerical work. Wartime conditions, however, helped to stimulate female employment in several ways: by the example of the WAAFS and ATS; by the pressure resulting from inflation and the reduction of middle-class family incomes; and by direct employment with the Allied armies: in 1945 over 4,000 women were employed by the British forces. Already before the war women had obtained a foot-hold in some professions, and today there are many women doctors, lawyers, teachers (including a few university professors and even heads of division), nurses, and social workers. Several thousand women occupy minor positions in the civil service, a few having risen to ranks as high as heads of departments, and a larger number work as typists and secretaries in private business. To these activities should be added the excellent work done by volunteers for such organizations as the Red Crescent (counterpart of the Red Cross) and the Women's Health Improvement Association.[1] There is little doubt that the present trend towards emancipation of women will continue and the rate of advance may well be accelerated in the next few years.

### ATTEMPTS TO RAISE THE LEVEL OF THE MASSES

The last twenty years have witnessed the first large-scale, con-certed effort to raise the level of the masses recorded in the millennia of Egypt's history. Until very recently the statement that 'responsible authorities in Egypt are not yet fully aware of the fact that the tiller of the soil and his family are at least as important as the soil and

[1] See Ruth F. Woodsmall, *Study of the Role of Women, their Activities and Organizations in Lebanon, Egypt, Iraq, Jordan and Syria* (NY, 1956).

its products'[1] was a true description of the situation, but the last few years have brought about important changes. These may be examined from the following angles: health, adult education, and rural centres; various schemes of social insurance are discussed in Chapter VIII. The measures described below are being taken by the government but until recently private associations also did some very useful work.

*Health*[2]

Outside a few large cities, health conditions in Egypt are among the worst in the world and poor health, more perhaps than any other single factor, is responsible for the wretchedness of the peasants. Before the Revolution important measures had been taken to remedy this state of affairs.[3] Expansion continued after the Revolution and by 1960 there was a total of 32,000 beds in all government and private hospitals, or one for every 800 inhabitants;[4] Egypt is thus as well provided as Syria, somewhat less than Turkey, and much less than Lebanon. Another 6,000 beds are to be added under the Five-Year Plan.

One of the main obstacles to progress was the shortage of doctors, the total number in the country in 1931 being only 2,700 and in 1951 5,200, or one for every 4,000 inhabitants; moreover the bulk of doctors was, and continues to be, concentrated in the larger cities. To break this bottleneck, a new medical school was established in Alexandria in 1942 and another in Cairo in 1950. By 1951 the number of students in medical schools had risen to 6,311; by 1960 to 9,467, when 826 obtained their degrees. As a result, the number of physicians in Egypt is now over 10,000, or one for every 2,700 inhabitants, though there seems to have been some decline in the quality of training. To relieve the shortage of physicians in the countryside, the government has made a two-year service in the villages compulsory after internship. Among other short-run measures taken was the sending to the villages, late in 1961, of

---

[1] Abbas Ammar, *The People of Sharqiya* (Cairo, 1944), i. 284.

[2] For an excellent, though slightly out-of-date, survey of health conditions see Simmons.

[3] 'In 1922 there were forty-five health institutions, as opposed to 700 by 1950. There were no village hospitals at all in 1922; in 1950 there were 250. General hospitals increased in number from 19 in 1922 to 100 in 1950. Free treatment is being given in all government health institutions.' (Address by the Egyptian Ambassador before the Inst. of the Council of World Affairs, Cleveland, Ohio, 1952.)    [4] *UAR Yb. 1961*, p. 934.

360 physicians and 120 pharmacists, accompanied by over 1,000 assistants. Simultaneously a six-year plan was launched to establish 2,500 rural health centres, each serving 5,000 inhabitants, at a cost of £E13·5 million.[1]

Already before the Revolution the scope of preventive measures had been greatly extended, and further progress has been achieved since. In 1960 over 3 million persons were vaccinated and nearly 3·8 million were treated with pesticides; inoculation against tuberculosis is being provided as is home treatment for patients; in 1960 over 750,000 school children were medically examined, inoculated and where necessary treated, special attention being paid to eye diseases; school children are also being provided with free meals; a few clinics for mother and infant care have been established; and, more generally, an extensive health propaganda is being carried out in the villages. The fight against narcotics has also continued, greatly reducing the flow.[2]

As has been seen, some success has been obtained, with the help of modern drugs, vaccines and pesticides, in reducing the incidence of malaria, eye diseases, smallpox, tuberculosis, and intestinal diseases. The chief scourge of the countryside, bilharzia, also seems to be very slowly yielding ground, although the magnitude of the task may be judged by the fact that in 1960 no less than 17,000 km. of irrigation canals and drains were treated against bilharzia.[3]

Some attempts are also being made to overcome the great shortage of housing. Shortly before the Revolution the government started to provide cheap housing for working men; by 1950 1,100 houses had been built in Cairo and the number rose slightly in the next two years. In the same year a law was passed laying down minimum standards for peasant houses on large estates but little was done to implement it either before or after the Revolution; at present the only attempts being made to provide better housing in rural areas, with their estimated 3 million dwellings, are the few houses being built by the Ministry of Agrarian Reform, at a unit cost of £E300–400, and as part of various schemes of land reclamation; however, experiments are being made to produce cheap building materials suitable for use by the peasants.

More is being done for the towns. In 1959 it was estimated that there were 1,800,000 urban dwellings and that 60,000 should be built each year to meet required replacement and an estimated

---

[1] *al-Ahram*, 11 Apr. 1962 and spec. issue of 12 May 1962.
[2] *UAR Yb. 1961*, pp. 896–912.　　　　[3] Ibid. p. 909.

population growth of 2·5 per cent per annum.[1] This would require an annual investment of £E36 million, which would be raised by the addition of other urban and rural housing to £E44 million per annum. Actual investment in housing in 1954–8 was put at £E47 million, or rather more than was required.[2] Since, however, too large a proportion of this consisted of higher-income housing, the government has embarked on a low-cost housing scheme. In 1960/1 13,100 such houses were built, at a cost of £E4·4 million, and attempts are being made to encourage the building of middle-class housing by various ministries, municipalities, co-operatives, and building companies.[3]

The schemes for providing drinking-water have, on the other hand, benefited mainly the villages. In 1936 it was estimated that pure drinking-water from government or municipal installations was available to 3·5 million city dwellers but not to any country dwellers; by 1952 these figures had risen to 5 and 2 million respectively and by 1957 to 9 and 5·7 million.[4] Under the current Five-Year Plan, which provides for an expenditure of £E17 million, these figures are to rise to 11 and 17 million respectively, covering practically the whole population.[5] Although it is often still necessary to overcome a certain reluctance on the part of peasants, who prefer Nile water as being 'richer', there is no doubt that this programme represents a great advance in the countryside.

## Adult Education

Although the first plan to stamp out illiteracy by opening 200 new schools each year for twenty-five years was drawn up as early as 1914, practically nothing was done for adult education until the last few years. Measures recently taken mark a start, but one which will have to be greatly accelerated if worth-while results are to be obtained. Legislation passed in 1944 made it compulsory for big landowners and employers to provide instruction to their employees,

[1] Of this it was judged that 55 per cent should consist of popular housing, at £E350, 35 per cent of middle-income at £E800, and 10 per cent of higher-income housing, at £E1,200.       [2] NPC, Memo. no. 242.

[3] *UAR Yb. 1961*, pp. 820–4; see also Abd al-Aziz Mari and Isa Abduh Ibrahim, *al-Mushkilat al-iqtisadia al-muasira fi'l-iqlim al-misri* (1961), pp. 616–25. Another measure which has been of considerable benefit to urban dwellers has been the extension of public gardens in the last few years and the opening of royal palaces and grounds, such as those of Abdin and Muntazah, to the public.

[4] Lecture delivered by Ahmad al-Halawani, Asst. Under-Secretary for Health, Cairo, 26 Apr. 1958.       [5] *UAR Pocket Yb. 1961*, p. 63.

and the government established evening schools for illiterates. In 1955 300,000 adult illiterates were being taught: 200,000 in government schools, 60,000 in the army and prisons, 30,000 in classes organized by employers, and 10,000 in classes set up by co-operatives and social centres.[1] These figures are identical with the ones for 1950 and little seems to have been done to extend the programme since then; total attendance between 1952 and 1960 was 1,135,000, of whom 66 per cent passed the final examinations.[2] The programme for industrial workers has 'met great opposition from both employers and workers . . . and . . . has fallen far short of the mark.'[3]

Another interesting development was started by Unesco which, on the basis of experiments carried out in 1951 in an Egyptian village, succeeded in shortening the time required by adults to learn to read from six months to six weeks; this was achieved by simplifying the Arabic script, by using a less stilted language than is customary in school books, and by the choice of interesting and relevant subjects. In January 1953 Unesco, in collaboration with WHO, FAO, ILO, and the Egyptian government, established the Arab States' Fundamental Education Centre at Sirs al-Layyan, near Cairo; this centre, which has trained scores of teachers, social workers, nurses, and others from nine Arab countries, has been of great benefit to the whole region.[4]

A useful innovation was the foundation, in Cairo in 1946, of the People's University, designed to provide free evening classes in general and vocational education; these proved very popular and branches were set up in the provinces. After the Revolution its place was taken by the Free Cultural University which by 1960 had 23 centres, with 10,000 students, in various parts of Egypt.[5] In addition centres with the name—full of East European associations—of Palaces of Culture are being established in the provinces. Three such centres are under way and it is planned to complete twenty-five under the Five-Year Plan, but progress has so far been slower than was anticipated. Their function was defined by the Minister of Culture as the awakening of political consciousness among the people and the bringing to them of elements of world artistic culture. An attempt is being made to supplement them with 'cultural caravans'—long trucks provided with a cinema and books and carrying a dozen persons who will perform plays before

[1] *Ég. indust.*, Jan. 1955.  [2] *UAR Yb. 1961*, p. 563.
[3] Harbison & Ibrahim, p. 113.  [4] See Unesco, *Sirs-el-Layyan* (Paris, 1955).
[5] *UAR Yb. 1961*, pp. 959-60.

villagers, lecture to them, and help them to start discussions; this programme started at the end of 1961. The Minister has also announced that he is studying the possibility of setting up a cultural unit in every village co-operative centre.[1]

With the spread of education there has been an appreciable rise in the number of books published in Egypt, from 750 in 1948 to 2,133 in 1960.[2] Part of this increase is, however, accounted for by the large number of propaganda pamphlets—150 were issued in 1960 by the Ministry of Education[3] and others by the Ministry of Culture. Output in 1948 was estimated at 6½ million copies and sales of local and imported books outside schools at only 2½ million; since then these figures must have risen considerably. One of the most useful developments has been the launching, in 1955, of the Thousand Books series, designed to make available in Arabic the world's masterpieces; 928 books had been published by 1960, of which all but 54 were translations.[4] The number of books in public libraries has slowly risen to 2,470,000 in 1959.[5]

## Rural Combined Units [6]

The object of these units, which constitute one of the most important measures of their kind carried out in the Moslem world, is to provide villagers with a variety of social services by resident specialists. Started as an experiment in 1939, by 1950 they numbered 150, each serving a population of 10,000. In 1954 the scheme was reorganized, the coverage of each unit being extended to 15,000 inhabitants, and by 1960 their number had risen to 250, serving a population of 4 million living in 1,026 villages. It is planned to build another 100 under the current Five-Year Plan, to serve 2 million inhabitants, and ultimately to raise the total to 868. Throughout the history of the units the limiting factor has been not the willingness of the villagers, who have put in hundreds of requests, but the lack of funds and, still more, of trained personnel.

The two basic principles underlying the units are: first, that the request must come from the villagers, who must contribute

[1] *al-Ahram*, 30 Nov. 1961 & 8 Jan. 1962.
[2] See breakdown in Fed. of Eg. Industries, *Yearbook 1961* (in Ar.), p. 210.
[3] *UAR Yb. 1961*, p. 571.
[4] Ibid. p. 562; a comparable project was launched in Turkey in 1940.
[5] See breakdown in *Ann. stat. 1958–9*.
[6] See Mohammed Shalaby, *Rural Reconstruction in Egypt* (Cairo, 1950); Beatrice Mattison, 'Rural Social Centres in Egypt', *Middle East J.*, Autumn 1951; *Atlas of Services*; and *UAR Yb 1961*, pp. 944–7.

2 feddans and £E1,500 as well as temporary quarters for the social workers; and secondly, that the social workers must live in the village, in a manner outwardly differing as little as possible from that of the community. These workers consist of an agricultural-social worker, and a health and welfare nurse, both of whom are carefully selected and trained. They are assisted by a young club leader, chosen from the local community and sent to Cairo for training, and, wherever possible, by a doctor and laboratory assistant. Village interest and self-government are stimulated by the holding of an annual assembly, which elects a council to carry on the business of the community. The council operates through joint committees: conciliation; economic and agricultural; charity; education and recreation; health and cleanliness. In 1960 an attempt was made to link the units more closely with the organs of local government by making the heads of services of the centres *ex-officio* members of the village councils and by transferring to the latter the powers formerly enjoyed by the councils of the units.

It will thus be seen that the activities of the units are manifold. They include: demonstration plots, livestock selection, poultry raising and the keeping of bees and silkworms, cottage industries, co-operatives; medical care, education, and recreation. Results achieved vary considerably. Much has been done to make the life of the peasant healthier, pleasanter, and more peaceful, and to dissipate the fog of ignorance which surrounds him. It has been noticed that the service which attracts peasants most is medicine; this serves as a bait which makes them accept the other activities. In the economic field less success has been registered. Auxiliary activities, such as bee-keeping, have made a small but welcome addition to farmers' incomes, and the introduction of new crops, or use of better varieties, has sometimes raised output appreciably. But, so far, the attempt to develop cottage and agricultural industries has made very little headway. Yet it represents one of the most promising ways of increasing incomes.

The Combined Units have their weaknesses, but their achievement has been impressive. To a large extent, the future of the Egyptian villages, and therefore of the nation as a whole, is bound up with their fate.

# VI

# National Income

---

*La vocation profonde de tous les hommes de parvenir à un meilleur statut, un meilleur sort et un niveau de culture plus élevé.* VOLTAIRE.

*Oh miserable distribution of mankind—one half lacketh meat, the other stomach.*
JOHN DONNE.

*Accumulate, accumulate! That is Moses and the prophets!* KARL MARX.

*The question of history is what each generation has done with its surplus produce. One bought crusades, one churches, one villas, one horses and one railroads.* EMERSON.


## STAGE OF DEVELOPMENT

The stage of economic and social development reached by Egypt is illustrated in Table 8 (p. 110), in which certain important indices of economic and social activity are compared with those of thirteen other countries of various degrees of development. These include representatives of three major underdeveloped regions—the Middle East, Latin America, and Asia—as well as more advanced countries in which climatic conditions, and especially the range of temperature, are not too dissimilar from those prevailing in Egypt. Greece has been included as reflecting economic and social conditions prevalent in south-eastern Europe before the Second World War and its aftermath. The table shows Egypt to be somewhat behind Turkey; distinctly below Greece, the Latin American countries, and Japan; and very far behind the United States, Australia, France, and Italy. On the other hand in both the economic and social fields Egypt is well ahead of India and of Pakistan. The asymmetry between economic and social development in Egypt relatively to other regions, has been discussed above (p. 90). Additional information, not shown in the table, renders it possible to make the following broad generalization: Egypt has reached a stage of development which is distinctly higher than that of Asia, with the important exception of Japan; is roughly comparable to

TABLE 8

*Indices of Economic and Social Development, 1959*

| Country | Nat. income[1] | For. trade[2] | Energy con-sumptn.[3] | Steel con-sumptn.[4] | Cement prodn.[5] | Merch. carried on rail[6] | Food con-sumptn.[7] | Textile con-sumptn.[8] | Life expec-tancy[9] | Literacy rate[10] | News-paper circ.[11] | Radio sets[12] |
|---|---|---|---|---|---|---|---|---|---|---|---|---|
| Egypt | 120 | 42 | 0·24 | 9 | 69 | 66 | 2,640 | 3·8 | 38·6 | 20 | 25 | 31* |
| India | 60 | 9 | 0·15 | 9 | 20 | 178 | 1,800 | 2·3 | 32·1 | 19 | 9 | 4* |
| Japan | 190 | 78 | 0·97 | 163 | 194 | 521 | 2,210 | 7·8 | 67·6 | 90 | 398 | 164* |
| Philippines | 150 | 39 | 0·15 | 15 | 27 | 7 | 1,980 | 2·2 | 51·1 | 60 | 19 | 11* |
| Argentina | 460 | 126 | 1·03 | 97 | 149 | 910 | 3,100 | 8·1 | 63·7 | 84 | 180 | 201 |
| Brazil | 230 | 51 | 0·33 | 37 | 74 | 220 | 2,540 | 4·6 | 42·4 | 49 | 63 | 77 |
| Chile | 360 | 152 | 0·79 | 59 | 139 | 371 | 2,330 | 4·5 | 51·8 | 80 | 74 | 117 |
| Mexico | 220 | 51 | 0·82 | 37 | 76 | 370 | 2,420 | 4·1 | 38·8 | 57 | 48 | 80 |
| Greece | 220 | 96 | 0·40 | 33 | 181 | 47 | 2,860 | 5·4 | 50·5 | 74 | 71 | 86* |
| Turkey | 210 | 32 | 0·25 | 14 | 62 | 178 | 2,850 | 5·4 | .. | 32 | 32 | 40* |
| Italy | 310 | 132 | 0·99 | 143 | 300 | 310 | 2,650 | 5·8 | 62·9 | 86 | 107 | 132* |
| France | 740 | 250 | 2·37 | 253 | 330 | 1,250 | 2,950 | 9·2 | 68·0 | 96 | 246 | 250 |
| Australia | 950 | 429 | 3·68 | 307 | 281 | 1,351 | 3,210 | 9·9 | 69·9 | 95 | 381 | 247* |
| USA | 1,870 | 174 | 7·83 | 491 | 333 | 5,100 | 3,290 | 16·4 | 69·6 | 98 | 327 | 900 |

\* Licensed sets only.

[1] US$, per capita, 1952–4. [2] Per-capita value of imports & exports, in US$, 1959. [3] Coal equivalent, in m.t. per capita, 1959. [4] kg. per capita, 1959. [5] kg. per capita, 1959. [6] Ton-km. per capita, 1959. [7] Calories per capita, 1957. [8] Cotton, rayon, & wool, kg. per capita, 1956. [9] At birth, ave. male & female. [10] Per cent. of pop. 14 yrs or over. [11] Daily circ., per 'ooo inhabitants, 1959. [12] Per ooo inhabitants, 1958.

*Sources:* UN, *Statist. Yb. 1960;* FAO, *Per Caput. Fiber Consumptn. Levels, 1948–58.*

that of most of the Middle East, but not its more advanced parts, such as Israel and Lebanon; and is well below the Latin American average, though above that of the poorer regions of Central America and north-western South America. Generalizing still further it may be said that, in an array of the sovereign states of the world according to their degree of development, Egypt stands very near the median; that the per-capita income of the Egyptian population is far below the world's weighted average; but that in an array of the world's inhabitants according to per-capita incomes, the Egyptian population stands somewhat above the median. In other words, the Egyptian standard of living, low as it is, is higher than the level of that of more than half of the human race, which inhabits southern and eastern Asia, most of Africa, and parts of Central America. And, as pointed out above (p. 47), although Egypt's per-capita income has risen appreciably in the last few years, its relative position has probably shown little change.

### RECENT TRENDS

In view of the unreliability and lack of comparability of most estimates of Egyptian national income, it is very difficult to determine the trend of real per-capita income with any degree of accuracy. An Egyptian economist has deflated the various series, which he admits are not comparable, by the wholesale price index and arrived at the following average per-capita incomes, in 1954 prices (£E): 1937–9 34·8; 1951–3 34·5; 1954–6 38·8.[1] A series prepared by the National Planning Committee put the per-capita domestic product, in 1950 prices (£E), at some 39 in 1938, 38 in 1945, 43 in 1950, and 42 in 1956.[2] Other series, notably those of Anis and Sherbini (see p. 34 above), point in the same direction, namely that following a sharp drop during the Depression there was a recovery in the late 1930's, a great decline during the Second World War, a recovery to the pre-war level by the early 1950's and a slight improvement since then.[3]

In Table 9 (p. 113), the two best series on agricultural and industrial

[1] A. Hosny, *The Econ. Structure of Egypt* (Am. Univ. of Cairo, Soc. Research Center, Nov. 1959, mimeo).

[2] Computed from series for 1938–56; in current and constant prices, reproduced in UN, *Dev. of Manufacturing*, p. 94.

[3] For indices of volume and gross value of agricultural crops covering the years 1924–8 to 1950 see Issawi, *EMC*, p. 79.

production[1] have been combined in a weighted index. The figures would seem to imply that, in spite of the post-war recovery, production did not catch up with population until 1957, but that there has been an appreciable rise in per-capita income since that date. In the last few years total production seems to have increased at a compound rate of about 4 per cent a year and per-capita production at about 1·5 per cent. However, the production figure for 1961 must have shown a drop, owing to the sharp decline in agricultural output which was not offset by the increase that took place in industrial production.

### PURCHASING POWER OF EGYPTIAN POUND

At the 1961 official exchange-rate of $2·87 to the pound, Egypt was one of the cheapest countries in the world.[2] A study made by the UN Statistical Office over the years 1958–60, for the purpose of comparing the cost of living of officials of international organizations stationed in various cities, put Cairo at the bottom of the list. The index (New York=100) was 65 for Cairo; for London and Geneva it was 82 and for Paris 87; other Middle Eastern figures were: Istanbul 77, Tehran 81, Beirut 85 and Baghdad 90.[3] Moreover this comparison considerably understates the cheapness of Egypt relatively to Western Europe or America. For, given the purpose of the inquiry, prices were collected from shops and dwellings patronized by foreigners; but in Cairo, as in other Middle Eastern cities, the gap between prices paid by nationals and foreigners is several times as high as it is in the more advanced countries.

Of the main constituents of the cost of living, food, rent, and services are relatively the cheapest; most kinds of food are abundant

[1] The latter may somewhat underestimate the growth of industrial production in recent years. An official estimate of the gross value of the output of the manufacturing industries, petroleum extraction, and electricity shows a rise between 1952 and 1957 of 52 per cent and between 1952 and 1958 of 63 per cent or, deflating by the wholesale price index of industrial goods, of 48 and 51 per cent respectively. This implies a simple rate of increase of slightly over 8 per cent p.a., compared to the one of 7 per cent recorded by the National Bank index (*UAR Pocket Yb. 1959*, p. 99 & *Coll. Basic Statist. Data*, p. 147). Another official index of manufacturing shows a rise of 33 per cent between 1950 and 1955, or some 6 per cent per annum (UN, *Dev. of Manufacturing*, p. 98; see also p. 172 below). On the other hand the agricultural index may exaggerate the increase. Thus an official estimate of net agricultural income from vegetable and animal production in constant prices fell from 111·4 in 1935–9 to 100 in 1952, rose to 109·2 in 1956 and 119·2 in 1957, and fell back to 115·9 in 1958 (NPC, Memo. no. 382).

[2] On 7 May 1962 the Egyptian pound was devalued, *de facto*, to $2·30.

[3] UN, *Monthly B. Statist.*, June 1961.

**TABLE 9**

*Quantum Indices of Agricultural and Industrial Production, 1935–60*

| Year | Crops[1] | Agric. prod.[2] | Indust. prod.[3] | Agric. & indust. prod.[4] | Popula- tion[5] |
|---|---|---|---|---|---|
| 1935–39 | 100 | 100 | (38) | (80) | 71 |
| 1947 | 93 | .. | (72) | (82) | 85 |
| 1948 | 108 | 111 | (81) | (95) | .. |
| 1949 | 106 | 109 | (89) | (95) | .. |
| 1950 | 102 | 108 | (90) | (92) | .. |
| 1951 | 97 | 105 | 91 | 90 | .. |
| 1952 | 106 | 110 | 95 | 96 | .. |
| 1953 | 98 | 109 | 97 | 91 | .. |
| 1954 | 110 | 121 | 100 | 100 | 100 |
| 1955 | 108 | 119 | 110 | 100 | .. |
| 1956 | 109 | 123 | 115 | 102 | .. |
| 1957 | 121 | 130 | 124 | 113 | .. |
| 1958 | 123 | 131 | 137 | 116 | .. |
| 1959 | 128 | 136 | 142 | 121 | .. |
| 1960 | (130) | .. | .. | (124) | 115 |

[1] Min. of Agric.; incl. all crops; 1946–50=100.

[2] Min. of Agric.; incl. animal & vegetable production; 1935–9=100.

[3] NBE; incl. manufacturing, mining & quarrying, & electricity; 1954=100. Index for 1938, based on est. increase of 138 per cent in industrial production between 1938 and 1951 (NPC, Memo. no. 34); indices for 1947–50 based on index for manufacturing production reproduced in UN, Dev. of Manufacturing, p. 98.

[4] Combined index of 1 and 3; a weight of 4 has been assigned to the first and of 1 to the second series; 1954=100; since the industrial production index has been rising more rapidly than the agricultural, this may somewhat understate the increase in total production.     [5] 1954=100.

the whole year round, rents are controlled—the vast majority at very low levels—and the price of services is determined by the very low level of wages; thus, to take a rough but not inaccurate index, a haircut in a good barber's shop costs about 20 cents, compared with 40–50 in Beirut, 50 in London, 75 in Geneva, and $1·25 in New York, and a tram or bus fare within the centre of Cairo 6 cents in the first class and 3 in second, while a ride to the suburbs costs 9–12 cents and about 6 cents respectively. Manufactured goods are, however, comparatively expensive, particularly durable consumer goods.

It is much more difficult to evaluate the purchasing power of the Egyptian pound in terms of working-class income, since the Egyptian pattern of consumption differs so completely from the

American or West European. It seems likely, however, that at present the Egyptian pound buys relatively more at lower income levels. This may be inferred from the fact that food, which absorbs over half the family budget, and rent are relatively inexpensive in Egypt.[1]

This conclusion regarding the relatively high internal purchasing power of the Egyptian pound is in no way contradicted by the fact that on the Egyptian black market its rate in 1950 was around $2·40 and in 1961 about $1·60.[2] For this depreciation is due solely to the effect, on a very narrow market, of the great demand for foreign exchange, for capital transfers and other purposes.

### NATIONAL INCOME

Official estimates of national income have been published for the years 1950-7,[3] the Five-Year Plan contains a detailed breakdown for 1959/60 and targets for 1964/5 and the Detailed Plan for 1960/1 has an estimate for that year.[4] In addition there is an unpublished estimate for 1961/2, prepared in October 1961, which claims to have taken into account the effect of the nationalizations of July 1961.[5] These figures, and especially the later ones, must be taken with great reservations, since they are based on very different concepts. The 1950–7 estimates refer to net national product at factor cost, or national income. The 1959/60–1964/5 estimates, however, almost certainly refer to GNP at market prices, although that fact is not stated specifically. In order to make the latter set comparable with the former, adjustments must be made for the rise in prices; for changes in indirect taxes, fees, and subsidies; and for depreciation.

---

[1] According to the Min. of Supply, investigations have shown that families with an annual income of £E100 spend 65–70 per cent of it on food while those with an income of £E600 or over devote only 35 per cent of it to food (*al-Ahram*, 13 Nov. 1961). The cheapness of food items of mass consumption may be illustrated by the following figures: a dozen eggs (year round) 30–35 cents; a loaf of bread (156 grammes or one-third of a pound) 1·5 cents; flour 10 cents a kilogramme; rice 9 cents a kg; tea $4·60, a very expensive item; rationed sugar 17 cents and unrationed sugar 38 cents; milk, 19 cents a litre; beef or veal with bone 65–70 cents a kg.; such vegetables as string beans, marrows, carrots, eggplants, and cauliflowers from about 5–12 cents a kg. in season to 15–25 cents out of season, and such fruits as oranges, dates, figs, grapes, bananas, and guavas from about 8–16 to 15–35 cents respectively.

[2] See quotations in Franz Pick, *Pick's Currency Yb. 1961* (NY, 1961).

[3] *Statist. Pocket Yb. & UAR Pocket Yb. 1959.*

[4] *Detailed Plan for Econ. & Social Dev. in First Year 1960/1* (Cairo, 1960, in Ar.), p. 243.

[5] NPC, Memo. no. 556. For 1964/5 targets see Table 2, p. 67 above.

Very recently, a consistent series for the years 1952/3–1961/2 has been released (see Table 10). The exact coverage of the figures is not given but they almost certainly refer to Gross Domestic Product at current market prices, excluding import and export duties but including other indirect taxes and fees. The latter swell the general total and have a particularly distorting effect on the industrial sector: thus whereas previous estimates put net industrial product at factor cost for 1954 at £E105 million, the table shows a figure for 1954/5 of £E155 million. Moreover, since indirect taxes and fees increased appreciably in 1952/3–1961/2, their inclusion exaggerates the amount of growth that actually took place during that period.

TABLE 10

*Gross Domestic Product,*[1] *1952–62*

*(£E m., at current prices)*

|  | 1952/3 | 1954/5 | 1956/7 | 1957/8 | 1958/9 | 1959/60 | 1960/1 | 1961/2 |
|---|---|---|---|---|---|---|---|---|
| Agriculture | 252 | 301 | 374 | 381 | 364 | 400 | 418 | 441 |
| Industry | 127 | 155 | 192 | 218 | 240 | 273 | 300 | 344 |
| Construction | 25 | 26 | 32 | 38 | 43 | 52 | 66 | 99 |
| Transport & communications | 54 | 58 | 58 | 65 | 72 | 97 | 105 | 114 |
| Rents of dwellings | 59 | 62 | 67 | 68 | 70 | 73 | 75 | 78 |
| Commerce & finance | 72 | 83 | 101 | 109 | 116 | 127 | 143 | 155 |
| Other services[2] | 217 | 235 | 243 | 247 | 252 | 260 | 290 | 325 |
| Total | 806 | 920 | 1,067 | 1,126 | 1,157 | 1,282 | 1,397 | 1,556 |
| Rest of world sector | .. | −13 | −5 | 2 | .. | — | — | −1 |
| Wholesale price index (1939=100) | 362 | 348 | 406 | 420 | 417 | 418 | 418 | 425 |

[1] Excludes import and export duties but includes other indirect taxes.
[2] Includes government administrative sector.

*Source:* Official estimates reproduced in Isam Ashur, *al-Dakhl wa'l-tatawwur al-iqtisadi fi'l-bilad al-arabiyya* (1962); figures on rest of world sector have been added.

Another point that should be noted is that the figures for 1959/60 are partly based on forecasts, while those for the two following years consist almost wholly of forecasts. The 10·8 per cent and 9 per cent increases shown in 1959/60 and 1960/1 are suspiciously high and the rise registered in some sectors, notably agriculture, commerce and government, seems exaggerated. The 1961/2 figures also seem very dubious; agricultural production in that year must have been distinctly lower than in 1959/60, in view of the disasters which struck the cotton, maize, and rice crops and there is no reason to believe that output in industry and construction increased in the proportions indicated.

The 1958/9 figure is 43·5 per cent higher than that for 1952/3 and the 1959/60 figure 59 per cent higher. In real terms, the increases are 24·4 and 38·2 per cent respectively, or simple annual rates of growth of 4·1 and 5·5 per cent. Since the later figures are probably inflated by higher indirect taxes and other factors, the compound rate of growth over the period may be put at about 4 per cent per annum, a figure which tallies with that given on p. 112 above. In the last few years, however, the rate of growth may have been higher.

The most striking change in the table is the rise in the share of industry from 16 per cent in 1952/3 to 21 in 1959/60; the extent of the actual shift is probably diminished by the inclusion of indirect taxes, which rose less than physical industrial output. The relative rise in industry will probably continue and it is anticipated that industrial output will exceed agricultural by 1964.

A forecast for GNP in 1962/3 has recently been published and is reproduced in Table 11 mainly because of the light it casts on the distribution between the public and private sectors; total consumption was expected to equal £E1,308·5 million and savings 302 million, or 18·8 per cent, compared to 10·6 per cent in 1959/60. It should be pointed out that the table greatly underestimates the extent of government control over the economy—e.g. the President has declared that 95 per cent of industry is either owned or controlled by the government (see above, p. 63).

A change has also taken place in the annual per-capita income earned in the various branches. Since the expansion in industrial output has been achieved with a relatively small increase in employment (see below, p. 174) the value added per head in that sector has sharply risen. In 1959/60 income per worker was £E123 in agriculture, 432 in industry, 306 in construction, 201 in commerce and finance, 213 in services, and 520 in transport and administrative

**TABLE 11**

*Forecast Gross National Product, 1962/3*

(*£E million*)

|  | Public sector | Private sector | Total |
|---|---|---|---|
| Agriculture . . . . | 28·5 | 440·7 | 469·2 |
| Industry . . . . . | 156·5 | 201·9 | 358·4 |
| Electricity . . . . . | 11·2 | 6·8 | 18·0 |
| Construction . . . . | 21·0 | 70·0 | 91·0 |
| Transport & communications . . | 92·9 | 30·7 | 123·6 |
| Rent of dwellings . . . . | — | 78·0 | 78·0 |
| Public utilities . . . . | 3·6 | — | 3·6 |
| Trade . . . . . | 30·5 | 116·0 | 146·5 |
| Finance . . . . . | 30·8 | — | 30·8 |
| Education . . . . . | 57·7 | 13·3 | 71·0 |
| Health . . . . . | 11·9 | 2·0 | 13·9 |
| Social services . . . . | 4·7 | 0·5 | 5·2 |
| Cultural & recreational services . . | 2·7 | 13·7 | 16·4 |
| Security, justice & defence . . | 81·0 | 3·1 | 84·1 |
| Other government services . . | 25·1 | — | 25·1 |
| Personal services . . . . | 1·2 | 97·8 | 99·0 |
| Total . | 559·3 | 1,074·5 | 1,633·8 |

*Source:* 1962/3 budget estimates, published in *al-Ahram*, 30 June 1962.

services.[1] Here again, however, the figure for industry must be taken with caution since the ratio between it and agriculture seems too high, and that between it and transport and communications (£E448) and commerce and finance too low, relatively to both the level prevailing in Egypt a few years ago and that to be found in other countries at a similar stage of development.[2]

## DISTRIBUTION OF INCOME AND CAPITAL

Before the measures taken by the revolutionary régime—the agrarian reforms of 1952 and 1961, the nationalizations of 1960 and 1961, the sequestrations of 1961, and the steeper taxation, prohibition of cumulation of posts and other restrictions gradually introduced

[1] *Cadre du Plan*, p. 21 and calculations based on table on p. 112.
[2] See Issawi, *EMC*, p. 83.

during the last ten years—the distribution of incomes in Egypt was marked by great inequality. No accurate breakdowns are available but the following figures give an indication. According to Anis's estimates[1] rents of lands and buildings absorbed 29 per cent of national income in 1937-9, 22 per cent in 1945, and 24 in 1950; the corresponding figures for profit and interest were 37, 40, and 38 per cent and for salaries and wages 31, 36, and 38 per cent; the balance was accounted for by government income. It will thus be seen that the share of salaries and wages rose appreciably, perhaps indicating some measure of equalization as well as structural changes in the economy. There was a further rise after 1950, and the social accounts for 1959/60 put the share of wages and salaries at 45 per cent.[2]

Some light is shed on the distribution by income groups by the tax returns. In 1960 the number of persons whose returns were examined for general income tax, which is payable on incomes of £E1,000 a year or over, was 42,000; of these 30,000 actually paid the tax. Those examined for the tax on commercial and industrial profits were 418,000.[3] Those examined for the tax on liberal professions (exemption £E100–150) numbered 23,000 and those for the tax on wages and salaries, with the same exemption, 16,000. Of course these figures should be raised to take tax evasion into account.[4]

Some rough estimates on distribution of income are also available. A United Kingdom Trade Mission gave the following breakdown: 1 per cent of the population, with family incomes of over £E1,500 per annum, absorbed 11 per cent of total national income and another 3 per cent, with incomes of £E600–1,500, absorbed a further 19 per cent; at the other end of the scale 60 per cent, with family incomes of £E48–96, accounted for only 18 per cent and 20 per cent, with incomes of £E96–240, for another 16 per cent.[5] An Egyptian economist has stated that some 30 per cent of gross income was concentrated in the hands of 75,000 families and two other economists that 'the richest tenth obtains around 45 per cent of net national income, whereas the poorest half of the population draws only 20 per cent. This compares with 30 and 40 per cent respectively

[1] In *Ég. contemp.*, 1950 & 1953.                  [2] *Cadre du Plan*, p. 102.
[3] Of these 252,000 fell below the exemption limit of £E100–500 a year, 133,000 between the exemption limit and £E500, 17,000 were in the £E500–1,000 group and 17,000 above the £E1,000 level; the last group was presumably included in the returns on general income tax.                  [4] See below, p. 283.
[5] U.K., Bd. of Trade, *Rep. of U.K. Trade Mission to Egypt, the Sudan and Ethiopia* (1955), p. 51.

in developed countries.'[1] The most ambitious, and most recent, attempt is summarized in Table 12 (p. 120). A correction is, however, necessary; in 1958–9 the total population was a little over 25 million, and not 27 million as stated by the authors. Since they have underestimated the percentage living in towns, their figure for urban population is correct but the one for rural population must be reduced to 17 million; this would presumably affect only the first category, i.e. the 'landless', whose number should be brought down to about 12 million. Another reservation concerns the figures used for national income, which are a blend of net domestic product and disposable income and which somewhat underestimate the total.

The share of the national income accruing to the government, in the form of taxes or as revenue of semi-government institutions and government concerns, has risen very sharply. Both before and immediately after the Second World War the figure was about 20 per cent. By 1959 the government's share was 35 per cent of the total, and at present it is over 60.

The pre-war value of the national capital was estimated by both the present author[2] and R. Adler[3] at about £E1,200 million. The main constituents of the latter estimate were: land £E660 million, residential houses 170 million, industry and commerce 130 million, state property 140 million; it was estimated that Egyptian securities held abroad and property in Egypt held by foreigners accounted for £E100 million, or one-twelfth of the total.

Recently an Egyptian economist[4] has estimated the national capital at £E2,300 million, excluding land. Of this the government owned or controlled through the Economic Development Organization and the Misr companies £E800 million, or some 35 per cent; this figure may have risen above 50 per cent as a result of the nationalizations and sequestrations of 1961. The addition of land would presumably raise the figure for total national capital to some £E4,000 million. In view of the repatriation of Egyptian securities during and after the Second World War and of the nationalization and sequestration measures carried out in 1960 and 1961, it may be taken that foreign ownership of Egyptian capital is negligible and is outweighed by Egyptian assets abroad (see below, p. 238).

[1] Samir Amin, 'Forces inflationistes et déflationistes dans l'économie égyptienne', *Ég. contemp.*, Oct. 1958, and El Sherbini & Sherif, ibid. July 1956.
[2] *Egypt*, pp. 56–58.     [3] In *Ég. contemp.*, 1943.
[4] Cited by A. R. Abdel Meguid, 'Monetary Management', ibid. Apr. 1961.

**TABLE 12**

*Distribution of Income, 1958*

| | Total population | | Total income (£Em.) | Per cap. income (£E) |
|---|---|---|---|---|
| | ('000) | (per cent) | | |
| **A. Urban:** | | | | |
| Employment unspecified | 2,983 | 37 | .. | .. |
| Domestic servants | 934 | 12 | 20 | 21·4 |
| Floating, unskilled workers | 186 | 2 | 5 | 26·8 |
| Handicraft workers | 400 | 5 | 16 | 40·0 |
| Workers in modern ind. & transport | 790 | 10 | 48 | 60·8 |
| Clerical employees | 1,117 | 14 | 118 | 105·6 |
| Handicraft employers | 736 | 9 | 94 | 127·7 |
| Middle classes | 614 | 8 | 83 | 133·5 |
| Bourgeoisie & aristocracy[1] | 240 | 3 | 203 | 845·8 |
| Total | 8,000 | 100 | 587 | 73·4 |
| **B. Rural:** | | | | |
| 'Landless'[2] | 14,000 | 73 | 50 | 3·5 |
| Poor peasants (below 1 feddan) | 1,075 | 6 | 7 | 6·1 |
| Intermediary strata (1–5 feddans) | 2,850 | 15 | 76 | 26·8 |
| Rich peasants (5–20 feddans) | 875 | 5 | 76 | 87·4 |
| Rural capitalists (above 20 feddans) | 150 | 1 | 116 | 773·3 |
| Total | 19,000 | 100 | 325 | 17·1 |

[1] Incl. landed aristocracy, est. at 50,000 persons; this presumably explains why figures for rural population do not add up to total.
[2] Those who do not run a farm either as landlords or as tenants.

Source: *Tiers-Monde*, July–Sept. 1960 & Apr.–June 1961.

As in other countries, capital is more unequally distributed than income. The concentration of ownership until very recently is indicated by figures given by President Abdel Nasser in his speech of 23 December 1961 (see above, p. 60) which would imply that property worth £E500 million was taken from 7,300 persons by the agrarian reforms of 1952 and 1961 and the July 1961 nationalizations. As was pointed out above the coverage of some of the figures is by no means clear, but there seems no reason to doubt that some 10,000 persons held a very large chunk of the national capital. Another estimate is that 10,000 persons held the bulk of securities and that 20,000 persons owned half the buildings and 100,000 the other half,[1] while 12,000 landlords held 30 per cent of the cultivated area. Moreover, there was much overlap between these categories.[2]

### CONSUMPTION

Egypt's relative level of living, compared to that of other countries, is indicated by some of the columns in Table 8 (p. 110). A more complete picture, covering a wider group of countries and more articles of consumption, is provided by M. K. Bennett's 'International Disparities in Consumption Levels', *American Economic Review*, September 1951. There are no significant differences in the relative position occupied by Egypt in the two studies.

Available evidence on consumption during the past decades points to the following conclusion: the upward trend in the level of living which had characterized the period preceding the First World War continued until the mid-1920's. This was followed by a decline which persisted until the late 1940's, after which the level started to rise again. These fluctuations in the average were accompanied by a widening disparity between the consumption levels of rich and poor until the revolutionary government proceeded, by drastic measures, to close the gap.

Perhaps the best single index available over a long period is consumption of the principal cereals (wheat, barley, maize, millet, and rice) and pulses (beans, lentils, and groundnuts). Total consumption of these foodgrains averaged 3,588,000 tons in 1914–16, rose to 4,463,000 tons in 1927–9, and fell to 3,915,000 tons in 1936–8; per-capita annual consumption amounted to 287, 309 and 245 kg. respectively.[3]

During the inter-war years consumption of various staples, such as tobacco and meat, as well as cereals, seems to have declined.[4] During the Second World War consumption was drastically reduced. Per-capita consumption of the four main cereals (wheat,

---

[1] *Tiers-Monde*, Apr.–June 1961.

[2] For comparable and closely similar figures on the pre-war period see Issawi, *EMC*, p. 84.

[3] Computed by J. I. Craig & Mahmoud Abdel Karim, *Cereals Consumption in Egypt* (Cairo, 1947).    [4] Issawi, *Egypt*, p. 55.

maize, millet, and rice) fell from 217 kg. in 1938/9 to 190 in 1940/1 and 192 in 1945/6. According to Anis, total personal expenditure on food, reckoned in constant prices, fell from £E94 million in 1939 to 83 million in 1941 and an average of 90 million in 1943/4.

As Table 13 shows, by 1948 the pre-war level had been surpassed and between that year and 1957 there was a rise in the level of consumption of some 10 per cent. It is probable that this trend has continued; thus according to an official estimate—which may err on the side of exaggeration—consumption of necessities (grains, tea, coffee, sugar, oil, meat, textiles and kerosene) rose by 6 per cent between 1959/60 and 1960/1, reaching the figure of £E376·5 million, out of a total consumption of 876·4 million, in the latter year.[1] This is a very satisfactory development, though it falls short of the one registered in many underdeveloped countries such as Greece, India, Iraq, Lebanon, Libya, Philippines, Syria, Turkey, and others during the same period. It was made possible by the growth in the national income, by much higher imports of grains and other foodstuffs—in recent years financed largely by American aid—and by the greater output of the local textile industry.

No information is available regarding the distribution among various groups and classes of this increment in consumption. But no one who was familiar with conditions previously existing in Cairo and Alexandria can fail to notice a distinct improvement in the clothing and general appearance of their working classes, and the increased variety of goods being sold in the poorer quarters is another indicator of progress. In the villages there seems to have been much less increase in private consumption, but the effect of the provision of such collective services as hygiene, education, and drinking water should not be ignored.

The most recent analysis of Egyptian family budgets was carried out by a French expert, who studied a sample of 6,373 families. Average per-capita expenditure during the month of December 1959 (PT) was 298. For governorates the figure was 473, of which food and drink absorbed 50 per cent, for other towns 334 and 57 per cent and for the countryside 231 and 69 per cent. Consumption in Lower Egypt was higher than in Middle Egypt which in turn came above Upper Egypt. The income elasticity of demand for food was put at 0·7, for grains at 0·35 (0·5 in rural and 0·2 in urban areas) for light and fuel 0·8, for household utensils, 0·75 and for 'personal expenses' 1·15.[2] These figures may be supplemented by a study

[1] NPC, Memo. no. 532.          [2] NPC, Memo. no. 421.

**TABLE 13**

### Per-Capita Consumption of Staple Products, 1938–57

|  | Pre-war | 1948 | 1951 | 1954 | 1957 |
|---|---|---|---|---|---|
| Calories (per diem) | 2,372 | 2,476 | 2,365 | 2,572 | 2,619 |
| Protein (gr. per diem) | 70 | 72 | 70 | 74 | 75 |
| Grains[1] (kg. p.a.) | 182 | 186 | 172 | 190 | 188 |
| Sugar (kg. p.a.) | 13·6 | 15·8 | 16·2 | 17·5 | 17·9 |
| Meat (kg. p.a.) | 12·4 | 9·2 | 11·9 | 11·9 | 14·2 |
| Fish (kg. p.a.) | 2·7 | 3·1 | 2·4 | 2·9 | 5·8 |
| Fruits (kg. p.a.) | 61 | 36 | 48 | 65 | 45 |
| Fresh vegetables (kg. p.a.) | 32 | 58 | 44 | 60 | 64 |
| Tea (kg. p.a.) | 0·48 | 0·71 | 0·82 | .. | .. |
| Coffee (kg. p.a.) | 0·56 | 0·54 | 0·27 | .. | .. |
| Cotton goods (kg. p.a.) | 2·4 | 2·8 | 2·8 | 3·0 | 3·9 |
| All fibres (kg. p.a.) | .. | 3·3 | 3·5 | 3·6 | 4·5 |
| Tobacco (kg. p.a.) | 0·35 | 0·63 | 0·65 | .. | (0·5) |
| Soap (kg. p.a.) | 3·32 | .. | 3·49 | .. | (3·1) |

[1] Another series gives the following figures on net supply of grains per capita: 1935–9 229 kg., 1940–4 217, 1945–9 208, 1950–4 202, and 1955–7 217 (NBE, Econ. B., no. 3, 1958).

Sources: Coll. Basic Statist. Data; Ann. stat.; FAO, Per Caput Fiber Consumption Levels, 1948–58; Ég. industrielle; NBE, Econ. B.

undertaken in 1957 which put the average private consumption of a family of five at £E166 a year. Of this food accounted for £E106, clothing 19, rent 12, fuel 4, household utensils 11, medical care 3, transport 8, recreation 2, and others 1. Public consumption was put at £E15 per family.[1]

[1] NPC, Memo. no. 40. In 1961 the following percentages of total expenditure were found in urban and rural areas respectively: food 47 and 63; clothing 8 and 8; housing 12 and 5; fuel 0 and 4; transport 4 and 2; education 4 and 0; health 3 and 2. See Z. Shabana, 'Market Structure for Egyptian Development', Ég. contemp., Jan. 1962. For earlier studies of family budgets see Issawi, EMC, pp. 87–88. For conditions of living in the villages see W. Blackman, The Fellahin of Upper Egypt (1927); Ammar, People of Sharqiya; H. H. Ayrout, The Fellaheen (Alex., 1953); J. Berque, Hist. sociale d'un village ég. au XXème siècle (1957); Ibrahim Amir, al-Ard wa'l-fallah (1957); and the article by J. M. Weir in J. Eg. Public Health Ass., 1952, based on the work of the Rockefeller Foundation in the village of Sindbis.

### SAVING AND INVESTMENT

There is evidence of a certain amount of capital accumulation between the two world wars. Private savings were invested in residential buildings and industry, were used to repatriate Egyptian securities held abroad, or were deposited in banks. Public investment went chiefly into irrigation works and railways.[1] But the volume of total savings remained small, being estimated by Anis at £E8 million in 1939, or just under 5 per cent of the national income.

During the war consumption was restricted and savings increased sharply. According to Anis they reached a peak of £E132 million, or 29 per cent of national income, in 1944. In 1945 and subsequent years they declined both in absolute size and as a percentage of the national income; in 1950 they stood at £E113 million, or 13 per cent. These savings are reflected in the expansion of the money supply: between 1939 and 1947 the combined volume of the note circulation and bank deposits rose by £E255 million, or 405 per cent, compared to a rise of 210 per cent in wholesale prices.

Some estimates of investment are available for the post-war years but they are tentative and hard to reconcile. They would seem to suggest that in 1946–56 gross investment averaged some £E100 million per annum, or about 12 per cent of GNP (see Appendix II, p. 317). Very recently, a series covering the years 1952/3 to 1961/2 has been released (see Table 14). The figures seem reasonable and those for the years 1952/3 to 1958/9 are consistent with other available information and show a gross rate of investment of 11·4 per cent for 1956–8; but those for 1959/60 to 1961/2 must be regarded as targets rather than calculations of actual investment. There is no doubt, however, that investment has sharply risen in the last few years, and it is scheduled to increase further under the Plan.

Estimates for 1961/2 put private consumption at £E1,060·9 million, collective consumption at 285·0 million and investment at 362·1 million or 21·7 per cent of the total. Investment was broken down as follows: government administration £E85·9 million, government enterprises 212 million, private business sector 57·8 million, and household sector 6·4 million. Another breakdown put the share of construction in investment at 48·3 per cent. External financing, as represented by the deficit in the balance of payments, was put at £E42·4 million, or 11·7 per cent of investment.[2] As pointed out before, however, these estimates seem very dubious.

[1] For details see Issawi, *EMC*, pp. 89–90 and sources cited therein.
[2] NPC, Memos. nos. 552 & 556.

### TABLE 14

## Gross Investment by Sectors, 1952–62[1]

### (£E million)

| Sector | 1952 | 1954 | 1956 | 1957 | 1958 | 1959 | 1960 | 1961 | Total[2] |
|---|---|---|---|---|---|---|---|---|---|
| Agric., land reclamation | 7 | 6 | 12 | 15 | 16 | 19 | 35 | 32 | 156 |
| Irrigation drainage | 7 | 9 | 7 | 7 | 9 | 9 | 17 | 22 | 105 |
| High Dam | — | — | 1 | 1 | 1 | 8 | 10 | 10 | 31 |
| Mining industry | 30 | 34 | 31 | 36 | 48 | 60 | 77 | 100 | 491 |
| Electricity | 6 | 7 | 9 | 8 | 7 | 8 | 9 | 13 | 87 |
| Transp., commun., storage | 19 | 24 | 16 | 24 | 27 | 33 | 63 | 71 | 319 |
| Suez Canal | — | — | 15[3] | — | — | 14 | 15 | 11 | 55 |
| Dwellings | 38 | 50 | 50 | 48 | 40 | 38 | 35 | 42 | 439 |
| Public utilities | 3 | 5 | 6 | 8 | 10 | 13 | 13 | 14 | 80 |
| Education | 4 | 5 | 7 | 7 | 8 | 9 | 10 | 11 | 72 |
| Health | 1 | 2 | 2 | 2 | 2 | 2 | 2 | 3 | 18 |
| Social services | 1 | 1 | 1 | 1 | 1 | 1 | 1 | 1 | 6 |
| Other services | 4 | 5 | 6 | 7 | 7 | 7 | 9 | 23 | 77 |
| Total | 119 | 146 | 162 | 160 | 175 | 220 | 295 | 355 | 1,937 |

[1] Fiscal year starting in year indicated; figures have been rounded.
[2] Investment in 1952/3–1961/2 inclusive.
[3] Investment in 1956/7–1958/9 inclusive.

*Source:* Official estimates reproduced in Ashur, *al-Dakhl.*

As for returns on capital, in 1928–39 the average return on paid-up capital was some 6–7 per cent, and on market value some 4 per cent although there were, naturally, wide variations between branches.[1] More recently, studies covering substantially over 50 per cent of joint-stock companies have shown that average gross profit on shareholders' funds was 23·4 per cent in 1954, 27·1 in 1955, 22·2 in 1956/7, 22·4 in 1957/8, and 22·9 in 1958/9; the percentage of dividends to paid-up capital was 11·3, 14·3, 11·7, 11·2, and 12·7 respectively.[2] The average return on the market value of shares on the eve of nationalization, in 1960, was 6·1 per cent.[3] Capital-output ratios have been discussed in Chapter IV (p. 70).

[1] See Hamdy, *Statist. Survey* and Tables IX & XII in Issawi, *EMC.*
[2] NBE, *Econ. B.* nos. 2, 1957; 2, 1959; & 3 & 4, 1960.
[3] CBE, *Econ. R.,* no. 2, 1961.

# VII

# Agriculture

*For the land, whither thou goest in to possess it, is not as the land of Egypt, from whence ye came out, where thou sowest thy seed and waterest it with thy foot, as a garden of herbs.*
                                                                                    DEUTERONOMY.

*And these gigantic enterprises may in their turn prove but the preliminaries of even mightier schemes, until at last nearly every drop of water which drains into the whole valley of the Nile . . . shall be equally and amicably divided among the river people, and the Nile itself, flowing for three thousand miles through smiling countries, shall perish gloriously and never reach the sea.*                    WINSTON CHURCHILL, 1899.

*I knew thee, that thou art a hard man, reaping where thou hast not sown and gathering where thou has not strawed.*                                                    ST MATTHEW.

Egypt differs from most underdeveloped countries in that it has already had its agricultural revolution. This process, which went on for over a century, shows four distinct stages: the introduction of cotton with perennial irrigation by canals under Muhammad Ali; the rapid expansion of cotton cultivation during the American Civil War; the huge irrigation works carried out by the British; and the various measures taken to intensify production after the First World War. As a result of these developments Egyptian agriculture, which is based on a uniform and very fertile soil 'équivalent à celui que nous trouvons en Europe chez les maraîchers',[1] is now marked by a highly developed system of irrigation; a labour-intensive technique; lavish use of fertilizers; and dependence on cotton. Until the recent agrarian reforms another characteristic was the very unequal distribution of property accompanied by absentee ownership, small-scale tenure and farming, and

---

[1] P. Fromont, quoted in Gabriel Saab, *Motorisation de l'agriculture et développement agricole au Proche-Orient* (1960), p. 16; this work is of fundamental importance for an understanding of Egyptian agriculture; another important book by the same author is *The Egyptian Agrarian Reform* (in the press). See also Platt & Hefny pp. 158–63 and A. F. Money-Kyrle, *Agricultural Development and Research in Eg.* (Beirut, 1957).

the presence of numerous intermediaries. In the last fifteen years agricultural output has increased by some 2 per cent per annum on a practically unchanged cultivated area, a noteworthy performance.[1] Nevertheless, it is clear that much more can be done, and indeed that Egypt is due for a second agricultural revolution, based on some mechanization, further intensification, and a shift to more valuable products.

## IRRIGATION[2]

'Thanks to the harnessing of the Nile, Egypt enjoys the equivalent of rainfall of three different natural regions: the Mediterranean in winter, the American Gulf in spring and early summer, and the Monsoon in late summer and autumn.'[3] This harnessing consists of dams designed to store water, barrages to raise the water level, drains and pumps for carrying off the water, and dykes for protecting the fields against the summer flood.

At present, there are four storage dams on the Nile, at Aswan, Gabal al-Awlia, Sennar, and Roseires. The Sennar dam on the Blue Nile, completed in 1925, serves exclusively the Gezira region of the Sudan, as does the Roseires dam. Under the Nile Waters Agreement of 1929 not more than 922 million cubic metres could be withdrawn at Sennar for the use of the Sudan. The agreement of 8 November 1959, however, fixes the 'vested rights' of the Sudan at 4 and of Egypt at 48 milliard cubic metres and the 'reserved rights' at 14·5 and 7·5 respectively, and provides that future development shall take place only by mutual agreement and that if the claims of other riparians to Nile water are allowed, each of the two countries will contribute half.

These dams and barrages are supplemented by an elaborate network of irrigation canals, aggregating 25,000 km., most of which are navigable. Fields are watered either by free flow or, during low flood, by mechanical means such as pumps, *saqias*, *shadufs*, or

---

[1] This was achieved by extending perennial irrigation still farther and thus expanding the cropped area; by the growth of the labour force; by greater use of animal draught power and machinery; by increased application of fertilizers and pesticides; and by the development and diffusion of improved seeds and breeds. For an analysis of these factors and further details see Abdel Moneim el Tanamly, 'L'Évolution de l'écon. rurale ég. dans les cinquante dernières années', *Ég. contemp.*, Oct. 1960 & CBE, *Econ. R.*, no. 2, 1961.

[2] For fuller details the reader is referred to Hurst, espec. the diagrams on pp. 55 & 282; Platt & Hefny, ch. 5; Besançon, ch. 4; Herbert Addison, *Sun and Shadow at Aswan* (1959).

[3] For details see Hussein Kamel Selim, *Twenty Years of Agricultural Development in Egypt* (Cairo, 1940), p. 4.

Archimedes' screws. No fee is paid for the use of irrigation water. The distribution of water, a highly complicated operation, is managed by the government engineers with great skill and equity, though the opposition of powerful landlords or other village groups has sometimes caused minor disruptions.[1] It should be added that, very recently, the government has started digging artesian wells for irrigation; this programme offers great possibilities since underground water is apparently abundant in the Nile valley and along its edges, but such irrigation is of course more expensive than that obtained from the river.

The need for drainage was realized only after the First World War when, with the spread of perennial irrigation, it was perceived that the absence of drains was responsible for the accumulation of salts in the soil, thus diminishing its fertility, and for raising the level of the underground water-table, which chokes the long cotton roots. Even today there is little doubt that the Egyptian farmer tends to be extravagant in his irrigation and that more economy would both raise yields and save water.[2] During the last thirty-five years much work has been done in this field and Egypt is now provided with 13,000 km. of drains. Most of the land is still drained by free flow, but 1 million feddans in Lower Egypt and 200,000 in Upper Egypt are served by lift drainage.

Nevertheless drainage is still a great weakness. Main drains are available everywhere, but they need deepening and more pumps, while field drains are inadequate, owing to the high cost of the land they occupy, and are moreover difficult to connect with the main collectors through neighbouring plots. Hence, since 1933, experiments have been made with pipe drainage, which at present serves 44,000 feddans in Lower Egypt. This system has raised yields by 50–100 per cent, made it possible to shift from maize to cotton, reduced salinity and economized water; it also requires less upkeep. The replacement of field by pipe drains would save some 750,000 feddans. Hence, in 1956, the government launched a scheme for the provision of adequate field drainage for the whole country; this is estimated to cost £E150 million and to require twenty-one years for

[1] Platt & Hefny, p. 211.

[2] Experiments have shown that optimum yields are obtained by applying only 60 per cent of the quantity of water generally used; the losses caused by the rise in the water table have been estimated at £E40 m. a year (see sources cited in Saab, *Motorisation*, p. 21). Another way of saving water is by lining canals with earth, concrete, asphalt, or plastic; losses by seepage are 8–10 per cent in the Delta and 50 per cent in desert areas (FAO, *Lower Cost Canal Linings for Egypt*, 1959).

completion, to which should be added another £E68 million to be spent on main drains in 1958–68. The scheme is expected to pay for itself in ten years.[1]

During many thousands of years the people of Egypt prayed for high floods. Today, however, a high flood constitutes a serious menace to the summer crops lying on either side of, and several feet below, the river and canals. Protection has so far taken the form of large earth banks, in certain places reinforced by masonry, while the Aswan dam is used to reduce the crest of the flood. Projects for fuller flood control included the diversion of flood water into Wadi Rayyan—a depression south of Fayyum—and the building of a storage dam at Merowe, near the Fourth Cataract. These schemes have been rendered unnecessary by the High Dam.

The High Dam has also replaced a set of projects, stretching from the northern Sudan to the Equator, which was being implemented since 1950 and was scheduled for completion by 1965.[2] These included reservoirs on Lakes Victoria and Albert and a regulator barrage downstream of Lake Kioga, to provide over-year or century storage; a dam on Lake Tana, also for century storage; and the Jonglei diversion canal, to carry water which would otherwise lose half its volume by evaporation in the Sudd marshes. Total costs were estimated at £E62·5 million, to which should be added those of Merowe (40 million), and Wadi Rayyan (30 million). These schemes would have made it possible to expand Egypt's cultivated area to 7·5 million feddans, and would have removed the danger of both floods and abnormally low years. Their chief drawback was that they were to be built outside Egypt, which entailed political risks, increased the outlay of foreign exchange, and deprived the country of the benefits of the generation of hydro-electricity. Another serious technical defect was that Egypt would have had to continue its present system of letting the flood water pass freely through the Aswan dam into the sea, for fear of silting, thus losing some 30 milliard of the total river flow of 84 milliard cubic metres.

The High Dam project was drawn up in 1947 by a Greek engineer resident in Egypt, was taken up by the government in 1954 and, after the setback due to Egypt's delay in accepting the American offer to finance it and the unfortunate withdrawal of that offer in

---

[1] *al-Majalla al-ziraia*, no. 12, Oct. 1960.

[2] For details see Hurst, and Yusif Simaika, *Mashruat istighlal miah al-nil* (1957). The implementation of some of these schemes, at a future date, is however once more under study (*al-Ahram*, 19 May 1962).

1956,[1] was started in 1958 with the help of Soviet engineers and of two Soviet loans aggregating 1,300 million roubles, or £E113 million. The scheme calls for the building of a rock-fill dam, the largest in the world, with a core of clay. It will create a lake with an area of 4,000 sq. km. and a volume of 130 milliard cubic metres. Because of this huge size, flood water can be retained, since it is estimated that it will require 500 years for the accumulated silt to fill the 30 milliard cubic metres allowed for. On the other hand evaporation will be high, some 10 milliard cubic metres a year.[2] A hydro-electric station with an aggregate capacity of 2·1 million kw. and a maximum output of 10,000 million kwh. will be set up; the dam will also make it possible to increase the electricity output of the Aswan dam. The present timetable calls for the provision of additional water by 1964, the completion of the main dam by 1967, the generation of electricity by 1967, and the attaining of full electric capacity by 1972. The cost of the dam has been estimated at £E112 million, of the turbines at 90 million, and of the necessary canals, drains, roads, &c, 104 million. Additional private investment required is put at £E98 million, giving a total of 404 million. The gross benefits to be derived are estimated as follows: cultivation of an additional 1 million feddans and the conversion of 700,000 feddans in Upper Egypt from basin to perennial irrigation, representing an increase of £E63 million in the national product; guaranteeing of water requirements for all crops in all years, improvement of drainage by lowering the water-table and provision of water for 700,000 feddans of rice plantations, representing £E56 million per annum; flood control and improvement of navigation, representing a gain of £E10 and £E5 million a year respectively; and electricity generated from the High Dam and increase in output of Aswan dam, £E100 million; a total of £E234 million per annum.[3]

By the end of 1961 total expenditure on the Dam amounted to £E16·5 million and the minister in charge announced that the first stage would be completed on schedule, by 1964,[4] but foreign observers were forecasting a delay of at least a year.

[1] The US offer was for $56 million and was accompanied by a UK loan of $14 million and one from the IBRD for $200 million; the latter two were withdrawn together with the American offer.

[2] For fuller details see Simaika; *UAR Yb. 1961*, pp. 401–17; & *UAR Pocket Yb. 1961*, pp. 81–87.

[3] On the other hand the Dam, by retaining the silt carried by the flood waters, will deprive Egyptian land of a precious fertilizer and at the same time make the reclamation of desert land more difficult.          [4] *al-Ahram*, 20 Jan. 1962.

## LAND RECLAMATION

During the last forty years the cultivated area has increased only slightly and now stands at 5,900,000 feddans but, as a result of the change-over from basin to perennial irrigation,[1] the crop area rose from 7,717,000 feddans in 1912 to 8,474,000 in 1938, 9,165,000 in 1948, and 10,349,000 in 1958. It should be added that, owing to the fact that Egypt can now rely on a steady water-supply, its total cultivated and crop areas show practically no variation from year to year, though the proportion under different crops does fluctuate in response to prices. This is in sharp contrast with other Middle Eastern countries, where annual variations in area of 20 per cent or more may be caused by changes in rainfall, while variations in yields are even more violent.

Two factors limit the extension of cultivation in the river valley: the topography and the amount of water available. Until recently, the maximum was put at 7·5 million feddans. This was based on the fact that the area lying within 10 metres of the river-level is a little under 8 million feddans, from which it is necessary to deduct the area occupied by public utilities as well as 'land unsuitable for cultivation'. This estimate has now been raised to nearly 10 million feddans, on the assumption that cheap power will be available—making it possible to extend cultivation to a level of 20 metres—and that savings can be made in the use of water.[2] But, to quote the leading authority, 'Our conservative estimate of 7½ million feddans may after careful investigation be extended a little, but 10 million feddans of perennial irrigation, together with development of the Sudan, would take more water than any scheme of projects could get out of the river'.[3]

Until recently practically all land reclamation was carried out in the river valley and relied on Nile water. By 1952 the government had developed some 300,000 feddans of state domains and by 1960 another 100,000 had been added. Land reclamation companies had

---

[1] The area still under basin irrigation is about 900,000 feddans; of these only 200,000 bear a single crop, the others supplementing their flow irrigation with pumps.

[2] The extra 3·8 m. feddans to be reclaimed consist of 279,000 of coastal lakes to be drained, 1,462,000 of 'black lands', mostly in the Delta, 1,560,000 of desert lands at a level of less than 10 metres above the river, also mostly in the Delta, and 670,000 of desert lands at a level of 10–20 metres, about equally divided between the Delta and Upper Egypt (Atef Sedki, 'L'Agric. égyptienne', unpub. thesis, Paris Univ., 1958, p. 541, quoted by Saab, *Motorisation*, p. 7).

[3] Hurst, p. 287.

also developed and sold to farmers some 150,000 feddans, mainly in the Delta. In 1953 a four-year plan for the reclamation of 235,000 feddans, at a cost of £E11·7 million, was drawn up but it has been only partially implemented.[1] Among the most successful schemes being carried out is the Egyptian American Rural Improvement Service covering 25,000 feddans near Alexandria and in Fayyum; work started in 1953 and is being jointly financed and executed by the Egyptian and United States governments. The Tahrir (Liberation) Province scheme has so far reclaimed some 25,000 feddans west of the Delta, at the very high cost of £E25–30 million;[2] the scheme has run into technical difficulties, because of insufficient preparatory study, and inefficiency and corruption. The current Five-Year Plan provides for the reclamation of 493,000 feddans by Nile irrigation at a cost of £E90·8 million, of 100,000 feddans in Tahrir Province by Nile and underground water irrigation at a cost of 20·5 million and, in addition, of 240,000 feddans of desert land at a cost of 62·1 million.[3] An Italian firm is helping in the reclamation of 140,000 feddans, at a cost of £E28 million. On the other hand private reclamation by companies or large landowners has entirely ceased.

It is only very recently that Egyptians have begun to consider the utilization of the deserts, which constitute 95 per cent of the country and are its only major untapped resource. Between the two wars, the success of the Gianaclis vineyards in Mariut and of the Italian farms in Cyrenaica drew attention to Egypt's Mediterranean fringe, which in Greco-Roman times was famous for its grain and wines.[4] At present the government is engaged in a systematic study of rainfall, underground water, and soil, and has launched a 20,000-feddan pilot scheme.[5] In addition there is a scheme for improving 60,000 feddans of pastures. The combined cost of both projects is £E5·5 million, to be spent over five years. A near-by project covers 50,000 feddans in Mariut, to be irrigated by a mixture of drain and Nile water, at a cost of £E12 million. The Wadi Natrun project aims at reclaiming 20,000 feddans, by means of wells, at a cost of £E3·6

---

[1] NPC, *al-Majlis al-daim li tanmiat al-intaj al-qaumi* (1955), pp. 65–69.

[2] Saab, *Eg. Agrar. Reform*, ch. 6; see ibid. ch. 10 for further details on land reclamation schemes.                                   [3] *Cadre du Plan*, pp. 34 & 200.

[4] After the Arab conquest vine growing declined sharply in Egypt, as in other Muslim lands, owing to the prohibition of wine drinking (see Xavier de Planhol, *The World of Islam* (Ithaca, NY, 1957), p. 50).

[5] For this and the following schemes see Gen. Desert Dev. Org., *UAR Desert Dev. & Land Reclamation Projects* (Cairo, 1961).

million. East of the Suez Canal, an area of 20,000 feddans, is to be irrigated by Nile water, carried by syphons across the canal, at a total cost of £E7·9 million. In Sinai small reservoirs have been built and a larger one is to be set up to store 160 million cubic metres of water and irrigate 20,000 feddans.[1]

But the most ambitious scheme is that of the New Valley, the name recently given to the series of depressions in the Western Desert punctuated by the oases stretching from Dakhla to Siwa. The cultivable land in these depressions has been put at 3 million feddans but the limiting factor is, of course, water. At present 10,000 feddans are under cultivation and current plans call for the reclamation of 121,000 feddans in 1960–5, at the high cost of £E21·6 million. It is hoped eventually to settle as many as 3 million people in the valley,[2] but that is evidently a matter for the distant future.

Looking farther ahead, greater potentialities may be discerned. Cheap electricity from the Qattara depression (see below, p. 322) could be used to lift water. Still wider vistas are opened by experiments to distil sea water by harnessing solar energy and by other methods. Much success has been achieved in this field in the United States,[3] the Soviet Union, Israel, France, and other countries, and the first experiments in distilling sea water by solar energy in Egypt took place in February 1962, in Suez.[4] Although present costs of these methods are still prohibitive for use in agriculture,[5] they are steadily coming down and there seems little doubt that in the not too distant future they will have dropped to a competitive level. Such a development will enable the Egyptians to break out of the narrow river valley in which they have been cooped up for the last six or seven millennia, ever since the desiccation of the Libyan and Eastern Deserts.

Lastly, mention may be made of reforestation. Egypt is a large importer of wood, as it has been for millennia, and the possibilities of greater local production deserve more attention than they have received. Poplar trees mature after twelve to fifteen years and, according to the estimate of an FAO expert, could be very profitably sold for £E4–8 per cubic metre, compared with the import price of £E16. Such trees could be planted along 15,000 km. of canals and

[1] *al-Ahram*, 31 Jan. 1962.

[2] See spec. issue of *al-Ahram*, 4 Dec. 1961, on the New Valley.

[3] US Dept. of Interior, *Saline Water Conversion Rep.* (ann.).

[4] *al-Ahram*, 12 Feb. 1962.

[5] Colin Clark, *The Economics of Irrigation in Dry Climates* (Oxford Univ., Inst. for Research in Agric. Economics), p. 31.

many more kilometres of roads, where they would serve as windbreaks for fruit and vegetable gardens. For desert areas such as Tahrir Province, Natrun, and the Mediterranean coast as far as Marsa Matruh improved breeds of Eucalyptus and Casuarina, as well as almonds, castor oil and other plants requiring little water are suitable.

### AGRICULTURAL TECHNIQUE[1]

Egyptian agriculture is still wasteful in its use of time, of seeds, of berseem as fodder, and of dung, which is used as fuel. But the absenteeism of many landlords and the illiteracy of the peasants has slowed down, though it has not stopped, the diffusion of technical improvements. The cheapness of labour and the skill of the fellah with his traditional instruments have held up the use of machinery, except for irrigation and drainage where, in 1957, there were 16,500 machines with an aggregate horse-power of 450,000. Further obstacles are the very small size of individual plots and the planting of many different crops over a small area, the poverty of the farmers, the weakness of co-operatives, the fact that the fields are cut into small patches by canals and drains and are not always accessible by road, the lack of near-by repair shops,[2] and the nature of cotton which does not lend itself readily to mechanization.[3] Table 15 shows how much greater are labour inputs per acre or per unit of output in Egypt than in the United States; it also brings out the comparative advantage enjoyed by Egypt in cotton, a labour-intensive crop.

In recent years, however, the number of tractors has risen sharply, from 1,200 in 1939 and 3,000 in 1945 to 7,600 in 1952 and 10,100, with an aggregate h.p. of 316,000, in 1957. This is thanks to the lower cost of tractors, compared to animal draught-power, on medium sized and large estates.[4] The yearly cost of animal power on farms of 10 feddans has been estimated at £E8·4 per feddan, while

[1] For the instruments and conditions of work see Samir Saffa, 'L'Exploitation écon. et agricole d'un domaine rural ég.', *Ég. contemp.*, 1949; Besançon; Platt & Hefny.

[2] These questions are exhaustively discussed in Saab, *Motorisation*, pp. 131–225.

[3] Mechanization of cotton plantations in the USA, which has made great advances since the Second World War, is discussed in J. H. Street, *The New Revolution in the Cotton Economy* (Chapel Hill, 1957); for mechanization in the Soviet Union see Akademia Nauk Uzbekskoi SSR, *Materiali obiedinennoi nauchnoi sessii po khlopkovodstvu* (Tashkent, 1958), ii. 448–683.

[4] In 1960 mechanical draught power and farm machinery were valued at £E40 m. (see Saab, *Eg. Agrar. Ref.*).

**TABLE 15**

*Labour Input in Egypt and United States*

| Product | Standard of comparison | Man-hour requirement for production | | |
|---|---|---|---|---|
| | | in USA | in Egypt | Ratio USA Egypt |
| Wheat | per acre | 6·1 | 160·0 | 1/26 |
| | per bushel | 0·4 | 6·0 | 1/16 |
| Corn | per acre | 28·7 | 357·5 | 1/12·5 |
| | per bushel | 1·1 | 9·1 | 1/9 |
| Cotton | per acre | 88·0 | 320·0 | 1/3·7 |
| | per bale (500 lbs.) | 271·0 | 322·0 | 1/1·2 |
| Barley | per acre | 8·5 | 115·2 | 1/13·6 |
| | per bushel | 0·4 | 3·9 | 1/10 |

*Source:* Mahmoud el Shafie, 'Population Pressure on Land and the Problem of Capital Accumulation in Egypt' (Wisconsin Univ. Ph.D. thesis, 1951).

that of a tractor was £E1·2–4·9 on farms of over, and £E4–8·35 on those under, 50 feddans.[1] Further effects of mechanization are: improved methods of ploughing and weed control; greater timeliness and regularity of operations; the release of land which would otherwise be put under fodder crops for draught animals; speedier reclamation of uncultivated land; decreased supply of manure; a rise in the productivity and wages of those labourers who operate the machinery; and a slight decrease in the volume of agricultural employment, although that has often been compensated by intensification of production.[2] Mechanization will no doubt be greatly

[1] For details see Saab, *Motorisation*.

[2] A study of a 500-feddan farm which replaced animal power by machines and at the same time intensified output of vegetables and dairy products showed, together with a marked rise in total production, a diminution of 17 per cent in the number of man-days and an increase of 1 per cent in woman- and child-days (ibid. p. 112). Recently it was estimated that mechanization of field work might displace 250,000 labourers, of whom 150,000 could be absorbed in pest-control operations and 20,000 in additional mechanical irrigation; the benefits were put at: a saving of £E9·5 m. in costs of ploughing and threshing; £E7·7 m. in saving of losses during threshing; and several millions in increased production of animals diverted from draught work (NPC, Memo. no. 33).

stimulated by the setting up of a tractor plant, scheduled to start operations in 1962 and to produce 3,000 units of 47 h.p. a year.[1]

There is one important respect, however, in which Egyptian agriculture is one of the most advanced: the utilization of chemical fertilizers. From about 1900 increasing use has been made of nitrates and superphosphates, and pre-war consumption averaged about 500,000 tons per annum. After a sharp setback during the war the upward trend was resumed and by 1960 1·4 million tons of fertilizers were used, of which 842,000 were nitrogenous; this was probably the highest input of fertilizer per cultivated acre in the world.

Nevertheless, even now the use of fertilizers is inadequate, and total requirements have been put at 1,140,000 tons of nitrogenous, 470,000 of phosphatic, and 19,000 of potash fertilizers.[2] It has been estimated that over half the area planted to wheat receives less than 50 kg. of nitrates per feddan a year; yet 100 kg. of nitrates, costing PT270, raised the yield of wheat by 37 per cent, or by PT562,[3] and increased the protein content from 9·8 per cent to 12·4.[4] The application of 100 kg. of sodium nitrate raised the yield of cotton from 3·89 to 4·48 cantars.[5] Experiments carried out by the Royal Agricultural Society showed that, in land left for two years without fertilizers, wheat yields fell by 34 and maize yields by 50 per cent.[6] It should not be forgotten that, under basin irrigation, the land lay fallow for several months and in addition was invigorated by an annual deposit of alluvium. With perennial irrigation, which involves constant use of the land and keeps off the alluvium-bearing flood, the soil would be rapidly exhausted were it not for the large-scale use of fertilizers.[7]

Mention may also be made of the rapidly growing use of pesticides, which have also amply paid for themselves, though annual losses because of insufficient pest control are put at £E20–25 million. The disastrous attack of the cotton-leaf worm in 1961,

[1] *al-Ahram*, 28 Sept. 1961.　　[2] NBE, *Econ. B.*, no. 4, 1961.

[3] NPC, Memo. no. 27.　　[4] *al-Majalla al-ziraia*, Dec. 1960.

[5] Saffa, in *Ég. contemp.*, 1949; for fuller details see Soc. d'Entreprises commerc. en Ég., *La Culture du coton* (1950), pp. 104–15.

[6] J. Anhoury, 'Les Répercussions de la guerre sur l'agric. ég.', *Ég. contemp.*, 1947.

[7] The amount of silt deposited on the basin lands of Upper Egypt was estimated at a yearly average of 1·03 mm. in 1929–31; on perennially irrigated land it was negligible (see John Ball, *Contributions to the Geography of Egypt* (Cairo, 1939), pp. 170–3).

which reduced the crop by some 34 per cent compared with 1960, also shows that much remains to be done in this field.[1]

Lastly, the increased use of selected seed may be noted. This process has gone farthest in cotton and sugar-cane but an appreciable progress has also been registered in grains.[2] Nevertheless losses due to insufficient use of selected seed are estimated at about £E10 million a year.[3]

The exhaustion of the soil is accentuated by the fact that the biennial crop rotation system is still followed. This cycle runs:

November–May: wheat or berseem (Egyptian clover).
June–July: fallow.
August–November: maize, millet, or rice.
December–January: fallow or berseem.
February–November; cotton.

It will be seen that this rotation yields three crops, including cotton, in two years but allows the land only a few months' rest. Under the triennial rotation, which is observed by a minority of progressive landowners and in the lands managed by the Agrarian Reform Committee, only 1 wheat, 1 maize, and 1 cotton crop are grown in three years, thus allowing for a long period of rest and summer flooding between the crops.[4] This rotation is much less exhausting for the soil and gives yields exceeding by as much as 20 per cent those of the biennial rotation. In the short run, however, the latter is the more remunerative rotation, since it permits the allocation of half the total area to cotton.

The necessity for following a rotation under which grain crops alternate with cotton, and not with other grains, was vividly demonstrated during the war years, when the restriction of the

[1] In a symposium on the causes of the crop failure of 1961 the following reasons were given: failure of the Ministry of Agriculture to provide enough pesticides; inadequate distribution by Agricultural Bank; insufficient co-operation of farmers with the authorities; and unfavourable climatic conditions (*al-Majalla al-ziraia*, Nov. 1961). The threat of renewed attacks by the cotton-leaf worm in 1962 led to the exposure of much incompetence and indifference in the government administrations and organizations responsible for agriculture (*al-Ahram*, 22 Apr., 5 May & 10 June 1962).
[2] See figures in *al-Islah al-zirai fi 9 sanawat*, p. 11.
[3] G. Saab, 'Rationalization of Agriculture and Land Tenure Problems in Egypt', *ME Econ. Papers*, 1960 (American Univ., Beirut).
[4] For details see Saab, *Motorisation*, pp. 18–20.

cotton acreage, combined with the lack of fertilizers, caused a sharp fall in yields. Experiments have shown that the succession of two cereal crops reduces yields by 20 per cent.

AREA AND VALUE OF MAIN PRODUCTS

Table 16 shows the relative importance of the areas under the main crops in 1935-9; in 1942-3, when wartime restrictions sharply reduced the cotton acreage and increased that of grains; in 1950-1, by which time wartime restrictions had been relaxed and Egyptian agriculture had reverted to its normal pattern; and in 1959-60, the latest year for which figures are available. The most interesting trends are the expansion in the rice acreage, thanks to the greater supplies of water, the increase in 'other crops', the relative decline in wheat and millet, and the absolute decline in barley and beans.

TABLE 16

*Percentage Area under Main Crops, 1935-9 to 1959-60*

| Crop | Area as percentage of total | | | |
|---|---|---|---|---|
| | 1935-9 | 1942-3 | 1950-1 | 1959-60 |
| Cotton | 21 | 8 | 21 | 19 |
| Maize | 19 | 21 | 16 | 18 |
| Wheat | 17 | 21 | 15 | 14 |
| Berseem | 20 | 18 | 24 | 24 |
| Millet | 4 | 8 | 5 | 4 |
| Rice | 5 | 7 | 8 | 7 |
| Beans | 5 | 4 | 4 | 4 |
| Barley | 3 | 5 | 1 | 1 |
| Other | 6 | 8 | 6 | 9 |
| Total | 100 | 100 | 100 | 100 |

Sources: *Ann. stat.*; CBE, *Econ. R.*, no. 2, 1961.

The wholesale value of the main crops, omitting berseem whose pre-war value was about £E13 million and in recent years about 50 million, has changed, as is shown in Table 17. It will be seen that cotton is the most variable element in Egyptian agriculture.

TABLE 17

## Values of Different Crops, 1924–58

### (£E million)

|                      | 1924   | 1929  | 1932  | 1937  | 1942  | 1950   | 1958   |
|----------------------|--------|-------|-------|-------|-------|--------|--------|
| Cotton & seed        | 65·0   | 40·0  | 14·7  | 27·6  | 23·0  | 218·5  | 140·9  |
| Wheat                | 12·2   | 11·7  | 10·2  | 10·4  | 24·4  | 22·4   | 34·8   |
| Maize                | 20·7   | 12·0  | 8·1   | 12·7  | 24·2  | 22·9   | 41·4   |
| Beans                | 4·2    | 3·5   | 2·5   | 2·5   | 5·9   | 7·4    | 9·5    |
| Rice                 | 2·9    | 2·9   | 2·4   | 2·2   | 12·7  | 24·3   | 18·9   |
| Millet               | 3·3    | 1·8   | 1·7   | 2·8   | 16·0  | 7·4    | 13·7   |
| Barley               | 2·4    | 1·7   | 1·2   | 1·4   | 5·1   | 2·0    | 3·7    |
| Sugar-cane           | 1·9    | 1·4   | 1·8   | 1·8   | 4·0   | 6·5    | 9·9    |
| Onions               | 1·2    | 1·0   | 1·1   | 0·6   | 0·4   | 5·8    | 7·0    |
| Lentils              | 0·6    | 0·5   | 0·3   | 0·5   | 1·0   | 1·9    | 2·4    |
| Helba (fenu-greek)   | 1·1    | 0·5   | 0·3   | 0·4   | 1·2   | 1·1    | 1·1    |
| Total                | 115·5  | 77·0  | 44·3  | 62·9  | 117·9 | 320·2  | 283·3  |

*Sources:* pre-war figures computed on the basis of wholesale prices and crop estimates; war and post-war figures from *Ann. stat. & Coll. Basic Statist. Data.*

### COSTS AND RETURNS OF MAIN CROPS

Table 18 (p. 140) gives some data on costs and returns of the main crops.[1]

In interpreting these figures the following factors should be kept in mind: the necessity of following a certain crop rotation; the period of growth, which varies from a few weeks for vegetables to several years for fruit trees and the consequent possibility of growing a secondary crop; and the risk involved and investment required. With these reservations, the following deductions may be drawn: livestock breeding and fruit yield the highest returns per acre but they also require the largest capital investment; in both respects they

[1] The table may be supplemented by calculations on livestock and dairy farming made by Saab in the late 1950's. For milk production with berseem as fodder and an output ranging from 2,400 to 4,500 kg., gross receipts per feddan were £E84–157·5; with maize as fodder and an output of 3,200–6,000 kg. the figures were £E128–240; net profits ranged from minus £E11·45 to 48·55 and from minus £E7·5 to 69·1 respectively. For meat, with berseem as fodder and an output of 420–900 kg., gross receipts were £E50·4–108 and net profits minus £E10·5–32·1; with maize as fodder and an output of 560–1,200 kg. gross receipts were £E67·2–144 and net profits minus £E14–41·8 (*Motorisation*, p. 352).

TABLE 18

*Costs and Returns of Main Crops, per feddan (£E), 1948–57*

| | Costs of cult$^n$ 1948–9 | Net income 1945–8 | Costs of cult$^n$ 1954–7 | Net income 1954–7 | Rent 1954–7 |
|---|---|---|---|---|---|
| **Summer Crops** | | | | | |
| Cotton | 16·7 | 29·2 | 21·7 | 44·6 | 20·4 |
| Rice | 15·3 | 11·9 | 17·9 | 17·1 | 8·1 |
| Millet | 9·9 | 6·2 | 16·6 | 9·4 | 7·5 |
| Sugar-cane | 29·9 | 30·3 | 38·4 | 49·3 | 24·1 |
| | | | | | |
| **Winter Crops** | | | | | |
| Wheat | 11·2 | 7·6 | 13·9 | 16·3 | 3·2 |
| Beans | 7·1 | 12·8 | 8·4 | 16·3 | 11·7 |
| Berseem | 6·6 | 23·5 | 7·6 | 29·8 | 13·5 |
| Onions | 21·1 | 34·4 | 25·7 | 40·9 | 14·4 |
| Barley | .. | .. | 9·1 | 12·5 | 9·6 |
| | | | | | |
| **Autumn Crops** | | | | | |
| Maize | 7·0 | 5·2 | 13·2 | 8·8 | 7·7 |
| | | | | | |
| **Vegetables** | | | | | |
| Summer | 23·0 | 25·7 | 32·5[1] | 11·0[1] | .. |
| Winter | 18·0 | 23·7 | 20·5[1] | 37·5[1] | .. |
| Autumn | 26·0 | 30·7 | 36·5[1] | 11·5[1] | .. |
| | | | | | |
| **Fruit** | | | | | |
| Oranges | 50·0 | 63·0 | | | |
| Grapes | 30·0 | 66·0 | | | |
| Mangoes | 30·0 | 65·0 | 68[2] | 100[2] | .. |
| Figs | 30·0 | 85·7 | | | |
| Bananas | .. | 77·0 | | | |

[1] Ave. of 1955–7.          [2] Approx. figure for all fruits.

*Sources:* for 1945–9, Gamal al-Din Said, *Iqtisadiat misr* (1951), pp. 170–4; for 1954–7, NBE, *Econ. B.*, no 1, 1960; for somewhat different figures see NPC, Memo. no. 382; rent is excl. from costs of cultivation and incl. in net returns.

are followed by vegetables.[1] Of the main field crops, cotton and the fodder crop, berseem, stand out as by far the most profitable.

[1] It has, however, been pointed out (ibid, p. 196) that the high profitability of vegetables shown in the table is attributable to the fact that the prices used for estimating returns were those prevailing in urban markets. Prices paid by canning plants were much lower, and an expansion of vegetable production would have to be largely absorbed by the canning industry.

Owing to the fact that most of the work is done by unpaid members of the farmer's family and that the draught animals used also belong to him, it is difficult to give an exact analysis of costs. A rough estimate made by the Ministry of Agriculture shows that labour accounts for 53 per cent of the total in cotton, 42 per cent in rice, 27 per cent in sugar, and 23 in wheat.

TABLE 19

*Labour Requirements and Labour Costs of Main Crops per feddan, 1950*

| Crop | Man-days | Child-days | Labour cost (£E) |
|---|---|---|---|
| Cotton | 41 | 87 | 10·75 |
| Wheat | 27 | 4 | 3·74 |
| Barley | 18 | 3 | 2·54 |
| Beans | 19 | 5 | 2·82 |
| Onions | 33 | 70 | 7·52 |
| Berseem | 25 | 3 | 3·15 |
| Millet | 42 | 11 | 5·14 |
| Maize | 25 | 10 | 3·71 |
| Rice | 35 | 40 | 9·26 |
| Sugar-cane | 76 | 31 | 11·07 |
| Groundnuts | 41 | 35 | 8·95 |
| Sesame | 28 | 4 | 4·20 |

*Source:* Muh. Husni al-Said, 'Inkhifad ujur ummal al-ziraa fi misr', *Ég. contemp.*, 1952.

Perhaps more significant is Table 19, showing the labour requirements and labour costs per feddan planted to different crops, which brings out very clearly the fact that cotton, rice, and onions, Egypt's traditional export crops, absorb much more labour than do cereals and once more demonstrates Egypt's comparative advantage in such crops.[1] Calculations by Saab[2] in the late 1950's show that a feddan of tomatoes requires 45 man-days and 62 child-days, for a total labour cost of £E12·125.

### COTTON GROWING AND MARKETING

In spite of the development of other resources during the last twenty or thirty years, cotton still forms the basis of Egypt's income. The reasons for its popularity, in addition to its remunerativeness,

[1] For somewhat different figures see *Nashrat bank al-taslif al-zirai wa'l-taawuni*, no. 2, 1960.        [2] *Motorisation*, p. 111.

have been that it is not consumable by peasants, and thus suited absentee landlords, that banks were always eager to lend against cotton, which can be easily graded and does not deteriorate, and that exporting firms were ready to advance to growers the funds necessary for cultivation in return for a lien on the forthcoming crop.[1]

Egypt occupies an outstanding place in the world of cotton, but it is steadily losing ground to its competitors. Thus in the 1950's it accounted for little over 4 per cent of the world crop, compared with 6 per cent in the 1930's and 7–8 per cent at the beginning of the century.[2] The reasons for this change are the large increase in world production—from 6·7 million tons in 1934–8 to 10·1 million in 1957–9—because of the expansion of production in the Soviet bloc, Latin America, and Africa; the failure to expand Egypt's cotton acreage significantly; and ·the drop in yields, caused by the rise in the water-table and attacks of diseases and pests, as well as a shift from higher-yielding medium staples to long staples.[3] Nevertheless, Egypt is still the second greatest exporter, coming after the United States and, since partition and the growth of internal consumption, ahead of India. However, the rapid increase in exports from the Sudan, Mexico, Peru, Syria, and other countries, and the consumption of an ever-rising share of the Egyptian crop at home, have combined to diminish Egypt's share in world exports, from 14·5 per cent in 1946–50 to 10·8 in 1951–5 and 9·0 in 1957–9.

Egypt's share in world output of long staples ($1\frac{1}{8}$–$1\frac{1}{2}$ inches, referred to in Egypt as medium staples) has remained at a little under 40 per cent but its share of exports has fallen from 75 per cent before the Second World War to some 50 per cent; here again the competition of the Sudan and Peru has been keen. In extra-long staples

[1] Egypt's soil and climate are ideal for cotton-growing; particular mention should be made of the warmth and steadiness of the climate, the abundance and reliability of the water-supply, and the depth of the soil, 7–12 metres, which allows the long cotton roots to strike deep; moreover 'nowhere is the clay content less than 20 per cent and it may be as high as 50 to 70 per cent' (Platt & Hefny, p. 161).

[2] In this and the following sections, figures on acreage, output, and yields have been kept at a minimum, since they are readily available, expressed in metric units, in the publications of the FAO and, expressed in Egyptian units, in the *UAR Statist. Pocket Yb.* A good study of cotton cultivation, marketing, spinning, and weaving in Egypt is Hasan Sidqi's *al-Qutn al-misri* (1950); see also C. H. Brown, *Egyptian Cotton* (1953) and Soc. d'Entreprises commerc. en Ég., *La Culture du coton.*

[3] Whereas in pre-war years Egypt's yield per ha., about 5·5 quintals, was far ahead of that of the Soviet Union's 3·5, Sudan's 3·1, and the USA's 2·4, by 1957–9 it was 5·7 quintals while the others were 7·1, 2·7, and 4·9 respectively.

($1\frac{1}{2}$ inches and over, referred to in Egypt as long staples) its share in output has fallen from 70 to well under 60 per cent, owing to greater production in the Sudan, Peru, and the United States. Egyptian long staples, such as Karnak, Menufi, Giza 45, and Giza 47 are, with the exception of Sea Island and Pima, the finest in the world as regards length, resistance and glossiness. Among medium staples Ashmuni, whose yields are well above those of long staples, continues to hold the field but has recently been joined by Dandara and Bahtim 185.

During the last eighty years Egypt has seen dozens of varieties come into favour, spread, and deteriorate owing to hybridization of plants in the fields or of seeds in the ginneries, or even owing to attacks of diseases or parasites, as was the case with Sakel. At first selection was carried out in an empirical way, mostly by Greek growers, several of whom are commemorated by the names of such varieties as Sakellarides, Pilion, and Casulli. But starting in 1912, and more systematically since 1920, the Cotton Research Board of the Ministry of Agriculture and the Royal Agricultural Society have done splendid work in the way of improving existing varieties and propagating new ones, superior as regards length of staple, yield, and resistance to disease. Many of the most popular varieties, such as Karnak and Menufi, have originated in the experimental farms of the Ministry which is at present evolving such new strains as Giza 59, outstanding for its high yields, its strong fibre, and its resistance to disease; Giza 68, with its early maturity, its high yield, and its toughness; and Giza 66 which has a higher yield than Ashmuni, is tougher and has a better fibre.[1] Other measures have included the spreading of improved methods of cultivation, for example earlier sowing and closer spacing; the control of cotton-seed by prohibiting the mixing of varieties in ginneries and destroying inferior seed and by planting certain varieties only in each region, thus raising the degree of purity from 80 per cent in 1926 to 98 per cent since 1933; and finally, the control of cotton pests and diseases. Thanks to all these measures, to improved drainage, and to ever-increasing use of fertilizers, the yield of Egyptian cotton rose by over 50 per cent in less than twenty years. The war caused a sharp drop in yields, owing to the exhaustion of the soil through over-planting of cereals and the lack of fertilizers, but in the last few years progress has been slowly resumed. A leading British authority has stated that, by the adoption of closer spacing and other improved methods, as well as a

[1] *al-Majalla al-ziraia*, Nov. 1960.

shift away from long to medium staples, the cotton crop could be raised from its present figure of 8–9 million cantars (about 400,000 tons) to 15 million.[1] The Five-Year Plan provides for an increase in cotton production of 25 per cent.[2]

In the United States the farmer markets his cotton crop but in Egypt his task usually ends with picking, in July or August. The cotton then passes to a ginnery, where it is ginned and pressed under hydraulic pressure, and from there to Alexandria, where it is steam-pressed, mixed into suitable types, and shipped abroad. The fact that Egyptian cotton is a high-quality and very diversified product has made it necessary to have a complex marketing organization, including many technical and financial experts who until very recently were mainly foreign; under this system Egyptian cotton became the best graded and packed in the world. Until recently the market operated as follows. Large growers often consigned their cotton to the ginning factory and sometimes even saw it through to Alexandria. Small growers, on the other hand, either sold it to the village merchant or carried it to the local *halaqa* (market) where it was sold by auction to brokers who in their turn disposed of it to merchants or exporters with up-country agencies. The cotton was then ginned, pressed, and dispatched to Minet al-Bassal Spot Market, usually after it had been pledged against an advance with a bank.

Following the closure of the Futures Market[3] in May 1940, a British Cotton Buying Commission was formed in September and was replaced by the Joint Anglo-Egyptian Cotton Commission in 1941 and the Egyptian Cotton Commission which has been functioning since 1942.[4] This Commission bought, at prices specified for

[1] Another suggestion for increasing output has been the replacement of Ashmuni by American Upland, since the latter yields in California and Arizona the equivalent of 10–11 cantars per feddan, against 6 for Ashmuni. This has, however, been opposed because of the danger of hybridization, of the inferior quality of Upland, and of the fact that experiments with such American staples as Acala, Delta, and Coker have given low yields (ibid. Sept. 1959). Recent experiments seem to indicate that cotton yields can be increased by 34 per cent by proper spacing and the application of the right amount of fertilizers at the appropriate time (*al-Ahram*, 6 Apr. 1962). [2] *Cadre du Plan*, pp. 64–66.

[3] A detailed account of the Futures Market, together with a study of the seasonal movement of cotton prices and the effect of this on growers is given in Issawi, *Egypt*, pp. 107–8; the organization of the Futures Market is described in NBE, *Econ. B.*, no. 2, 1949. Costs of production and distribution of cotton are discussed in Said, *Iqtisadiat*, pp. 127–48.

[4] See M. E. Airut, 'Historique et activités de l'Egyptian Cotton Commission de 1942 à 1959', in *Mahad al-dirasat al-masrafia* (1959).

each variety and grade, all cotton offered either at Alexandria or up-country, stored it, and resold it to mills and exporters; when market prices were above those fixed by the Commission the latter was by-passed. The Futures Market was reopened in 1948 but, after an orgy of speculation and manipulation during the Korean boom and a subsequent collapse in prices, was shut down in 1952;[1] it was reopened in 1955 but under strict government supervision and, being 'narrow and virtually isolated from world markets' and in addition 'dominated by occasional large-scale deals by foreign government and buying organs' functioned very unsatisfactorily.[2] On 22 June 1961 the Futures Market was once more closed for an indefinite period. Henceforth all cotton is to be sold to the Commission, which is charged with exporting and supplying the needs of local mills. For good measure, in July the government also nationalized all cotton-pressing establishments and took over 50 per cent of the capital of cotton export firms, through whom the Commission continues to channel sales abroad.[3] In March 1962 the Spot Market was also closed down.

It is now possible to discuss the factors which determine the price of Egyptian cotton. Professor Bresciani-Turroni, working on the years 1899–1925, showed that there was a marked correlation between the *ratio of the sizes* of the Egyptian and American crops on the one hand and the *ratio of their prices* on the other.[4] His conclusion was confirmed by the present author for the decade 1923–33.[5]

In other words, although Egyptian cotton formerly enjoyed a practical monopoly for certain uses, such as aeroplane tyres and sewing thread, most of the crop had to compete with foreign staples and, since marginal uses determine price, the bigger the Egyptian crop the smaller is its premium over other cottons. The basic world price is, however, not significantly influenced by the size of the Egyptian crop.

In the post-war period a further complication was introduced by the dollar shortage. As a 'soft currency' article, Egyptian cotton was the object of intensified demand after 1947, and its premium over American increased greatly in 1948 and 1949; narrowed during the United States recession of 1949–50, and reached unprecedented

[1] See NBE, *Econ. B.*, no. 4, 1952.  [2] CBE, *Econ. R.*, no. 2, 1961.
[3] For details see ibid. The difference between the buying prices, fixed by the government, and export prices represents the profits or, as in 1961, the losses made by the ECC.
[4] 'Relations entre la récolte et le prix du coton ég.', *Ég. contemp.*, 1930.
[5] *Egypt*, p. 67.

heights in the scramble for raw materials touched off by the Korean war, but this phase ended abruptly in 1951. More recently American cotton-export policy has introduced still another factor in the determination of world prices of cotton.

Little information is available regarding the price and income elasticities of demand for Egyptian cotton but it may be surmised that income elasticity for Egyptian cotton, a high-quality product, is above the fairly high figure for cotton in general. Similarly the price elasticity of demand for Egyptian cotton must be very high, since the latter constitutes only a very small fraction of total supply; an exception may, however, exist in certain specialized uses in which Egyptian cotton can be replaced only with difficulty.

As for the price elasticity of supply of Egyptian cotton, a study was made for the periods 1914–38 and 1948–56, correlating the ratio of the cotton area to that of other crops on the one hand with the index of the relative price of cotton to that of other crops on the other. The results show a close correlation and an arc elasticity 'somewhere between 0·4 and 0·6', which is fairly high.[1] Government regulations have played an increasingly important part in the determination of cotton acreage, but there is no doubt that Egyptian farmers are responsive to changes in prices and profitability.

### GRAIN CULTIVATION AND MARKETING

The area sown to grains (wheat, maize, rice, millet, and barley) increased from an average of 4,040,000 feddans in 1935–9 to 4,930,000 in 1940–4 owing to wartime restrictions on cotton, fell back to 4,396,000 in 1950–4, and rose again to 4,592,000 in 1955–9. Total output of these grains rose from 4,227,000 tons in 1935–9 to 4,449,000 in 1945–9 and, after a decline in 1950–4, to 5,179,000 in 1955–9. This represents an increase of 16·4 per cent in twenty years, compared with a population growth of over 50 per cent.

Yields dropped sharply during the war, owing to the disruption of rotations caused by over-extension of cereals and to shortage of fertilizers, and for most crops did not regain the pre-war level until the mid or late 1950's. In 1955–9, wheat yields averaged 6·5 ardebs per feddan (23·2 quintals per ha.) compared with 5·9 before the war, maize 6·27 ardebs (21·3 quintals per ha.) compared with 7·45, millet 9·09 (30·3 quintals) compared with 9·11 and barley 8·12 (23·0 quintals) compared to 7·29. Rice yields surpassed their pre-

[1] R. M. Stern, 'The Price Responsiveness of Egyptian Cotton Producers', *Kyklos*, 1958.

war level in the early post-war period and by 1955–9 averaged 2·24 daribas per feddan (50·4 quintals per ha.) compared with 1·63 in 1935–9.[1]

Except for rice, the performance of cereals in recent years has thus been disappointing and may be contrasted with the inter-war period (see above, p. 35). It is true that, even at their present level, Egyptian yields are among the highest in the world. An application of Kendall's ranking coefficient, based on nine cereals and pulses, gave Egypt seventh place in 1946 after Belgium, Denmark, the Netherlands, New Zealand, the United Kingdom, and Ireland.[2] Nevertheless Egypt's wheat yields compare unfavourably with those of Western Europe, its maize yields with those of the United States, and its rice yields with those of Spain and Italy. And the scope for improvement is shown by comparing average yields with those obtained from imported seeds or on experimental farms. The Five-Year Plan calls for an increase of 35 per cent in the output of cereals, mainly through higher yields.[3]

Wheat and millet show the highest yields in Middle Egypt and maize in the Delta; in recent years efforts have been made to extend the use of hybrid maize and the farms managed by the Agrarian Reform Committee are trying to meet part of the country's needs for selected wheat seed.[4] The cultivation of rice has greatly expanded and the old mixture of South-East Asian varieties has been replaced by superior Japanese breeds. Another factor explaining the rise in yields has been the extension of rice cultivation southward, to more fertile areas; formerly it was grown exclusively in the north of the Delta, on land which was being desalinated. Since rice requires three or four times as much water per unit area as cotton, and three times as much as maize, its acreage is strictly determined by the water supply and in years of a very low Nile it has to be curtailed.[5]

Starting in 1942 the government has ordered that a minimum proportion of each holding be devoted to wheat; the most recent figure is 33 per cent except in certain specified areas.[6] But in fact the

---

[1] CBE, *Econ. R.*, no. 2, 1961. In 1955–9 acreage of maize averaged 1,851,000 feddans and production 1,624,000 tons, of wheat 1,501,000 and 1,464,000, of rice 654,000 and 1,385,000, of millet 451,000 and 574,000, and of barley 135,000 and 132,000 tons.

[2] L. Dudley Stamp, *Land for Tomorrow* (Bloomington, Ind., 1952).

[3] *Cadre du Plan*, pp. 64–66.  [4] *al-Ahram*, 31 Oct. 1961.

[5] For further details on cereals see Soc. d'Entreprises commerc. en Ég., *Le Riz dans l'écon. ég.* (Cairo, 1949) & *La Culture du maïs en. Ég.* (Cairo, 1951); Besançon, pp. 233–42; Platt & Hefny, pp. 168–74.  [6] *al-Ahram*, 9 Jan. 1962.

regulations have been evaded and in the 1950's the cotton area regularly exceeded that of wheat by 10–20 per cent. During and after the war growers were also obliged to surrender to the government a certain proportion of their wheat crop at fixed prices but in recent years, as urban needs came to be increasingly met by imports, this obligation has been relaxed.[1] Prices continue to be fixed by the government, to support certain crops. In recent years they have been considerably raised and, as a consequence of that and the drop in world prices, whereas in 1952 local wheat prices were only 46 per cent of c.i.f. Alexandria prices, and maize only 53 per cent, by 1958 the figures were 126 and 132 respectively. But this did not lead to an increase in the share of the area allotted to grains since cotton-supported prices rose even higher and cotton and rice continue to be more profitable than wheat, maize, millet, or barley.[2]

The marketing of grains is much less elaborate than that of cotton. The normal procedure has been for the grower to sell his crop to the village trader who sometimes deposits it in a bank *shoona* (open store). The grain is then either sold to the village agent of one of the big city traders or sent by boat to the riverside markets of Cairo (Rod al-Farag and Atar al-Nabi) or Alexandria, where it is bought by a city trader. Large growers, however, often short-circuited the village trader, depositing their crop in a bank *shoona* and selling it directly to a city trader either through his village agent or in Cairo or Alexandria. Similarly mills often bought their requirements direct from up-country. Lately an increasing proportion of the crop has been handled by the Agricultural Bank.

Until recently the cereals market received very little attention from the government and suffered from the wide variations in grading and purity, and the absence of standardization in weights and measures. Attempts to enforce higher standards have, however, been made and the metric system has become compulsory. In January 1962 the government took over a 50 per cent interest and control over 98 large flour mills, 77 rice decorticating mills, and 77 bakeries.[3]

A more useful measure has been the provision of better storage. The bulk of cereals continues to be stored in *shoonas*, which involves

---

[1] The government continues to sell to consumers at lower prices; thus in December 1961 it brought down the price of maize to PT15 per kg.; as the cost to the government was PT34, it was estimated that it would bear a loss of £E7 m. on its projected imports of 200,000 tons of maize (ibid. 3 Dec. 1961).

[2] NPC, Memo. no. 382 & CBE, *Econ. R.*, no. 2, 1961.

[3] *al-Ahram*, 1 Feb. 1962.

a loss of some £E8 million a year through deterioration. By 1952 seventy small silos, with a total capacity of over 40,000 tons, had been set up and since then a 58,000-ton silo has been built in Cairo and a 48,000 one in Alexandria at a combined cost of £E2·9 million. Present plans call for the building of 49 silos, with storage space of 646,000 tons, by 1965; total costs amount to £E35 million, of which the United States will cover $25·1 million.[1]

### OTHER CROPS[2]

The most important of these is berseem (Egyptian clover) which covers some 2 million feddans, a larger area than any other Egyptian crop, and forms an indispensable item in any crop rotation, restoring the nitrogen taken out of the soil by other plants. Berseem, which yields some 20–30 tons per feddan, forms the main green fodder in winter and when dried provides summer fodder.

Beans share the restorative properties of berseem and are the main summer fodder; they also constitute an important item in working-class diet. About 350,000 feddans are put under beans each year, giving a crop of over 350,000 tons. Onions, one of Egypt's oldest export crops, are also one of the most remunerative. Present acreage is about 50,000 feddans and production nearly 500,000 tons. There has also been an expansion in groundnuts and sesame, each with an acreage of about 40,000 feddans; yields are among the highest in the world and the two crops aggregate some 50,000 tons. In recent years exports of oil-seeds have been significant.

Sugar-cane occupies an acreage of about 110,000 feddans.[3] Table 18 (p. 140) would seem to indicate that it is one of the most remunerative crops, but since the sale price of sugar-cane to the factories is arbitrarily fixed, these figures have little meaning. Egypt has certain advantages for sugar-cane: its short period of growth, its high yields—80 tons per ha., compared with over 400 in Hawaii and 80 in Indonesia but only 35 in Cuba and 65 in Puerto Rico—and its very high labour requirements. As against that must be set the relatively cold winter and the enormous water intake. It is a moot point whether land as precious as that of Egypt, and capable of being switched to other crops, should attempt to compete with the cheap soil of tropical producers, and it is a fact that Egyptian raw sugar is

[1] Ibid. 15 Feb. 1962.

[2] For further details see Besançon, pp. 242–52 and Platt & Hefny, pp. 175–86.

[3] See Soc. d'Entreprises commerc. en Ég., *La Culture de la canne à sucre en Ég.* (Cairo, 1952).

far more expensive than imported sugar.[1] In the last twenty years output of raw sugar has risen to 320,000 tons, or double the pre-war average.

Output of vegetables has greatly increased in the last few decades. The 1939 census put the total area under vegetables at 172,000 feddans, compared with 144,000 in 1929 and, after a sharp rise during the war and a small decline after the war, by 1951 the figure stood at 207,000 and by 1959 at 476,000 or 8·2 per cent of the cultivated area, and total output amounted to 3,280,000 tons. Particularly striking has been the extension of potato acreage, to 53,000 feddans in 1959; output has reached 370,000 tons and small quantities have been exported, though imports are still larger. Tomato acreage has been about 130,000 feddans and output 700,000 tons. At the same time methods of cultivation have improved and a certain localization of crops has come about. But much remains to be done in the way of developing better seeds; fighting animal pests and plant diseases; experimenting with different methods of planting, watering, and fertilizing; improving the grading and packing of vegetables; providing refrigeration and factories for preserving and canning; facilitating and reducing the cost of marketing both at home and abroad; and, above all, standardizing the different varieties and delimiting the regions most suited to each crop.[2]

Fruit acreage has also increased, from 28,000 feddans in 1913 to 75,000 in 1939, 86,000 in 1950, and 126,000 in 1959, or 2·2 per cent of the cultivated area. Most of the expansion has taken place in the south-eastern Delta, between the markets of Cairo and the Canal Zone, and near Alexandria and much of it has taken the form of citrus orchards, which account for nearly half the total area. Other important fruit crops include grapes, mangoes, guavas, pomegranates, bananas, and figs. Quality has also markedly improved. Output in 1959 totalled about 850,000 tons, of which citrus accounted for 200,000 and dates for 330,000; Egypt is the second largest producer of dates, after Iraq. Although in recent years imports have been drastically curtailed by high tariffs and prohibitions, and exports have been expanded, Egypt is still a net importer of fruit.[3]

[1] In 1929–30, before the Egyptian crop was protected, Java sugar was selling at £E8·300 per ton c.i.f. Alexandria, and Cuban at 6·475, against 13·104 for Egyptian (*Mauduat al-mutamar al-zirai al-thani* (Cairo, 1945), i. 57). There is no reason to believe that relative costs have greatly changed since then.

[2] This subject is discussed in ibid. pp. 216–42.

[3] For details see *Coll. Basic Statist. Data*, p. 72.

As Table 18 (p. 140) shows, fruit is by far the most profitable of Egypt's crops. Expansion continues, however, to be held up by several factors. First, there is the poverty of the population, which severely limits the internal market. Secondly, high capital costs are involved: a feddan of mangoes requires a total expenditure of £E440–480 before it comes to fruition, while the wooden props for vines alone cost £E50–150 per feddan.[1] Thirdly, a long time must elapse before any return is obtained on outlay—two years for figs, four for vines, and ten for mangoes—during which much capital and effort may be lost because of an attack by pests or disease. Fourthly, fruit-growing requires technical knowledge which the average farmer does not possess. Fifthly, there are the high costs of grading, packing, and transport. Lastly, there is the lack of processing, canning, and refrigeration facilities, including refrigerated transport. And, of course, the cumbrous governmental restrictions and regulations, especially as regards export, hit particularly hard perishable commodities such as fruits and vegetables.

### LIVESTOCK, POULTRY, AND FISHERIES

In recent years net income from livestock and poultry has accounted for a little over 30 per cent of net agricultural income, a figure well below those of Western Europe.[2] Livestock herds have shown a rapid increase[3] but in the 1950's output of milk showed no increase, standing in 1957 at 2,400 million lb.[4] Milk yields continue to be low, the average per cow being under 2,000 lb. compared with 9,079 in Holland, 6,438 in the United States, and 4,454 in France; the scope for increase is also shown by the fact that improved herds yield 4,300 lb.[5] Meat yields are also low and total output is well below 500 million lb., and Egypt imports some 65,000 head of livestock each year, as well as frozen meat. As for wool, the clip is about 5·8 million lb., or some 4·5 lb. per head, compared with 12 in

[1] Said, *Iqtisadiat misr*, p. 183.

[2] In 1956–7 slaughters and production brought in £E92·8 m., the estimated value of animal work was £E51·4 m., and that of manure 8·3 m., giving a gross income of 152·3 m. and, allowing for consumption by the animals, a net income of 76·2 m. (NBE, *Econ. B.*, no. 1, 1960).

[3] Between 1917 and 1958 the number of buffaloes rose by 147 per cent, to 1,395,000, of cows by 170 per cent, to 1,390,000, of sheep by 56 per cent, to 1,259,000, and of goats by 134 per cent, to 723,000.

[4] *Coll. Basic Statist. Data*, tables 35 & 36; about seven-eighths of the milk is used for cheese or butter.

[5] *al-Majalla al-ziraia*, Oct. 1959; butter-fat content is, however, high, being 7–8 per cent compared to 5 in the USA.

New Zealand, 10 in Australia, and a world average of 5·4; moreover Egyptian wool is used only for rugs and blankets, wool for cloth being imported.[1]

Two main obstacles are impeding progress.[2] First, 80 per cent of livestock is in the hands of small farmers,[3] who value the animals for draught work and are little interested in fattening or milking qualities. Secondly, there is the lack of green fodder in summer owing to the prohibition on the cultivation, after May, of berseem in which the cotton worm can breed, and the lack of silage. Other adverse factors include the high capital investment required, the poverty of the internal market, and the lack of refrigeration and processing facilities. In recent years, however, some progress has been made in diffusing better breeds, devising improved feeds—for example by mixing cotton-seed cake with bran and molasses—and securing greater purity and cleanliness, and extending free veterinary services to farmers.

Before the Second World War poultry farming used to provide a sizeable export of eggs, mainly to Britain. But production in the 1950's has been well below the pre-war figure of 900 million and in addition 'as the result of stock deterioration and poor feeding the eggs have so fallen off in size and protein content that they now find little acceptance in the foreign market'.[4] Attempts to improve breeds by importing chicks from the United States have had some success. The number of hens is put at some 16 million.

Egypt's fisheries employ some 50,000 men and 15,000 boys and yield a catch officially estimated at 80,000 tons but judged by the Minister of Supply to be about 140,000 tons.[5] But even the latter figures works out at only 5 kg. per capita, compared to 40 in Japan and 30 in Britain. The Mediterranean and Red Sea provide 25 per cent of output, the lakes 60, and the Nile and canals 15 per cent. Costs are high partly because of bad methods of distribution but mainly because of the primitive methods used in fishing: although there are some 400 motor boats engaged in deep-sea fishing they are poorly equipped and the bulk of the catch is still provided by sailing boats.[6] Among recent improvements are the restocking of lakes, the

---

[1] *al-Majalla al-ziraia*, Aug. 1959.

[2] For further details see Saab, *Motorisation*, pp. 354–84. The same author judges that milk yields can be increased by 250 per cent and beef yields by 60–100 per cent on a profitable basis.  [3] NPC, Memo. no. 33.

[4] Platt & Hefny, p. 190.  [5] *al-Majalla al-ziraia*, Nov. 1960.

[6] For details see FAO, *Yb. of Fishery Statist.* & *Fisheries B.* and *Ég. indust.*, Apr. 1958.

provision of a small amount of refrigeration, and the building, with Japanese help, of a canning factory for sea food. Plans for the future include the building of a large shipping fleet, with Italian help, and the reorganization of the fishing industry.[1] Another project is the exploitation of the lake formed by the High Dam, which is estimated to yield 50,000 tons a year.[2] A more distant possibility is the lake to be formed in the Qattara depression.[3]

### AGRICULTURAL INCOME AND ITS DISTRIBUTION

The figures given in Table 20 (p. 154) show a significant increase in both gross and net agricultural income between 1952 and 1958. However, comparison with pre-war figures shows much less progress, the substantial increase in gross income being largely absorbed by higher costs in the form of more fertilizers and greater inputs of labour and work by animals and machines. Similarly, another series covering the years 1950–7[4] shows that the 1950 figure for net income was not regained until 1957. The latter series also shows that animal produce accounted for under a fifth of gross income and that, except for the sharp fluctuations in the value of the cotton crop, the constituents of gross income changed little. No later estimates are available but between 1958 and 1960 the index of crop production (see Table 9, p. 113) rose by some 5·5 per cent; this was, however, followed by a sharp drop in 1961.

An interesting feature of Table 20 is the rising share of net income absorbed by rent, until the agrarian reform of 1952 and the drop in cotton prices began to make themselves felt, and the corresponding decline in the returns on capital and work of farmers. It is possible to trace, with some degree of precision, the movement of rents during the last seventy years. The 1892–1907 cadaster put

---

[1] *al-Ahram*, 1 Oct. 1961 & 14 Jan. 1962.      [2] Ibid. 18 Jan. 1962.

[3] The draining of the northern lakes for land reclamation has aroused an interesting controversy. Proponents of drainage point out that the present annual catch is only 47 kg. of fish, worth £E5, per feddan, to which should be added a further small sum for the birds, reeds, and grass derived from the lakes; the cost of reclamation is not more than £E130, and the net return after four years £E15, per feddan. Adversaries claim that present yields of fish are greatly underestimated and that with restocking the catch could be raised to over £E40 per feddan which, since costs of production are low, would give a higher net return than agriculture. A compromise solution is to drain completely Mariut and Idku lakes, where reclamation has already resulted in a sharp drop in the catch, but to reclaim only the edges of the other northern lakes, leaving the centres for fishing (*al-Majalla al-ziraia*, June, 1960).

[4] *Coll. Basic Statist. Data*, p. 85.

**TABLE 20**

*Agricultural Income, 1935–58*

(£E million, in 1952 prices)

| | 1935–9 | 1952 | 1953 | 1956 | 1957 | 1958 |
|---|---|---|---|---|---|---|
| Gross income[1] | 340·4 | 381·8 | 381·0 | 416·4 | 438·3 | 437·5 |
| Expenses: | | | | | | |
| Labour | .. | 29·1 | 25·5 | 30·9 | 32·7 | 31·5 |
| Machines | .. | 7·2 | 7·6 | 9·2 | 9·5 | 9·8 |
| Fodder | .. | 79·1 | 88·9 | 88·6 | 84·2 | 92·7 |
| Chemical fertilizers | .. | 22·7 | 19·5 | 19·9 | 23·0 | 22·3 |
| Seeds | .. | 24·0 | 26·3 | 27·0 | 26·4 | 25·9 |
| Other | .. | 1·6 | 0·8 | 2·5 | 2·5 | 2·4 |
| Total | 97·3 | 163·7 | 168·6 | 178·1 | 178·3 | 184·6 |
| Net income | 243·1 | 218·1 | 212·4 | 238·3 | 260·0 | 252·9 |
| Rents | 140·9 | 150·6 | 151·4 | 164·5 | 163·1 | 161·2 |
| Returns on capital & work of farmers | 102·2 | 67·5 | 60·9 | 73·8 | 96·9 | 91·7 |

[1] Vegetable & animal production.

*Source:* NPC, Memo. no. 382.

the total rental value of Egyptian land at £E16,356,000, or 3·6 per feddan. The 1935–7 cadaster gave a total of £E33,610,000 or 5·7 per feddan. Thus both total and average rentals rose considerably over the period. But this long-term trend masks a violent cyclical movement during the depression: by 1932 rentals had fallen to 40–50 per cent and in 1937 they stood at between 60 to 70 per cent of their level in 1928.[1]

During the Second World War rents tripled. The Land Tax Committees put the total rental value in 1945–6 at £E109,934,000 or 18·4 per feddan. A similar increase is shown by the Ministry of Agriculture, which puts the average rent at £E7·2 in 1935–9, 17·1 in 1946, and 25·0 in 1951. It would seem that the increase was highest on the poorer lands, and least on the richer.[2]

[1] A. Lambert, 'Divers modes de faire valoir les terres en Ég.', *Ég. contemp.*, 1938.
[2] The last set of figures is taken from *Monthly B. Agric. Statist.*

The sharp fall in cotton prices in 1951 and the agrarian reform brought down rents appreciably and the tax assessment of 1956 put the national average at £E22·6; average rents ranged from £E30–33 in the provinces nearest Cairo, i.e. Qaliubia, Minufia, and Giza, to 24–29 in the richer parts of Upper Egypt, i.e. Minia, Asiut, Suhag, around 17–20 in the remoter provinces of the Delta such as Behera, Sharqia, and Kafr al-Shaikh, and were lowest in the farthest districts of Upper Egypt (9·3 in Aswan), in Suez (10·9), and in Fayyum (13·3).[1]

Less data are available regarding wages. Expressed in terms of maize, the staple food of the peasants, they rose by some 30 per cent between 1912 and 1929, but relatively to the urban cost-of-living index they fell by about 35 per cent. In the slump both money and real wages fell by nearly 50 per cent.[2]

During and after the Second World War wages followed the increase in the cost of living, with a time-lag. On a farm near Cairo they rose from PT3 (per day) in 1939 to PT5 in 1941 and PT9 in 1944; during this period they failed to catch up with the price of necessities consumed by labour, especially maize.[3] In the post-war years the gap was closed. In 1945 the government fixed a minimum of PT10 per day, and by the summer of 1952 wages ranged between PT10 and PT15, except in the north of the Delta where, owing to the scarcity of labour, a wage of PT25 was not uncommon.[4] Children picking cotton earned some PT6–7 per day.[5] The minimum was raised to PT18 in the autumn of 1952 but government surveys in Daqahlia in 1955 and in Minia in 1956 showed that agricultural wages averaged PT10 a day and that labourers were employed for not more than 150 days a year,[6] which seemed to imply a resumption of the downward trend.

A survey of the last fifty years shows that the Ricardian analysis of rents and wages applies remarkably well to Egypt. An increase in population and wealth was accompanied by a considerable rise in the remuneration of the scarce factor, land, and by a fall in that of the abundant factor, labour. Indeed wages seem to have reached the minimum level, described by early nineteenth-century economists, below which they can hardly descend.

[1] *Coll. Basic Statist. Data*, p. 61.

[2] See details in Issawi, *Egypt*, pp. 77 & 80. Wages of unskilled labourers stood at 25–30 m/m in 1914, 60–80 m/m in 1920, 40–45 in 1928, 20–25 in 1933, 25–30 in 1939 (A. Lambert, 'Les Salariés dans l'entreprise agric. ég.', *Ég. contemp.*, 1943).

[3] Saffa in *Ég. contemp.*, 1949, pp. 412–15.    [4] Said, ibid. 1952.

[5] Anhoury, ibid. 1947.    [6] Saab, *Motorisation*, p. 95.

## LANDOWNERSHIP AND TENURE

Table 21 shows the pattern of landownership in 1952, on the eve of the first agrarian reform; in 1961, after the completion of that reform and before the second reform had been put into operation; and the anticipated effects of the second reform. These measures are discussed in the following section.

TABLE 21

*Distribution of Landholdings, 1896–1961*

('ooo feddans and holdings)

| | 1896 | | 1952 | | 1961 | | After reform of 1961 | |
|---|---|---|---|---|---|---|---|---|
| | No. of owners | Area owned | No. of owners | Area owned | No. of owners | Area owned | No. of owners | Area owned |
| Under 5 feddans | 611 | 994 | 2,642 | 2,182 | 2,870 | 2,660 | 2,920 | 3,040 |
| 5–10 ,, | 144 | 1,816 | 79 | 526 | 79 | 530 | 79 | 530 |
| 10–50 ,, | | | 69 | 1,291 | 69 | 1,300 | 69 | 1,300 |
| 50–100 ,, | | | 6 | 429 | 11 | 630 | 11 | 630 |
| 100–200 ,, | 12 | 2,192 | 3 | 437 | 3 | 450 | 5[1] | 500[1] |
| over 200 ,, | | | 2 | 1,117 | 2 | 430 | — | — |
| Total | 767 | 5,002 | 2,801 | 5,982 | 3,034 | 6,000 | 3,084 | 6,000 |

[1] These figures presumably apply to estates of exactly 100 feddans.

*Sources: Ann. stat.; NBE, Econ. B., no. 3, 1961.*

A comparison of the figures for 1896, the earliest available, with those for 1952 brings out the great rise in the number of landowners, owing to growing population pressure and the relatively small increase in the cultivated area. The table would seem to indicate that the area belonging to large and medium landowners remained unchanged, and that all the increase went to the small owners. Actually the process was somewhat different, as newly reclaimed land was usually taken up by large or medium owners whose properties were, however, constantly being broken up among their heirs.

A striking feature has been the great increase in dwarf holdings of under 1 feddan, from 943,000 in 1913 to 2,058,000 in 1957; the area in such farms increased from 406,000 to 827,000 feddans. At the other end of the scale, in 1952 less than 200 persons owned nearly half a million feddans. Land distribution was more unequal in Upper than in Lower Egypt.

The 1950 agricultural census brings out the pattern of land operation and tenure; 61 per cent of the land was owner-operated, 20 per cent leased, and 19 per cent in mixed enterprises.[1] The agrarian reform seems to have slightly increased tenancy since by 1956 these figures were: 59, 22, and 19 per cent.[2] In the latter year 730,000 owners cultivated 3,690,000 feddans and 346,000 tenants 1,351,000 feddans, while 1,172,000 feddans were run in mixed enterprises by 178,000 persons. It will be noticed that owner-operators, together with mixed farmers, account for less than 30 per cent of the total number of landowners; in other words most land-owners are absentees. This phenomenon is mainly explained by the fact that dwarf farmers lease out their plots, which are too small to support them; thus in 1950 there were only 183,000 owner-operators or mixed farmers of under 1 feddan. About a third of the land in ownerships of 1–5 feddans is similarly leased; most of this probably belongs to city dwellers. But many of the larger landlords also leased part, or occasionally all, of their land, either in plots of 2–5 feddans to tenant-cultivators or in plots of 10–50 feddans to farmers employing hired labour.[3]

It will thus be seen that only about a quarter of landowners can live on the produce of their farms. The rest must supplement their income either by renting additional land or by working as hired labourers for part of the year. There is also a growing number of landless labourers.

Conditions regulating the farming of land vary widely.[4] Cash rents are prevalent near cities and on large estates. Rents in kind are mostly paid on land which is being improved and where labour is scarce, the amount paid by the tenant varying with the fertility of the soil; under this system tenants may, if they choose, pay the market cash value of the amount specified. A third variant is a combination of cash and kind; the rent is fixed in cash, but in addition the landlord gets a share of some or all of the crops. Finally, there is *métayage* which is to be found in most provinces; generally speaking the landlord used to provide the costs of cultivation and get the bulk of the crop while the tenant did the work and received the smaller

[1] *Coll. Basic Statist. Data*, p. 64.      [2] NBE, *Econ. B.*, no. 1, 1957.
[3] Groupe d'études, in *Tiers-Monde*, July–Sept. 1960.
[4] For fuller details see Mahmud al-Sibai, *al-Tatawwurat al-iqtisadia fi misr* (n.d.).

share; this type of contract was usually made for the duration of a single crop. *Métayage* became more widespread following the inflation caused by the Second World War and is estimated to have covered 500,000 feddans in 1952.[1]

Under all these forms, the landlord regulated matters of water, drainage, and rotation. He also supervised the gathering of the crops and had them deposited in his *shoona* so as to ensure payment of rent. It should be added that land was never leased for more than two or three years; annual leases are more common, and very often the land is let for the duration of one crop only. The changes in tenancy brought about by the land reforms are discussed in the next section.

Owing to the pressure of population on the very limited land resources, and because of the absence of alternative employment, land values have risen enormously. Whereas in the United States in 1945 'an average acre of farm land was worth the equivalent of less than 10 days of the average farm worker's wages, in Egypt an equivalent farm land area claimed a price equal to about 20 years of the average worker's wages.'[2] A consequence of this situation is the very depressed condition of tenants. On large estates, where part of the land is operated by the owner and part leased out, 'the rents charged were in some cases higher than the net output from the land operated by the owner. This shows that tenants in Egypt frequently are little better off than agricultural labourers.'[3]

High land values, high rents, short leases, and the general scarcity of capital combine to starve most of the land of working capital which in 'farms of 5 feddans and less does not exceed £E60, i.e. £E12 per cultivated feddan, less than 4 per cent of total capital invested (working capital *plus* value of the land and buildings)';[4] however it should be remembered that part of the high value of the land is due to man-made improvements such as irrigation works and drains.

### AGRARIAN REFORM

Before discussing agrarian reform, a few words may be said about the abolition of *waqf* (mortmains). Family *waqf* (*ahli*), which amounted to nearly 600,000 feddans, vested the usufruct of the land in the heirs in perpetuity, and thus the land itself became inalienable.

---

[1] P. Pissot, 'La Réforme agraire en Ég.', *Économie rurale* (Paris), Oct. 1958.
[2] Moh. Abdel Wahab Ezzat, in *Al Haiyat* (Karachi), 1952.
[3] Ibid. See also Mahmud Riad al-Ghunaimi, *Hiazat al-aradi fi misr* (1956).
[4] Saab, in *ME Econ. Papers*, 1960.

The effect was that no bank would advance money to *waqf* beneficiaries since it could secure a lien only on the income, not the
property itself, and similarly the beneficiaries themselves could not
sell any part of the property; hence most *waqf* land remained un-
improved. Moreover the multiplicity of beneficiaries often reduced
the share of each to ridiculous proportions and encouraged unlimited abuse on the part of administrators and bailiffs. In September
1952 existing family *waqf* was divided between the beneficiaries and
the creating of new ones was forbidden, a measure which has brought
nothing but good to both the beneficiaries and the country at large.[1]
In 1957 this was followed by the application of the Land Reform
Law of 1952 to charitable (*khairi*) *waqf*, where the usufruct was
vested in a religious or charitable organization; the area affected was
put at 150,000 feddans and here too the transference of management
from bailiffs to small farmers under the supervision of the Ministry
of Agrarian Reform is likely to be very beneficial.

Agrarian reform bills were introduced in Egypt in 1945 and 1950
but were decisively rejected by the landlord-dominated parliament
and nothing was done until the law of 9 September 1952 was
promulgated by the military régime. This well-thought-out and
carefully executed measure provided for: fixing minimum wages
for agricultural labourers and permission to form trade unions;
regulation of tenancy relations; redistribution of large estates; and
the formation of multi-purpose co-operatives.[2] The first of these
provisions has remained largely inoperative and the last will be discussed in the following section.

Except for uncultivated land in process of reclamation, agricultural landholdings were limited to 200 feddans, but up to another
100 could be transferred to the owner's children and up to 5 feddans
could be sold, before requisition, to each farmer previously cultivating the land.[3] The surplus was to be taken over by the government
within five years, a supplementary tax at the rate of five times the
original tax being levied on all unrequisitioned land above the
maximum. Compensation was payable in bonds. The land thus

---

[1] A bill abolishing *waqf* had been introduced in 1937 but rejected by parliament.
[2] See text and analysis in Sayed Marei, *Agrarian Reform in Egypt* (Cairo, 1957)
and also Sir Malcolm Darling, 'Land Reform in Italy and Egypt' in *Yb. Agric.
Co-operation, 1956* (Oxford); Warriner, *Land Reform and Development in the Middle
East* (1957); and P. Pissot, in *Économie rurale*, Oct. 1958.
[3] These provisions were tightened in September 1958 and September 1959,
reducing to 300 feddans the maximum allowed to a man, his wife, and their
minor children and prohibiting such a family from leasing additional land.

requisitioned was to be distributed to farmers owning under 5 feddans, at the rate of not less than 2 and not more than 5 feddans, could not be subdivided, and was to be paid for by them in instalments. Land belonging to the royal family, about 180,000 feddans, was taken over without compensation. It has been estimated that a total of 566,000 feddans was due for expropriation.

Expropriation started on 26 October 1952 and has proceeded at a deliberate pace since then; by the end of 1960 an area of 478,000 feddans had been taken from some 1,700 owners.[1] Law No. 127 of 25 July 1961 prohibited any individual from owning more than 100 and any family more than 300 feddans of agricultural land, including uncultivated and desert land;[2] it has been estimated that 300,000 feddans will be affected by this measure.[3] In November 1961 10,000 feddans were sequestrated from fifteen families as part of an operation designed to 'liquidate feudal influence in landownership'. And at the beginning of 1962 measures were being taken to expropriate, with compensation, all agricultural land held by foreigners; it was estimated that 2,614 owners, with total holdings of 141,000 feddans, would be affected,[4] but this estimate fails to take into account the large amount of foreign owned land sold to small Egyptian farmers since 1952.

Distribution has, rightly, been somewhat slower than expropriation. By the end of 1960 311,000 feddans of the expropriated land had been distributed and it was decided, for various reasons, to withhold from distribution 130,000 feddans of the balance. To this should be added 85,000 feddans distributed from *waqf*, and small amounts from State Domains and various land-reclamation projects. In all, by the end of 1960 431,000 feddans had been transferred to 163,000 families. It was planned to distribute another 160,000 feddans in July 1962.[5] It seems likely that a total of about 1 million feddans will eventually change hands and that over 250,000 families will benefit from the various measures of redistribution, a significant

---

[1] See details in Min. of Agrar. Reform, *al-Islah al-zirai fi 9 sanawat*, pp. 18 & 39–58.

[2] However, according to President Abdel Nasser, the 100-feddan limit is to be interpreted as applying to total family holdings and families owning over 100 feddans are advised to sell the extra (*Draft of the Charter*, p. 66).

[3] NBE, *Econ. B.*, no. 3, 1961. Expropriation started on 1 Nov. (*al-Ahram*, 1 Nov. 1961). A figure of 250,000 feddans, from 3,200 owners, is given by Saab (*Eg. Agrar. Ref.*, ch. 11).

[4] *al-Ahram*, 23 Nov. 1961 & 25 Feb. 1962.

[5] Ibid. 25 Mar. & 17 June 1962.

number even if it represents less than 8 per cent of the number of rural families.[1]

As regards terms of compensation, the 1952 law stipulated that it was to equal ten times the estimated rental value of the land, which in turn was fixed at seven times the land tax imposed before the decree, plus that of buildings, machinery, and trees. By the end of April 1961 government bonds to the value of £E42·4 million had been issued in compensation for 221,300 feddans, or an average of £E193 per feddan, and a further £E4·9 million was to be paid for another 24,800 feddans.[2] Although this average figure is distinctly below the market value of land before the Revolution—£E400–600 per feddan in 1948–52—it is not unreasonable, especially in view of the drop in land prices by some 30–40 per cent during the post-Korean deflation.[3] If it be assumed that the same rate will be applied to the rest of the expropriated land, a total of some £E77 million will be paid for the land, other than that of the royal family, taken under the 1952 reform; the value of the land taken under the 1961 reform has been put at £E24 million,[4] giving a grand total of about 100 million.

Under the terms of the 1952 law, compensation was to be paid in 3 per cent non-negotiable bonds redeemable in thirty years. Conversely, beneficiaries were to pay an amount equal to that given by the government to the original owner plus 15 per cent for expenses; this charge was to carry 3 per cent interest and to be repayable within thirty years. In other words, agrarian reform was to be a self-supporting operation. In September 1958, as has been seen, the terms of both compensation and payment by beneficiaries were changed: interest was reduced to $1\frac{1}{2}$ per cent and the maturity of the bonds and period of repayment was extended to forty years. Under the 1961 law compensation is payable in fifteen-year 4 per cent negotiable bonds; payment by beneficiaries is to equal half the amount paid as compensation to owners and is to be made in forty years, at $1\frac{1}{2}$ per cent interest.[5]

The second main measure of the law of 1952 was the regulation

[1] To this should be added the 145,000 feddans sold by landowners to small farmers, in lots of 5 feddans or less, under the provision of art. 4 of the Agrarian Reform Law.  [2] *al-Islah al-zirai*, p. 44.  [3] Pissot, in *Écon. rurale*, 1958.

[4] This figure is puzzling, since it represents only about £E80–100 per feddan and there is every reason to believe that the land due for expropriation under the 1961 law is more valuable than that taken under the 1952 law.

[5] It has been estimated that the concessions made to beneficiaries of the 1952 and 1961 reforms will cost the state over £E50 million (see Saab, *Eg. Agrar. Ref.*, ch. 11).

of tenancy relations by five provisions. First, all leases are to be set down in writing. Secondly, land may be leased only to those who cultivate it; this is designed to eliminate all intermediaries between landlord and farmer. Thirdly, the minimum duration of a lease is set at three years whereas previously, as noted, leases ran for one year or less. Fourthly, tenants may not be evicted by landlords unless the latter intend to cultivate the land themselves. Lastly, rent may not exceed seven times the value of land-tax, and under *métayage* is not to absorb more than half the crop. The 1961 law added a further provision: no individual or nuclear family may either lease out over 50 feddans or rent any land if it already owns 50 feddans or more. It has been estimated that at least 50 per cent of the area, and 4 per cent of the farms, have been affected by the 1952 measures and that the average reduction in rent was 33 per cent, being considerably higher in Upper Egypt; it has also been stated that the law has been observed by large and medium landlords, who did not want to get into trouble with the authorities, but not by small landlords, many of whom are absentees.[1]

In attempting an overall judgement of the land reform the following observations may be made. The first objective of the reform was completely successful: the breaking of the power of the landlords. The second, the improvement of the living conditions of the rural population, has also been partly attained. It is true that the law has brought no relief whatsoever to the poorest section of the population, landless rural labourers, whose position has if anything deteriorated owing to the rise in prices and the reduction in the demand for hired labour following the break-up of estates, but the income of tenants has gone up appreciably as a result of rent reductions, which have been estimated at a total of £E40 million.[2] And that of the beneficiaries of redistribution has gone up still more since the instalments they pay to the government are far below their previous rents and since they also gain from co-operative marketing (see below, p. 166) and, in most cases, from greater production. The following examples, which are probably not typical, of the increase in net income per feddan have been given: Simbilawain from £E10 to 45·7; Shibin al-Kom from 20 to 23·5; Minia from 17 to 24·42; Nag Hamadi from a level which sometimes fell as low as 7 to 40·66,[3] and Behera province from 16·34 to 24·58.[4] More generally,

---

[1] Saab, in *ME Econ. Papers, 1960*. Pissot puts the reduction in rents at 25–35 per cent.
[2] *al-Islah al-zirai*, p. 36.
[3] Ibid. p. 35.
[4] Pissot, in *Écon. rurale*, 1958.

incomes are stated to have doubled, but this seems to be an over-statement; Saab accepts Miss Warriner's estimate of an average increase in money incomes of 50 per cent above the 1951/2 level but points out that in the meanwhile the cost of living rose by 10–15 per cent.[1]

The third objective of the law was to divert capital from agriculture to industry by discouraging further land purchases and by allowing landlords to use their bonds for investment in approved enterprises. As has been seen, the latter aim was not at all successful and the capital that was diverted went into high-income apartment houses; the government had therefore to pass a law, in 1956, limiting investment in building (see above, p. 53). The Agrarian Reform Committee itself did, however, invest some of its funds in various industrial projects, notably the fertilizer plant at Aswan.

The final objective, to raise agricultural output, is by far the most difficult to assess; on balance there seems to have been some increase, but its extent does not seem to have been very considerable and its incidence has been by no means universal. Official publications show a marked increase in selected areas; thus cotton yields in eight districts are stated to have risen by an average of 25 per cent following the land reform.[2] On the other hand reliable observers told the author that in some expropriated estates, especially fruit orchards, output had decreased drastically. The following judgement probably best sums up the situation:

> The crop yields of the new landowners, though slightly lower than actual (i.e. present) yields of neighbouring big landowners, are on the average at the same level as those of the evicted landowners in 1952; in some cases striking increases in yields have been achieved. This is especially true in the fertile lands of Upper and Middle Egypt as well as in the Central Delta. . . . Yields are nearly always equal to those of the neighbouring small landowners (less than five feddans). In many instances, the yields of the beneficiaries of the Land Reform are superior to those of the neighbouring *independent* small landowners. . . . Little has been achieved to really intensify and diversify production on the holdings of the new landowners.[3]

As for tenants, the greater security they now enjoy seems to have encouraged them to make some improvement in the land and to

---

[1] *Eg. Agrar. Ref.*, ch. 6, where further details are given.
[2] *al-Islah al-zirai*, pp. 34–5; see other examples on p. 18.
[3] Saab, in *ME Econ. Papers*, 1960. For a detailed and slightly more favourable evaluation see his *Eg. Agrar. Ref.*, ch. 5.

adopt better methods of cultivation. Some landlords, after the loss of part of their estates, have intensified cultivation on the remaining part[1] and many have planted orchards. But as against that must be set a considerable amount of disinvestment due to fear of another land reform,[2] a fear that materialized in the law of 1961.

It may be added, in conclusion, that the increase in income has been absorbed by greater consumption, including a rise in marriage rates, and has not resulted in more investment.[3]

### CO-OPERATIVES

A few agricultural credit co-operatives were founded before the First World War and after the achievement of independence the government helped the movement by favourable legislation and the provision of cheap loans through Misr Bank. By 1931 there were 539 co-operative societies of all kinds with a membership of 53,000. The foundation in that year of the Agricultural Credit Bank, which advanced to individuals or co-operatives alike, removed the main attraction of the latter and the rate of expansion slowed down considerably. In 1939 the number of co-operatives was only 792, membership 78,000, advances and sales £E1,125,000, and paid-up capital and reserves £E327,000. Nor did the matter end there. The fact that the Bank advanced to co-operatives at a lower rate than to individuals was best appreciated by *large* landowners, who began to join the co-operatives and secure control over them.

During the Second World War the government relied heavily on the co-operatives for the distribution of supplies and fertilizers; as a result, between 1939 and 1944, membership increased tenfold. After that growth in numbers once more slowed down, but activity increased and by 1955, the latest date for which overall figures are available, there were 2,671 co-operatives of all kinds with 868,000 members, capital and reserves of £E4·8 million and advances and sales of 23·7 million.[4] By 1960 there were 3,101 agricultural credit co-operatives, with 674,000 members; and loans advanced by them amounted to £E20·4 million;[5] in 1961 the number rose to 3,788, which means that practically every village has a co-operative.[6] Marketing co-operatives are still, however, few in number and

---

[1] *al-Islah al-zirai*, p. 35.    [2] Saab, in *ME Econ. Papers, 1960.*
[3] Ibid.; for more details see his *Eg. Agrar. Ref.*, ch. 6.
[4] *Coll. Basic Statist. Data.*
[5] Agric. & Co-op. Credit Bank, *Rapports, 1960.*
[6] *al-Ahram*, 21 Nov. 1961.

limited in scope.[1] In the meanwhile, laws had been passed in 1944 and 1957 reorganizing the co-operatives and extending government control over them and in 1949 the Agricultural Credit Bank had been reorganized, to allow co-operatives to participate more fully in its activities (see below, p. 262). The result of these two measures was that 'many societies—600, said one authority—merely act as post offices between the bank and their members. . . . One great merit it can claim, however; it has replaced the indiscriminate lending of the professional money-lender by a system of controlled credit, linked moreover with marketing.'[2] And although the co-operatives do perform various social and cultural services for their members, the rather severe judgement made by the same observer seems in many cases justified: 'Better farming has been encouraged, but not better living.'

In the last few years attempts have been made to widen the scope of agricultural co-operatives. In 1960 Law No. 267 created General Co-operative Organizations, each of which is charged with the supervision of a specific kind of co-operative, e.g. agricultural, consumers, &c; the Agricultural and Co-operative Credit Bank was put under the Organization for Co-operative Agricultural Credit.[3] In January 1961 co-operatives were reorganized and put under the supervision of officials of the Ministry of Agriculture. More recently it has been sought to make co-operatives more democratic by stipulating that two-thirds of the members of their councils shall be farmers owning less than 5 feddans. An attempt is also to be made to link up agricultural and consumer co-operatives.[4]

Since 1952 another kind of agricultural co-operative has developed. The Agrarian Reform Law stipulated that all beneficiaries must join a multi-purpose co-operative which would perform such services as loans, supply, sale, and organization of production. By 1960 there were 330 such societies, with nearly 200,000 members, each covering an area of about 1,000 feddans and managed by a Supervisor appointed by the Ministry of Agrarian Reform;[5] co-operatives within each administrative district are under the direction of the Delegate of the Ministry. The co-operatives supply their members with selected seeds, chemical fertilizers, pesticides, and gunnies; in

[1] See details in *Nashrat bank al-taslif al-zirai wa'l-taawuni*, no. 2, 1960.
[2] Darling, 'Co-operation in the Middle East', *Yb. Agric. Co-op.*, 1951.
[3] Agric. & Co-op. Credit Bank, *Rapports, 1960*.
[4] *al-Ahram*, 22 & 27 Nov. 1961.
[5] In 1959 membership in such co-operatives was opened to neighbouring small owners and tenants but few, if any, have joined (see Saab, *Eg. Agrar. Ref.*, ch. 4).

1960 the value of such supplies was £E4·5 million.[1] They also provide credit, including supervised credit and loans in kind, amounting in 1960 to £E4·4 million, and market members' crops; observers agree that marketing has been very successful and it has been estimated that, on average, farmers get £E2–3 per cantar of cotton above the price paid by local merchants.[2] The co-operatives have moreover tried to improve cottage industries and to provide their members with various social services.[3] But the most far-reaching change introduced by them has been co-operative production, under which each member's holding is divided into 'three equal plots situated each within the area allotted to one of the three main crops . . . entering in the triennial rotation'.[4] In many cases this has been accompanied by mechanization on a co-operative basis.[5]

There seems little doubt that the new co-operatives have performed valuable services to their members and have reduced some of the disruptions which the removal of landlord control might have created. There is equally little doubt that these societies are co-operative in little more than name; in fact they are strictly controlled by government officials. Moreover, they could quite easily and imperceptibly be transformed from co-operatives to collectives, and mark the beginning of the end of private ownership in the one important sector where it is still predominant. But, in view of the crushing burden which the government has assumed in the other sectors of the economy, and considering the manifest failure of collectivized agriculture from East Germany to China, it is perhaps not unreasonable to hope that such a step will not be taken in the immediate future.

### AGRICULTURAL POLICY

Under the influence of landlords or cotton speculators, and in pursuit of an unattainable self-sufficiency, Egyptian governments

---

[1] *al-Islah al-zirai*, p. 24.

[2] Saab, in *ME Econ. Papers, 1960*. However, since 1958 most of the cotton crop has been sold to the Egyptian Cotton Commission, at prices which dissatisfied farmers (see Saab, *Eg. Agrar. Ref.*, ch. 5).

[3] For details see ibid. ch. 6.     [4] Saab, in *ME Econ. Papers, 1960*.

[5] More recently an attempt has been made to deal with the problem of fragmentation, a very serious one in Egypt, in areas not covered by Agrarian Reform Co-operatives; this is to be done by pooling all village lands and cultivating the whole area in plots of 20–50 feddans devoted to a single crop; after an initial success in two villages it was decided to try out this method in 103 villages and, if favourable results were obtained, to generalize further (*al-Islah al-zirai*, pp. 21–23). For details on the pilot project at Nawag see Saab, *Eg. Agrar. Ref.*, appendix.

have, since the early 1920's, repeatedly attempted to regulate the growing and marketing of cotton and cereals, generally with most unfortunate results (see above, p. 36).

In the last ten years, following the 'Korean boom', when the government encouraged bullish speculation in cotton and pushed prices upwards by fixing high minima and buying large quantities of cotton, with disastrous results during the collapse of 1951–2, government policy has been cautious.[1] But two criticisms may be made. First, by fixing buying prices for cotton and grains it has abolished the market mechanism to which, by and large, farmers have shown themselves responsive (see above, p. 146) and which secures a far better allocation of land.[2] Secondly, it has unduly encouraged the cultivation of grain, a policy which is certainly mistaken. It is perhaps to be deplored that an agricultural country like Egypt cannot feed itself, but the hard fact remains that its soil is much too precious and its water much too scarce to be wasted on wheat and maize, which are best left to countries practising extensive cultivation like Australia and Argentina, or even on rice, in which Egypt can compete only with difficulty with the monsoon countries. Exclusive reliance on cotton admittedly is dangerous[3] and diversification is necessary, but it must be a diversification which increases the real wealth of the country, not merely swells the monetary value of certain crops by inflating prices and taxing the consumer.

Egypt's agricultural policy is clearly dictated by its climate, its location, and its factor endowment. Its first agricultural revolution, based on cotton, took the maximum advantage of these conditions, and cotton has come to stay. Evidently Egypt's first task is to expand its cotton crop as far as possible and to improve its quality still further. But a second revolution is demanded by the great increase in Egyptian population, by the development of air transport and refrigeration, and by the very rapid growth of the three neighbouring regions of Western Europe, the Middle East, and Eastern Europe. Everything in Egypt—soil, climate, location, compactness,

---

[1] See Zaki Shabana, 'Econ. Effects of the Cotton Policy of the Principal Countries' (in Ar.), *Ég. contemp.*, Oct. 1958.

[2] With the reservation, however, that the alternative returns from the various possible crop combinations should be calculated not at farm prices but at prices based on export prices for crops like cotton and on import prices for ones like wheat and maize.

[3] However, one argument against cotton can easily be dismissed, the fear that in time of war or other emergencies Egypt might not be able to feed its population, for a shift from cotton to grain can be effected at a few months' notice.

and abundant labour supply—point to it as a vast vegetable, fruit, and flower garden and an exporter to these regions of fresh and canned fruit and vegetables, jams, flowers, and dairy produce. This must be accompanied by a shrinkage in the area under cereals and rice and an increase in mechanization which will release a large number of animals from farm work and devote them entirely to meat and dairy production. Such a shift would simultaneously increase returns per acre severalfold, absorb a much larger amount of labour and, by reducing rice cultivation, save an appreciable amount of water.[1]

Without going into details it may be pointed out that many Egyptian fruits could compete on the European market because of their late maturity (for example, Valencia oranges) or early maturity (Clementine tangerines) or because Egypt is the only producer outside the tropical zone (mangoes). Similarly Egypt can sell, in winter and spring, onions, tomatoes, potatoes, garlic, string beans, peas, marrows, cucumbers, carrots, artichokes, and other vegetables. A few enterprising landowners have shown that there is a market abroad for gladioli, roses, tuberoses, and other flowers.[2] Lastly, a much greater production of meat and dairy produce is needed to feed the rapidly growing urban population, and export possibilities, especially to Arab countries, are not negligible.

This is the goal to be aimed at, and there are some indications that the Egyptian government has understood its importance.[3] But, clearly, it is surrounded by formidable obstacles, many of them of the government's own making; these will be discussed in Chapter XIII.

[1] See the examples given in Saab, *Motorisation*, pp. 197–202, where a threefold increase in net income is envisaged and idem, in *ME Econ. Papers* where he states that 'it is possible by combining vegetable crops, cotton and intensive animal breeding to raise the yearly rate of absorption of manpower per cultivated feddan to 80 man days and 120 woman or child days, instead of the 55 man days and 60 woman or child days with the usual three crop rotation'.

[2] *al-Majalla al-ziraia*, Jan. & Feb. 1959.

[3] For e.g., a report by the Ministry of Agriculture aiming at increasing agricultural income by £E112 m. (26 m. by extension of cultivation and 86 m. by intensification) was recently discussed by the President and Cabinet. The two measures which seem to have been most strongly stressed were better means of fighting cotton pests and increasing the production and export of fruit and vegetables (*al-Ahram*, 25 Jan. 1962).

# VIII

# Industry

No nation can keep up with others in civilization if deprived of manufacturers, and thereby brought down to a mere agglomeration of clodhoppers. FRIEDRICH ENGELS.

*Nowadays part of the definition of nationhood is industrial development.* LORD FRANKS.

*The argument for industrialization as a means of general economic development is, initially at any rate, stronger in the densely populated countries than in the sparsely settled regions.* RAGNAR NURKSE.

### INDUSTRIAL POLICY

Industry is the fastest growing sector of the Egyptian economy and the one on which the greatest hopes are laid. To quote the Five-Year Plan: 'While agriculture is considered as the first sector, which constitutes the framework of the whole of production, industry is considered as the only path to economic progress and continued development.'[1] But it is perhaps the one which is most difficult to analyse. This is not for lack of certain kinds of data: both official publications and the press are full of information regarding the discovery of mineral deposits, the opening of factories, and the increase in production, and industrial production censuses are both frequent and reliable. But what is almost wholly lacking is recent information on such subjects as capital investment, costs of production and productivity, which alone make it possible to determine how far Egyptian industry is competitive, to what extent it is actually helping to raise the real national income, and whether the funds invested in it could not be better employed elsewhere.

The available data will be analysed below, but in the meanwhile the following judgement may be made. Only a handful of Egyptian industries can be considered competitive; yet the government is basically right in seeking rapid industrialization, even though some

[1] *Cadre du Plan*, p. 14.

individual projects are obviously misguided and even though, more fundamentally, there may well have been

failure to understand the by no means self-evident proposition that . . . productivity determines the level of living an economy will yield. In the absence of full understanding of the causes of high living standards, it is easy to be misled by the very real connection between industrialization and high living standards into assuming an overly simple connection.[1]

In the author's opinion, the following reasons justify the industrialization of Egypt. From the short-term, purely economic, point of view, capital investment in industry is justified wherever the value added by labour using that capital is greater than the value added by a corresponding amount of labour using an equal amount of capital would have been in other sectors. In a country such as Egypt, where new land can be brought under cultivation only at great cost, where intensification of agriculture has been carried very far, where transport does not constitute a serious bottleneck, and where for various political reasons the scope of services bringing in foreign exchange cannot be greatly extended, this may well occur even if all machinery, fuels and raw materials used in manufacturing have to be imported.[2]

This is reinforced by longer-term considerations connected with internal and external economies. First, there are the economies of scale: a firm whose costs are high at a given level of production may greatly reduce them when the growth of the market enables it to expand its output to optimum dimensions. Secondly, there are what may be called 'the economies of experience': continued production alone can suggest means for making improvements and reducing costs. Thirdly, there are the economies of complementarity, external to the firm or even to the industry, arising from the development of other industries—which take its products or by-products and supply it with raw materials or equipment—or of power, transport, water supply, repair shops, and other services. These three sets of

---

[1] Everett E. Hagen, in Mass. Inst. of Technology, *Investment Criteria*, p. 60.

[2] It will be noticed that this argument focuses on the scarce factor, capital, and not on the abundant factor, labour. No assumption regarding zero productivity of labour in agriculture is made, as it is for instance in UN, *Econ. Survey of Europe since the War* (p. 219) where it is stated that: 'the existence of vast surpluses of manpower in agriculture creates a situation where money costs in industry are higher in relation to agricultural money costs than is warranted by comparative real costs in the two branches of the economy'; but of course there is a connexion between the two arguments.

factors justify the protection and nurturing of many an 'infant industry' in Egypt.

To these economic arguments may be added two social ones. First, it seems likely that social patterns associated with urbanization can help to slow down the rapid growth of population and, although until recently Egyptian towns were marketing rather than industrial centres, no economic basis for further urbanization other than industry seems to be at present available.[1] Secondly, although it is true that in Europe science, rationalism, and even technological progress had been developing for generations or even centuries before modern industrialism,[2] in Asia and Africa the sequence is liable to be reversed and industrialization is likely greatly to stimulate the growth of a scientific spirit.

Two political and psychological arguments in favour of industrialization have also had great appeal in Egypt, as in other backward countries: the promise of self-sufficiency and the promise of power. Neither stands close examination, at least for the short run. Industrialization enables a country to meet its needs for consumer goods but, at any rate for several decades, only at the cost of greater dependence on the outside world for capital goods and often even for producer goods.[3] As for power, it is difficult to see the use of making at home steel sheets or even motor car engines and small arms as long as the jets, tanks, radar, rockets, and other weapons without which modern war cannot be waged have to be imported. But in both respects the existence of home industries does give the country a certain leeway.

It remains to mention the very recent landmarks in Egypt's industrial development, which owe much to the Soviet lines of credit opened since 1958, as well as to other foreign aid (see below, p. 238). In 1953–7 the number of industrial joint-stock companies rose from 184 to 259 and their paid-up capital from £E66·3 to 99·7 million, or by just over 50 per cent.[4] In 1958 an industrialization plan

[1] There is evidence from Japan and Puerto Rico that birth-rates among women working in factories or offices are distinctly lower than those not only of women who have no paid job or are engaged in agriculture but also of women engaged in cottage industries (see A. J. Jaffe and K. Azumi, 'The Birth Rate and Cottage Industries in Underdeveloped Countries', *Econ. Dev. & Cult. Change*, Oct. 1960).

[2] Hagen, in *Investment Criteria*, p. 77.

[3] A related argument, that industrialization justifies itself both politically and economically in wartime, when a country may be cut off from its sources of supply, has been rendered largely obsolete by the nature of contemporary warfare.

[4] For a detailed study see *R. of Indust. Bank* (in Ar.), no. 1, 1958–9.

was launched, aiming at a total investment of £E277 million over 1958–63, with an anticipated increase in employment of over 70,000, in gross output of £E202 million, and in net output of 84 million.[1] This was later replaced by the general Five-Year Plan 1960–5 (see above, p. 66) which provides for an investment of £E579 million, a rise in employment of 215,000, and an increase in gross output of £E720 million and in 'value added' of £E267 million.

The targets set by the Plan for investment in industry, including manufacturing, mining, and power, seem, so far, to have been attained. Investment during 1961 was put at £E88 million and was expected to rise to 120 million by 1962.[2] The revised figures for 1961/2 put investment at £E113 million, of which 99 million were in the public sector and 14 in the private; by the end of 1961, gross industrial output was running at the rate of £E1,189 million, compared with 1,094 million in 1959/60. And it was announced that in 1962 78 new factories, costing £E97 million, would start production.[3]

### RECENT GROWTH AND STRUCTURE

Since the late 1930's Egyptian industry has grown very rapidly; between 1938 and 1951 production rose by 138 per cent, or a simple annual rate of increase of just over 10 per cent (see above, p. 112), and this pace was maintained after the Revolution. The National Bank's index of industrial production (1954=100) rose from 91 in 1951 to 124 in 1957 and 142 in 1959. The industrial production censuses show that 'value added' by establishments employing 10 persons or more increased from £E79 million in 1952 to 130 million in 1959 and, according to a press item, 149 million in 1960; since the index of industrial prices rose by 7 per cent in that period the total increase in real terms was 77 per cent, or a simple rate of nearly 10 per cent.[4] During the first half of 1961 output of establishments employing 100 or more persons was 26·2 per cent higher than during the first half of 1960;[5] output of establishments employing 500 persons or more was, according to the above-mentioned press item, 7·3 per cent higher in the second half of 1961 than in the second half

[1] UAR, *al-Taqaddum al-sinai fi'l-iqlim al-misri* (1959).
[2] Interview given by President Abdel Nasser, *al-Ahram*, 20 Jan. 1962.
[3] Ibid. 11 Nov., 3 & 10 Dec. 1961.
[4] An official estimate puts the total increase in industrial production between 1952 and 1960 at 109 per cent which, adjusting for the rise in prices, would mean that it just about doubled, giving a simple rate of increase of some 12 per cent p.a. The figures, however, refer to gross output, not 'value added' (ibid. 10 Dec. 1961). See also NBE, *Econ. B.*, nos. 2 and 3, 1962.          [5] Ibid. no. 3, 1961.

TABLE 22

## Industrial Production, 1938–61
('000 tons)

|  | 1938 | 1946 | 1952 | 1957 | 1959 | 1960 | 1961[1] |
|---|---|---|---|---|---|---|---|
| Cotton yarn | 21 | 33 | 56 | 78 | 91 | 105 | 111 |
| Cotton cloth | (12) | (25) | 40 | 59 | 60 | 64 | 73 |
| Rayon fabrics | — | (1) | 4 | 10 | 8 | 9 | 9 |
| Refined sugar | 162 | 191 | 210 | 250 | 287 | 338 | 330 |
| Canned fruits & vegetables | .. | 20[2] | 2·6 | 7·9 | 10·3 | 9·1 | .. |
| Cotton-seed oil | 53 | 74 | 100 | 85 | 103 | 104 | .. |
| Sulphuric acid | 8 | 11 | 44 | 89 | 93 | 103 | 103 |
| Caustic soda | — | 5·0 | 2·0 | 2·5 | 4·0 | 3·5 | .. |
| Paper & cardboard | 7 | 30[2] | 20 | 39 | 41 | 49 | 50 |
| Tyres[3] | — | — | — | 157 | 195 | 280 | 315 |
| Superphosphates | 20 | 15 | 106 | 177 | 167 | 190 | 180 |
| Nitrates | — | — | 111 | 208 | 246 | 330 | 590 |
| Soap | 45 | (55) | 67 | 75 | 80 | 80 | .. |
| Glass | 2 | 12[2] | 12 | 25 | 36 | 45 | .. |
| Iron and steel products | — | — | 70 | 148 | 243 | 327 | (400) |
| Motor cars [4] | — | — | 1,282 | 1,271 | 1,700 | 1,838 | |
| Cement | 375 | 588 | 951 | 1,466 | 1,784 | 2,047 | 2,141 |
| Crude petroleum | 226 | 1,128 | 2,379 | 2,362 | 3,155 | 3,319 | 3,800 |
| Electricity[5] | 288 | 431 | 992 | 1,706 | 2,125 | 2,639 | 4,800 |
| Index of Indust. prod.[6] | (38) | (68) | 95 | 124 | 142 | .. | .. |

[1] Preliminary.  [2] 1945.  [3] '000 units.

[4] Units; until 1959 assembly only; in 1960 731 units were assembled and 1,107 manufactured.  [5] Million kwh.  [6] 1954=100.

Sources: Fed. of Industries in Eg. Region, Yb. 1961 (in Ar.); UN, Dev. of Manufacturing; Akher Saa, spec. issue; CBE, Econ. R., no. 3, 1962.

of 1960. It is, however, probable that production in the smaller establishments was dislocated by the sequestration to a greater extent than that in the larger establishments; moreover, it is likely that even before nationalization and sequestration the smaller establishments increased output less rapidly than larger ones. It may therefore be surmised that in 1961 total output rose by some 10 per cent.[1] Table 22 shows the increase in the principal branches since 1938.

[1] Output of nationalized industries in July–February 1961/2 was £E252 m., against 230 m. in July–February 1960/1 (al-Ahram, 15 Apr. 1962); total gross output in 1961 was £E738 m., against 661 m. in 1960 (CBE, Econ. R., no. 3, 1962).

Employment increased much less than output, indicating a marked rise in productivity. Employment in establishments with 10 or more persons, which had risen from 155,000 in 1937 to 279,000 in 1947, dropped to 273,000 in 1952 and 263,000 in 1956 but thereafter rose slowly until 1958 and then rapidly to 327,000 in 1960.

## Location

The structure of industry in Egypt shows few peculiarities.[1] In 1958 just over half of those working in establishments employing 10 or more persons were in Alexandria and Cairo, 28 per cent in the former and 23 in the latter;[2] other small nuclei are the textile centre of Mahalla al-Kubra and the petroleum and petrochemical centre of Suez. Excluding the province of Giza, only 5 per cent were employed in Upper Egypt, but it is hoped to build up a large industrial base around the Aswan dam and High Dam. The reasons for this concentration in the capital and main port, which is typical of backward countries, are the high purchasing power of Cairo and Alexandria; their good communications; the presence of cheap and reliable electric power and repair shops; the relative abundance of skilled labour; and the concentration in them of the foreigners who started so many of Egypt's industries.

## Size

In 1958 establishments employing 10–49 workers accounted for 79 per cent of the number of enterprises with more than 10 persons, employed 19 per cent of their workers, and produced 17 per cent of the 'value added'; the corresponding figures for the 50–499 group were 19, 32, and 32 per cent respectively and for establishments employing 500 or over 2, 49, and 51 per cent respectively. The share in employment of the largest establishments rose slightly from 47 per cent in 1952, while their share in 'value added' rose from 57 in 1952 to 63 in 1956 and 67 in 1959.[3] The general increase in size is shown by the fact that whereas in 1952 average employment in establishments with more than 10 workers was 79 and average gross output £E80,000 the corresponding figures for 1960 were 97 and £E153,000 respectively.[4]

[1] For further details see UN, *Dev. of Manufacturing* & Issawi, *EMC*, pp. 155–62.
[2] *Coll. Basic Statist. Data*, pp. 109–13. In previous censuses Cairo occupied first place and 'greater Cairo', which includes the adjacent provinces of Giza and Qaliubia, is by far the largest centre of industry; if the figures for these provinces are included, Cairo's share rises to 40 per cent of the total.   [3] Ibid. p. 104.
[4] In 1937 average employment in such establishments was 62 and in 1927, 38 (UN, *Dev. of Manufacturing*, p. 36).

As regards establishments employing less than 10 persons, the latest data refer to 1947, when about 224,000 persons worked in such establishments and 181,000 in those employing 10 or over.[1] The former figure compares with 168,000 in 1937 and 153,000 in 1927 but it may be doubted whether this rate of growth has been maintained in recent years.

As regards the various branches, a United Nations study concluded that in 'some branches such as sugar refining, petroleum refining, and the making of paper, fertilizer and cement, the average number of workers in the existing plants in Egypt, Israel and Turkey is high and approximately the same as in more industrialized countries (perhaps in some cases even higher)'. These are usually new industries, with few units and in which technology sets a minimum size. In the older industries, however, 'notably the making of clothing and shoes, and leather tanning, not only do handicrafts play a much more important role than in industrial countries, but the industry itself consists of much smaller units. This applies even to the textile industry, especially to cotton weaving.'[2]

The preponderance of small and very large enterprises, and the weakness of the middle group, which is characteristic of so many industrializing countries, has important political and social consequences; in part it explains the weakness and vulnerability of the Egyptian bourgeoisie.

*Motive Power and Capitalization*

Data on motive power are scarce. A United Nations report put the total installed capacity in all 'productive' manufacturing establishments (i.e. those not engaged in repair work) at 326,000 h.p. in 1947 and 453,000 in 1950; horsepower per worker was estimated at 0·9 and 1·5 respectively.[3] Table 23 (p. 181) shows that installed power in manufacturing was about 515,000 h.p., which would give an average of about 2 h.p. if divided by the number of workers in *all* establishments with 10 or more workers and of about 1 h.p. if divided by the total number engaged in manufacturing. These figures are comparable to those in countries at a similar level of industrial development, such as Turkey and Lebanon.

Data on capital investment are even scantier. Paid-up capital of establishments engaged in manufacturing was put at £E65 million in 1947 and 102 million in 1950, or £E200 and 340 per worker; the latter is equivalent to $975, a figure below that of Israel or Lebanon

[1] Ibid. p. 103.       [2] Ibid. p. 37.       [3] Ibid. p. 111.

but close to that of Turkey.[1] In plants set up in recent years, however, capitalization per worker has been much higher; thus a study of sixty-seven projects, costing £E50·5 million, which began producing in 1960/1, shows that investment per worker was £E2,431. The figure is, however, greatly swollen by the presence of a nitrates fertilizer plant and if that is excluded investment per worker would drop to £E1,127, or some $3,250.[2]

## Concentration, Integration, and Monopoly

The preponderance of large establishments, noted above, is one aspect of the concentration and monopolistic conditions prevailing in Egyptian industry until the recent nationalizations. Other aspects were the small number of firms in several industries, or the large percentage of output accounted for by one firm; the large extent of vertical and lateral integration; and the existence of cartels or selling arrangements in some industries.

Concentration may be illustrated from the sugar, nitrate fertilizer, and tyre industries, which were complete monopolies; the alcohol, beer, steel, salt, cigarette, and cement industries, which consisted of two or three firms; and the rayon and vegetable-canning industries where one firm, and the cotton spinning and paper industries where two firms, produced the bulk of output.

Several factors explain the concentration of Egyptian industry. First, there is the narrowness of the market, which in certain industries does not leave room for more than a few firms of adequate size; there seems no doubt however that, especially in textiles, some Egyptian firms have passed well beyond the size needed to secure economies of scale. Secondly, there is the dearth of entrepreneurial ability. Thirdly, lack of industrial credit and of funds for investment in industry made it difficult for small entrepreneurs to set up businesses. Lastly, and most important, there was the desire to obtain monopoly profits.

At present all the larger enterprises are fully owned or controlled by one or other of the Organizations (see above, p. 64); it has been announced that competition between firms is to be encouraged but it is not yet clear how this policy is to be implemented.

Vertical integration is widespread in Egypt. The short time in which Egyptian industry evolved and the absence of well-developed sources of power, repair shops, &c, forced many firms to undertake

---

[1] UN, *Dev. of Manufacturing*, pp. 114–15.    [2] NPC, Memo. no. 555.

several of the successive processes of production.[1] Another cause of vertical integration has been the desire to ensure an adequate and stable source of raw material; examples are provided by the sugar, wine, and linen industries. A third factor has been the amalgamation of independent firms carrying out different stages of production, such as sugar crushing and refining. Finally, there has been the desire to use by-products, or to create new outlets for part of the output, which has, for example, led the cement company to manufacture concrete products and the sugar company to make alcohol.

Lateral integration, also existing in Egypt, can be traced to the existence of excess capacity at certain stages resulting from vertical integration which led to the emergence of certain discontinuities. Other reasons have been the desire to find outlets for surplus profits, especially during the war; the relative ease with which established firms could raise capital for new projects; and the difficulty of expanding production in existing fields, because of the narrowness of the market, resulting in a desire to develop new products.

There seems little doubt that in Egypt both types of integration have been carried well beyond the optimum; hence, certain recent tendencies towards simplification. It will be interesting to see whether the managers of the nationalized industries will try to break up some of the enterprises they have acquired into smaller units or whether they will, on the contrary, build them up into still larger combines.

Monopolist conditions were to be found in most branches of Egyptian industry. In addition to the factor of size, mentioned above, several causes combined to promote monopolies. Among them were the dearth of capital and the small number of entrepreneurs interested in founding firms; the localization of industry; the protective effect of the tariff; and the attitude of the government, which helped the sugar and textile combines, encouraged the formation of cartels in transport and cotton processing, and urged further amalgamation in the textile industry.[2] It should, however, be added that the government exercised increasing control over many monopolies, both by fixing prices and rates and by sharing their monopoly gains.

[1] Thus the Sugar Company had to build its own narrow-gauge railway and even a river fleet; the Rayon Company installed a complete mechanical workshop capable of making all spare parts required by it; the cotton-textile factories both spin and weave, and the two largest ones also dye, bleach, and print; many factories have their own generators of electricity; and many carried their products into wholesale, or even retail trade.

[2] al-Gritly in *Ég. contemp.*, 1947, p. 250.

Before the nationalizations the form taken by monopoly varied. Some attempts at cartellization succeeded, e.g. in the cotton ginning and pressing industries, which had suffered from excess capacity. Sales agreements were prevalent in several industries, e.g. cement, beer, and salt. And, as mentioned earlier, some industries consisted of only one firm.

## Organization and Finance

Lastly, a brief description may be given of the legal and financial conditions prevailing before the nationalizations and sequestrations. Since then, the bulk of Egyptian industry has been wholly or partially owned, and controlled, by the government (see above, p. 63); the rest consists of small firms most of which are unincorporated while others are joint-stock companies unaffected by the nationalization decrees.

As regards nationality, the share of foreigners, formerly very considerable, had fallen sharply. The 1956 Census of Industrial Production showed that of 3,514 enterprises employing 10 persons or more, 632 belonged to foreigners and 84 were of mixed nationality; the sequestrations of 1956 and the various measures taken in the next four years (see above, p. 55) greatly reduced the number of foreign establishments and by 1960 practically all industry was in Egyptian hands.

Until 1953 the share of the government in industry was negligible, consisting of a petroleum refinery, some printing presses and repair shops for railways, cars, and ships. After the revolution the government participated, together with private capital, in a few large schemes notably iron and steel works, fertilizers, and railway equipment, and it acquired a few public utilities by nationalization. But until 1960 nearly the whole of industry was privately owned. Government investment in industry in 1959–60 was £E183·7 million.

The greater part of industrial activity was carried out by companies. In 1956 the 266 joint-stock and limited-liability companies employed 55·5 per cent of all workmen in establishments with more than 10 persons and produced 72·1 per cent of their net output; the balance was accounted for by private companies and partnerships of various kinds or by individually owned enterprises.

One of the striking aspects of Egyptian industrial companies was their very sparing use of either debentures or preference shares. Thus a study of 91 industrial companies with an aggregate paid up capital of £E100·2 million in 1959 showed that all their long-term liabilities, which included items other than debentures, amounted to only 8·3 million.[1] Moreover debentures were almost always issued after the company had been well established, not at the time of incorporation. The great reliance put by Egyptian companies on ordinary share capital can be explained by the fact that most of them were launched by a small group of promoters, who wished to retain control in their hands and not relinquish it to debenture holders; by the lack of enthusiasm, until very recently, for industrial investment on the part of the Egyptian public; and by the very legitimate desire of not saddling a new enterprise with heavy fixed charges.

Until the establishment of the Industrial Bank in 1949 (see below, p. 264), and with the exception of the Misr group, growth was largely financed by ploughing back profits. This was motivated by the usual reasons: the difficulty of raising capital; the absence of long- or medium-term industrial credit; the desire to retain control in the founding group; and the wish to make dividends look reasonable and to pay less taxes. Short-term credit was furnished to large and well-established firms by commercial banks, through overdrafts, but smaller firms often found it difficult to borrow from banks. The above-mentioned study showed that of a total net increase in liabilities of £E24·9 million in 1958/9, 6·3 million came from depreciation and similar provisions, 3·6 million from retained profits, 10·6 million from bank overdrafts and other short-term resources, and 4·4 million from capital issues. It will thus be seen that Egyptian industry was ploughing back nearly 20 per cent of its net profits, which in 1958/9 were £E18·7 million.[2]

The quite rapid increase in the capital of industrial companies, through both retention of profits and new issues, is shown by the fact that the paid-up capital of an unspecified group of industrial companies rose from £E41·7 million in 1951 to 62·6 million in 1960.[3] During the same period total net dividends (i.e. after payment of taxes, which were increased from 15 per cent in 1951 to 22 by 1960) rose fairly steadily from £E4·9 to 10·3 million, i.e. roughly from 12 to 16 per cent of paid-up capital and from 5 to 7 per cent of the market value of the shares.[4]

---

[1] NBE, *Econ. B.*, nos. 3 & 4, 1960.　　　　　　　[2] Ibid.

[3] CBE, *Econ. R.*, no. 2, 1961; the market value of the shares of these companies rose from £E103·9 m. to 157·8 m.

[4] Dividends were highest in the foodstuffs and chemicals groups and lowest in the mining and metallurgy and the electricity and engineering groups, with textiles, building materials, and cotton ginning and pressing in between.

## BRANCHES OF INDUSTRY

During the first half of 1961 establishments employing 100 persons or more accounted for some 10 per cent of all establishments with 10 or more persons, produced 73 per cent of the 'value added' by them, and had a gross output of £E231·3 million and a 'value added' of 95 million, or a yearly rate of £E462·6 and 190 million respectively.[1] For 1959/60 gross output of the whole industrial sector, including very small establishments, was put at £E1,094·2 million and 'value added' at 273·4 million.[2] For 1960/1 the figures were estimated at £E1,185·2 and 301·11 million, compared with target figures of 1,188·7 and 300·2 million respectively.[3]

The relative importance of the main branches of industry at the beginning of 1961 is shown in Table 23. Consumer goods industries account for about two-thirds of total output, a proportion characteristic of countries in the earlier stages of industrialization whereas in mature economies, such as those of the major industrial countries after the First World War, it may fall to one-third or below.[4] The Plan aims at raising the share of what are called 'industries of an essentially productive nature', i.e. mining, power, metallurgy and machinery, and chemicals, from 16·5 per cent of total gross output in 1959/60 to 30·9 in 1964/5 and eventually to 33·6 in 1969/70; correspondingly the share of consumer goods industries is to fall from 61·7 to 51·0 and 50·7 respectively.[5] A detailed description of the main branches of Egyptian industry is given in Appendix III (p. 319).

## EFFICIENCY OF INDUSTRY

Two general statements may be safely made about the productivity of Egyptian industry: it is rising rather rapidly; and it is still very low compared to that of advanced countries. As a result, in spite of low wages, the vast majority of industries are not competitive, but where they enjoy the benefits of cheap raw materials as well they can hold their own in local, and very occasionally in foreign markets.

Three studies of productivity per worker are available. Net output per person employed in Egypt was put by Gamal al-Din Said at £E56 in 1944 and at 74 in 1947, both figures calculated in 1937

---

[1] NBE, *Econ. R.*, no. 3, 1961.  [2] *Cadre du Plan*, p. 51.
[3] NPC, Memo. no. 531.
[4] W. Hoffman, *The Growth of Industrial Economies* (Manchester, 1958), statist. app.  [5] *Cadre du Plan*, p. 17.

TABLE 23

*Main Branches of Industry,[1] First Quarter 1961*

| | No. of establish- ments | Installed motive power ('000 h.p.)[2] | Persons employed | Gross output (£E'000) | Value added (£E'000) |
|---|---|---|---|---|---|
| Mining & quarrying | 16 | 2 | 10,841 | 4,648 | 3,844 |
| Water, gas, electricity | 4 | 353[3] | 3,833 | 1,400 | 856 |
| Food & beverages | 75 | 235 | 37,219 | 20,769 | 7,146 |
| Tobacco | 11 | 2 | 7,827 | 14,615 | 1,659 |
| Textiles[4] | 159 | 86 | 129,330 | 30,911 | 17,042 |
| Clothing & shoes | 5 | .. | 3,224 | 796 | 236 |
| Wood, cork, furniture | 16 | 3[5] | 3,320 | 697 | 235 |
| Paper & printing | 32 | 3[6] | 11,978 | 2,553 | 1,107 |
| Leather & rubber | 10 | 2[7] | 2,896 | 2,553 | 827 |
| Chemicals | 27 | .. | 14,800 | 6,847 | 4,440 |
| Petroleum products | 2 | 14 | 3,517 | 1,486 | 1,063 |
| Non-mineral products | 27 | 23[8] | 12,528 | 3,307 | 1,711 |
| Basic minerals | 13 | .. | 9,811 | 4,268 | 2,463 |
| Mineral products | 17 | .. | 3,619 | 547 | 293 |
| Machinery[9] | 39 | 17 | 8,862 | 3,071 | 1,117 |
| Miscellaneous | 5 | 130[10] | 1,650 | 258 | 106 |
| Total | 458 | 870 | 265,255 | 98,726 | 44,145 |

[1] Establishments employing 100 persons or more. [2] Figures are for 1957, incl. all establishments in industry, and are only approximate. [3] Electricity only. [4] Ginning, pressing, spinning, & weaving. [5] Carpentry only. [6] Paper only. [7] Tanning only. [8] Cement only. [9] Manufacture & repair of machinery, electric instruments & transport equipment. [10] Incl. all industries listed above for which no figures or incomplete figures are given.

*Sources: Census of Ind. Production, 1st qr. 1961 (in Ar.); Ann. stat., 1957 & 1958.*

prices; these figures compared with 264 in the United Kingdom, 294 in Germany, and 595 in the United States in 1935-7.[1] Between 1947 and 1958 employment in establishments with 10 or more workers dropped by nearly 3 per cent while 'value added' in real terms (i.e. deflating by the price index of industrial goods), rose by some 73 per cent; in other words productivity per man' rose at a simple rate of about 7 per cent per annum. Between 1958 and 1960 however, according to the press item mentioned above,

[1] *Iqtisadiat misr*, p. 275; see table reproduced in Issawi, *EMC*, p. 165 for fuller details.

employment in such establishments increased by 27 per cent and 'value added', in real terms, by 32 per cent, or a simple rate of increase of only 2 per cent per annum.

TABLE 24

*Physical Output per Worker, 1954*

|  | Egypt (1954) | Israel (1951) | Turkey[1] (1950) | UK[2] (1948) | USA (1947) |
|---|---|---|---|---|---|
| Grain milling (tons) | 140[3] | 320 | .. | 250 | 480 |
| Beer (hl.) | 290 | 730[4] | 250 | .. | .. |
| Cigarettes (kg.) | 1,230 | 5,700[4] | 4,400 | .. | 6,860[5] |
| Cotton fabrics ('000 of sq. metres) | 7[6] | .. | 6 | 20 | 32 |
| Paper (tons) | 12 | 65[7] | 8 | .. | 104[5] |
| Matches (millions) | 13[8] | 24 | .. | 27 | 68 |
| Petr. refining (tons) | 500 | 1,300 | .. | 730 | 1,890 |
| Cement (tons) | 470 | 600 | 260 | 900 | 1,040 |

[1] Output per production worker.    [2] Establishments with 11 or more workers.
[3] Excl. rice milling & small grain mills in villages.
[4] 1956.         [5] Output per production worker 1939.
[6] Members of Chamber of Textile Industry, producing about 70 per cent of total output.        [7] 1955.
[8] Members of Chamber of Chemical Industry, producing about 70 per cent of total output.

*Source:* UN, *Dev. of Manufacturing*, p. 71.

For 1954 a United Nations study[1] put 'value added' per person in manufacturing establishments employing 10 or more persons at $900, compared with $1,500 for Turkey in 1950, $1,800 for Israel in 1951/2, and $5,200 for the United States in 1947; the comparable figure for Lebanon in 1955 was nearly $1,500.[2] Table 24 gives some figures on physical output per worker in certain industries, which indicate a level of productivity, at the respective dates, roughly equal to that of Turkey, less than one half that of Israel and from a ninth to a third that of the United States.

The third study covers 67 projects, with an aggregate investment of £E50·5 million, which started production in 1960/1.[3] Net output per worker was put at $3,800 in the mineral products industry, $8,900 in chemicals, $4,500 in food processing, $2,500 in engineering and metals, and $2,700 in textiles. The author of the

[1] *Dev. of Manufacturing*, p. 70.        [2] Indust. Census of 1955.
[3] NPC, Memo. no. 555.

study, however, believes that the estimates of output are exaggerated, and points out that they are out of line with both those of other countries[1] and those for 1957 which were: $750, $880, $1,000, $850, and $1,100 respectively.

Output per worker is the most commonly used measure of productivity. Other measures are the capital-output and the net to gross ratio. As regards the first, in 1947 the over-all ratio of capital to 'value added' in manufacturing industry was 1·10; in food processing it was 1·04, in textiles 0·56, in chemicals 2·77, in mineral products 1·84, and in engineering and metal products 2·61.[2] The abovementioned study of 67 projects showed that in 1960/1 the capital-output ratio had risen to 1·72; the corresponding ratios for the various branches were: food 0·55, textiles 1·77, chemicals 3·0, minerals 0·20, and engineering 0·99, but too much significance should not be attached to these changes since the number of projects studied was small.

As for the net to gross ratio, it is rather low and has not shown any definite trend. The ratio of 'value added' to 'value of total output' was 0·32 in 1947, 0·29 in 1952, 0·35 in 1956, 0·27 in 1958, and 0·29 in 1960. The first reason for the lowness of this ratio is the nature of Egyptian industry; most branches confine themselves to relatively simple processing and few have reached the stage of elaboration where raw materials form a very small part of total costs. Secondly, there is the relatively high cost of many raw materials and the high proportion of rejects in severa lfactories. Other factors are the low capital investment, which means that the value added by capital is correspondingly small, and the low productivity of labour and hence the low level of wages.

The factors affecting the productivity of Egyptian industry may be studied under the following headings: size of market; availability and cost of power and transport; cost and quality of raw materials; state and use of equipment; efficiency of managers and technicians; efficiency of labour; and government policy.

### Size of Market

The Egyptian population is sufficiently big to support most industries at an adequate scale.[3] But this is largely offset by the low

[1] UN, Dept. of Soc. Aff., *Patterns of Industrial Growth* (NY, 1960), pp. 60–61 and Jan Tinbergen, *The Design of Development* (Baltimore, 1958), p. 73.
[2] See Issawi, *EMC*, Table XXII, p. 144.
[3] The most exhaustive discussion of this subject is E. A. G. Robinson, ed., *Economic Consequences of the Size of Nations* (1960).

per-capita income owing to the small percentage of the population engaged in the labour force and the low productivity per man, especially in agriculture and some services. As a result, the total output of Egypt is probably not much larger than that of a city like Baltimore with a million inhabitants.

The purchasing power available for industrial goods is, however, much smaller than that of Baltimore. In the first place, a study of family budgets in 1957 showed that 64 per cent of total expenditure went to food and only 20 per cent to such items of industrial origin as clothing, fuel, and household utensils, to which should be added a substantial fraction representing the amount spent on processed foods.[1] Demand for industrial goods will increase only slowly and a projection for 1977 shows 61 per cent still being absorbed by food.

Secondly, there is the heterogeneity of the consumers, which breaks up the market into several small sectors. This is best seen in dress, where the differences between town and country, westernized and traditional, are obvious.

Thirdly, Egyptian consumers, having for long drawn on the products of all the leading nations, are quality-conscious and prefer foreign to domestic goods. Until very recently this was aggravated by the class structure which put a large proportion of the country's purchasing power in the hands of the rich, whose purchase of domestic products was very small. But, on the one hand, the quality of many Egyptian goods has greatly improved. And more important, the prohibition of imports and the various measures taken by the government against the rich have both levelled incomes and diverted purchasing power from foreign to local goods.

The market for Egyptian industry has been enlarged mainly by import substitution and whereas twenty-five, or even fifteen, years ago most goods in the shops were of foreign origin, today the vast majority of consumer goods, including durables, is Egyptian. But this process is approaching its end, since imports of consumer goods now represent only a very small fraction of total sales. Henceforth the market will have to be widened by raising productivity, a much slower process.

*Transport and Power*

Within the valley, transport costs in Egypt, whether by rail or river, are moderate but the extreme length of the country relatively

---

[1] NPC, Memo. no. 40A; of the 64 per cent spent on food 50 was on food products and 14 on agricultural produce.

to its area constitutes a handicap. In the deserts, however, where practically all Egyptian mining takes place, lack of adequate transport greatly adds to costs and makes it uneconomical to exploit certain deposits.

In the past Egyptian industry was burdened by the high cost of imported fuels, first coal and then oil, and by the unreliability of electric power and its high cost arising from dear fuel, small scale of production, and low load factor. The position gradually improved and by 1954 electric power, though still expensive to household and other consumers, was being delivered to industry at 1·3 cents per kwh., compared with 0·6 in Italy, 0·8 in the United States, and 1·1 in the United Kingdom.[1] The increasing provision of cheap hydro-electricity, and greater efficiency in thermal plants, may gradually narrow these differentials and expensive power is no longer a major impediment.

## Raw Materials

The lack of a cheap and abundant supply of raw materials has not prevented countries which possess capital, enterprise, and skills, such as Switzerland, from attaining the first rank of industrial powers, but it undoubtedly constitutes a further obstacle in addition to the many facing Egypt. In recent years several new minerals have been discovered and some are being exploited, but inadequate transport, lack of water, and the poor mining equipment used raise costs greatly. Thus good glass sand is to be found in Sinai but its delivered price in Cairo is twice as high as that of imported Belgian sand,[2] and chrome and copper are also expensive. Similarly imports have replaced soda ash formerly produced in Wadi Natrun, after the deposits had deteriorated. And the costs of iron ore carried from Aswan to the steel mill near Cairo must be very high indeed.

The position is much better as regards agricultural raw materials but here too there are grave deficiencies. In the first place such basic materials as wood, rubber, jute, tobacco, and silk are not available. Secondly, some products, although cheap, are of inferior quality, for example wool, or flax, the latter being well below medium-grade Belgian fibre and having to be mixed with it before becoming fit for use;[3] or are spoiled in the course of processing, such as hides where annual losses due to the use of sharp instruments have been put at

[1] UN, *Dev. of Manufacturing*, p. 78.
[2] Arthur D. Little, Inc., *Final Report* (Cambridge, Mass, 1954), p. 108.
[3] Ibid. p. 79.

£E150,000 and only 75 per cent of skins are judged to be of first-class quality.[1] Thirdly, it is often impossible to rely on a large supply of uniform quality; this is most apparent for vegetables and fruits. Fourthly, agricultural produce often contains an inordinate amount of impurities; thus milk has for long been a subject of complaint and recently industries using sesame and cotton seed drew attention to the large admixture of foreign matter in them.[2] Lastly, owing to protection and the high costs of production, the price of many Egyptian products is higher than that prevailing in most other countries, for example, sugar, milk, maize, and wheat; and, in a few cases, local exigencies have led to the use of a more expensive raw material—for example, glucose is made from maize, not potatoes as in other countries, which raises its cost.

A special case is that of Egyptian cotton which, owing to the prohibition on the importation of foreign staples, is the only kind available to the local textile industry. In other countries Egyptian cotton is used for counts of 30 to 180, but in Egypt it is used for counts of 16 for which Indian cotton, which is 40 per cent cheaper, is used elsewhere. The paradoxical result is that the best cotton in the world is woven into cheap cloth for mass consumption, accounting for 60 per cent of the cost of the cloth; it is as though mahogany were used for kitchen tables. As pointed out below, however, the Egyptian government has at last decided to import American cotton, releasing Egyptian for export (p. 324).

Still worse is the fate of industries purchasing intermediate goods from another Egyptian industry. The outstanding example at the moment is steel, which is both expensive and below foreign standards. Egyptian refractory bricks have also been found unsatisfactory by other industries. In 1953 one of the caustic soda plants was selling its products for £E65 a ton, compared to an import price of 40.[3] In 1959 the bottling industry was complaining that domestic caps were expensive, of poor quality, and delayed in delivery; that local bottles were dear and, not being coloured, unsuitable; and that the price charged for sugar was very high.[4] Egyptian industries also pay more for their paper boxes and bags, their glass jars and above all their tin cans than do their foreign competitors.

[1] NPC, Memo. no. 454. See also A. D. Little, Inc., *Opportunities for Industrial Development in Egypt* (Cairo, 1955), pp. 86–90.
[2] Fed. of Ind., *Yb. 1961*, pp. 156 & 182.
[3] A. D. Little, Inc., *The Egyptian Chemical Industry* (Cambridge, Mass., 1955).
[4] *Ég. indust.*, Jan. 1959.

The great dependence of many Egyptian industries on imported raw materials also constitutes a severe handicap; examples are the match industry which imports all its raw materials except glue and cardboard and where in 1955 imports amounted to £E400,000 and sales to 1·1 million;[1] the pharmaceutical industry where in 1959 the corresponding figures were £E1·1 and 1·8 million;[2] the cigarette industry, which depends almost entirely on imports; brewing, which uses foreign malt and hops; and the rayon and rubber industries. This dependence leads, in the first place, to relatively high costs for certain products which Egypt does not import in bulk. Secondly, and far more important, there are periodic shortages caused by lack of foreign exchange; in 1960 this occurred in the electric bulbs, storage batteries, radios, building materials, and ice industries.[3] Alternatively, a sudden change in sources of supply, or in commercial policy, may lead to sharp rises in prices, for example the price of certain raw materials used by the metallurgical industry 'rose in certain cases to 70 per cent as compared with the previous year, as importation was often possible only under the barter system'.[4] The situation is often aggravated by the fact that relatively high duties continue to be levied on producers goods used by certain industries.[5]

The combined effect of all these factors is reflected in the high proportion of the cost of raw materials, which in 1956 represented 67 per cent of the gross value of output, compared with 65 in 1947.

### Equipment

In its early stages, Egyptian industry relied heavily on second-hand equipment. This policy was justified in so far as it reduced the proportion of a scarce factor, capital, relatively to an abundant one, labour, but it naturally also reduced both labour productivity and the output-input ratio. During the war machinery deteriorated rapidly, owing to intensive use and inadequate maintenance. In the post-war period there was much re-equipment, in 1954 imports of second-hand machinery were prohibited, and the large expansion of the last few years has been based entirely on new equipment. All this has appreciably raised productivity and decreased the amount of

[1] Ibid. Jan. 1956.   [2] Ibid. Feb. 1960.
[3] Fed. of Ind., *Yb. 1961*, pp. 73, 75, 104, & 152.
[4] NBE, *Econ. B.*, nos. 3 & 4, 1960.
[5] See complaints of electrical equipment industry in Fed. of Ind., *Yb. 1961*, pp. 76–77.

waste but, given Egypt's 'factor mix', one wonders whether this process has not been carried too far under the influence of technicians who naturally want the best available machinery and are unfamiliar with the economics of production.[1]

Another factor reducing productivity is the existence of excess capacity. This was particularly great in the early post-war period, when the effects of war-time expansion were reinforced by shortage of raw materials.[2] A United Nations study showed that in 1952–4 utilization of capacity ranged from 4 per cent in fruit preserving and 8 in canning to 88 in cement and 96 in sugar.[3] A study by the Industrial Bank in 1957 put excess capacity in both rice decortication and cotton ginning at 50 per cent.[4] In recent years demand has caught up with capacity in several industries but shortages of raw materials often hold up production. And it remains true that in most industries correction of imbalances and improvement of organization would give higher returns than the introduction of new machinery.[5]

### Efficiency of Managers and Technicians

As in other backward countries, lack of entrepreneurship and managerial skills is the biggest single obstacle impeding industrial progress, and nationalization, far from enabling the country to by-pass it, has merely strung red-tape across the path. The most authoritative study on this subject concluded that all the 58 plants studied 'suffered from critical shortages of competent administrators, experienced professional staff, and trained supervisors'. It drew a sympathetic picture of managers in private enterprises: 'There are few top managers in any country who spend more time and money keeping abreast of world-wide developments in their industries than the managing directors and general managers of Mehalla, Kafreldawar, and Misr Rayon Company.' In contrast the 'old-line government enterprises [e.g. public works and until recently the railways] give the impression of being overstaffed and unduly burdened with red-tape'. On the other hand the new Organizations, such as the Suez Canal Authority and Oil Refinery, 'are headed by young and competent administrators, in a great many cases by officer-engineers

---

[1] Harbison & Ibrahim, p. 53.     [2] Said, *Iqtisadiat misr*, p. 289.
[3] *Dev. of Manufacturing*, p. 81.     [4] *Ind. Bank R.*, no. 2, 1957.
[5] Thus, in the paper industry, 'quality could be raised appreciably by technical improvements in methods of production and by the modification of existing equipment' (Little, *Final Rep.*, p. 108).

drawn from the Egyptian Army, who are eager to adopt any procedure or technique, foreign or domestic, which they think will work'. But even in the refinery, 'it was difficult to develop a new spirit in the old working forces which were accustomed to the routines of government bureaucracy'.[1]

* The general overstaffing of administrative and clerical grades, partly owing to nepotism and partly to inadequate management, is shown by the fact that in 1956 there were, in addition to 3,300 employers, 29,000 salaried employees compared with 263,000 workers in establishments with 10 or more persons, and that the remuneration of the employees was £E9·9 million compared to 25·7 million for the workers.[2] A study made some years ago by Said showed that, compared with the United Kingdom, the proportion of salaried employees to the total labour force was higher in six out of the seven industries analysed.[3] At the same time the inadequacy of the foremen and other intermediary personnel is generally admitted to be one of the major weaknesses of Egyptian industry.[4]

The government has attempted to develop managerial skills by founding, with the help of the International Labour Organization and the United Nations, a Vocational Training and Productivity Centre, and Institutes of Public Administration and of Personnel Management.[5] It may be safely stated, however, that the beneficial effects of these measures will be outweighed by the adverse consequences of the nationalizations and sequestrations.

As regards technicians, there has been a very marked improvement in recent years, owing to the entry into industry of many thousands of Egyptians who have studied abroad. The great expansion of local engineering faculties has also helped considerably: 'In the opinion of outside observers, training for engineering, particularly at Cairo University, is fairly up to date by Western standards.'[6] But it goes without saying that shortage of technicians is still a major problem in many industries; thus in 1960 both the cotton textile and the ice industry complained of the lack of qualified personnel.[7]

[1] Harbison & Ibrahim, pp. 50, 63, 66 & 67.

[2] *Census of Indust. Production, 1956* (in Ar., 1959), p.27.

[3] *Iqtisadiat misr*, p. 260.

[4] See Yusif Sayigh, 'Management–Labour Relations in Selected Arab Countries', *Internat. Labour R.*, June 1958.

[5] For details see Harbison & Ibrahim, pp. 124–9.

[6] Ibid. p. 119.

[7] Fed. of Ind., *Yb. 1961*, pp. 37 & 152.

*Efficiency of Labour*

It is certain that the efficiency of Egyptian workmen has considerably risen during the last forty years. Thus in the post-war period
the Mehalla company has doubled its production and decreased its labor
force by 40 per cent. Within eight years the Kafreldawar company tripled
its output with no net additions to its labor force. . . . Some of the
reduction in employment is undoubtedly the result of laborsaving
machinery. Most of it, however, is probably attributable to the more
permanent commitment of a stable industrial labor force.[1]

But there is equally no doubt that the productivity of Egyptian
workmen is still far below that to be found in the developed countries. 'In many factories which we visited in Egypt, six to eight
workers were employed to produce what one, with comparable
machinery and equipment, would turn out in the United States.'[2]

Many factors account for the low productivity of Egyptian workmen. First there is their poor health, congested housing, and inadequate food. Secondly, there is the prevailing illiteracy and lack of
training. This is gradually being remedied by the spread of technical
and general education and by the growing habit of providing in-
training. Nevertheless lack of skill still shows itself in the high
percentage of waste products. Thus, to take only one example, in the
finer counts of cotton yarn, waste amounts to 12 per cent, compared
with 4–5 per cent in England, and the Misr textile works installed
labour-saving machinery primarily to reduce waste of raw materials.[3]
A third important factor is absenteeism and the high turnover of
labour, owing to the fact that Egyptian workmen, like those of most
underdeveloped countries, have not completely cut their rural ties
and often leave the factory to help in the picking of cotton on their
relatives' farms. Thus a study of one factory showed that, between
its foundation in 1938 and the end of 1953, its 'separation rate' was
535 per cent.[4] This, however, has been partly overcome by the
provision, by the larger firms, of canteens, housing, and other
amenities. Thus the building of a 'workers city' at Mahalla, for
employees of the Misr Spinning and Weaving Company, reduced
absenteeism from 9 per cent in 1946 to 5 per cent in 1949 and the
percentage of workers leaving from 35 to 5 per cent.[5]

Other adverse factors include the lack of financial or other

[1] Harbison & Ibrahim, p. 53.                [2] Ibid. p. 136.
[3] Said, *Iqtisadiat misr*, p. 245; Harbison & Ibrahim, p. 52.
[4] Harbison & Ibrahim, p. 82.
[5] Rep. to ann. meeting of shareholders, 17 Dec. 1949.

incentives for greater productivity and the sense of frustration produced by the unfamiliar factory discipline. To these should be added inadequate leadership and supervision.

Briefly, most of the alleged deficiencies of industrial labor are attributable to more fundamental deficiencies of management. Haphazard recruitment, lack of training, excessively high accident rates and low productivity are evidences of the unwillingness or inability of employers to invest in effective development of the human resources they employ.[1]

The Egyptian workman has shown himself to be intelligent and adaptable and given better leadership and training, as well as more favourable living conditions, there is no reason why he should not equal those of other countries.

Low wages must, however, be set off against low productivity. In 1954 average hourly earnings in manufacturing in Egypt were 11 cents, compared with 10 in India, 20 in Mexico, 23 in Japan, 28 in Italy, 38 in France, 40 in Germany, 52 in the United Kingdom and Puerto Rico, and 181 in the United States,[2] and since then the gap between Egypt and the more advanced countries has widened. In some industries Egyptian labour costs are higher than those of all but the most high-wage countries, but in others they are lower. Thus in 1951 the average number of workers per 1,000 spindles was about 16 and in some modern plants it was as low as 6; the corresponding figures for Western Europe was 5 and for the United States 4; in Egypt a worker tended 2–4 looms against 6 in Europe.[3] At that time Egyptian wages in textiles averaged 11 cents an hour, coming near the bottom of the international scale.[4] But the measures taken in 1961, shortening the working week, prohibiting overtime, and forcing establishments to take on extra workers (see below, p. 194) are bound to raise labour costs.

## Government Policy

The help given to Egyptian industry by the government has been immense; indeed it is no exaggeration to say that without it most industries would not have survived. This help has primarily taken the form of prohibitive duties or outright prohibitions on imports

---

[1] Harbison & Ibrahim, p. 138.          [2] UN, *Dev. of Manufacturing*, p. 75.
[3] F. Ungricht, in *J. du commerce & de la marine* (Alex.), 6 Nov. 1961; Abdalla Abaza in *al-Ahram*, Apr. 1952. It is interesting to note that for both spinning and weaving the Egyptian figures for 1951 were almost identical with those for Lebanon in 1961 (see Ind. Inst. of Lebanon, study on textile industry, mimeo).
[4] ILO, *Textile Wages: an internat. study* (Geneva, 1953).

of competing goods; of exemption from duty of imported capital goods; of generous fiscal treatment of depreciation charges and reserves; of advancement of credit; and, more recently, of large export subsidies. Further helpful measures have been the recent standardization of weights and measures;[1] the consolidation funds set in the textile and other industries which fix specifications, control quality, carry out research, give financial assistance to members, and promote exports;[2] and a certain amount of prospection and research. The government's expansion of technical and vocational education, and the various measures taken by it to provide training,[3] have also been of assistance to industry.

On the other hand industry has suffered from certain government measures. Price controls have often been clumsily applied. Excise duties are levied on many products used as raw materials by other industries, for example sugar, and the same applies to customs duties on certain products. The wood-working industry has complained of the quarantine restrictions on imported wood.[4] The prohibition of import of cotton, to protect local growers, has already been mentioned and more generally the attempt simultaneously to protect both agriculture and industry has deprived the latter of many of the benefits of the tariff. Lastly, many industries have greatly suffered from bureaucratic restrictions and red tape. Thus in 1958 the mining industry complained about the restriction of movement in mining zones by the military and about the multiplicity of authorities charged with enforcing laws applicable to it, such as those on industrial and commercial establishments, quarantine, supply, customs, traffic, security and social legislation, as well as those on mining and quarrying.[5] The nationalization of industry could be used to simplify some procedures but it would be optimistic to believe that it will be. And, needless to say, the removal of hundreds of managers and owners under the nationalizations and sequestrations of 1961 and their replacement by government officials or army officers has already had a harmful effect on efficiency.

### LABOUR CONDITIONS

There is reason to believe that, in the early 1930's, real wages in industry were lower than in 1914.[6] The expansion of industry, the

---

[1] Berque, *Les Arabes*, pp. 100–2.     [2] *Akher Saa*, spec. issue on industry.
[3] For an account of the work done and the results achieved see Min. of Ind., *Productivity & Vocational Training Dept.* (n.d.).
[4] Fed. of Ind., *Yb. 1961*, pp. 36, 76, & 110.     [5] *Ég. indust.*, Apr. 1958.
[6] M. Clerget, *Le Caire* (Cairo, 1934), ii. 154–8.

growth of trade unionism and government intervention on behalf of labour have, however, resulted in distinct improvement. This has taken the form of somewhat higher wages, much shorter hours, better working conditions, and the provision by the larger firms of various amenities.

### Wages, Hours, and Unemployment

Real wages declined during the Second World War, as prices outstripped money wages. According to a study made by the National Bank, the pre-war level had not quite been recovered by 1955, but this conclusion is open to grave objections and it seems much more probable that real wages had returned to that level by 1951 or 1952 at the latest.[1] Since then money wages have risen appreciably, from PT189 a week in January 1951 and 199 in January 1952 to 233 in January 1959, while the cost-of-living index remained practically unchanged.[2]

A regional breakdown for 1957, the latest available, shows the Frontier Provinces, Suez, and the Canal Zone to be far above the average, with PT542, 496, and 302 respectively; Cairo at and Alexandria just below the average, with 232 and 213 respectively; and the rest of the country below the average.[3] These differences are mainly because of the presence in the former zones of the petroleum industry, whose wages are far above the average; other high-wage industries are basic metals, transport, electricity, and gas and water.[4]

The reasons for the lowness of wages are clear enough. There is the low productivity of labour, owing to malnutrition, lack of training, poor equipment, and inadequate management. There is also the continual drift to the towns from the enormous surplus rural population, resulting in a large reserve of unemployed who depress wages; for, low as they are, money wages in the towns are twice as high as in the country and real wages are also higher. Finally, there

[1] NBE, *Econ. B.*, no. 2, 1957. Since no official figures are available before 1942, the Bank's study assumes that wages in that year were equal to the pre-war ones; but by 1942 the cost-of-living index was 80 per cent higher than in 1939 and on both *a priori* grounds, given the great wartime demand for labour, and in the light of available information it is impossible to assume that wages remained unchanged; in 1938 weekly wages were about PT50–60.

[2] The official index actually showed a small decline, but there is reason to believe that it does not reflect the real rise in prices in recent years.

[3] *Statist. of Employment, Wages & Working Hours*, July 1957 (in Ar.).

[4] *Statist. Pocket Yb. 1959.*

was the very strong bargaining position of the employers, which the trade unions were not able to match.

Money and real wages changed little between 1955 and 1961 but remuneration of workmen was appreciably increased by Law No. 111 of July 1961 which states that 25 per cent of net profits (after deduction of 5 per cent for reserves and 5 per cent for purchase of government bonds) should be distributed to employees and workers as follows: 10 per cent to be given to them directly, 5 per cent for social services provided by the enterprise, and 10 per cent for 'central social services'.[1] In February 1962 the minimum wage, formerly PT16–22, was raised to PT25 and wages above that level were increased by up to 10 per cent.[2]

One last remark may be made regarding the wage structure.

It would be very difficult indeed to introduce a system of equal pay for equal work in Egypt. The high cost-of-living allowances and the practice of annual increases are now firmly rooted in the minds of both employers and workers. Even piece rates are seldom, if ever, based upon systematic job studies. . . . In fact we know of no company in Egypt which applies a wage scheme based on a systematic study of work incentives as a means of increasing labor productivity.[3]

Working hours have been steadily reduced, from a pre-war average of about 55 per week to 51 in the early post-war years and 50 in 1957. Even more important was the sharp reduction in the proportion of firms working excessively long hours. In the 1937 census 57 per cent of the establishments indicating the number of hours worked had a working week of over 60 hours and 17 per cent worked 80 hours or more. By 1951 these percentages had declined to 13 and 2 and in 1957 only three small industries had a working week of over 60 hours. There is no evidence that this reduction decreased productivity and the limitation of the working week to 48 hours by Law No. 46 of 1958 was probably a wise measure. The same cannot however be said of Law No. 113 of 1961, which not only fixed a 7-hour 6-day week but prohibited overtime.

The proportion of women employed is small, but has shown a slight rise over the pre-war figure. In 1957 nearly 7 per cent of workers in transformation industries were women but in other

[1] The average share of employees and workmen in the profits of 13 industrial companies in 1961 was £E20·3 (*al-Ahram*, 18 Apr. 1962). A ceiling of £E50 a year per worker has been imposed (ibid. 28 Apr. 1962).          [2] Ibid. 26 Feb. 1962.
[3] Harbison & Ibrahim, p. 94; for further details see pp. 88–94.

branches they accounted for less than 1 per cent; women are mainly concentrated in the textile and clothing industries. As for children, although their employment has diminished, they 'constitute a very important, though not officially recognized, segment of the industrial labor force', especially in the smaller enterprises.[1]

No reliable statistics exist regarding unemployment. The sample labour survey of 1960 put the unemployed at 4·2 per cent of the whole labour force, but it is difficult to interpret this figure since the treatment of rural unemployment is not clear.[2] There is relatively little seasonal unemployment—because seasonal industries, for example cotton ginning and sugar crushing, recruit their labour mainly from the countryside—or cyclical unemployment, because of the stable character of Egyptian industry. On the other hand there is a large reserve of wholly or partly unemployed labour; a rough calculation put underemployment in 1958 at about 10 per cent of working time.[3] As in other countries, skilled labour suffers relatively little from unemployment.

## Working-Class Organization and Action

The earliest Egyptian trade unions were founded at the beginning of this century, and in the 1930's there were several union-led strikes, but the movement did not receive official recognition until 1942.[4] Law No. 85 of that year authorized the formation of unions, except for state and municipal employees, hospital workers, and agricultural workers; unions were allowed to form federations but were forbidden to engage in political activities and close supervision was maintained over them. By the end of 1951 488 unions with 145,000 members had been registered, compared with 200 with 80,000 in 1942.

In 1952 the revolutionary government modified the previous law by extending permission to form unions to all workers and employees, except for government and municipal officials; by authorizing the formation of a Confederation of union federations; by providing that wherever three-fifths of the workers of any given factory are members of a union the remaining two-fifths become members

[1] Ibid. p. 76.   [2] *Coll. Basic Statist. Data*, p. 51.
[3] NBE, *Econ. B.*, no. 2, 1960.
[4] For the history of the labour movement in Egypt see Issawi, *EMC*, pp. 172–4; al-Gritly in *Ég. contemp.*, 1947, pp. 534–54; M. T. Audsley, 'Labour and Social Affairs in Egypt', *M.E. Affairs* (St Antony's Papers, no. 4, 1958); Harbison & Ibrahim, pp. 174–82.

automatically; and by compelling employers to deduct union subscriptions from wages and salaries if requested to do so by the union. The next few years saw a rapid spread of unions and by 1958 there were 1,377 with a membership of 433,000. In 1959 Law No. 91 reorganized the structure of the trade union movement, reducing the number of unions to 59. Most unions form part of industry-wide federations and in 1957 a Confederation of Labour was established. By then, although agriculture and small enterprises remained untouched by unionization, practically all workers employed in large or medium factories or trading establishments, as well as transport workers, were organized and it was judged that 'Egypt's statistical proportion of union membership compares favourably with that of Western Europe, and it probably exceeds that in nearly all other economically under-developed countries'.[1] Rather more than half the total are plant unions and the rest craft unions. Union officials must be employed in the respective establishment, which has prevented the emergence of a full-time leadership.

Until recently unions were in a weak bargaining position and tended to be dominated by their employers although long before nationalization this had been replaced by government domination. In the first place Law No. 105 of 1948 provided for compulsory arbitration in 'vital' industries and Decree No. 319 of 1952 extended this to all industries. Secondly, union leaders are in practice nominated by, and work closely with, the government officials in charge of labour relations. Lastly, the defence of workers against employers and the determination of the relationships between management and labour have been increasingly undertaken by the government, not the unions. And it goes without saying that the recent nationalizations have greatly increased government control over the unions since practically the sole employer is now the government. The new role reserved for trade unions has been thus described:

They are no longer groupings for the seizing of rights or defence of interests in opposition to employers but have become centres for the concentration of workers and parliaments for the expression of their opinions; unions are no longer charitable societies helping the distressed and treating the sick—they must become centres of revolutionary radiation and instruments for pushing forward the wheels of production.[2]

[1] Harbison & Ibrahim, p. 183. In 1961 it was estimated that 28 per cent of all industrial workers and 11 per cent of commercial workers belonged to unions (*al-Ahram*, 8 Dec. 1961).

[2] *al-Ahram al-iqtisadi*, 1 Dec. 1961.

*Social Legislation*

In Egypt, as elsewhere, industrialization was allowed to produce many horrors before any attempt was made to regulate it and protect its victims; however, during the last thirty years, the record of the Egyptian government in the field of social legislation has been a good one. No attempt will be made here to survey the various measures,[1] but only to summarize the most recent laws on labour and social insurance.

Law No. 91 of 1959, codifying previous legislation, fixes the working day at 8 hours for adults (reduced in 1961 to 7) and 6 for juveniles; grants a weekly rest, annual and sick leave to all workers; prohibits the employment in any industry of children under 12; grants maternity leave to women; fixes minimum wages; grants indemnities for layoffs and limits the employer's right to dismiss workers. Earlier laws had made provisions for free clinical and medical treatment, for cheap food and, in places distant from inhabited localities, for living accommodation, all at the expense of the employer. The law also provides for the establishment of Workers' Councils to ensure co-operation between labour and management. In July 1961 Law No. 114 decreed that boards of directors of companies, which were not to consist of more than seven members, should contain one workers' and one employees' representative. It may therefore be concluded that the Egyptian worker's basic rights are at present very well protected by legislation, but it remains to be seen how the laws will be applied now that the government has so largely replaced private employers. There is also much to be said for raising further the minimum age of employment.

In addition the larger establishments have, over the years, developed extensive social-welfare services in the form of canteens, restaurants, medical care, recreational facilities, co-operative stores, transport, housing, mosques, educational facilities, and savings, pension and insurance schemes[2] and some unions had their own insurance and welfare plans.[3]

In 1936 legislation defined employers' liability for accidents affecting industrial and commercial workers; in 1942 insurance against work accidents was made compulsory, and in 1950 benefits were

---

[1] For details see Issawi, *EMC*, pp. 175-8; Mahmud Gamal al-Din Zaki, 'Qanun al-amal', in *Buhuth*, pp. 595-618; Audsley in *M.E. Affairs*; Harbison & Ibrahim, pp. 149-69.    [2] See details ibid. pp. 95-96.
[3] See, for e.g., the account of the textile workers of Mahalla's scheme in *al-Ahram al-iqtisadi*, 1 Nov. 1961.

extended and workmen were granted compensation for occupational diseases. Law No. 202 of 1958 extended the coverage of such legislation to all workers except agricultural labourers and domestic servants and replaced the lump sum previously payable by a pension.

Social insurance was first attempted in 1950, in the form of social security for the aged, the disabled, widows, and orphans, but the scheme was soon abandoned. In 1955 Law No. 419 introduced a plan for disability and life insurance and old-age pensions. The insurance funds are financed by contributions by the employers of 7 per cent of their payrolls, 2 per cent being for insurance against death and disability and 5 per cent for old-age pensions; workers contribute 5 per cent towards the pensions. Coverage was greatly extended by Law No. 92 of 1959 and by the end of the year 269,000 workers belonged to the insurance schemes and the income of the funds had risen to £E4·2 million.[1] Lastly, mention may be made of the plan under way to provide compulsory health insurance for 1·5 million employees and workers, together with their families. The scheme is to be started in the main towns and gradually extended to the countryside. It provides for hospitalization, physician care, laboratory facilities and medicine as well as payment for partial or total disability. Costs are estimated at £E48·8 million over a ten-year period and are to be financed by contributions equal to 7 per cent of wages, 6 from the employer and 1 from the worker.[2]

[1] *Coll. Basic Statist. Data*, pp. 196–7; see also below, p. 254.
[2] *al-Ahram*, 2 Nov. 1961 & 27 Mar. 1962.

# IX

# Transport and Communications

---

*Good roads, canals and navigable rivers, by diminishing the expense of carriage, put the remote parts of the country nearly on a level with those in the neighbourhood of a town; they are, on that account, the greatest of all improvements.* ADAM SMITH.

*The legitimate object of government is to do for a community of people whatever they need to have done, but cannot do at all, or cannot do so well for themselves, in their separate and individual capacities.* ABRAHAM LINCOLN.

Broadly speaking, it may be said that in contrast to many under-developed countries, such as Iran and Turkey in the Middle East and most countries of Latin America, Egypt is not seriously handicapped by inadequate transport facilities. Until very recently transport problems were much the same as those of other countries and the remedies proposed and adopted differed only in that the mainly state-owned and managed Egyptian railways were in a much stronger position to combat road and river competition, which they fought by legislative and administrative as well as by economic action. However, between 1956 and 1961 railways, airlines, country bus lines, shipping and inland water transport, as well as bus and tramway lines within cities, were successively nationalized, and now practically the whole of public transport is government-owned and operated.

## RAILWAYS

It has already been seen that Egypt's railway system developed early and rapidly, and by 1914 was adequate for the country's needs. It consisted of the standard-gauge Egyptian State Railways, which until recently accounted for some 85 per cent of traffic, and three light railway lines, built and operated by private capital.

During the First World War Egypt's railways were linked to those of Palestine but after that there was little further extension until 1940. Once more, however, wartime construction increased the length of the State Railways from 5,766 km. in 1939 to 6,799 in 1945, while post-war construction raised the total to 7,102 in 1949. In 1959 the light railways totalled over 1,400 km., of which 1,126 were open to traffic.

Egypt thus has some 14 km. of railway for every 100 km. of inhabited area, a figure which approaches the Western European standard and is well above that of other underdeveloped areas. Expressed in terms of population, the comparison is much less favourable to Egypt, which has little over 2 km. of line for every 10,000 inhabitants.[1]

As regards transport, the country falls into three zones: Upper Egypt, the Delta, and Fayyum. The Nile valley south of Cairo bears a double-track line as far as Suhag; from there a single line runs to Shallal, just south of Aswan. In 1960 this was extended to the site of the High Dam. Three factors have recently appreciably increased traffic on the southern lines: the construction of the High Dam, the large-scale production of chemical fertilizers at Aswan, and the transport of iron ore from Aswan to Cairo. Fayyum is served by a branch line, supplemented by a network of light railways. The towns of the Delta and Canal zone are connected by double tracks with Cairo, while light railways provide slow cross-country transport.

Passenger traffic rose rapidly until the 1930's, when the effects of the Depression were aggravated by competition from motor buses. The number of passengers carried on all state railway lines grew from 12·6 million in 1902 to 35·3 million in 1939; the corresponding number of passenger-km. was 601 and 1,318 million respectively. During the Second World War traffic increased sharply, and the rise continued, to a peak of 88·7 million passengers and 3,188 million passenger-km. in 1956, but after that competition from buses once more made itself felt and by 1959 the number of passengers had dropped to 65·0 million. There was the same trend in the traffic of the light railways, which carried 18·5 million passengers in 1939, a peak of 28·1 million in 1951, and 12·4 million in 1959.[2]

Merchandise traffic followed a similar pattern, but the rate of growth was much slower. In 1902 3,974,000 tons of merchandise were carried 813 million ton-km. on the State Railways and by 1939 6,660,000 tons. Traffic reached a peak of 8,496,000 tons and

[1] For comparable figures on the density of railways, roads, and motor vehicles in Eastern Europe and post-war India, Pakistan, and the Middle Eastern countries see Issawi, *EMC*, ch. 8.

[2] NBE, *Econ. B.*, no. 1, 1954; *Ann. Stat.* 1957/8; *Coll. Basic Statist. Data.*

1,695 m. ton-km. in 1945 and in 1957 stood at 6,355,000 tons and 1,658 m. ton-km., at which level it remained in the next two years. In the last thirty years freight carried on the light railways has fluctuated between a peak of 1,195,000 tons in 1949 and a trough of 429,000 in 1953.[1]

Increased traffic during the war, coupled with the impossibility of replacement, put a heavy strain on rolling-stock and in the early post-war years the railways were not allowed enough funds for replacements; thus between 1933 and 1946 annual expenditures on renewals averaged only £E368,000.[2] In 1954 the Permanent Council for Production reviewed the situation and in view of the large proportion of equipment due for replacement drew up a programme for renewal and improvement involving a total expenditure of £E23·4 million.[3] In 1959 it was estimated that 40 per cent of the track, 40 per cent of steam locomotives, 24 per cent of passenger cars, and 19 per cent of freight cars were over-age.[4] The current plan, for 1960–5, provides for a total investment of £E100 million.[5]

Much progress has been made in implementing these renewal programmes, with considerable United States aid, including loans of nearly $33 millions in 1960.[6] Diesel engines began to be widely used after 1948 and had replaced steam on all lines south of Cairo by the end of 1961; the same process is scheduled for completion in the Delta by 1963.[7] There has also been considerable renewal of passenger and freight cars. In 1959 the State Railways' rolling-stock consisted of 721 locomotives, 1,583 passenger cars, and 18,307 freight cars, the two latter figures being very slightly above the corresponding pre-war ones.

Less progress has, however, been made in renewing track and signalling equipment. In recent years a conflict, which has its counterpart in other underdeveloped countries such as Turkey, has

---

[1] The State Railways are now carrying some 400,000 ton-km. per km. of line, against 500,000 in India, 350,000 in Pakistan, 1 m. in pre-war Poland, 500,000 in pre-war Hungary, and 400,000 in pre-war Yugoslavia. It would therefore seem that the railways network can adequately handle existing merchandise traffic.

[2] *al-Majlis al-daim li tanmiat al-intaj al-qaumi* (1955), p. 393.

[3] See details ibid. pp. 394–6.          [4] NPC, Memo. no. 201.

[5] *Cadre du Plan*, p. 37; see details on pp. 225–6.

[6] For a list of the main projects executed in 1952–60 see *UAR Pocket Yb. 1961*, pp. 229–32.

[7] Diesel locomotives consume 2 kg. of diesel oil per km. while steam locomotives consume 17 kg. of fuel; the complete conversion to diesel is expected to save £E4 m. a year (ibid). During and after the Second World War conversion from coal to oil had saved some £E1·5 m. p.a.

arisen between the local steel manufacturers who make rails and the railway authorities who consider the latter as falling below standard. Local rails have been used only for sidings and the shortage of foreign exchange has held up renewal of main tracks. Another bottleneck has been inadequate crew training, but this is being overcome by special programmes.

The capital value of the State Railways was officially put in June 1957 at £E86·1 million on the basis of a valuation made in 1905 plus the cumulative purchases and a certain proportion of capital expenditures and renewals since that date; allowances for depreciation brought the figure down to £E53 million.[1] In the 1930's and during the Second World War fixed capital formation in the railways averaged about £E1 million per annum but in 1948-54 it rose to some £E4 million and is now several times that figure.[2]

Before the Second World War rates had been continuously reduced, in response to the general fall in the price level and to meet motor competition. Moreover the railway tariff had been adjusted so as to encourage exports, and to help local agriculture and industry by carrying certain bulky products at reduced rates.[3] During the Second World War both passenger and freight rates were raised by 100 per cent but in 1949 passenger rates were reduced by a quarter. This increase, together with a slight rise in merchandise traffic and a considerable increase in passenger traffic, both military and civilian, raised receipts threefold. Expenses also rose, owing to higher wages and, at first, increased fuel costs because of inexperience in the use of oil; on the other hand little was spent on renovation. During the period 1940-9 net profits were £E36 million; of this it has been estimated that £E20 million represents the amount that would have normally been spent on improvements and renovations.[4]

After the war some rates were reduced, traffic declined, and much was spent on development. Consequently, the ratio of expenses to receipts, which had fallen from 85 in 1938/9 to a minimum of 48 per cent in 1944/5, rose to 83 per cent in 1946/7 and thereafter was very close to, and in some years actually exceeded, 100. At present third-class fares on main lines are reckoned at 2 millièmes per km. for trips up to 300 km., as against 1·25 millièmes in the pre-war period,

---

[1] NPC, Memo. no. 166. The corresponding adjusted figure for 1933 was £E26 m. (Abdul Aziz Mehanna & Hussein Fahmy, *Iqtisadiat al-sikak al-hadidia* (1950), p. 90.)  [2] NPC, Memo. no. 128.

[3] Hussein Fahmy, *An Inquiry into the Present Position of the Egyptian State Railways* (Cairo, 1931), p. 65 and Mehanna & Fahmy, *Iqtisadiat*, p. 206.

[4] Ahmad Abu Ismail, 'al-Nataij al-malia', *Ég. contemp.*, Jan. 1952.

and 1·4 millièmes for longer distances; second-class fares are twice as high and first-class fares four times; fares on suburban lines are much lower. These figures are somewhat below the level prevailing in other countries and there is a constant pressure to reduce them, to meet the needs of the low-income groups who form the vast majority of the passengers, or to grant special fares to various categories. As for freight rates, before the Second World War they consisted of 16 categories which ranged from 1 to 30 millièmes per ton-km. for journeys up to 250 km. During and after the war the number of categories was reduced to 11 and most rates were doubled, though some were raised in a lower proportion. Rebates are granted for bulk transport of such goods as sugar, phosphates, cement, and chemical fertilizers.[1] On the whole, local freight rates are in line with those prevailing in other countries. But although in the pre-war period merchandise traffic contributed twice as much to earnings as passenger traffic, since 1943 the latter has contributed more than freight and it would seem as though, since 1945, freight has actually been carried at a loss.[2] Present plans envisage a 25 per cent increase in passenger traffic and a rise in merchandise traffic to 10 million tons, or 20 per cent above the 1959 level, by 1965.[3]

## RIVER NAVIGATION

The navigable waterways of Egypt total 3,100 km., divided almost equally between the Nile and canals. The Nile is navigable from the southern frontier to Cairo, nearly 1,300 km. and thence along the Rosetta branch to the sea, over 200 km., but the Damietta branch can carry only small boats. Most of the irrigation canals are navigable the whole year round for boats drawing up to 120 or 150 cm. The lakes in the north of the Delta and Lake Qarun, in Fayyum, are also used for navigation.[4]

The configuration of Egypt is such that most waterways run parallel to railways, bringing the two into inevitable competition. Moreover the canals are designed primarily for irrigation, not navigation. Hence it is not surprising that water transport should have been systematically neglected. Tow-paths are inadequate and uneven, certain parts of the Nile in Upper Egypt are blocked by sand banks, river ports and landing stages are poorly equipped, and some canals

[1] NBE, *Econ. B.*, no. 1, 1954.   [2] NPC, Memo. no. 128.
[3] *UAR Pocket Yb. 1961*, p. 232.
[4] For fuller details see NBE, *Econ. B.*, no. 4, 1955 and *al-Majlis al-daim*, pp. 359–71.

are too narrow or too shallow. More serious still is the multiplying number of road and railways bridges which prevent the passage of motor vessels and impede the movement of sailing craft, which have to lower their masts. If to this is added the multiplicity of authorities whose regulations affect inland navigation and the fact that irrigation needs are given priority over those of navigation in the opening of locks and sluices, it is not surprising to discover that in many important ways the situation is less satisfactory than it was before the First World War.

In 1958 the river fleet consisted of some 12,000 units.[1] The volume of freight carried in 1932–9 averaged 4·6 million tons; in 1940–7 4·9 million tons, and in 1948–56 5·1 million.[2] Until very recently the bulk of the motorized traffic belonged to twenty-four companies, with a combined capital of £E5 million. Of these, by far the most important was Misr-Fluviale.

In 1953 the Permanent Production Council drew up an investment programme for 1954–9 totalling £E5·2 million.[3] The Plan provides for an investment of £E6·7 million in 1960–5, mainly in 54 river wharves for fuel and dry goods—including one at Aswan and another at Helwan for the transport of iron ore—and the building of a motorized river fleet, of 56 500-ton vessels, with the help of an Austrian firm. Progress has so far been slow, but in 1960 a contract was signed for the purchase of 30 motorized and 46 other barges. Another measure to help river navigation is the decision to make all new bridges or replacements of the swing or lift type.

### ROAD TRANSPORT

In spite of considerable improvements effected during the last twenty-five years, roads are still the weakest link in Egypt's transport system. Road-building outside the cities started in 1913 but proceeded very slowly, owing to opposition from the railways, and by 1936 there were only 400 km. of paved roads and another 7,000 of dirt roads. In that year, however, work began on several highways

---

[1] Of these 191 were tugs aggregating 24,000 h.p., 30 motor barges for oil with 4,500 h.p., 314 motor barges for dry goods with 37,000 h.p. and a capacity of 71,000 tons, 125 passenger steamers, 499 barges with a capacity of 68,000 tons, and 4,700 sailing boats with a capacity of 234,000 tons (NPC, Memos. nos. 128 & 142).

[2] River navigation carried an average of 3·6 m. passengers in 1940–5 and 12·4 m. in 1947–56.

[3] For details, see *al-Majlis al-daim*, pp. 364–71. Capital formation in river navigation averaged c. £E250,000 p.a. in 1929–39, fell to £E100,000 in 1940–5, and ran at a little below £E1 m. in 1948–54.

stipulated by the Anglo-Egyptian Treaty and during and after the Second World War road-building was intensified. In 1959 there were 2,621 km. of paved and 12,860 km. of unpaved roads in the cultivated part of the country and 3,169 km. of paved and 871 of unpaved roads in the deserts, a grand total of 19,521.

Egypt thus has 40 km. of roads for every 100 square km. of cultivated area, a proportion roughly equal to that of Eastern Europe and above the Middle East average. However, there are only 7 km. of road for every 10,000 inhabitants, a figure below that of India, Eastern Europe, and almost all Middle Eastern and Latin American countries. As with canals, most of the roads run parallel to the railways, thus causing further duplication.

The number of vehicles increased rapidly, from about 4,000 in 1920 to 34,000 in 1939 and a peak of 95,000 in 1955, but by 1959 it had fallen to 86,000. The number of motor-buses and lorries, which had declined during the depression years from 5,300 in 1932 to 4,000 in 1937, rose rapidly during the war and post-war years to 20,000 in 1951, at which figure it has since remained. This means that there are 10 buses and lorries and 35 passenger cars for every 10,000 inhabitants, figures well below the Middle Eastern and Latin American averages but distinctly above the Indian figure.

The quantity of goods carried by road has risen rapidly in recent years, from an annual average of 4·5 million tons in 1929–39 and again in 1940–7 to 8·9 million in 1948–56.[1] Motor-buses were estimated in 1955 to carry 39 million passengers.

Before the Second World War the amount collected by the government in taxes on motor-cars, spare parts, and petrol was roughly equal to that spent on the construction and repair of roads and bridges. In the post-war period, however, receipts have exceeded expenditures by several million pounds,[2] for example by £E4·4 million in 1954. Total fixed capital formation in road transport rose from an annual average of about £E1 million in 1932–9 to about 1·4 million in 1940–5 and around 8 million in 1948–54.

In the last few years highway construction has been accelerated. An excellent road now links Cairo with Alexandria via the Delta, supplementing the older one across the desert, and work is proceeding on a new Cairo–Port Said highway. The road to the Libyan frontier has been improved, large sections of the Upper Egypt road

[1] NPC, Memo. no. 128.
[2] Anwar Bakir, 'Contribution à l'étude du problème de la coordination des transports en Ég.', *Ég. contemp.*, July 1951.

to Aswan and the Red Sea coastal road have been paved, and work is proceeding on a road from Asiut to the Western Oases. The Plan provides for a total government investment of £E20 million on roads between cities and 6 million on roads within cities, and for another 15 and 7·2 million respectively on trucks and buses; private investment during this period is estimated at 5 million.[1] The resulting saving in time, fuel, maintenance and increased value of goods transported is put at £E4·5 million a year.[2]

## PIPELINES

In 1960 there were two products pipelines in Egypt, both originating at the Suez refineries.[3] A 6-inch pipeline, 120 km. long and with an annual capacity of 540,000 tons of benzine and kerosene, was laid between Suez and Cairo by the British army in 1943 and handed over to the Egyptian government in 1955; it is being replaced by a 10-inch 140-km. pipeline with an annual capacity of 1·8 million tons, scheduled for completion by the end of 1961, at a total cost of £E1·7 million. In 1956 the government completed a 12-inch pipeline, 131 km. long, from Suez to Mostorod, near Cairo. Designed for diesel and fuel oils, it has an annual capacity of 2·3 million tons. Total investment in this pipeline amounted to £E3·5 million and it was estimated that it would save £E1 per ton as compared with railway transport.[4] Construction is also proceeding on a 12-inch pipeline, with a capacity of 1·8 million tons, connecting Mostorod with Helwan, 40 km. away. Scheduled to start operations in 1962, its total cost is put at £E254,000.

Two other pipelines are also due for completion in 1962. A 31-km. 6-inch line is to connect Alexandria with Kafr al-Dawar; its annual capacity will be 500,000 tons of benzine and kerosene and its estimated cost £E600,000. The other is a 12-inch line from Alexandria to Tanta, 140 km. away; a branch will be extended to Mahalla al-Kubra and other branches to various points between Alexandria and Tanta; the capacity of the pipeline is 2 million tons of fuel oil and its estimated cost is £E4 million.

## AIR TRANSPORT

As in other countries, air transport has greatly developed during the last twenty-five years. The compactness of the Delta reduces one

---

[1] *Cadre du Plan*, p. 37; see details on pp. 226-7.
[2] *Akher Saa*, spec, issue on Arab industries.
[3] *al-Betrol fi'l-gumhuria al-arabia*, pp. 161-6.
[4] *al-Majlis al-daim*, p. 336.

of the chief advantages of flying-speed, but in Upper Egypt flying results in a considerable saving of time. The country now has ten airports in use: Cairo, Alexandria, Port Said, Luxor, Marsa Matruh, Aswan, Asiut, Minia, Embaba, and El Tor.[1]

Egypt's first airline, Misr Airwork, started operations in 1933; helped by wartime conditions, it extended its services in the early post-war period as far as Turkey, Iran, Ethiopia, Saudi Arabia, and Switzerland.[2] Investment in fixed capital in air transport rose from an annual average of around £E200,000 in 1932–9 to 300,000 in 1940–5 and 800,000 in 1948–54.[3]

In 1960 Misr line was nationalized and at the end of the year Misr and the Syrian airlines merged to form the United Arab Airlines. By the end of 1961 UAA was operating a route structure of 39,000 km., compared with 16,000 in 1950 and 18,000 in 1956.[4] On domestic flights the revenue-passenger load factor was 72 per cent and the revenue-weight load factor 79 per cent, but on international flights these figures fell to 49 and 60 per cent respectively, in spite of the fact that the UAA handle all government traffic and are given a priority in certain other fields; hence it is not surprising that domestic traffic shows a profit and international a loss.

Several new flights were inaugurated in 1961, including ones to Mogadiscio via Aden and Asmara; to Karachi via Dahran; to Moscow via Prague; to London; and to Lagos and Accra. Further plans for the near future include flights to New York, Conakry, Morocco, Bombay, and Tokyo via Hong Kong; some of these plans were carried out in 1962. For them longer-range aircraft are required and negotiations are under way for the purchase of 5 Boeing 320's, at a cost of $50 million, and 2 Comets, to supplement the 5 Comets, 6 Viscounts, 5 Dakotas, and the dozen other planes which constituted the fleet at the end of 1961.[5] Plans have also been made for the purchase of 11 freight-carrying aircraft.[6]

The crews are exclusively Egyptian; training teams are brought

[1] For data on activity in these airports see Min. of War, Civil Aviation Dept., *Ann. Statist. Rep. & Monthly Statist. Rep.*

[2] Another airline, Société Aérienne Internationale d'Égypte was formed after the war and operated a service to Italy but was liquidated in the early 1950's.

[3] NPC, Memo. no. 128.

[4] In 1960 2,154,000 revenue-km. were flown on domestic services and 5,528,000 on international; the number of passengers carried was 132,000 and 114,000 respectively, for a total of 56·2 and 142·7 m. passenger-km.; freight carried amounted to 680,000 and 1,442,000 ton-km. respectively.

[5] *al-Ahram*, 4 Nov. 1961.    [6] Ibid. 8 Nov. 1961.

over with new types of planes but local personnel take over within a few months. In 1961 a Civil Aviation Training Centre was established near Cairo under a joint project whereby the United Nations was to contribute slightly over $1 million and the UAR $870,000.

COMPETITION AND CO-ORDINATION

Like most countries, Egypt has been the scene of fierce competition between road, rail, and river during the last forty years. A comparison of the annual averages for 1947–56 with those for 1929–39 shows that all three forms of transport shared in the general increase in freight from 14·9 to 21·4 million tons. However, the relative share of the railways fell from 38 to 34 per cent and that of water transport from 31 to 24 per cent, while roads increased theirs from 31 to 42; it should, however, be noted that freight carried by truck travels on average a much shorter distance than that carried by rail. In passenger traffic, which rose from 188·8 to 207·7 million respectively, the railways did better, raising their share from 15 to 25 per cent. This was achieved by cutting rates, offering new services, and consequently greatly reducing profits; thus their return on capital fell from 8 per cent in 1925 to 3 per cent in 1935.[1] Moreover the railways used the power of the state to restrict other activities. Thus the State Railways had the first option in organizing transport on roads parallel to their lines and were entitled to hold 51 per cent of the stock of certain road carriers. In 1939 a Consultative Transport Council was formed, to frame and carry out a policy of co-ordination; it contained no representatives of navigation companies, road carriers, or even private railways. In 1941 river navigation was subjected to stricter control. In 1950 motor-bus transport was regulated by a law, which divided the country into zones in each of which one company was to be granted an exclusive concession, being subjected to stricter control on rates, timetables, safety regulations, speed, &c.

The whole question took on a new aspect in 1960 when all bus and river navigation lines of any consequence were nationalized. Hence, except for independent truckers and small river boats, all transport, both within and between cities, is now government owned and operated. No overall plan of co-ordination has yet been announced but it would appear that the government is closing down all light railways, replacing them by either standard-gauge lines or bus routes. It is developing new routes to serve the poorer markets,

[1] Mehanna & Fahmy, p. 121.

which tended to be neglected in the past. Some 200 new buses have also been imported to renew the rolling stock, which had run down owing to the inability of the former companies to secure import licences.

## EXTERNAL COMMUNICATIONS

Surrounded on three sides by wide stretches of desert, which lead to the relatively poor countries of Palestine, Cyrenaica, and the Sudan, Egypt from earliest antiquity relied mainly on shipping for contacts with the outside world until the exigencies of war spanned the deserts. During the First World War the Egyptian railways were connected with those of Palestine, and in 1942 a bridge was laid down across the Suez Canal, avoiding the ferry at Kantara; at the same time the Palestinian and Turkish railways were connected by a line running along the Lebanese coast. Since the Palestine war of 1948, however, the borders between Egypt and Israel and Lebanon and Israel have been closed. The Western Desert railway was during the Second World War extended beyond Marsa Matruh to Tobruq, 370 km. away, where it joins the trunk road through Cyrenaica and Tripolitania. At the present time, however, this line is not in use beyond Marsa Matruh.

To the south a desert road now connects Aswan with Wadi Halfa, bridging the gap between the Egyptian and Sudan railways. Shortly after the Second World War preliminary surveys were also made for a railway line along the eastern bank of the Nile connecting the Egyptian and Sudanese railways, which are of a narrower gauge. The project was estimated to cost £E5 million, and a small amount of work was carried out. In April 1960 an agreement was reached between the two governments for linking the railway systems of both countries by extending the Egyptian standard-gauge line to Wadi Halfa, and for relocating sections of the Sudanese track south of Wadi Halfa, which will be flooded by water impounded by the High Dam.

However, the mass of traffic still enters and leaves Egypt by sea. Goods landed in 1960 amounted to 6,359,000 tons and goods shipped to 5,408,000 tons.[1] This discrepancy between imports and exports is caused by the light weight of cotton exports, compared with metals, grains, fertilizers, and other articles of import. Consequently ships are compelled to leave Egyptian ports in ballast or, more often, loaded well below capacity. This fact may mean that bulk goods produced in Egypt can enjoy the benefit of cheap freight to foreign lands.

[1] UN, *Statist. Yb. 1961.*

Alexandria handles the bulk of exports, being by far the most important point of exit for cotton and rice; and in 1952–6 it also accounted for 66 per cent of the volume and 81 per cent of the value of imports. It is Egypt's main point of contact with Europe and America and also handles a sizeable part of the Far Eastern trade. With its outer and inner harbour sheltering 640 and 186 ha. respectively, Alexandria has the largest water area of any Mediterranean harbour. Moreover it has excellent rail, road, and canal connexions with the interior. But in spite of considerable progress since the war, including a dry dock, a petroleum port, grain elevators, new quays, and improved canal connexions, it still compares unfavourably in such matters as dock repair facilities, mechanical loading equipment, and number of floating cranes and tugs with its main Mediterranean rivals.[1]

Both Port Said and Suez owe their importance mainly to the Canal, through which well over 90 per cent of ships calling at either harbour pass. Both ports, particularly Suez, have recently been improved. Both are among the principal fuelling stations on the Europe–Asia route, formerly supplying mainly coal imported from Western Europe and now oil from the Persian Gulf area. Port Said handles certain exports such as onions and potatoes and in 1952–6 accounted for 4 per cent of the volume and 8 per cent of the value of imports; it also carries on a significant amount of transit trade; its main contacts are with the Far East and the Eastern Mediterranean. Suez serves as a collecting port for petroleum, phosphates, and manganese mined in the Sinai and Red Sea areas and also receives petroleum and Far Eastern produce; in 1952–6 it accounted for 29 per cent of the volume and 8 per cent of the value of imports.

The Western Desert ports of Marsa Matruh, Sidi Barrani, and Sallum have no commercial importance. The old harbours of Rosetta and Damietta do not take steamers and carry on a small amount of trade with Lebanon, Syria, and Turkey by means of sailing ships; a project for a deep-water port at Damietta is under study. The Red Sea ports of Tor, Abu Zanima, Qusair, Ghardaqa, and Safaga were formerly served by British, Italian, and Egyptian ships which carried the manganese, phosphates, and oils mined near-by to foreign countries or to Suez for transhipment; however, by a decree of 25 June 1961 all coastal shipping has been reserved for Egyptian ships. Current plans envisage the construction of two new

[1] NPC, Memo. no. 202 and *al-Majlis al-daim*, pp. 377–80.

Red Sea ports, at Abu Ghusun and Marsa Alam, and the improvement of existing ports.

Before the Second World War Egyptian shipping lines, with the help of a subsidy, expanded the merchant fleet from 32,000 tons in 1932 to 108,000 in 1939. During the war many ships were sunk and by 1954 the total registered tonnage of dry-goods vessels was 82,000 tons, and they handled 2 per cent of Egypt's foreign trade.[1]

The revolutionary government helped the three shipping lines by granting them a combined subsidy of £E125,000 plus tax remissions of £E93,000 per annum and by encouraging them to buy a few small tankers. In 1957 the Economic Organization formed a fourth line which in 1959 took over two of the existing lines. In July 1961 the third line was nationalized, bringing all shipping into government ownership.

At the end of 1961 the Egyptian fleet consisted of 95,000 tons of usable cargo ships, together with 23,000 tons of over-age ships, and 79,000 tons of tankers plus 18,000 of over-age vessels; it was handling 12 per cent of Egypt's exports and imports of dry goods and 30 per cent of its oil. Current plans envisage the diversion of 50 per cent of total foreign trade to Egyptian ships by the procurement of 67 ships aggregating over 300,000 tons for cargo and 10 tankers aggregating over 120,000 tons. Most of these will have to be purchased abroad since Egypt's only functioning shipyard, at Port Said, cannot turn out vessels exceeding 3,000 tons, while the one under construction in Alexandria is limited to 6,000.

Air communications with the outside world have greatly developed during the last thirty years.[2] Thanks to its geographical position and excellent weather conditions, as well as to the recent improvement in its facilities, Cairo has once more caught up with Beirut as the main airport on the Europe–Far Eastern route, a position it had lost in the early 1950's. The principal field, Cairo Airport, covers 850 ha.; the main runway is 3,350 m. long and is covered with concrete while the secondary runway is being extended to 3,100 m. and strengthened with concrete. The Flight Information Centre of Cairo serves the area bounded by latitudes 20 to 35 N. and longitudes 20 to 40 E. In 1960 no less than 28 foreign airlines, in addition to UAA, called at Cairo (a figure that rose to 30 by 1961) and two at Alexandria, on scheduled flights; these effected 183 flights per week in summer and 171 in winter, of which UAA accounted for 38 and 37 flights respectively; there were also many

[1] *al-Majlis al-daim*, p. 372.  [2] NPC, Memo. no. 203.

unscheduled flights to these and the smaller airports. Passenger traffic through Cairo is running at over 850,000 per annum, freight at 5,000 tons and mail at 400 tons.

TABLE 25

*Suez Canal Shipping, 1910–61*

| | No. of ships passing through | Net transit tonnage (millions) | Goods traffic (m. tons) | Passengers ('000) | Revenue from tolls[1] |
|---|---|---|---|---|---|
| 1910 | 4,533 | 16·6 | 22·4 | 234 | 127 |
| 1920 | 4,009 | 17·6 | 17·0 | 500 | 145 |
| 1930 | 5,761 | 31·7 | 28·5 | 305 | 1,023 |
| 1938 | 6,171 | 34·4 | 28·8 | 480 | 1,626 |
| 1942 | 1,646 | 7·0 | .. | 1 | 457 |
| 1945 | 4,206 | 25·1 | .. | 984 | 1,882 |
| 1950 | 11,751 | 81·8 | 72·6 | 664 | 26,980 |
| 1955 | 14,666 | 115·8 | 107·5 | 521 | 32·2 |
| 1956 | 13,291 | 107·0 | 101·0 | 320 | 29·4 |
| 1957 | 10,958 | 89·9 | 81·3 | 188 | 24·5 |
| 1958 | 17,842 | 154·5 | 139·4 | 342 | 42·1 |
| 1959 | 17,731 | 163·4 | 148·3 | 326 | 44·5 |
| 1960 | 18,734 | 185·3 | 168·9 | 367 | 50·4 |
| 1961 | 18,148 | 187·1 | 172·4 | 323 | 51·9 |

[1] Until 1950 in m. French francs, thereafter in £E m.

*Sources: Le Canal de Suez; Suez Canal Reports; NBE, Econ. B.*

### THE SUEZ CANAL

Table 25 shows the continuous increase in Suez Canal traffic, an increase interrupted only in the early 1930's, during the Second World War, and in 1956–7 when the Canal was totally blocked, and then resumed operations only partially, as a consequence of the hostilities of October–November 1956.[1]

Until its nationalization, on 26 July 1956, the Canal had been owned and managed, quite efficiently and after the initial difficulties had been overcome very profitably, by the Compagnie Universelle du Canal, whose original share capital was 200 million gold francs and whose concession was due to run until 1968. Between 1876 and 1934 six improvement programmes had been carried out, at an

[1] Most of the figures and information in this section have been taken from *Le Canal de Suez: documents statistiques* (1950); *Compagnie universelle du Canal* (1947), and the ann. reps. of the Suez Canal Authority, *Suez Canal Report*.

aggregate cost of 951 million gold francs, which had been met by issuing debentures of 423 million francs and drawing on reserves for 528 million. Further improvements in 1947–54 totalling 55 million gold francs, and in 1955 amounting to 12 million, were met from reserves. The balance sheet drawn up at the end of 1955 showed assets of 83·6 milliard French francs, or roughly £E83·6 million. Of these buildings, machinery, and stocks, almost all held in Egypt, amounted to £E22·2 million. The bulk of the remaining assets consisted of securities; almost all of these were held outside Egypt, mainly in France and the United Kingdom.[1]

Although the company was legally Egyptian, until the Second World War it had constituted a foreign enclave which had little impact on the Egyptian economy. The bulk of the company's shares was held abroad, mainly in France and England, and less than 5 per cent in Egypt. As late as 1946 only 2 of the 28 members of the board of directors were Egyptian, and the greater part of pilots, technicians, and administrative personnel were foreigners. Direct payments to the Egyptian government amounted to £E1·5 million per annum and much larger sums were disbursed by the company in local purchases and in wages to its workmen, the bulk of whom were Egyptian; expenditures by foreign employees stationed in Egypt were also far from negligible. In addition, there were, and are, considerable indirect benefits; several thousands of navvies and shop-keepers thrive on the transit traffic and there is a large number of quick trippers who spend a day or two in one of the Canal ports or cut across to Cairo for the night. Moreover the contribution of the Canal to the Egyptian economy was rapidly growing. In March 1949 an agreement was concluded between the Egyptian government and the company which provided for an increase in the number of Egyptian directors and administrative and technical personnel, and raised the government's share to 7 per cent of gross profits. By 1956 direct payments to the government were running at £E6 million per annum, or 3 per cent of total government revenue; the total contribution of the company to the Egyptian economy was estimated at £E13 million, or some 40 per cent of the amount collected in dues and about 1·5 per cent of national income.[2] Of the administrative and technical personnel, 42 per cent were Egyptian, as was the bulk of the 5,100 workers.

[1] NBE, *Econ. B.*, no. 3, 1956.
[2] UN, Dept. of Econ. & Soc. Aff., *Econ. Developments in the Middle East* (NY, 1957), p. 101.

The nationalization of the Canal was initially achieved with little disruption. Most of the foreign pilots left, but the Egyptian pilots, helped by new recruits from Egypt and Eastern and Central Europe, did a splendid job in maintaining services. The hostilities in October and November 1956 resulted in the blockage of the Canal but with international help a passage was cleared and traffic resumed in April 1957, first on a partial and then on a full scale. On 29 April 1958 a settlement was reached with the shareholders of the company. The company was to retain all assets located outside Egypt and in addition to receive from the Egyptian government £E28·3 million, in instalments ending at the beginning of 1964.[1] In the meanwhile, the replacement of foreign by Egyptian personnel continued; its extent may be judged by the fact that at the end of 1960 129 pilots out of a total of 216 were Egyptians—most of the rest being Greeks, Russians, Yugoslavs, Poles, and Germans—as were 858 out of 900 employees, and since then several foreign pilots have left.[2] Before nationalization, the company had started its eighth programme for improvement. This was resumed, in a modified form, in September 1958 and completed in the spring of 1961; it was designed to provide passage for ships drawing up to 37 feet and to widen the passage, at 11 metres draught, from 60 metres to 90 and in places to 100. Simultaneously work started on the 'Nasser' programme, which aims ultimately at doubling the Canal over its whole length. The completion of the first stage of this programme, in 1963, will increase the capacity of the Canal by 20 per cent; it involves the removal of 94 million cubic metres of soil, or 20 million more than the amount removed during the construction of the original Canal in 1859–69. Total costs of all improvement works during the five years 1959–63 have been estimated at £E62·8 million and they are being partially covered by a loan of $56·5 million granted by the International Bank in December 1959.[3] Other noteworthy improvements include the setting up in Port Said of a floating dock capable of handling ships of up to 30,000 tons deadweight, which will make it possible to carry out locally repair work now being sent to Palermo or Bombay, and the signing of a contract for the installation of underwater television. In recent years an average of £E12·5 million per annum has been spent on improvements, a noteworthy advance on the previous level.

The importance of the Canal in international trade needs no stressing. It has been estimated that in 1955 some 13 per cent of sea-

[1] NBE, *Econ. B.*, no. 3, 1958.　　　[2] *Suez Canal Report, 1960.*　　　[3] Ibid. *1959.*

borne trade passed through it; for tankers the figure was 19 per cent. Its importance to the countries bordering on the Red Sea and Persian Gulf may be judged from the fact that in 1955 the percentage of their total exports passing through the Canal was about 70 per cent for Kuwait, Bahrain, and Qatar, 65 per cent for Iran and the Sudan, 40 per cent for Iraq, and 35 per cent for Saudi Arabia.[1]

A breakdown by nationality of ships using the Canal shows a marked decline in the share of the United Kingdom, from nearly 50 per cent before the Second World War to 36 per cent in 1949 and 21 in 1960. Recently there has also been a decline in United States shipping, from 13 per cent in 1949 to 3 in 1960, but this is largely because of the transfer of ships to flags of convenience; thus in 1960 Liberia was the second largest user of the Canal, with 16 per cent, followed by Norway, with 13 per cent.

The large increase in merchandise movement through the Canal is mainly thanks to the great expansion in northbound traffic, which rose from 19 million tons in 1933–7 to 48 million in 1949 and 140 million in 1960; the corresponding figures for southbound traffic were 9, 13, and 29 million. This great increase is accounted for by the rising output of the oilfields of the Persian Gulf area; in 1960 oil accounted for 82 per cent of the sub-total, compared with 25 per cent in 1933–7, while merchandise originating in or destined for countries bordering on the Persian Gulf accounted for 67 per cent of all goods passing through the Canal.[2]

Dues levied on loaded ships were slowly lowered after the First World War to 5·9 shillings, or PT28 per ton, in 1938. In January 1941 they were raised to PT39, at which level they remained until September 1951, when they were reduced to PT36·5; a further reduction, to PT34, was made in 1954.[3] In view of the rise in prices, dues form a much smaller proportion of c.i.f. prices than they did before the war; thus in 1921–30 they constituted 1·5–3 per cent of that of Australian wheat in England, but in 1954 only 0·8 per cent.[4] In 1954 it was estimated that Canal dues on crude petroleum amounted to about 10 cents a barrel, or some 3 per cent of the c.i.f. price; for such commodities as jute, rubber, and manganese tolls

[1] UN, *Econ. Dev. ME*, p. 99.

[2] For a discussion of the problems of production and transport of petroleum see Charles Issawi and Mohammed Yeganeh, *Economics of Middle Eastern Oil* (NY, 1962).

[3] In August 1958 a 3·5 per cent surcharge was added to dues, by the UN, to pay for the clearing of the Canal; this was abolished in March 1961.

[4] Henri Poydenot, *Le Canal de Suez* (1955), p. 63.

represented 0·2–1 per cent of c.i.f. prices.[1] Nevertheless Canal dues were one of the factors which induced the petroleum companies to build the pipeline from Saudi Arabia to the Mediterranean. So far, the enormous increase in oil production has kept both pipeline and Canal fully occupied but the limited capacity of the Canal and the potential political dangers have stimulated the building of super-tankers which can carry oil around Africa at a unit cost no higher than that of oil carried through the Canal by smaller ships.[2]

### MEDIA OF COMMUNICATION

With 7,000 post offices of all kinds and over 15,000 km. of telegraph lines, Egypt is well provided with postal facilities. Land and sea cables link it with all parts of the world and in the last few years direct wireless communication with twenty-eight countries has been established. In recent years the post office has introduced a certain amount of mechanization but the effects of this have been more than offset, for both letters and telegrams, by the censorship which greatly delays communications as well as by a general decline in efficiency. The telephone service is still inadequate; the number of telephones has risen from 66,000 in 1940 to 122,000 in 1951 and 196,000 in 1959 and it is planned to add another 203,000 by 1965.[3] Service is unsatisfactory, apparently not so much because of the shortage of lines compared with the number of subscribers as to the inordinate average length of conversations.

Since the early 1930's, when commercial broadcasting was allowed, radio has been a state monopoly. By 1951 there were five medium-wave transmitters, with an aggregate power of 71 kw., and a 10-kw. short-wave transmitter which provided satisfactory reception throughout Egypt and were heard in neighbouring countries. The importance attached to broadcasting by the revolutionary régime may be judged from the fact that the aggregate power of the transmitting stations, of which there are now nine, has risen to 1,434 kw.; broadcasting time has similarly risen from 22

---

[1] Claude E. Boillot, 'Suez Canal Transit Tolls', *Oil Forum* (NY), Nov.–Dec. 1954.

[2] Before the recent improvements, the largest tanker to pass the Canal partly laden drew 35 feet and carried 44,000 tons of oil; the largest yet to pass in ballast displaced 106,600 tons (*Petroleum Press Service*, June 1959 & *al-Ahram*, 14 Mar. 1962). In 1957 it was estimated that 65,000-ton tankers sailing around the Cape could deliver oil to Western Europe at the same cost as 35,000-ton tankers passing through the Canal (*Oil Forum*, Jan. 1957).

[3] *Coll. Basic Statist. Data*, pp. 160–1 and *UAR Yb. 1961*, pp. 862–72.

hours a day to 198 on medium waves and 130 on short waves. A new transmitting station is under construction and is to start broadcasting on medium waves in 1963; with a power of 1,000 kw., it will be the strongest station in the world; it will cost several million dollars.[1]

The number of registered radio sets has also greatly increased, to 853,000 in 1959, or 33 per 1,000 inhabitants.[2] But this per-capita figure gives a misleading impression of the coverage of broadcasting in Egypt, first because there are many unregistered sets;[3] and secondly because—as in other Middle Eastern and Mediterranean countries—it is regarded as a sign of meanness to keep the sound of one's radio to oneself and each set has dozens of listeners in cafés, neighbouring houses, or public places. It may therefore be said that Egypt is not too badly supplied with radio facilities.

As regards the content of the broadcasts, the main programme continues to consist chiefly of light music and religious subjects, but propaganda of all kinds occupies a rapidly rising share. Following the fashion set by President Abdel Nasser, the language used is becoming increasingly colloquial, which makes it more intelligible to the masses. The Second Programme, inaugurated in 1957, is on the air for three hours a day and provides more scholarly talks in classical Arabic, and classical Western music, while the local European programme concentrates on music and news. Finally there is the Voice of the Arabs, inaugurated in 1953 and estimated to have a budget smaller than that of the Soviet foreign broadcasts but comparable to that of the Voice of America. This programme, which is beamed to other Arab countries for fifteen hours a day, has to be heard to be believed: for sheer venom, vulgarity, and indifference to truth it has few equals in the world.

In addition, there have been, since 1953, foreign-language programmes directed to various parts of the world. At the time of writing use was made of twenty languages, for $23\frac{1}{2}$ hours a day, including all the principal Asian, African, and European tongues.[4]

Television broadcasts started in 1960 and there are two channels in use and some 50,000 sets or 2 per 1,000 inhabitants, compared to the minimum desirable figure of 20 set by Unesco. Better coverage

[1] *al-Ahram*, 16 Jan. 1962.

[2] This compared with 4 in India, 14 in Iraq, 40 in Jordan, 45 in Turkey, 60 in Syria, 60 in Lebanon, 93 in Greece, 121 in Italy, 163 in Japan. A Unesco report has recently set 50 as the desirable minimum (*Mass Media in the Developing Countries*, 1961, p. 35).

[3] In 1961 the radio registration fee was abolished.

[4] *UAR Yb. 1961*, pp. 999–1023.

is being provided for Upper Egypt and the capacity of the local factory, which produces 19- and 23-inch screen sets, is to be raised to 40,000 sets per annum. Sets have been placed in many of the squares and public gardens of Cairo. Much reliance is placed on foreign films, mainly American, the rest of the time being taken by locally produced plays and shows, news, political speeches, and educational programmes.

The number of cinemas has risen rapidly in the last few years, from 194 in 1949 to 260 in 1951 and 375 in 1961; the seating capacity has similarly increased to some 400,000 or 1 per 65 inhabitants.[1] Attendance reached a peak of 84 million in 1953 and stood at 73 million in 1959, 2·9 per capita.[2] In the early 1950's it was estimated that 20 per cent of screen time was taken by Egyptian films, 55 per cent by American, and 25 per cent by British, French, and Italian; since then the proportion of Egyptian films has gone up as has that of films from the Soviet bloc, India and Pakistan, and Germany. In 1960 of 312 films imported into Egypt, 261 were American or British, 15 Soviet, 10 Italian, 7 French (an abnormally low figure, because of the strained political relations between the two countries), and 6 Greek.[3]

In 1959 Egypt, with 60 films, was the eleventh most important producer of long films in the world. Production started in an experimental way before the First World War and by the 1920's some commercial films were being turned out. The first well-equipped studio, that of Société Misr, was founded in 1934. The use of sound track, making it possible to introduce singing which is so popular with the masses, and the reduction of foreign competition during the Second World War, gave the industry a great stimulus; production of long films rose steadily from an annual average of 3 in 1929–31 to 25 in 1944–6.[4] In the mid-1950's there were no less than 120 producers. In 1957 the Organization for the Consolidation of the Cinema was established by the government and its powers were extended in 1960; it advances loans to producers or participates in their costs; produces short documentary films on its own; has founded a Higher Institute for the Cinema; and assists in marketing

[1] This compared with 1 per 12 in the UK and Spain, 1 per 11 in Italy, 1 per 10 in the USA and 1 per 50 set as the minimum by Unesco.

[2] This compared with 1·4 in Sudan, 2·7 in Jordan, 3·5 in India, 10·4 in Spain, 12·3 in Japan, 14·5 in the UK, and 15·0 in Italy. For a good account of the film industry see J. Landau, *The Arab Theater and Cinema* (Philadelphia, 1956).

[3] Fed. of Ind., *Yb. 1961*.

[4] See art. on the cinema industry in *Ind. Bank R.*, no. 2, 1957.

Egyptian films abroad. Several producing firms were affected by the nationalization measures of 1960 and 1961.

Egyptian films have considerably improved during the last thirty years in content, acting, and technique and have greatly helped in modernizing the outlook of the masses. But a study made in 1957 listed the following weaknesses: poorness of script; defects in scenario; inadequacy of direction; insufficient care in matters of sound; restricted number of actors and low level of acting. Average costs of production were estimated at £E35,000 for long films, 19,000 for medium, and 12,000 for short; of these totals 60 per cent was absorbed by payments to actors, directors, and workmen and only 5 per cent by scenery, props, costumes, &c. As regards receipts, 53 per cent of the total came from showings in Egypt and the rest from abroad: 18 per cent from Lebanon and Syria, 13 from Iraq, and the balance from the Sudan, North Africa and other countries ranging as far as Indonesia and North and South America where the presence of Lebanese and Syrian emigrants provides a market:[1] the number of copies of films exported annually rose to 1,720 in 1959 but fell to 1,187 in 1960.

The press has been one of the most prominent casualties of the Revolution. Already long before its nationalization, in May 1960, its spirit had been completely broken by censorship and by the suppression of newspapers that showed any independence, such as the pro-Wafdist *al-Misri*. Today it is merely a raucous loudspeaker, transmitting the voice of the government. The saddest aspect of this development is that it has occurred in a country which could boast of what was by far the most developed press in the Arab world and of a couple of dailies which could stand comparison with the best of many European countries.

Together with this decline in quality there has been an increase in quantity. Total circulation of dailies increased threefold between the pre-war years and 1952, reaching 515,000 in that year, and has since probably risen by half. This gives an average of about 25 to 30 per thousand inhabitants, compared with 9 in India and Pakistan, 10 in Iraq, 19 in Syria, 20 in Jordan, 32 in Turkey, 100 in Lebanon, 107 in Italy and 398 in Japan; the desirable minimum set by Unesco is 100. Three newspapers dominate the field: *al-Ahram* and *al-Akhbar* with a circulation of nearly 200,000 each and *al-Gumhuria* with 100,000; the difference between these papers is negligible. The leading evening newspaper is *al-Misa*, with a circulation of about

[1] Ibid.

20,000. As a result of the *Gleichschaltung* of the Egyptian press, and of the strained relations between the Egyptian and other Arab governments, foreign sales have greatly fallen off; thus those of one of the leading dailies have declined from 20,000 to 5,000.

Until the mid-1950's there was a very active weekly or fortnightly press, consisting of three kinds: satirical illustrated party papers written partly in colloquial; pleasantly illustrated and entertaining magazines; and organs of non-party political, economic, or social opinion. The first and last groups have disappeared but the second survives, with the official political line grafted on to it. The leading weekly is *Akhbar al-Yaum*, with a circulation of about 300,000, followed by such magazines as *al-Musawwar*, *Akhir Saa*, *Rosa al-Yusif*, and *Sabah al-Khair*. The monthly reviews, which in the previous seventy years had done so much to spread western culture, as well as a better knowledge of Arab history and literature, have also suffered greatly. One of the oldest and best reviews, *al-Muqtataf*, has ceased publication as has another excellent journal, *al-Kitab*. However, *al-Hilal* still survives and, together with the recently founded *al-Majalla* and the Arabic version of the *Reader's Digest*, *al-Mukhtar*, strives to meet the needs of the more serious public.

As against this retrogression must be set an important gain, the growth of a large body of technical periodicals issued by the various government departments and organizations and covering the economic, financial, industrial, agricultural, social, educational, and other fields; a list of many of these publications is provided in the bibliography.

This brief account makes it clear that Egypt is sharing the experience of many countries that are passing through a communist or social-nationalist revolution. On the one hand there has been a great and highly desirable extension of media of communication, and a much larger proportion of the population is being provided with radio and television programmes, films, and newspapers. And, on the other, most of these media have been reduced to instruments of government propaganda and the nature of the message that is being communicated through some of them is such as to offset much of the benefit of the increase.

# X

# Foreign Trade and Balance of Payments

---

*There is no theory probably more flattering to princes and statesmen, or to a whole nation, than to institute measures which hold out independence of all other nations, by producing and manufacturing at home all that is considered necessary and luxurious.*

JOHN MACGREGOR, 1847.

*Toutes les questions si débattues du libre échange et de la protection se réduisent à ces mots si simples; par des droits modérés et justement calculés, assurer la préférence au produit national.*

A. THIERS, 1868.

*The foreign-trade monopoly is the shield and protection of our young socialist industry.*

STALIN, 1927.

*The balance of payments commands, the balance of trade obeys, and not the other way round.*

BÖHM-BAWERK.

## COTTON AND FOREIGN TRADE

The price of cotton is still the most important single element influencing the size of Egypt's foreign trade, and until very recently it was by far the most important. For, in the first place, cotton and its by-products accounted for 80–90 per cent of the value of exports and, given the relative stability of the quantity of cotton exports, price was the main factor determining the total value of cotton exports. And in the second place, exports accounted for the bulk of foreign-exchange proceeds and thus determined the value of imports. Hence, when average cotton prices were $20–40 per cantar, between 1921 and 1929, imports stood at £E45–55 million. When, after 1930, prices sagged to $10–13, imports fell to £E25–35 million. Between 1947 and 1950 cotton prices ranged between $50 and $100, while imports rose to £E100–200 million.[1]

In recent years the link between cotton and imports has become much looser. First, the share of cotton in total exports has fallen

[1] For further details see Issawi, *EMC*, pp. 196–7.

owing to greater consumption at home and expanded exports of other products; in 1956–60 it averaged well below 70 per cent. Secondly, because of the growth of receipts from Suez Canal dues and other invisibles, the share of exports in total receipts has declined, to an average of 65 per cent in the 1950's.[1] Since the outbreak of the Second World War, imports have greatly exceeded exports in every single year; in the period 1940–60 inclusive the import surplus amounted to £E710 million, or an annual average of 35·5 million. Lastly, in every post-war year, except 1949 and 1954, there has been a sizeable deficit on current account; the total for 1946–59 inclusive was £E269 million or an annual average of 19·2 million; these deficits were covered first by drawing on the sterling balances accumulated during the Second World War and then by the credits granted by the United States, the Soviet Union and other countries.

### FOREIGN TRADE AND NATIONAL INCOME

In recent years imports have represented a fifth to a quarter of Egypt's national income while exports have been somewhat lower. Egypt's ratios are thus at the lower end of the range (20 to 40 per cent in 1949) of those of most underdeveloped countries. In these countries development has been brought about mainly by foreign capital, which expanded the production of one or more raw materials required by the industrial complexes of Western Europe and North America; hence, although both per-capita incomes and per-capita exports and imports are low, the ratio between them is high.[2]

In view of the very tentative nature of available national income

[1] NBE, *Econ. B.*, no. 2, 1961; this issue contains a good statistical analysis of Egypt's foreign trade and balance of payments in the 1950's.

[2] In contrast to this group five other groups may be distinguished. First the self-sufficient developed continental economies, the USA and the Soviet Union; in 1949 the US import ratio was as low as 3 and the export ratio was 5 per cent; the Soviet figures were even smaller around 2 per cent, owing to still larger size, lower development, and great self-sufficiency. Secondly, the developed countries of Western Europe, where the export ratios were 10–20 per cent and the import ratios 15–25. Thirdly, regions of recent settlement, e.g. Canada and Australia, where high per-capita income is more than matched by large exports and imports and where the export ratios were 25–35 per cent and the import ratios 20–30. Fourthly, mineral exporters such as the Persian Gulf oil producers and N. Rhodesia where exports sometimes actually exceed national income. And lastly a miscellaneous group whose ratios are low either because they combine great size with a low degree of development, e.g. India and China, or because they have not yet been drawn into the network of international trade, e.g. Yemen.

estimates, it is impossible to determine with accuracy the trend of the export or import ratios. Available figures suggest, however, that before the First World War and in the inter-war period both ratios remained remarkably stable, around 20 per cent of national income. In 1950 an export ratio of 20 was once more registered, while the import ratio rose to 25. After that, however, exports lagged behind the growth of national income and by 1958 and 1959 the ratio had fallen to 15–16 per cent. The import ratio remained at around 20 per cent, and in 1958 and 1959 averaged about 22 per cent.

It may therefore be tentatively concluded that the marginal propensity to import remained fairly constant until quite recently. Since the Second World War, however, many factors have interfered with the normal adjustment of imports to income: in the immediate post-war period pent-up demand accompanied by large reserves of foreign exchange—a result of forced savings during the war; for some years, shortages in the supplying countries of certain goods desired by Egypt; and more recently increasing government restrictions on imports. At present two sets of factors are affecting, in opposite directions, the propensity to import. On the one hand the mass exodus of foreigners and the drastic fall in income suffered by the richer classes have sharply brought down the demand for imported consumer goods while the growth in local industrial production has increased the possibility of import substitution. But on the other hand industrialization has made Egypt increasingly dependent on foreign supplies of capital equipment, raw materials, fuels, and semi-processed goods; to this should be added the increased dependence on imported foodstuffs for the ever-growing population.[1] The government evidently expects the former factors to predominate since in the current Five-Year Plan imports are scheduled to fall from £E229·2 million in 1959/60 to 214·9 in 1964/65, or from 18 to 12 per cent of GNP. At the same time exports are expected to rise from £E168·8 to 229·3 million, maintaining the ratio of 13 per cent of GNP. The import surplus is thus expected to decline from £E60·4 to — 14·4 million.[2] However, the

---

[1] The overall propensity to import is a function of three factors: the import content of various sectors of demand, the relative importance of these sectors and their rates of growth. A very rough estimate for Egypt, based on input-output tables, put the marginal propensity to import of private consumption at ·14, of government consumption at ·10, of investment at ·54 and of re-exports at ·07 (NPC, Memo. no. 470); it should be noted that the government plans a large increase in investment, the import content of which is high.

[2] For details, see *Cadre du Plan*, pp. 82–88.

experience of other countries which have launched similar development plans shows that export possibilities tend to be exaggerated and, still more, that import needs tend to be seriously underestimated. As Professor Ragnar Frisch pointed out, in a discussion of the time it takes for an investment to pay back the foreign indebtedness incurred because of it, 'It is surprising how long this recuperation period is for many projects.'[1]

## MAIN EXPORTS AND IMPORTS

Egypt's export trade is still essentially based on cotton, but its structure has undergone some important changes during the last fifty years. On the eve of the Second World War, the share of cotton had dropped to just over 70 per cent, but the addition of its by-products and derivatives (cotton seed, cotton-seed oil and cotton-seed cake) raised the proportion to 80 per cent; the balance included cigarettes, rice, onions, petroleum, phosphates, manganese, and skins and hides. In the post-war period the by-products and derivatives of cotton practically disappeared from the list of exports, owing to increased internal consumption. As for cotton itself, the post-war and Korean booms raised its share to an average of 87 per cent in 1950–3 but the subsequent break in prices reduced it sharply to under 70 per cent in 1956–60. The balance consisted of such traditional exports as rice and onions, of certain newer agricultural exports such as fruits, groundnuts, and potatoes, of minerals such as petroleum, phosphates, and manganese, and of manufactured goods such as cotton yarn, cotton piece-goods, rayon fabrics, sugar, cement, and shoes. Table 26 shows the main items of exports.

Taking the 1950's as a whole, raw materials accounted for 85 per cent of Egypt's exports; of the balance, the share of articles having undergone 'advanced transformation' has steadily increased and in 1959 was actually greater than that of articles having undergone 'simple transformation'.[2]

The structure of imports is more diversified and has changed more fundamentally. Until 1930 textiles were the leading item, accounting for 25–30 per cent of imports; half of the sub-total consisted of cotton piece-goods. Foodstuffs accounted for 20–25 per cent of imports, half of the sub-total consisting of cereals.[3] Coal formed a

[1] NPC, *Current Notes*, no. 17, 1960.
[2] For details see NBE, *Econ. B.*, no. 2, 1961.
[3] See Abd al-Moneim al-Kaissouni, 'Bad mazahir al-tijara al-kharijia' in *Buhuth*, pp. 131–56.

TABLE 26

Main Exports: Quantity, Value, and Percentage, 1938–61

('000 tons and £E million)

| | 1938 | | | 1950 | | | 1960[1] | | | 1961[1] | | |
|---|---|---|---|---|---|---|---|---|---|---|---|---|
| | Quantity | Value | Percentage | Quantity | Value | Percentage | Quantity | Value | Percentage | Quantity | Value | Percentage |
| Cotton | 359 | 21·3 | 72 | 389 | 152·3 | 88 | 374 | 134·7 | 68 | 295 | 104·6 | 62 |
| Cotton seed | 337 | 1·6 | 6 | 1 | 0·1 | — | — | — | — | — | — | — |
| Cereals | 79 | 0·8 | 3 | 182 | 7·8 | 5 | 282 | 9·9 | 5 | 205 | 7·3 | 4 |
| Vegetables | 155 | 1·0 | 3 | 93 | 2·3 | 1 | 321 | 5·8 | 3 | 195[2] | 4·9[2] | .. |
| Petroleum | 214 | 0·5 | 2 | 372 | 2·0 | 1 | 1,055 | 4·5 | 2 | 2,042 | 7·4 | 4 |
| Phosphates | 403 | 0·3 | 1 | 502 | 1·1 | 1 | 302 | 1·4 | 1 | 421 | 1·5 | 1 |
| Cotton yarn | — | — | — | 5 | 2·3 | 1 | 20 | 9·1 | 5 | 17 | 7·7 | 5 |
| Cotton piece-goods | — | — | — | 0·3 | 0·3 | — | 13 | 6·7 | 4 | 10 | 6·1 | 4 |
| Sugar, molasses, & confectionery | 41 | 0·2 | 1 | 7 | 0·1 | — | 98 | 2·0 | 1 | 126 | 2·9 | 2 |
| Others | .. | 3·5 | 12 | .. | 4·6 | 3 | 2,702 | 23·7 | 11 | 3,075 | 26·5 | 17 |
| Total | .. | 29·2 | 100 | .. | 173·0 | 100 | 5,167 | 197·8 | 100 | 6,386 | 168·9 | 100 |

[1] Excluding trade with Syria.    [2] Potatoes and onions only.

Sources: Dept. of Statist. & Census, Monthly Summary of Foreign Trade; NBE, Econ. B.; CBE, Econ. R.

little over 10 per cent of imports and machinery, metals and metal products some 10–15 per cent. Following the 1930 tariff, imports of consumer goods began to decrease while those of machinery and raw materials rose sharply; in the 1940's petroleum replaced coal and the growth of population led to a rapid increase in imports of cereals and other foodstuffs. All these trends were accentuated in the 1950's. Textiles practically disappeared from the list of imports, and were followed by an ever increasing number of consumer goods which were manufactured locally. A few producer goods also began to feel the effects of greater local production, such as cement, sulphuric acid and, more recently, fertilizers and iron and steel products. Petroleum imports grew rapidly, as local production failed to keep pace with Egypt's rising energy needs, while those of coal shrank. Imports of wheat also rose rapidly, frequently passing the million-ton mark; Egypt is now one of the world's leading importers of wheat.[1] Above all, there was a several-fold increase in machinery and metals, the share of which rose from 20 per cent of total imports in the late 1940's to nearly 40 per cent by 1960.[2] Over the whole 1950's, raw materials constituted 24 per cent of imports, articles having undergone 'simple transformation' 28 per cent, and articles having undergone 'advanced transformation' 44 per cent; the balance consisted of unspecified items. A more meaningful classification, for 1960, puts the share of consumption goods at 25 per cent of total imports, against 29 in 1959; of producer goods at 42 per cent, against 38; of investment goods at 23 per cent, against 24; and of unspecified goods at 10 per cent, against 9 per cent.[3] Table 27 shows the main items of imports during the pre-war and post-war periods.

### DIRECTION OF FOREIGN TRADE

Since 1952 drastic shifts have taken place in the direction of Egypt's foreign trade. On the one hand the secular fall in the share of Egypt's former main partners, the United Kingdom, France, and Belgium has continued; this shift was partly owing to the decline of the British textile industry, partly to increased competition from other industrial countries—e.g. Germany, Italy, Japan, and the

[1] In 1958 Egypt was the ninth largest importer of wheat (FAO, *Trade Yb. 1959*).

[2] Recorded imports do not cover 'capital goods imported within the framework of foreign credit facilities' (CBE, *Econ. R.*, no. 1, 1961).

[3] For details see ibid.

TABLE 27

## Main Imports: Quantity, Value, and Percentage, 1938–61
### ('000 tons and £E million)

| | 1938 | | | 1950 | | | 1960[1] | | | 1961[1] | | |
|---|---|---|---|---|---|---|---|---|---|---|---|---|
| | Quantity | Value | Percentage | Quantity | Value | Percentage | Quantity | Value | Percentage | Quantity | Value | Percentage |
| Cereals | 16 | 0·1 | — | 614 | 17·6 | 8 | 1,186 | 26·6 | 11 | 1,194[2] | 27·3[2] | 11 |
| Tea & coffee | 17 | 1·1 | 3 | 22 | 8·6 | 4 | 23 | 8·2 | 4 | 27 | 9·7 | 4 |
| Cotton cloth | 19 | 3·3 | 9 | 6 | 5·8 | 3 | 0·2 | .. | .. | .. | .. | .. |
| Silk & woollen cloth & yarns | 5 | 2·0 | 6 | 15 | 14·3 | 7 | 1·3 | 0·9 | .. | .. | .. | .. |
| Chemicals | 27 | 0·8 | 2 | 60 | 5·6 | 3 | 131 | 14·0 | 6 | 99 | 10·4 | 4 |
| Fertilizers | 514 | 3·0 | 8 | 684 | 12·4 | 6 | 626 | 9·0 | 4 | 552 | 7·1 | 3 |
| Wood | 303 | 1·7 | 5 | 374 | 9·9 | 5 | 218 | 8·2 | 4 | 281 | 10·5 | 5 |
| Coal | 1,548 | 2·0 | 5 | 219 | 1·0 | 1 | 175 | 1·6 | 1 | 329 | 3·1 | 1 |
| Petroleum & products | 698 | 2·4 | 6 | 1,167 | 9·0 | 4 | 3,340 | 24·3 | 11 | 3,467 | 21·5 | 9 |
| Iron & steel & products | 219 | 3·1 | 8 | 348 | 13·8 | 7 | 232 | 17·9 | 8 | | 18·3 | 8 |
| Machines | 28 | 2·4 | 7 | 61 | 17·6 | 8 | 86 | 38·6 | 17 | 87 | 42·1 | 17 |
| Motor vehicles & parts | 10 | 1·2 | 3 | 15 | 6·0 | 3 | 13 | 7·2 | 3 | 11[3] | 4·5[3] | 2 |
| Gold ('000 gr.) | 1 | 0·1 | — | 32 | 16·2 | 8 | .. | 0·1 | .. | .. | .. | .. |
| Others | .. | 13·7 | 37 | .. | 74·6 | 35 | .. | 75·9 | 31 | .. | 89·3 | 37 |
| Total | .. | 37·0 | 100 | .. | 212·7 | 100 | 6,535 | 232·5 | 100 | 7,472 | 243·8 | 100 |

[1] Excl. trade with Syria.  [2] Wheat, wheat flour, and maize.  [3] Motor cars and buses.

Sources: Dept. of Statist. & Census, Monthly Summary of Foreign Trade; NBE, Econ. B.; CBE, Econ. R.

United States—and partly to the deterioration in their relations with Egypt. On the other hand there was the dramatic rise of the Soviet bloc to a position of predominance after 1955. Table 28 brings out the long-term changes in relative position of the main areas trading with Egypt and Table 29 shows the country's trade with its chief partners in the last three years.

TABLE 28

*Direction of Trade, 1885–1960*

*(percentage of total value)*

|  |  | 1885–9 | 1913 | 1929 | 1938 | 1950 | 1955 | 1959 | 1960 |
|---|---|---|---|---|---|---|---|---|---|
| Soviet | imports | 6 | 8 | 9 | 11 | 7 | 7 | 32 | 28 |
| bloc[1] | exports | 10 | 8 | 3 | 10 | 1 | 22 | 54 | 51 |
| U.K. | imports | 38 | 31 | 21 | 23 | 19 | 13 | 7 | 6 |
|  | exports | 63 | 43 | 33 | 32 | 22 | 6 | 3 | 3 |
| W. Europe | imports | 27 | 35 | 39 | 40 | 36 | 47 | 34 | 33 |
|  | exports | 23 | 36 | 35 | 36 | 35 | 34 | 22 | 18 |
| USA | imports | 1 | 4 | 5 | 7 | 6 | 12 | 14 | 18 |
|  | exports | — | 8 | 13 | 2 | 9 | 7 | 1 | 5 |
| Others | imports | 28 | 22 | 26 | 19 | 32 | 21 | 13 | 15 |
|  | exports | 5 | 5 | 16 | 20 | 33 | 31 | 20 | 23 |

[1] Soviet Union, Albania, Bulgaria, Czechoslovakia, Hungary, Poland, Rumania, Yugoslavia, E. Germany; the share of Yugoslavia in Egypt's imports was 2·4 per cent in 1959 and 6·5 in 1960 and in exports 2·2 and 7·0 per cent respectively.

*Sources: Ann. stat.; Monthly Summary of Foreign Trade.*

Tables 28 and 29 may be supplemented by a few remarks on trade relations with certain countries. In the 1950's the Arab countries accounted for some 6 per cent of Egypt's imports; the main suppliers were the Sudan, with livestock, and Saudi Arabia, with petroleum; in 1960 the Arab countries, including Syria, supplied a little over 8 per cent of Egyptian imports. Exports to them averaged 8 per cent of the total for the 1950's; the main articles were cotton piece-goods, silk fabrics, rice, sugar, and printed matter; the main markets were the Sudan, Saudi Arabia, and Lebanon. In 1960 the Arab countries, including Syria, took just over 10 per cent of Egypt's exports. Trade with the Soviet bloc has been greatly expanded by the Czech arms deal, the Soviet credits, and the conclusion of a series of bilateral

TABLE 29

*Import and Export Trade with Principal Customers, 1959–61*

(£E million)

| | 1959 | | 1960 | | 1961 | |
|---|---|---|---|---|---|---|
| | Imports | Exports | Imports | Exports | Imports | Exports |
| United States | 30·0 | 2·1 | 40·0 | 10·0 | 46·7 | 10·4 |
| Soviet Union | 26·8 | 28·3 | 22·9 | 30·9 | 27·7 | 25·4 |
| West Germany | 27·9 | 7·6 | 32·1 | 9·3 | 26·8 | 5·2 |
| Czechoslovakia | 8·1 | 16·2 | 8·0 | 13·0 | 6·0 | 23·8 |
| China | 8·3 | 11·7 | 6·8 | 15·5 | 6·6 | 5·1 |
| East Germany | 8·9 | 10·5 | 8·8 | 10·1 | 7·9 | 6·1 |
| Italy | 10·9 | 7·3 | 11·2 | 7·2 | 8·1 | 7·5 |
| United Kingdom | 15·5 | 4·2 | 13·6 | 4·6 | 17·7 | 4·0 |
| India | 5·5 | 6·8 | 10·0 | 13·4 | 10·7 | 8·1 |
| France | 5·8 | 3·2 | 8·8 | 3·7 | 5·9 | 4·4 |
| Switzerland | 5·2 | 3·8 | 4·2 | 2·2 | 4·4 | 2·0 |
| Yugoslavia | 5·2 | 3·4 | 6·5 | 13·5 | 6·3 | 1·0 |
| Japan | 3·0 | 4·7 | 4·0 | 5·3 | 8·2 | 5·0 |
| Belgium | 3·1 | 1·4 | 3·2 | 1·5 | 1·4 | 1·0 |
| Total[1] | 214·4 | 154·3 | 232·5 | 197·8 | 243·8 | 168·9 |

[1] Excl. trade with Syria and incl. other countries.

*Sources:* Dept. of Statist. & Census, *Monthly Summary of Foreign Trade*; NBE, *Econ. B.*; CBE, *Econ. R.*

agreements. Trade with the United States has increased over the last few years, mainly because of higher Egyptian imports paid for by the rapidly rising United States aid; at the same time it may be noted that in 1960 the United States became Egypt's principal market for piece-goods, followed by the Sudan. The main markets for cotton yarn are East Germany, West Germany, and Yugoslavia, and for silk fabrics the Sudan and Saudi Arabia. Of the other exports, phosphates go mainly eastwards, to Japan and Ceylon, and manganese and onions to Western Europe; markets for rice are widely scattered, including India and Pakistan, East and West Germany, Lebanon and Jordan, and Yugoslavia and Cuba. The main direction of cotton exports may be judged from the figures for total exports; in recent years the principal markets have been the Soviet Union, Czechoslovakia, and China, followed by India and Japan.

An interesting feature of Egypt's recent import trade has been the widening range of sources for several commodities. Thus the main suppliers of wheat and flour have been the United States, the Soviet Union, Italy, and France; of petroleum and products the Soviet Union, Rumania, the United States, and Saudi Arabia; and of iron and steel West Germany, the Soviet Union, Czechoslovakia, China, France, Italy, and the United Kingdom. On the other hand many goods are still imported from traditional sources, including not only such raw produce as colonial goods from South East Asia and tropical America and timber from Eastern Europe but also pharmaceuticals, machinery, motor cars and spare parts from the United States, West Germany, the United Kingdom, Italy, France, and Switzerland.

### QUANTUM AND TERMS OF TRADE

The long-term growth of the quantum of Egypt's exports, as well as the fluctuations in their purchasing power, are indicated, albeit roughly, in Table 1 (p. 28). This shows that between 1870 and the end of the century, when cotton prices fell by almost two-thirds, Egypt, together with most primary producing countries,[1] suffered a deterioration in its terms of trade but that there was a rapid recovery thereafter until the First World War. A somewhat more accurate picture can be given for the years 1910–37, based on indices of export and import prices calculated by Abd al-Moneim al-Tanamly[2] and the period after 1938 is covered by indices of quanta and prices prepared by the National Bank of Egypt. The quantum of exports fell by nearly 40 per cent between 1910 and 1920, doubled between 1920 and 1929 and, after declining during the early 1930's and rising to a record figure in 1935–7, stood in 1938 at the 1929 level, or about 20 per cent above that of 1910. As for imports, they too fell by a little over 20 per cent between 1910 and 1920, almost regained the pre-war level by 1929, fell sharply during the depression, and in 1938 stood at about two-thirds of the 1910 level. The terms of trade (1928=100) fell from 113 in 1913, to a low of 53 in 1918, stood at a peak of 137 in 1925, and dropped to 44 in 1939. The changes since 1938 are shown in Table 30. After deteriorating during the war years, the terms of trade improved rapidly in the

[1] See League of Nations, *Industrialization and Foreign Trade* (1945) and UN, Dept. of Econ. Aff., *Relative Prices of Exports and Imports of Underdeveloped Countries* (1949).

[2] 'al-Iqtisad al-zirai', in *Buhuth*, pp. 122–4. The export index covers cotton and the import index about 50 per cent of total imports.

post-war period and were pushed up to a record level in 1951 by the Korean War. Thereafter there was an equally sharp break in 1952 and 1953, followed by an appreciable improvement.

TABLE 30

*Indices of Quantum and Terms of Trade, 1938–59*

(*1938=100*)

| Year | Exports | | Imports | | Terms of trade |
|------|---------|---------|---------|---------|----------|
| | Index of quantum | Index of price | Index of quantum | Index of price | |
| 1939 | 117 | 100 | 84 | 109 | 91 |
| 1943 | 42 | 202 | 34 | 312 | 65 |
| 1945 | 57 | 249 | 53 | 311 | 80 |
| 1948 | 109 | 439 | 154 | 303 | 145 |
| 1951 | 86 | 798 | 188 | 349 | 229 |
| 1953 | 104 | 445 | 118 | 402 | 111 |
| 1954 | 92 | 505 | 112 | 388 | 130 |
| 1955 | 94 | 495 | 125 | 397 | 125 |
| 1956 | 89 | 539 | 125 | 404 | 133 |
| 1957 | 97 | 598 | 116 | 425 | 141 |
| 1958 | 108 | 515 | 162 | 399 | 129 |
| 1959 | 112 | 466 | 164 | 353 | 132 |

Source: NBE, *Econ. B.*, no. 1, 1951 & subs. issues.

A study of Egypt's foreign trade over the years 1946–57 by a United Nations expert shows that changes in the 'balance of trade have been to a greater extent the result of volume changes than of changes in the terms of trade'. It also shows that 'in general, a favourable volume effect as compared to the base year was accompanied by losses from trade (i.e. an unfavourable terms-of-trade effect) while an unfavourable volume effect was usually accompanied by gains from trade, with the result in either case that the change in the trade balance was moderated'.[1]

## BALANCE OF PAYMENTS

Table 31 (p. 232) shows the principal items in Egypt's balance of payments during the post-war years. It will be seen that in every

[1] NPC, Memo. no. 16.

**TABLE 31**

*Principal Items in Balance of Payments, 1946–61*

(£E million)

| Item | 1946 | 1949 | 1952 | 1955 | 1958 | 1959 | 1960 | 1961 |
|---|---|---|---|---|---|---|---|---|
| **Current Transactions** | | | | | | | | |
| *Credit:* | | | | | | | | |
| Proceeds of exports | 51·9 | 138·7 | 145·6 | 133·1 | 161·0 | 164·3 | 200·2 | 161·3 |
| Shipping | — | 7·9 | 6·8 | 9·1 | 8·7 | 12·5 | 15·2 | 8·2 |
| Suez Canal | — | 23·0 | 26·6 | 31·8 | 43·0 | 44·4 | 50·1 | 51·2 |
| British army expenditures | 20·7 | 11·5 | 5·8 | 4·8 | — | — | — | — |
| Other credit items | 30·4 | 35·8 | 33·9 | 48·5 | 37·5 | 43·7 | 36·2 | 35·4 |
| Total | 103·0 | 216·9 | 218·7 | 227·3 | 250·2 | 264·9 | 301·7 | 256·1 |
| *Debit:* | | | | | | | | |
| Payments for imports | 88·6 | 158·3 | 210·5 | 190·3 | 214·0 | 235·3 | 255·2 | 224·3 |
| Shipping | — | 8·8 | 6·9 | 9·3 | 10·7 | 11·5 | 14·8 | 7·8 |
| Interest, dividends, and other revenues | 12·1 | 13·7 | 16·9 | 17·1 | 2·2 | 2·2 | 3·2 | 4·5 |
| Travel & maintenance | 4·7 | 10·4 | 11·6 | 10·2 | 5·0 | 8·9 | 12·2 | 9·7 |
| Other debit items | 16·2 | 15·5 | 26·2 | 34·4 | 38·4 | 43·0 | 39·9 | 49·6 |
| Total | 121·6 | 206·7 | 272·1 | 261·3 | 270·3 | 300·9 | 325·3 | 295·9 |
| *Balance of Current Transactions* | −18·6 | 10·2 | −53·4 | −34·0 | −20·1 | −36·0 | −23·6 | −39·8 |
| *Capital remittances & compensations, net* | −0·8 | −5·3 | −2·0 | 2·2 | −3·8 | 11·4 | 11·1 | 20·4 |
| *Overall balance Accounted for as follows:* | −19·4 | 4·9 | −55·4 | −31·8 | −23·9 | −24·6 | −12·5 | −19·4 |
| Changes in sterling balances | −11·8 | −23·6 | −41·0 | −34·9 | 2·3 | −18·9 | −30·6 | }−23·4 |
| Changes in gold & foreign exchange | — | 19·4 | −17·7 | 2·6 | −12·9 | 2·1 | 3·2 | |
| Increase (−) or decrease in non-resident accounts held in Egypt | — | 9·5 | 1·8 | 0·9 | −6·6 | −6·9 | 14·2 | −2·8 |
| Balance of unrecorded items, errors, & omissions | −7·6 | −0·4 | 0·6 | −0·4 | −6·7 | −0·9 | 0·7 | 6·8 |
| Total | −19·4 | 4·9 | −55·4 | −31·8 | −23·9 | −24·6 | −12·5 | −19·4 |

*Source:* NBE, *Econ. B.*; CBE, *Econ. R.*

year there was a heavy import surplus but that invisible items showed a surplus. Except in 1949 and 1954, however, this failed to offset the import surplus, and a deficit was registered on current account.

On the credit side the most important item has been exports which, during the 1950's, averaged 65 per cent of total receipts. This was followed by Suez Canal dues, whose importance has risen steadily because of the rapid increase in traffic. During the 1950's Canal dues averaged 14 per cent of total receipts, their share rising from 10 per cent in 1950 to nearly 17 per cent in 1960. Until its nationalization, in 1956, the *net* contribution of the Canal to Egypt's balance of payments consisted of payments to the government and local expenditures in the form of wages and payments for services (see above, p. 213). Since 1956 the net contribution has consisted of the amount collected in dues minus payments for goods and services purchased by the Canal Authority abroad together with compensation to shareholders of the former Canal Company. Until 1956 another important credit item was the expenditure of the British army stationed in Egypt, which accounted for some 5 per cent of total receipts. Tourism also forms a significant item (see below, p. 234).

On the debit side, imports absorbed 77 per cent of total payments during the 1950's. The next most important item is government expenditures abroad—presumably largely for political purposes—which accounts for 8–9 per cent of the total; in 1959 expenditure under this heading reached the record figure of £E27·9 million. Payments to foreign shippers continue to absorb 3–4 per cent of total disbursements. Formerly the second most important debit item was interest and dividend payments to holders of shares and bonds of companies operating in Egypt, including the Suez Canal Company; in the early 1950's it amounted to 5–6 per cent of total payments and in 1954 reached a peak of £E18·1 million, or over 8 per cent. However, the nationalization of the Canal and other foreign companies greatly reduced this item, to less than 1 per cent of the total. On the other hand Egypt has had to make compensation payments to former shareholders and to the United Kingdom and Sudan governments (see below, p. 239); this item, which is shown under capital transactions, amounted to £E5·3 million in 1958, 6·5 million in 1959, 33·4 million in 1960, and 8·0 million in 1961.

Over the post-war period by far the most important item on capital account has been releases from sterling balances, carried out under successive agreements with the United Kingdom.[1] As a result, the total balance held in London by banks operating in Egypt fell from £E347 million in July 1947 to 180 million in December 1952 and 24 million in July 1960. Sterling releases, plus the increasing volume of foreign grants and loans received by Egypt (see below, p. 238), have made it possible to increase slightly gold and dollar reserves. At the end of 1960 gold reserves (which had been revalued) amounted to $174 million and all foreign-exchange reserves to $117 million.

A few words may be added regarding the regional distribution of the balance of payments. Transactions with the American monetary area show a heavy deficit on merchandise trade; this is partly compensated by a surplus on other transactions, mainly owing to payment of Suez Canal dues; the resulting overall deficit on current account has been covered by various forms of United States aid. The same pattern may be observed in dealings with Western Europe and the sterling area; with the last mentioned, however, receipts from Canal dues and shipping are so high that there has generally been an overall surplus on current account. With the Soviet bloc, merchandise transactions have generally shown a surplus and other transactions a deficit, leaving an overall deficit on current account. The current account with the Middle East also shows an overall deficit, due to both merchandise and other transactions.

### TOURISM

Traditionally (and largely because of the Pyramids and other monuments so frequently decried by economists as conspicuous

[1] The most important of these was concluded on 30 June 1947; it provided 'for the departure of Egypt from the sterling area and the blocking of the sterling assets held by the banks operating in Egypt . . . and for the release of a series of amounts in sterling'. The British government also undertook 'not to restrict the use of free sterling or the sterling proceeds of our exports for the payment of current transactions in any monetary zone'. The suspension, a few weeks later, of convertibility of sterling into dollars deprived the last clause of its value (NBE, *Rep. of 48th Ord. Gen. Mtg, 1947*). Egypt, however, drew about $125 m. between 1 Jan. 1945 and 15 July 1947 and was allocated $131 m. in 1947–51 inclusive. On 1 July 1951 a new agreement was signed providing for the release of £150 m. during the subsequent 10–13½ years; between 1951 and 1960 annual releases were to be £10 m., Egypt having the right to draw an additional £5 m., up to a total of £35 m., should its free balances fall below £45 m. This arrangement was interrupted during the Suez crisis, when Egypt's sterling holdings were blocked, but releases were resumed in 1957. For the general framework in which these events took place see Philip Bell, *The Sterling Area* (Oxford, 1956).

examples of wasteful expenditure!) Egypt has attracted large numbers of foreign visitors. The tourist trade received a great stimulus with the building of a set of superb hotels in Cairo, Alexandria, and Upper Egypt at the end of the last century and the beginning of this one, but the Depression gave it a heavy blow. By the 1930's, owing to the large expenditures of the richer Egyptians and foreign residents who spent their summers in Europe and Lebanon, as well as to the outlays of Moslem pilgrims to the Holy Cities of Arabia, Egypt probably had a net deficit on tourist expenditure. In the early post-war years political tensions and the Palestine war reduced the inflow of tourist traffic, and tourist expenditure probably continued to show a deficit. But more recently the position has changed, and Egypt now earns a substantial amount under this heading.

On the one hand travel of Egyptians abroad has been severely restricted; exit visas are granted only for reasons of health, business, or study, except where special arrangements have been made, as with Lebanon; moreover in all such cases the amount of foreign exchange granted is strictly limited. These measures have greatly curbed the outflow of funds.[1] And on the other hand, and more important, the number of tourists visiting Egypt has greatly increased, from 149,000 in 1955 to 285,000 in 1960. Owing to a shorter average stay, however, the number of guest nights spent rose only from 4,396,000 to 4,560,000. In addition, there were 210,000 passengers in transit. In 1960 tourist expenditures were estimated at £E22·4 million, compared with 22·7 million in 1959. Of the total number of visitors in 1960 44 per cent were Arabs, 32 per cent West Europeans, and 12 per cent Americans, but the pattern of expenditure was different, Europeans spending £E9·3 million, Arabs 9·2 million, and Americans 2·6 million.[2]

Vigorous efforts are being made to increase the inflow of tourists. Some excellent hotels have been built in Cairo and Upper Egypt

---

[1] It goes without saying that these restrictions, which have given the middle classes and the intelligentsia a feeling of intense claustrophobia, are extremely unpopular. There is no doubt that the Egyptian government is perfectly justified in wishing to conserve its scarce foreign exchange and in seeking to curtail drastically the amounts spent abroad by Egyptians. But this could have been achieved equally effectively by limiting the amount of foreign exchange granted, without adopting restrictions on travel reminiscent of those used behind the iron curtain, and in some respects more rigorous than in Poland.

[2] NBE, *Econ. B.*, no. 2, 1961. For various reasons, figures on expenditure do not agree with those published in the balance-of-payments estimates.

and 'tourist cities' (hotels, restaurants, and recreational centres) have been set up on the Red Sea and Mediterranean. By the end of 1960 Egypt had available for tourists 174 hotels with 8,052 rooms, and work is proceeding on several new projects. Visa and customs formalities have been simplified. Tourist offices have been opened in many foreign cities and expenditure on advertising has greatly increased. But much remains to be done before Egypt can fully exploit the potentialities offered by its superb winter climate, its unparalleled Pharaonic and Moslem monuments, and its beautiful beaches. Internal airline schedules, systems of transport, and hotel reservation often cause tourists unnecessary inconvenience. Although visa, customs, and exchange-control formalities have been greatly simplified, they still present a more formidable combination than is encountered in almost any Mediterranean country. Lastly, although tourists are actually met with great courtesy, and even friendliness, the general hostility to foreigners exuded by the press and even by certain official pronouncements cannot but have a discouraging effect on would-be travellers to Egypt.

### FOREIGN INVESTMENTS

Egypt's large export surplus during the First World War enabled it to invest in foreign securities estimated, in 1920, at well over £E100 million. During the inter-war years there was a large-scale exchange of foreign for Egyptian securities; in 1934 Egyptian holdings of foreign securities amounted to only £E38 million, while foreign indebtedness had been reduced from the 1914 level by £E47 million on the Public Debt and 26 million on share and debenture capital.[1]

In 1933 total foreign investment (excluding the Suez Canal) amounted to £E81 million. Of this, French investments, mainly in mortgage banking and public utilities, accounted for £E39 million. British interests followed with £E32 million, of which the greater part was in industrial firms and mortgage banks. Then came Belgian capital with £E7 million, mainly in land companies; Italian with 2 million, and Swiss with 1 million.[2]

During the Second World War Egypt once more redeemed a large part of its foreign debt, of which only 38 per cent was by then held abroad. The national debt was converted into Egyptian pounds (see above, p. 42) and a substantial amount was purchased from foreign owners. Thus some £E1 million of government bonds held

---

[1] Crouchley, *Investment*, pp. 81 & 165.       [2] Ibid. p. 201.

in France at the time of conversion were redeemed as well as a further 8 million of securities.[1] British holdings of securities were liquidated to an extent of 12 million.[2] Much Italian capital, and what there was of German, was lost as a result of war-time sequestration.

During the post-war years there was little foreign investment in Egypt, but some British and American capital, together with local capital, participated in industrial enterprises. Some Lebanese capital was invested in Egypt during the war and post-war years, and substantial amounts of Kuwaiti and Saudi Arabian capital after the war; most of this was in urban real estate.[3]

In 1948 foreign capital in Egypt was estimated at approximately £E100 million, at current stock-exchange quotations; this represented a substantial diminution in real terms from the pre-war figure. About £E45 million belonged to French interests and an approximately equal sum to British interests.[4] This would leave £E10 million for Belgian, Swiss, and United States capital, a figure which seems a considerable underestimate. Thereafter there was little direct foreign investment. American capital participated in a few enterprises such as petroleum, tyres, and chemicals and British in engineering and chemicals. The total value of outstanding United States direct investments in Egypt and the Sudan rose from $17 million in 1943 to $40 million in 1950; investments in Egypt stood at about $62 million in 1961.[5] In 1954 German private capital participated, to the extent of £E2·1 million, in setting up a steel mill and further amounts were later invested in other enterprises while Belgian and Italian capital went into petroleum. According to President Abdel Nasser, the total amount of foreign capital invested in Egypt between 1952 and 1961 was £E8·7 million, of which 5·2 million went into petroleum.[6]

The decreasing dependence of Egyptian business on foreign

[1] L. Topuz, 'Les Capitaux étrangers en Ég.', *R. écon. & financ.*, 24 Aug. 1948.

[2] Cleona Lewis, *The US and Foreign Investment Problems* (Wash., 1948).

[3] The value of property belonging to Lebanese, excluding those who have acquired Egyptian nationality, has been estimated at £E30–35 m. (*L'Orient*, 6 May 1962).

[4] Topuz, in *R. écon. & financ.*, 24 Aug. 1948. Cleona Lewis estimated British holdings in Egypt and the Sudan in 1947 at only £E29 m.; this figure, however, represents nominal values which were much lower than current prices.

[5] US Dept. of Commerce, *Survey of Current Business; Pick's Currency Yb. 1961*, p. 143.

[6] *al-Ahram*, 26 Nov. 1961. This figure presumably represents new foreign capital investment and therefore includes neither retained profits of foreign capital nor new capital from Arab countries.

capital in the post-war period is brought out by the fact that whereas the Egyptian share in the total capital of joint-stock companies operating in Egypt in 1933 was only 9 per cent, it rose to 47 per cent in companies established in 1934–9, 66 per cent in those established in 1940–5, and 84 per cent in those established in 1946–8.[1] At the same time the purchase by Egyptians of foreign-owned shares and bonds of companies operating in Egypt continued, and it is possible that by 1956 half the total capital of joint-stock companies registered in Egypt was Egyptian owned.

Since 1956 a massive liquidation of foreign investments has taken place. Following the Suez attack, British and French property was sequestrated; some of it later returned to its former owners, but the greater part remained in Egyptian hands. In 1959 Egypt agreed to pay the United Kingdom a sum of £27,600,000 in settlement of claims and counter-claims,[2] and a further undisclosed sum was paid to France. In December 1960 Belgian investments worth about £E7 million were nationalized or sequestrated. And in July 1961 most of the remaining foreign investments in the private sector were taken over by the government, as part of the general nationalization measures (see above, p. 58). Except for oil companies, foreign investment in the private sector is now negligible.

On the other hand foreign grants and loans to the Egyptian government, or to enterprises partly owned and managed by it, have been very considerable. The chief donor, as in most parts of the world, has been the United States. Between July 1945 and the end of 1951 the United States granted Egypt $500,000 and advanced loans amounting to $18 million. And between 1952 and the end of 1961 United States aid to Egypt totalled $567 million; of this $73 million consisted of grants, $432 million of loans repayable in Egyptian currency—most of which is re-lent to the Egyptian government for development purposes—(at 4 per cent interest, repayable in 30 years) and $62 million of loans repayable in hard currency. In recent years United States aid has been running at about $130 million and by the beginning of 1962 at nearly $200 million. The next most important source of aid has been the Soviet Union, which opened three lines of credit: the first, in 1958, for £E61 million (700 million

[1] Estimate by Abd Allah Abaza, published in Rashid al-Barawi, *Haqiqat al-inqilab al-akhir* (1952), p. 65.

[2] In connexion with this settlement, the claimed value of British property to be desequestrated was estimated at about £130 m. and that of Egyptianized or nationalized British property at about £50 m. (statement by Chancellor of the Exchequer in House of Commons, 2 March 1959).

roubles) for technical assistance, equipment, and machinery, and the other two, of £E35 and 90 million respectively, for the first and second stages of the High Dam; credits extended bear interest at 2½ per cent and are repayable in twelve years in Egyptian goods or in a currency acceptable to the Soviet Union. The other main lender has been West Germany, which in 1958 opened a credit of £E44·5 million (DM545 million) for economic development. In addition, in July 1961 West Germany opened further credits not shown in Table 32: a credit of DM500 million was granted to cover the foreign-exchange costs of the Euphrates dam, in Syria; one of DM150 million was opened for various projects in the UAR, such as dams, bridges, roads, &c (it bears 3 per cent interest and is repayable in 12–16 years); and credits totalling DM400 million will be extended for 7–10-year periods, at rates prevailing in international markets.[1]

In 1959 a loan of £E19·7 million ($56·5 million) was granted to Egypt by the International Bank for improving the Suez Canal.

No detailed breakdown is available on the utilization of these credits. Table 32 (p. 240) shows the position in March 1961, but it is misleading in one very important respect, namely the extent of United States aid, since the figure given represents well under half the total amount extended since 1952; presumably the table shows only credits opened since a later date. Moreover the table lumps together grants, long-term loans, lines of credit and short-term credit facilities extended by some countries for the promotion of their exports.

By March 1962 western credits granted since 1958 were $722 million, or £E252 million, and Soviet bloc credits $628 million, or £E219 million; of these $375 and $347 million respectively were still unused. In May 1962 an agreement for a credit of $42 million was concluded with the International Monetary Fund and one for $164 million with the United States. In addition, the Minister of Economy announced that further loans, totalling $477 million, would be soon advanced by the United States, of which 450 million would be for the purchase, over three years, of wheat, oils, and tobacco and 27·5 million for railway equipment.[2]

In addition to running down its foreign-exchange reserves and contracting large debts, Egypt has also incurred certain other liabilities. Compensation to the Suez Canal Company (see above, p. 214) and to the British and French governments has already been mentioned. In addition Egypt agreed in 1957 to pay to the Sudan

[1] *al-Ahram*, 6 and 7 July, 1961.    [2] *Arab News and Views* (NY), 1 June, 1962.

TABLE 32

## Foreign Loans and Credit Facilities, 1961

### (£E million)

| | Amt of loan or facility | Amt contracted or utilized[1] | Balance |
|---|---|---|---|
| *Western countries:* | | | |
| United States | 68·1[2] | 41·3 | 26·8 |
| W. Germany | 53·1[3] | 30·0 | 23·1 |
| Italy | 34·3[4] | 15·9 | 18·4 |
| Japan | 17·0 | 11·4 | 5·6 |
| France | 10·0 | — | 10·0 |
| United Kingdom | 5·4 | 5·4 | — |
| Netherlands | 5·0 | 0·5 | 4·5 |
| Switzerland | 4·0 | 1·9 | 2·1 |
| Sweden | 3·3 | 3·3 | — |
| Others | 6·3 | 6·3 | — |
| Total | 206·5 | 116·0 | 90·5 |
| *Soviet bloc:* | | | |
| Soviet Union | 186·0 | 32·6 | 153·4 |
| East Germany | 9·5 | 3·4 | 6·1 |
| Czechoslovakia | 9·2 | 7·1 | 2·1[5] |
| Hungary | 5·9[6] | — | 5·9 |
| Yugoslavia | 7·0 | 4·3 | 2·7 |
| Total | 217·6 | 47·4 | 170·2 |
| *IBRD* | 19·7 | 11·2 | 8·5 |
| Grand Total | 443·8 | 174·6 | 269·2 |

[1] Until Mar. 1961.

[2] Of which £E5·3 m. in grants and 46·3 m. repayable in local currency. Figure incomplete, see text.

[3] Of which £E12 m. in short-term credits.

[4] Of which £E14·2 m. for land reclamation and 18·4 m. for industrial projects.

[5] Expired 31 Oct. 1961.

Incl. Syrian region of UAR.

Source: *Exposé on Budget Project for FY July 1961–June 1962.*

£14 million in return for the withdrawal of Egyptian banknotes from the Sudan and in 1959 to pay £E12 million as compensation for the flooding of the northern Sudanese districts by the waters held by the High Dam; the last instalment was paid early in 1962. In March 1961 Egypt extended to Mali a loan, repayable in seven years and bearing 2½ per cent interest, for the purchase of equipment, machinery, and materials, and in May 1961 a similar loan, for £E6 million, was extended to Guinea; the latter provides that the amounts repaid will be used by Egypt for the purchase of imports from Guinea.[1] Another loan has been granted to Somalia.

It will thus be seen that in a few years' time Egypt will be faced with very heavy liabilities arising from interest charges and repayment of principal. Of course the huge investment financed by these foreign loans will make it possible to carry out much import substitution and reduce Egypt's imports of consumer, and many producer, goods. But no one can doubt that for many years to come Egypt's balance of payments will be subjected to a great strain.

## COMMERCIAL POLICY AND ORGANIZATION

On the outbreak of war in 1939 Egypt imposed a system of exchange control on foreign transactions and subjected imports and other foreign-exchange payments to licensing.[2] Licensing did not apply to transactions with the sterling area until July 1947, when Egypt ceased to be a member. By March 1948 it was found that supplies of sterling were sufficient to permit the removal of restrictions on imports from the sterling area, and this was gradually followed by the abolition of licensing on imports from all but 'hard currency' areas. In October 1952, however, owing to the severe strain on Egypt's balance of payments, all imports were made subject to licensing.

During this period Egypt's commercial policy was dictated by two facts. On the one hand until 1952 the supply of sterling was abundant, but the sterling area was unable to furnish all the goods required by Egypt; on the other hand dollars required for certain imports were scarce. Egypt therefore pursued the double objective of maximizing its receipts of hard currencies and reducing, wherever possible, its imports from the dollar area. A further goal was to widen the market for Egyptian cotton, by means of bilateral or barter agreements.

[1] NBE, *Econ. B.*, no. 2, 1961.
[2] Mustafa Saqqaf, *al-Riqaba ala'l-naqd al-ajnabi fi misr* (1954).

Since the revolution, as Egypt's balance of payments worsened, as its sterling balances were rapidly run down, and as its cotton exports met with growing competition and buyers' resistance in their main markets, two main instruments of policy were increasingly used: bilateral payments and trade agreements, and unofficial devaluation to stimulate exports and reduce imports.

The greater part of Egyptian foreign trade is now conducted under a series of bilateral payments agreements, which fix the total value of exports and imports between the two partners, sometimes allow for a 'swing' or other form of credit, and stipulate that balances shall be paid in a convertible currency, and of trade agreements which specify the products to be exchanged.[1] Such agreements have allowed Egypt to divert nearly half its trade to the Soviet bloc, a development welcomed by most Egyptians. However, two main drawbacks should be noted. First, since Egypt has been very anxious to dispose of its cotton and since the prices of the goods exchanged have been determined by negotiation, the Soviet bloc suppliers have been able to set very high prices for their goods; the losses incurred by Egypt under this heading have run into several million pounds a year. Secondly, some Soviet bloc purchasers of Egyptian cotton, notably Czechoslovakia, have resold Egyptian cotton in various western markets at discounts running up to 30 per cent; this too has inflicted further heavy losses on the Egyptian economy. The magnitude of the costs incurred in such trading has gradually been realized and recently efforts have been made to shift exports once more to Western countries, but it is difficult to recapture a lost market, especially where spinners have adapted their machines to other qualities. However, the shift is being eased by the facilities offered by certain countries; thus late in 1961 a British firm offered Egypt a credit of £5 million, to be used for the purchase of capital goods and to be partly paid for by £2½ million worth of Egyptian cotton.

There has been no formal devaluation of the Egyptian currency since 1949, but *de facto* exchange depreciation has been achieved by various means.[2] Thus in 1949 the system of Export Pound Accounts was instituted under which the Egyptian pound stood at a discount in free markets.[3] In 1953 Import Entitlement Accounts were intro-

---

[1] For a summary of the various agreements and a list of those in force at any given time see NBE, *Econ. B.* and CBE, *Econ. R.*

[2] See ibid. and IMF, *Ann. Rep. on Exchange Restriction* (Washington, D.C.).

[3] NBE, *Econ. B.*, no. 2, 1953.

duced, leading to the emergence of a premium of 5–10 per cent for certain currencies such as the dollar, pound sterling, and mark.[1] In February 1958, when exports to western countries had sunk to a very low level, an effort was made to stimulate them by a new system of Export Pound Accounts under which premia of up to 30 per cent were originally offered, later reduced by steps to 17·6 per cent on earnings of free currencies, while importers paid a premium of 9 per cent on purchases of foreign exchange. In September 1959 these accounts were abolished, but the system of premia and discounts was retained. By 1960 exporters of raw cotton and cotton and silk products to countries with convertible currencies were being offered a premium of 6·4 per cent, exporters of most other products 17·5 per cent, and tourists 27·5 per cent. On the other hand a premium of 10 per cent was paid on purchases of foreign exchange for imports and most invisible payments in addition to a payment of 9·9 per cent on import licences. In September 1961 premia on exports of cotton and textiles were abolished. Finally, on 30 December 1961, four important decrees were issued.[2] Payments for imports were subjected to an overall surcharge of 20 per cent, instead of the previous 10 per cent premium and 9·9 per cent duty. Exporters were granted a uniform premium of 20 per cent, irrespective of the kind of goods exported (but for petroleum, rice, onions, and groundnuts this was offset by a 20 per cent export tax) or of the market of destination. This was said to be more in conformity with international ethics and to demonstrate Egypt's economic neutralism and in fact was designed to bring down prices of imports from the Soviet bloc and other bilateral agreement areas. The official exchange-rate was declared binding for certain payments such as Suez Canal dues and disbursements by airline and shipping companies. Lastly, the bringing into Egypt of Egyptian banknotes was prohibited. These decrees were followed by a sharp drop in the rate of the Egyptian pound in foreign markets.[3]

As regards commercial organization, mention has already been made of the fact that the government successively monopolized the importation of such commodities as tea, wheat, fertilizers, and pharmaceuticals and that in June 1961 cotton exports and practically

---

[1] Ibid. no. 3, 1953.

[2] *al-Ahram*, 31 Dec. 1961 & NBE, *Econ. B.*, no. 4, 1961.

[3] On 7 May 1962 a uniform premium of 25 per cent was applied to all bank transfers in settlement of exports and payment for services; in other words the Egyptian pound was devalued, *de facto*, to $2·30. Suez Canal dues will continue, however, to be payable at the old rate of $2·87 (*al-Ahram*, 7 May 1962).

all imports were confined to government-owned or controlled companies (above, p. 59). Since that time, the export of cotton has been effected through the Egyptian Cotton Commission. That body works through the former cotton exporting houses, 50 per cent or more of whose capital is now owned by the government; many managers of these firms have been changed and close control is exercised by the Commission. Most other exports have remained in private hands, but they are being slowly strangled by the red-tape of the customs administration and other bodies charged with the supervision of exports.[1] As regards the nationalized industries, the Ministry of Industry has declared that each enterprise is to be allowed to export its own products, in competition with other enterprises.[2]

As for imports, in October 1961 the 86 groups of commodities which constitute the Egyptian customs classification were allotted to 18 government companies. Some of these groups are assigned exclusively to one company, for example living animals and meat, others to several companies, while some, such as cereals, may be imported by all eighteen companies.[3] A cross classification, showing the items allotted to each company, does not reveal any logical connexion between them.[4] However, it has been announced that the organization of export trade is to be rationalized by amalgamating companies and co-ordinating their activities.[5]

At the end of 1961 the system of importation was working along the following lines. Foreign exporters would contact the government company or companies to which their product had been allotted, giving it the agency name. The government company would then assign the article to its former agent or distributor who would do the actual handling, giving the government company a commission of 3–10 per cent. In other words, imports were still coming in through their former channels, but only after being

---

[1] See the examples given by the Min. of Nat. Econ. in *al-Ahram* 15 Dec. 1961. Of the numerous ones reported to the present writer the following will suffice. An attempt to export tomatoes necessitated the collection of over 20 official signatures, and a certain amount of bribery; by that time the merchandise was unfit to be exported. A merchant who wished to export handicraft work to the United States and had a few hundred catalogues printed was informed that he needed export permits to send these catalogues to his correspondents; as an ultimate concession he was told that he could send all the catalogues to one of his prospective buyers in the States, who could then distribute copies to his competitors; this attempt at export, too, was abandoned.

[2] *al-Ahram al-iqtisadi*, 1 Dec. 1961.
[3] See list in NBE, *Econ. B.*, no. 3, 1961.
[4] *al-Ahram*, 27 Sept. 1961.　　　　[5] Ibid. 8 Feb. 1962.

subjected to numerous formalities which slowed them down and raised their cost. As against that must be set the possibility that these companies may be in a better position to exert pressure on foreign suppliers and force them to lower their prices as well as stricter control over foreign-exchange disbursements. Another point to be noticed is that the same company handles several competing products—for example several brands of American and British as well as Soviet and other tractors—which opens the door to possibilities of abuse. Lastly, although in principle factories in the private sector are allowed to import their own requirements directly, cases where permission to do so has been refused have already occurred.[1]

[1] For a fuller discussion of objectives and methods see ibid. 9 June 1962.

# XI

# Finance

*The advantage of this [i.e. an international standard] is that it prevents individual follies and eccentricities. The disadvantage is that it hampers each Central Bank in tackling its own national problems.*                                               J. M. KEYNES.

*Better banks can facilitate but cannot provide the foundation for economic development.*
                                               R. S. SAYERS.

*Economic expansion cannot, for long, be based on monetary disorder.*

PER JACOBSSON.

No sector of the Egyptian economy has changed more profoundly since the Second World War than the financial one. A sterling-exchange standard has been replaced by a managed currency. A system under which there were absolutely no restrictions on movements of funds abroad has given way to the strictest form of exchange control. The insurance business, formerly mainly in the hands of foreign firms, was first egyptianized and then nationalized. Similarly the banking system, in which branches of foreign commercial banks played an important—and until recently a predominant—part, has been revolutionized. First a few gaps in the credit system were filled by founding special banks, sponsored and partly owned by the government, and by increasing the power of the Central Bank. Then, in 1956, measures were taken to egyptianize all banks. Lastly, in 1960 and 1961, the whole banking system was nationalized and is now operated by the government.[1]

### CURRENCY SYSTEM

The successive steps by which Egypt severed its link with gold have already been mentioned (above, p. 31). The declaration that

[1] The most useful sources on the financial system in Egypt are the various publications of the NBE: the *Ann. Reports*, the quarterly *Econ. B.*, the annual *Credit & Banking Developments*, and the commemorative volume, *The National Bank of Egypt, 1898–1948*. To these should be added the *Econ. R.* of the CBE, which started publication in 1961. For details on the period before 1952 see Issawi, *Egypt*, ch. 10.

the National Bank's notes would be legal tender and the substitution of sterling securities for gold backing did not mean that Egypt adopted a sterling-exchange standard, since there was no obligation to convert Egyptian notes to sterling. However, a 'gentleman's agreement' between the National Bank and the other banks provided for the transfer to and from London of sums exceeding £E50,000. The effect of this arrangement was that Egypt was virtually on a sterling-exchange standard and that there were absolutely no obstacles—not even transfer charges—to the movement of funds between Egypt and London.

This system had several advantages for Egypt such as cheapness, simplicity, and flexibility of operations and the fact that the cover of the note issue earned interest instead of being immobilized in bullion. But as against that it had two major drawbacks. First, it was an automatic system, which tied Egypt's currency to its balance of payments. An increase in the note issue was possible only if a surplus was secured which could be used to provide the necessary sterling cover, and conversely a deficit necessitated the liquidation of foreign assets and, usually, a consequent reduction in the note issue. All this meant that Egypt, unlike so many backward countries, enjoyed a sound currency, with which the government could not tamper and which was safeguarded against inflation caused by internal factors such as a budget deficit. But, by the same token, it meant that the government could not manage the currency but had to accept passively changes originating from outside. The second defect was that the Egyptian pound was closely tied to sterling. This again helped to ensure its soundness but made it dependent on external factors and strengthened Anglo-Egyptian financial and economic relations, a fact which became most apparent in moments of crisis, such as the devaluation of sterling in 1931 and the two world wars with the massive British army expenditures in Egypt (see above, p. 31 and below, p. 269). Given the sentiments prevailing in Egypt towards Britain, it was inevitable that the link with sterling should be blamed for all Egypt's woes, including both the depression of the 1930's and the inflation of the 1940's.[1]

Egypt's departure from the sterling area, in July 1947, was followed by the promulgation in July 1948 of Law No. 119 of 1948. This provided that all increases in the note issue should henceforth be covered by 'bills of the Egyptian Treasury in respect of the

[1] For a discussion of Egypt's monetary system see Ahmad Nazmy Abd al-Hamid, 'Nizam al-naqd fi'l-khamsin sana'l-akhira', in *Buhuth*, pp. 11-37.

portion of the issue which must be covered by gold' and by Egyptian
government or government-guaranteed securities or by bills of the
Egyptian treasury in respect of the portion of the issue which must
be covered by the securities. The government was authorized to use
as cover up to £E50 million in treasury bills. In 1950 the limit was
raised to £E100 million to make possible an expansion of the note
issue required to finance the cotton crop at the very high prices then
prevailing and in 1957 it was again raised to £E200 million. As a
result of the 1948 law, the agreement regarding the conversion of
sterling into Egyptian pounds, and vice versa, came to an end; such
conversion became 'subject to the exchange control, like operations
in other currencies'.[1] In the following years the gold cover of the
note issue was both revalued and increased, and at the end of 1960
it amounted to £E60·6 million, compared with 162·4 million in
securities. The Issue Department of the National Bank continued to
remain distinct from the Banking Department and when, at the end
of 1960, the National Bank was divided into a Central Bank and a
National Bank, the former retained the distinction between the two
departments.

As regards the evolution of the note issue, the First World War
led to widespread use of banknotes and the issue (end of year
figures) rose from £E2·7 million in 1913 to a peak of 67·3 million
in 1919, but owing to the deflation of the late 1920's and 1930's the
1938 figure was only 22·2 million. During the Second World War
there was a large expansion, to £E148 million in 1945, which
continued, reaching 191 million in 1950. Thereafter the rise was
slower, and was interrupted by setbacks, and at the end of 1960 the
note issue stood at £E223 million, while deposit money greatly
increased (see below, p. 251). 'Thus while the previous decades saw
a transition from coins to Bank-Notes, the last decade witnessed a
strong tendency towards augmenting the role played by deposit
money.'[2]

### STRUCTURE OF CREDIT INSTITUTIONS

The outbreak of the 1952 Revolution found the Egyptian commercial banking system divided into three main sectors: the partially
and increasingly egyptianized National Bank, fulfilling many of the
functions of a Central Bank and working closely with the government, but maintaining a certain degree of independence (see above,

---

[1] NBE, *Rep. of 49th Ord. Gen. Mtg.*, 1948.

[2] NBE, *Econ. B.*, no. 1, 1961; this issue contains useful information on currency
and banking during the 1950's.

p. 41); the purely Egyptian Misr Bank; and branches of foreign banks, or banks registered in Egypt but owned mainly by foreigners. Of the twenty-five registered commercial banks three were British, two were French, two Greek, two Turkish, and two Palestinian. The remaining fourteen were incorporated in Egypt, but except for the National and Misr Banks they were mainly foreign owned and still largely managed by foreigners or members of minority groups. The banks with the widest network were Misr and the National Banks, Barclay's, and the Ottoman Bank.[1] The two principal mortgage banks (Crédit Foncier and Land Bank) were incorporated in Egypt, but both were predominantly French in capital and management. The Agricultural Credit Bank, the Crédit Hypothécaire Agricole, and the Industrial Bank were jointly owned by the government and the principal banks. The insurance business was still mainly in foreign hands, and foreign companies handled 60 per cent of life insurance policies in 1948, a figure somewhat below the pre-war one.[2]

Egyptian interest in the stock exchange had considerably increased in the previous fifteen years, but most of its clients were still foreign or egyptianized residents. Levantines, and in particular Jews, played an important part. It was indicative that the leading Arabic dailies such as *al-Ahram* gave less information on the stock exchange than did the small foreign dailies.

This situation changed radically after 1956. Following the Suez attack, British and French banks were sequestrated, and on 14 January 1957 Law No. 22 of 1957 was promulgated. This provided that all commercial banks must take the form of Egyptian joint-stock companies with a paid-up capital of not less than £E500,000, in the form of nominative shares owned by Egyptian subjects, and with Egyptian management. Banks were allowed a period of one year, later extended to five, to carry out the necessary changes. The sequestrated British and French banks were taken over by the Economic Development Organization, which merged them with Egyptian banks founded after the Second World War by private capital alone or in association with public bodies. Thus Barclay's was merged with the Bank of Alexandria, the Ottoman and Ionian Banks with al-Goumhouria Bank, the Crédit Lyonnais and Comptoir National d'Escompte with the Bank of Cairo, and the Banque du Crédit d'Orient with the Union Commerciale. The magnitude

[1] For further details see ibid. no. 1, 1952 and Issawi, *EMC*, p. 213.
[2] NBE, *Econ. B.*, no. 3, 1950.

of the changes involved may be judged from the fact that the capital of commercial banks owned mainly by foreigners amounted at the end of 1956 to £E5·2 million and deposits with them to about £E100 million, or half the total deposits in all commercial banks, while the sequestrated banks, in turn, accounted for well over half of the activity of foreign-owned banks.[1]

In the course of the next three years the smaller banks registered in Egypt, as well as the branches of Greek, Japanese, Turkish, Saudi Arabian, Lebanese, Palestinian, and United States banks, either closed down or joined one of the Egyptian banks.

In 1960 two further steps were taken: in February both the National and Misr Banks were nationalized and in December the Banque Belge et Internationale en Égypte suffered the same fate, its name being changed to Port Said Bank. The Banque Belge was the most important of the eight remaining banks which, although registered in Egypt, were still mainly foreign owned but were in the course of merging with an Egyptian-owned bank in order to effectuate their egyptianization before the deadline of 13 January 1962 set by the law of 1957.[2] The eight remaining branches of foreign banks, which between them accounted for about 13 per cent of commercial banking activity in Egypt, were also in the course of selling out or closing down.[3] This meant that, by the beginning of 1961, the government owned wholly, in addition to the National Bank, three leading banks (Misr, Alexandria, Port Said), which between them accounted for 57 per cent of the aggregate balance sheet of all banks operating in Egypt, and partly three other banks (Cairo 45·2 per cent, al-Goumhouria 25·2, and Banque de l'Union Commerciale 25·1), which accounted for a further 30 per cent. The government also owned, wholly or mainly, the mortgage, agricultural, and industrial banks. The last step was taken on 20 July 1961, when under the provisions of Law No. 117 all banks and insurance companies in the UAR were nationalized.

The latest published figures on the number of bank branches refer to the end of 1960.[4] Including the National Bank, there were 264 commercial bank offices, of which 59 were in Cairo, 33 in Alexandria, and 20 in the Canal Zone. In other words, Egypt has a bank for

[1] NBE, *Econ. B.*, no. 1, 1961.
[2] In 1961 the National Bank took over the two main foreign banks, Banca Commerciale Italiana and Banca Italo-Egiziana, as well as two Greek and one American banks.     [3] Ibid.
[4] See details in CBE, *Credit & Banking Developments in 1960.*

every 100,000 persons, a figure which may be compared with 60,000 in India, under 10,000 in Italy, and under 3,000 in Australia.[1] More-over, as the above figures show, the distribution of facilities is very uneven, the heavy concentration in Cairo, Alexandria, and the Canal being matched by scarcity in the provinces. Ideally, nationali-zation should make it possible to remedy this defect and also to introduce a certain amount of specialization between the different banks.

It remains to be added that some Egyptian banks have established branches abroad; in 1960, there were 17 such branches in Syria, 8 in the Sudan, 7 in Saudi Arabia, and 2 in Libya, the Gaza strip, and Lebanon. The former branches of the National Bank in the Sudan closed down when the Bank of Sudan was established in 1960.

## CUSTODY AND TRANSFERENCE OF SAVINGS

The growth of deposit banking in Egypt dates from the First World War and in the inter-war period expansion continued. By the end of 1939, private deposits in all banks operating in Egypt, including foreign branches of the National Bank, amounted to £E65 million.[2] The number of depositors was about 100,000.

During the Second World War the rise in the national income (in money, not real terms) and the shift to profits that took place com-bined to raise greatly the volume of deposits, and the number of depositors also increased, though in a much smaller proportion. In the post-war period deposits declined; but after 1952 the rise was resumed. Total private deposits increased from £E215·3 million at the end of 1954 to 354·1 million in 1960 and 370·9 million in 1961.[3]

At the end of February 1959, of the £E250 million constituting total deposits in the commercial banks, 48 per cent were in the hands of the two largest banks, Misr Bank and the Bank of Alexandria, and 82 per cent in the hands of the six largest, the balance being shared by 19 small banks.[4] At the same date deposits in the National Bank amounted to £E53 million. In the late 1940's, current deposits constituted about 80 per cent of the total deposits of commercial banks, time deposits about 14 per cent, and savings deposits about

---

[1] al-Gritly, in *Buhuth*, pp. 197–202; this study contains a wealth of information.
[2] Gritly, in *Buhuth*.                    [3] NBE, *Econ. B.*, no. 4, 1961.
[4] Gritly, in *Buhuth*. February was chosen as the midpoint of the cotton season. The regional concentration of deposits is illustrated by the fact that 80 per cent of those in the Bank of Alexandria were in Cairo and Alexandria.

7 per cent. In the 1950's the share of current deposits slowly fell, and in 1959 it stood at 76 per cent of total private deposits.[1] The stability of deposits and their low velocity of circulation may be illustrated by the fact that the proportion between bank clearings and deposits was about 3 to 1 in both pre-war and post-war years, being a little lower in recent years. However, deposits show a marked seasonal fluctuation, increasing during the cotton season with the rise in incomes.

Rates of interest seem to have risen in recent years. In 1952 it was stated that the rate on time deposits 'varies between 0·5 per cent and 1·5 per cent, depending on the size of the account and the time during which the deposits are left with the banks. Rates of 2·5 to 3 per cent are not, however, uncommon.'[2] But by 1960 it was reported that rates on current deposits were 1·25 per cent and those on deposits for a year or more 3 per cent.[3]

Although the volume of private deposits has increased, it is still rather small, amounting to less than £E15 per capita. In the past this was owing to the following economic and social factors: the absence of a large and prosperous middle class; the prevailing illiteracy and distrust among the poorer classes; the preference shown for investment in land or hoarding of gold; the emphatic Koranic prohibitions against usury, only partly offset by Muhammad Abdu's *fatwa* authorizing the taking of interest on Post Office Savings Bank deposits; the absence, until 1937, of any legislation regarding the drawing of cheques, leading to a general distrust of cheques and reluctance to open bank accounts;[4] and, not least important, the fact that until quite recently, and more particularly before the foundation of Misr Bank, few bank managers (who were almost always foreigners) were able to establish close contacts with Egyptians and persuade them of the advantages of opening an account.

In recent years several of these factors have disappeared, and even before the measures taken in 1957 the gradual egyptianization of bank personnel and the growth of education had done much to spread the habit of deposit banking, as had the guarantee by the government of deposits in certain banks. But fairly heavy, and rising, stamp duties and the liability of bank deposits to seizure by the Department of Taxation acted as deterrents and the extent of hoarding of banknotes was shown by the fact that, when those

[1] NBE, *Econ. B.*, no. 1, 1961.  [2] Ibid., no. 1, 1952.  [3] Gritly, in *Buhuth*.
[4] Even today some government administrations refuse to accept cheques in settlement of payments.

denominations were withdrawn in 1959, more than £E50 million of £E50 and £E100 notes were outstanding.[1] Still more recently, the nationalizations and sequestrations of 1961 have led to a withdrawal from deposits.

The Post Office and other savings banks, opened at the beginning of the century, were designed to attract small savings, since the minimum deposit allowed was 5 millièmes and the maximum £E500, a figure subsequently raised to £E2,000. Their rapid growth in pre-war years to a total of 487,000 accounts aggregating £E9·6 million in 1938 was partly thanks to the relatively high rate of interest allowed, 3 per cent. During the war and post-war period the expansion of deposits was accelerated, in spite of a decline in the interest rate, and at the end of 1948 there were 728,000 accounts aggregating £E29·8 million.[2] In recent years deposits have grown rapidly, helped by a rise in interest rates to 2·5 per cent and by the granting of greater autonomy to the Post Office in 1954. By the middle of 1962 the number of depositors in its savings banks was around 1 million with accounts totalling £E53 million. But the total number of depositors in such accounts was still only 4 per cent of the population, a very low figure.[3]

Another important channel for the draining of savings has been life insurance, supplemented recently by various forms of social insurance. Until 1928 there was only one Egyptian insurance company, founded in 1900 by the National Bank, but by 1939 the number had risen to 6 and by 1956 to 13, with a nominal capital of £E25 million of which 17·2 had been paid up; foreign interests, mainly British, accounted for 44 per cent of the paid-up capital of these companies.[4] At the same time there were over 110 branches of foreign insurance companies, which between them accounted for about half the total business transacted in Egypt—53 per cent in 1954 and 47 in 1955. The share of foreign companies had been showing a steady drop since the early 1930's.

In 1957 Law No. 23 decreed the egyptianization of all insurance companies within five years and Law No. 162 raised the minimum authorized capital from £E200,000 to 500,000. As a result of these measures, by 1960 the number of companies had decreased to 49, of which 17 were Egyptian. In July 1961 all insurance business was

---

[1] Gritly, in *Buhuth*.     [2] NBE, *Econ. B.*, no. 2, 1953.
[3] Savings deposits with commercial banks, which allow the same rate of interest, amounted in 1959 to £E26·5 m. (ibid. no. 1, 1961 & *al-Ahram*, 2 June 1962).
[4] Ali Ahmad al-Shafi, 'Bahth an al-tamin fi khamsin sana', in *Buhuth*, pp. 157–96.

nationalized and further amalgamation reduced the number of companies to 9 by the beginning of 1962.[1]

In 1958, the latest year for which figures are available, 164,000 individual and collective life assurance policies were outstanding, for a total value of £E152·2 million (compared with 74·7 million in 1954[2] and an incomplete total of 48 million in 1948). Other insurance business included capital redemption assurance, for £E9 million, and general insurance (fire, accident, transport, &c.) for 6·2 million.

Government control was first extended to insurance companies in 1939, and was tightened by Law No. 156 of 1950 which compelled life assurance companies to keep in Egypt amounts equal to their mathematical liabilities while other undertakings had to keep reserves of not less than 40 per cent of total premiums collected in the country during the previous financial year. Investment of reserves was also specified; thus 25 per cent was to be kept in Egyptian government bonds.[3] In 1957, to ease the disruption caused by the break of relations with Britain and France, the Egyptian Company for Reinsurance was formed, with capital subscribed by Egyptian insurance companies and public bodies; it began operations in 1958. As a result of all these measures the insurance item in the balance of payments, which in the late 1940's showed an annual net debit of about £E1 million, is now in balance.

Lastly, mention must be made of social insurance. A law of 1955 set up an Institute for Insurance and Savings of Workmen and ordered all firms employing fifty or more workers to establish provident funds (half the contribution to be made by employers and half by workers) and to contract life assurance policies whose premiums were to be borne by the employer. A law of 1958 transferred workmen's compensation insurance to this institution and also replaced lump-sum payments for major injuries by a pension. In 1959, however, this institution was replaced by an Institute for Social Insurance under a new law (abrogating the two previous laws), which also provided for old-age insurance in addition to insurance against risks of death or total disability and extended the coverage to all urban workers.[4] By the end of March 1961 235,000 employers and 350,000 workers were covered by insurance and pension schemes,[5] and by June 1962 nearly a million.

The relative importance of various forms of savings in recent

[1] *al-Ahram*, 17 Jan. 1962.   [2] CBE, *Econ. R.*, no. 1, 1961.
[3] See Shafi, in *Buhuth*.   [4] CBE, *Econ. R.*, no. 1, 1961.
[5] *Exposé on the Budget Project*, p. 109.

years is shown in Table 33; the figures given differ from those in other sources, but the discrepancy is not great.

TABLE 33

*Savings through Various Institutions, 1956–60*

(*End of year, in £E million*)

| Year | Banks | Post Office | Invest- ments of insurance Co. | Ins. & pension funds | Inst. for Social Insurance | Total |
|------|-------|-------------|-------------------------------|---------------------|---------------------------|-------|
| 1956 | 55·4 | 32·6 | 33·2 | 24·4 | 0·9 | 146·5 |
| 1957 | 61·5 | 37·8 | 41·4 | 36·9 | 2·4 | 180·0 |
| 1958 | 73·2 | 41·5 | 47·1 | 49·2 | 4·9 | 215·9 |
| 1959 | 88·1 | 45·7 | 53·5 | 54·4 | 8·0 | 249·7 |
| 1960 | 94·2 | 47·4 | 57·5 | 71·3 | 11·0 | 285·6 |
| 1961/2 | 104·0 | 53·0 | 58·0 | 126·0 | 21·0 | 362·0 |

*Sources:* NPC, Memo. no. 504; *al-Ahram*, 2 June 1962.

The stock exchanges, of which there is one in Cairo and one in Alexandria, were closed down in July 1961 and their future is uncertain in view of the great transformations that have taken place in the economy but it would seem that they will be reopened to handle government bonds and securities of nationalized and non-nationalized companies. These markets were rather narrow, the nominal value of securities quoted in the Cairo Stock Exchange being in the early 1950's about £E200 million and their market value fluctuating between 300 and 400 million. This narrowness and the mercurial character of the clientele explain the sensitiveness of the market to any shock and its liability to sharp price fluctuations. Until 1961 government intervention in the market had taken the form of occasionally fixing minimum quotations, as well as forbidding futures operations.

## SHORT-TERM CREDIT OPERATIONS

Egypt's chief short-term credit has, since the 1820's, been the moving of the cotton crop. Until quite recently, this required an annual inflow and outflow of foreign funds. Up to 1914 this took the form of a seasonal influx of gold but after that banks operating in Egypt transferred the required funds through the National Bank and the note issue was correspondingly increased. Later, as farmers began repaying loans and making disbursements, and as the seasonal import surplus in spring and summer replaced the export surplus normally achieved in autumn and winter, the note issue contracted and the banks transferred their surplus funds to the London and other money markets.

The growth of deposits gradually reduced this dependence on foreign money centres, which had occasionally transmitted to Egypt shocks originating abroad, and the imposition of exchange-control on transactions with the sterling area in 1948 cut the last links between the Egyptian and London money markets. On 28 February 1961 the paid-up capital of all commercial banks in Egypt amounted to £E17·3 million and their reserves and undivided profits to 33·3 million, or 9·8 per cent of total liabilities, which amounted to 518·9 million; deposits amounted to £E360·4 million and borrowings from the Central Bank to 19·5 million or 70·0 and 3·8 per cent respectively.[1]

Turning to the assets, it may be noted that the banks have a fair degree of liquidity. The reserve ratio of the commercial banks, after rising during the war from a pre-war average of 10–15 per cent, has shown a falling trend, from 21·2 per cent in 1952–5 to 17·7 in 1956–9; at the end of 1960 it stood at 19·6 per cent. The amount of cash held by banks varies little throughout the year but their balances with the Central Bank (see below, p. 267) fluctuate much more. At the beginning of the cotton season the reserve ratio falls sharply and later recovers—in the 1959/60 season from 19·3 per cent at the end of July 1959 to 13·8 at the end of November, gradually returning to 15·7 at the end of March 1960 and 19·2 at the end of July. This cycle is accompanied by a corresponding movement in the note issue, which in the 1950's showed an average rise of £E24·1 million between the end-of-July trough and the end-of-November peak.[2]

A similar cycle is observable in loans and advances, which account for a little over 15 per cent of total assets and which are also greatly influenced by cotton.[3] Loans and advances are at their minimum in

[1] The 1961 figures include, for the first time, the balance sheet of the NBE in the aggregate figures for commercial banks. The balance sheet of the CBE is naturally not included.

[2] See details in NBE, *Econ. B.*, no. 1, 1961.

[3] The ratio of loans and advances to deposits has shown a marked rise, from 71·8 per cent in 1952 to a peak of 88·1 per cent in 1959; this shows the increasing activity of commercial banks (ibid).

August and rise sharply to a peak around the end of the year.[1] Advances on cotton and grains are made to merchants, or to a much smaller extent to growers, who deposit the produce pledged in a bank *shoona* (open store); loans secured by bills and securities are used to finance a wide range of operations and hence show very little seasonal fluctuation. Rates of interest vary according to both the status of the borrower and the type of collateral.

Advances, like deposits are heavily concentrated. In February 1959 five banks, with advances of over £E10 million each, accounted for 76 per cent of the total and two other banks for another 9 per cent. As for regional distribution, Cairo absorbed 51 per cent of the total and Alexandria 24 per cent.[2]

Another asset closely tied to cotton was bills discounted, since the bulk formerly consisted of three-month exporters' bills, which were discounted at a rate close to that ruling in London and which showed a marked seasonal variation. In recent years, however, the position has changed. In the first place the volume of exporters' bills discounted may have actually decreased, or at any rate has not increased substantially, and it seems to be less concentrated seasonally than before; among the factors responsible for this change are the shift in exports to the Soviet bloc and, more recently, the nationalization of cotton exporting. Secondly, there has been a marked growth in inland bills because banks sometimes finance instalment buying by means of bills and much of the cotton purchased by local mills is similarly financed; discount rates for inland bills are usually 5–7 per cent.[3] As a result, the total amount of bills discounted by commercial banks rose from £E8·8 million in 1952, or 4·5 per cent of assets, to 20·6 million in 1960. Moreover the seasonal fluctuation in bills is much smaller; thus in the 1959–60 season the minimum was £E14·2 million and the maximum 20·1 million.

There has also been a marked increase in the discounting of treasury bills and bills drawn by public bodies, such as the Economic

---

[1] In 1959/60 the rise was from £E146·2 m. in August to 221·1 m. in November; of this total, advances on cotton amounted to £E8·6 m. and 77·4 m. respectively, accounting for practically the whole increase. In the past the share of cotton was much larger, amounting to 50 per cent or over of total advances during the seasonal peak but it has been reduced by the growth of other types of advances. These, too, are usually covered by some kind of collateral, unsecured loans forming only 10–15 per cent of the total. Thus in February 1961, of a total of £E227 m. of outstanding loans, unsecured loans accounted for 31 m., cotton for 70 m., other agricultural produce for 9 m., other merchandise for 28 m., securities for 17 m. and bills for 12 m.          [2] Gritly, in *Buhuth*.          [3] Ibid.

Development Organization. Short-term treasury bills began to be issued on a large scale during the Second World War but the commercial banks have been reluctant to take them up because of the low rate of interest they bear, around 1 per cent. Thus in February 1960 all the £E175 million of treasury bills issued were held by the National Bank (124 million in the Issue Department and 51 million in the Banking Department), while a year earlier only £E4·3 million had been held by commercial banks.[1] In February 1961 the total amount of Egyptian treasury bills held by the commercial banks, including the National Bank, was £E17 million, of foreign treasury bills 1 million, and of commercial paper 21·2 million.

The last item on the assets side to be considered is investments. Formerly a sharp contrast was presented by the National Bank, where investments (chiefly in Egyptian and foreign government securities) represented about 60 per cent of total assets, and the commercial banks, where they represented only 7 per cent, a figure well below that prevailing in other countries. Moreover this figure included participation in the capital of subsidiary companies, chiefly by Misr Bank, which accounted for about 80 per cent of all the investments made by commercial banks. About one-third of the investments was in Egyptian government securities.

This situation has considerably changed. In the first place, foreign government securities have practically disappeared from the balance sheet of the commercial banks, including the National Bank, though a very small amount is still held by the Central Bank. Secondly, holdings of Egyptian government securities have considerably increased. The latter bear 2·5–3·5 per cent interest, are exempt from taxes on income, and may be included in the calculation of the minimum liquidity ratio and are therefore attractive to banks.[2]

Other investments rose much less, from £E9·4 million in 1952 to 14·8 in February 1961. The greater part of these securities continued to be held by Misr Bank, the holdings of the Bank of Cairo in cotton and insurance companies formed by it having been sold to the Economic Development Organization in 1959.[3]

This section may be concluded by a few remarks on the distribu-

[1] Bills issued by the Economic Organization carry 3 per cent and are more acceptable; in 1959 a total of £E10 m. was held by the commercial banks. In summer, however, commercial banks invest some of their idle funds in treasury bills; the annual maxima were £E11·7 m. in August 1959 and 14·6 m. in 1960.

[2] Holdings of Egyptian government and government-guaranteed securities rose from £E7·7 m. in 1952 to 30·9 m. in 1959; in February 1961 the total, including the National Bank, was 81·8 m. (Gritly, in *Buhuth*).   [3] Ibid.

tion of credit facilities. First, as regards size, at the end of 1960 all the banks, including the National Bank, had extended total credit facilities aggregating £E236·2 million to 488 large clients, i.e. those having facilities of 100,000 or more; facilities to the 1,924 medium clients amounted to 56·4 million and those to the 1,409 small clients (below £E10,000) to 5·1 million. Large loans are most prevalent in industry and in cotton wholesale trade.[1]

As regards distribution by sector, the last few years have witnessed a large increase in the share of industry and a corresponding decline in that of trade. In 1958 industry absorbed 27 per cent of total facilities (a figure much higher than in previous years), trade 69 per cent, and agriculture 4 per cent. By 1960 the share of industry was 37 per cent and that of trade 49 per cent while agriculture, services, and other activities shared the balance.[2] The relative growth of industry and decline of wholesale trade has resulted in a corresponding rise in the importance of Cairo, to 43 per cent of the total, at the expense of Alexandria, which received 22 per cent.

Table 34 (p. 260) shows the main items in the balance sheets of the commercial banks, National Bank, and Central Bank. It brings out one further point not noted in the above discussion; formerly the National Bank used to hold a large amount of money at call in London but neither it nor the Central Bank does so any more.[3]

### AGRICULTURAL CREDIT

In view of the great importance of agriculture in the Egyptian economy, the predominance of small-scale farming, and the impecuniousness of the mass of the rural population, cheap short-term agricultural credit is more necessary than any other form. Yet until 1930 there was no institution specializing in agricultural credit except the Agricultural Bank (see ch. ii).

Farmers obtained their requirements from different sources. Growers of sugar-cane received advances from the Sugar Company; cotton growers were sometimes financed by local brokers or merchants or branches of exporting firms, in return for a lien on the crop. These merchants in turn often borrowed from the banks, so

---

[1] CBE, *Credit & Banking Developments in 1960*, p. 27.

[2] See details in ibid. p. 25.

[3] A few words may be added on credit extended by non-banking institutions. At the end of 1960 the Insurance and Pensions Funds Administration had £E27·5 m. outstanding, the Post Office Savings Bank 4·3 m., the insurance companies 2·3 m. and the Social Insurance Organization 1·8 m., a total of £E35·9 m.; of this, no less than 25 m. went to industry (ibid. pp. 28–30).

**TABLE 34**

*Main Items in Balance Sheet of Banks, end of year, 1950 and 1961*

(£E million)

| | Cash & balance with Central Bank | Money at call | Bills dis-counted | Invest-ments[1] | Ad-vances | De-posits |
|---|---|---|---|---|---|---|
| **1950** | | | | | | |
| National Bank (Banking Department) | 7·3 | 50·3 | 0·5 | 143·2 | 31·9 | 241·5 |
| Clearing Banks | 36·2 | — | 5·6 | 9·5 | 104·9 | 143·2 |
| Total | 43·5 | 50·3 | 6·1 | 152·7 | 136·8 | 384·7 |
| **1961** | | | | | | |
| Central Bank (Banking Department) | 18·2 | — | 5·0 | 72·2 | 73·9 | 22·9 |
| Commercial Banks | 67·0 | — | 18·6 | 157·3 | 231·7 | 384·4 |
| Total | 85·2 | — | 23·6 | 229·5 | 305·6 | 407·3 |

[1] Incl. treasury bills.

*Sources:* NBE, *Econ. B.*; CBE, *Econ. R.*

that the rate of interest charged to farmers was relatively high.[1] Small mortgage loans were also rendered inaccessible or expensive by the fact that, owing to the legal difficulties standing in the way of recoveries, the Crédit Foncier confined itself to large loans. The bulk of credit requirements was supplied by village usurers, who charged rates of 30 or even 40 per cent.[2]

In 1931 the Agricultural Credit Bank was founded with a capital of £E1 million, of which the government supplied one half and the

[1] In Egypt, as in other countries, it has always been very difficult for commercial banks to meet the credit needs of all but very large farmers. Brokers and merchants, who are intimately acquainted with local farmers, serve as necessary intermediaries for the channelling of bank credit to the villages. In recent years banks charged such cotton merchants and brokers rates of 5–6·5 per cent, compared with 4·5 per cent charged to cotton exporters (Gritly, in *Buhuth*).

[2] J. Zannis, *Le crédit agricole en Égypte* (1937), p. 38.

principal banks the other. The government guaranteed shareholders a minimum dividend of 5 per cent, in return for which it retained control over the Bank's activities. It also advanced funds to the Bank —raised from £E6 million before the war to 16·8 million in 1960— first directly and then through the National Bank, at rates of interest which were gradually reduced from 2·5 per cent in 1931 to 1·5 in 1938 and 1 in the post-war period.[1] The Bank was exempted from the provisions of the Five-Feddans Law, and in addition utilizes the services of tax-collectors to recover its instalments, a feature which both reduces costs and ensures prompt repayment.

The Bank developed very rapidly; by 1940 it had over 100 branches and nearly 500 *shoonas*, distributed all over the country, and during the war the government relied on it heavily for the collection of grain and the distribution of fertilizers. This led to further expansion and by 1960 there were 142 branches and 1,151 silos, *shoonas*, and stores for various products.

The object of the Bank was the financing of small growers; but in view of the very reasonable rates charged, big landowners sought increasingly to make use of its services, at first through the medium of dummy cultivators and then by inducing it to advance loans to owners of up to 200 feddans instead of only up to 40, thus covering over 99·9 per cent of the landowners. Nevertheless, the fact that in 1948 the total number of loans made was as high as 373,000, giving an average of under £E20 (compared with £E8 in the pre-war period), suggests that the original purpose of the Bank, i.e. the financing of small cultivators, was being at least partly achieved. The agrarian reform of 1952 naturally decreased the proportion of business transacted with large holders and by 1960 of the Bank's 531,000 clients 69 per cent were smallholders (under 5 feddans) who absorbed 23 per cent of advances, 27 per cent were medium holders who absorbed 37 per cent, and 4 per cent large holders (over 30 feddans) who absorbed 40 per cent. The agrarian reform and sequestrations of 1961 will no doubt further decrease the share of the large owners.

In the meanwhile the Bank's business with co-operatives was increasing rapidly. In 1933 co-operatives took 5 per cent of total advances, in 1938 20, and in 1943 a peak of 29, dropping back to the pre-war level by the late 1940's. In 1948 the Bank's capital was raised

[1] In addition, the Bank found it necessary, starting in 1956, to issue 3 per cent bonds. In 1961 the total outstanding was £E25 m. (Credit Agric. & Coop., *Rapports, 1960*).

by £E500,000, of which half was subscribed by the government and half by 1,955 rural and consumer co-operatives and its name was changed to Agricultural and Co-operative Credit Bank.[1] Deposits of co-operatives increased rapidly, to £E3·7 million by 1960. In addition to performing various services for the co-operatives, such as collecting their bills, issuing letters of guarantee on their behalf, and selling them seed and fertilizer at a discount, the Bank has gradually channelled the greater part of its transactions through them; the percentage of total advances absorbed by co-operatives rose rapidly from 38 per cent in 1956 to 50 in 1958 and 84 in 1960.

At the end of 1960, total advances amounted to £E36·7 million, compared with 29·4 million in 1959, 17·7 million in 1956, and 12·9 million in 1951. Of this, short-term loans (up to fourteen months) for seasonal expenses (seed, fertilizers, pesticides, marketing) amounted to £E35·1 million, medium-term loans (up to ten years, for the purchase of livestock or machinery or for land improvement) 1·5 million, and long-term loans only to 32,000. Since 1957 the volume of supervised credit, extended through co-operatives, has increased rapidly and more recently a few 'Village Banks' were set up to supervise this and other forms of credit, with fewer formalities than those used by the Agricultural Credit Bank.

The Bank undertakes many other activities. In 1960 it accounted for 77 per cent of all chemical fertilizers sold in Egypt, the balance being provided by merchants who bought them from the Agricultural Organization or the local fertilizer companies; the Bank aims at taking over all fertilizer distribution.[2] It also sells to farmers selected cotton, wheat, rice, and other seed, the total in 1960 being nearly 1·2 million ardebs. Lastly, it undertakes large supply operations on behalf of the government such as delivering domestic and imported wheat and flour to local mills.

All these activities have been quite remunerative and, coupled with efficient management, enabled the Bank to show an appreciable profit in every year of operation.[3] The rates of interest charged were successively reduced from 7 per cent for individuals and 5 for co-operatives before the war to 5 and 3 respectively after the war: in 1961 all loans were made interest-free, surely a misguided measure.

---

[1] In 1960 the Bank, which since 1957 had been under the supervision of the Economic Development Organization, was transferred to that of the Co-operative and Agricultural Organization and its name was once more changed to Agricultural and Co-operative Credit.    [2] Ibid.

[3] These profits made it possible to raise reserves to £E2·8 m. by the end of 1960.

It remains to add that, in view of the government's intention to give co-operatives an ever-increasing role in agriculture, the part played by the Bank is likely to gain in importance during the coming years.

### MORTGAGE CREDIT

Mortgage loans on agricultural land, which loomed so large in the period 1880–1914, have steadily lost their former importance. The First World War and post-war prosperity led to a repayment of loans and considerable reduction of mortgage debt, which fell from £E45 million in 1914 to 30 million (of which about half was owed to the Crédit Foncier) in 1924, remaining around that figure until the outbreak of the war in 1939. In 1936 the mortgaged area represented 18 per cent of the cultivated area, and aggregate debts amounted to 5 per cent of the estimated value of the cultivated land of Egypt.[1] The number of landowners involved was put at 160,000 or 6 per cent.

Although the rate of interest charged was not exorbitant (averaging 7 per cent in 1932) the fall in prices after 1930 greatly increased the debt burden. Hence in 1933 the government concluded an arrangement with the main mortgage banks by which the latter spread out the annuities payable by debtors while the government took over two-thirds of the overdue interest. This proved to be only the first of a succession of such agreements in the interests of debtors.[2] The effect of these settlements, together with the rise in agricultural prices, was to ease considerably the burden of debt.

During the Second World War mortgage indebtedness declined sharply; repayments exceeded new lending, and outstanding advances of the two leading banks fell from £E16 million in 1940 to 8 million in 1945. After the war loans once more increased, but the greater part is now secured by urban property and is used for construction of buildings. Thus the ratio of outstanding loans against agricultural land to total loans was only 25 per cent at the end of 1960 compared with 64 per cent in 1950.[3] Total outstanding mortgage loans by all mortgage banks other than the Crédit Hypothécaire at the end of 1960 were £E12·8 million while other loans were 300,000;[4] of these 10·9 million were accounted for by the Crédit Foncier Égyptien which since its inception had advanced a

---

[1] E. James, 'L'Organisation du crédit en Ég.', *Ég. contemp.*, 1939.
[2] A full account may be found in Economides, in *Ég. contemp.*, 1952.
[3] NBE, *Econ. B.*, no. 2, 1961.
[4] CBE, *Credit & Banking Developments in 1960*.

cumulative total of 127 million in mortgage and short-term loans. The average rate charged by mortgage banks is about 5·5 per cent.

The Crédit Hypothécaire was founded by the government in 1932 as a branch of the Agricultural Credit Bank and was made an independent institution in 1935 and put in charge of some of the mortgage debts taken over by the government from other institutions. The Bank was designed to help small farmers, and individual loans were not to exceed £E1,200, a figure subsequently raised to 4,000. At first there were numerous applications, but as conditions improved demand fell off and there was a further decline during the Second World War. In 1956 the Bank was reorganized, its capital was increased, and it was put under the Economic Development Organization. Since then it has concentrated on loans to co-operatives, municipalities, and individuals for housing projects. It supplements its own funds by low-interest loans from the National Bank; at the end of 1958 such loans amounted to about £E2 million while the Bank's own outstanding loans were 4·4 million; the rate charged to co-operatives, which absorbed half the total, was 3 per cent.[1]

### INDUSTRIAL CREDIT

Until very recently this was the least developed branch of credit in Egypt, and there is little doubt that the lack of adequate facilities was one of the obstacles impeding industrialization. It is true that, beginning in the 1920's, the foreign commercial banks often made short-term advances to the larger local industries and occasionally directly participated in the creation of a new enterprise.[2] But the first important steps taken to remedy the shortage of industrial credit were due to Misr Bank,[3] whose deposits have continuously increased, since its inception in 1920, reaching £E17 million in 1938, 61 million in 1951, and 120 million in 1960 and which may be said to have done more to spread the banking habit among Egyptians than any other bank.

In addition to its other activities Misr Bank set itself to foster local industry in three ways:

1. *By direct participation.* Twenty-seven 'Misr' companies were formed with an aggregate paid-up capital of £E20 million and

---

[1] Gritly, in *Buhuth.*     [2] For details see ibid.

[3] For a detailed and critical account of Misr Bank, see Gritly, in *Ég. contemp.*, 1947, pp. 443–5.

activities ranging from spinning and weaving to insurance, fisheries, airlines, and films.[1]

2. *By advances*. In 1936 advances to the seven Misr companies whose balance sheets were available aggregated over £E1·5 million.

3. *By industrial loans*. Starting in 1932 the government provided Misr Bank with funds to be used for advancing to industry. At the outbreak of war these aggregated £E1·1 million, most of which was absorbed by the Misr group.

This method of borrowing on short term and lending on long term caused difficulties, culminating in a run on the Bank at the outbreak of war, but the war boom enabled the Misr companies to repay practically all the Bank's advances. The Bank itself was also thoroughly reorganized, repaid the government advances, and achieved a very sound position which it maintained until its nationalization in 1960.

Nevertheless it was generally recognized that Misr Bank was not well equipped to supply the rapidly growing need for industrial credit. The projects for an Industrial Bank bore fruit in 1949; of the capital of £1·5 million the government subscribed 51 per cent and banks and other institutions 30 per cent, the balance having been offered to the public. The government guaranteed a 3·5 per cent dividend on share capital, as well as the principal and interest on debentures up to five times the Bank's capital, and was authorized to advance up to £E2 million for working capital. This was subsequently increased and at the end of 1960 the Bank's balance sheet showed a debt of £E6·9 million to the National Bank, guaranteed by the government. Moreover in 1959 the Bank was authorized to issue up to £E3 million of bonds guaranteed by the government, and did so in 1960; in the latter year the authorization was increased to 7·5 million. The Bank may participate in industrial enterprises; supply them with raw materials or machinery; advance short-term loans (up to one year) guaranteed by merchandise, medium-term loans (up to 10 years) to newly established firms, and long-term loans (up to 20 years) for the creation of new enterprises; help graduates of technical schools, by loans of up to 5 years, in setting up businesses; and invest its funds in industrial securities.

[1] After the Second World War the Bank ceased to found new companies. However, it continued to finance and reinforce existing Misr companies and participated in several mixed enterprises launched by the government, such as the steel mill, a large chemical plant and a hotel company. In 1958 stock of Misr companies accounted for £E7·9 m. out of the Bank's total investment of 19·3 m.

The Bank had a slow start. Among its handicaps were the fact that applications for loans were ill prepared; that, in the absence of proper book-keeping it was impossible to judge the financial soundness of borrowers; and that various administrative formalities delayed and complicated matters. The rates charged to borrowers have also aroused complaints although they are actually lower than those charged by commercial banks—5·5–6 per cent compared with 6·5. Lastly, the absence of industrial co-operatives has greatly restricted loans to small and medium businesses, as well as to cottage and village industries.

Since 1953, however, many of these obstacles have been gradually overcome and in the last few years business has appreciably expanded. Loans rose from £E2 million in 1958 to 4·2 million in 1960. The leading recipients were the engineering and mechanical, the textile and the building materials industries. In 1960 loans to large borrowers (over £E100,000) absorbed 71 per cent of advances, to medium borrowers 27 per cent, and to small borrowers (under £E10,000) only 2 per cent. In recent years the share of medium and long-term loans has appreciably increased, to 38 per cent of the total in 1960; the balance consisted of short-term loans and credits. Lastly, there has been a decline in the share of loans absorbed by Cairo, from 88 per cent in 1958 to 70 per cent in 1960.[1]

As noted on p. 259 above, advances by commercial banks to industry have greatly increased in the last few years. Needless to say, the nationalization of the bulk of large-scale industry in the past two years has greatly changed the credit needs of that sector.

### CENTRAL BANKING

Until 1951 the National Bank fulfilled the following functions normally entrusted to central banks: monopoly of note issue; custodian of the bulk of the government's funds; financial adviser to the government and agent for dividend payments, loan flotations, treasury bill tenders (since 1941), &c. The three main functions, denied to it were those of bankers' bank (though in practice banks kept balances with the National Bank), lender of last resort, and controller of the volume of credit through changes in the rediscount rate and open-market operations.

In spite of these limitations the National Bank on many occasions played the part of a central bank, to the great advantage of the

[1] Indust. Bank, *Ann. Rep. for 1960* (in Ar.).

country.[1] In addition, there seems little doubt that on several occasions the Bank succeeded in imposing, by moral suasion, a general policy on other banks. During the war years the Bank, whose staff had been rapidly egyptianized after 1940, played the leading part in the exchange-control system, and balances kept with it by the other banks greatly increased, from £E600,000 in 1938 to 30·4 million in 1950. In 1951, after prolonged discussion, a law was passed giving it more of the powers enjoyed by other central banks and at the same time increasing the control exercised over it by the government. Commercial banks were to hold liquid assets in form and proportion to be fixed by the Minister of Finance and the newly formed Supreme Monetary Committee, which included government representatives and determined the policy of the Bank. They were also required to keep interest-free deposits with the National Bank, the ratio being determined by the Committee.[2] In return for these increased powers, the National Bank was to 'refrain from the smaller commercial operations not required by the public interest' and from making advances with the funds deposited with it by the commercial banks'.[3]

The National Bank had thus acquired a powerful means of control over the volume of credit, i.e. the determining of bank deposits with it; this was reinforced by the fact that commercial banks came to meet their peak seasonal requirements by borrowing from it.[4] It was also authorized to rediscount treasury bills and approved commercial bills, but the very sparing use of the latter in Egypt and the absence of a call market obviously precluded any major operations.[5] Nevertheless, one of the advantages to be had from rediscounting, the fixing of uniform interest rates, was attained by moral suasion and by common action of the banks through their conference.[6]

[1] See examples in Issawi, *EMC*, pp. 227–8.

[2] The reserve ratio was fixed at 15 per cent and subsequently lowered to 12·5 during March–October and 10 per cent during November–February; in 1960 the latter figure was, exceptionally, lowered to 7·5, to facilitate the issue of a £E25 m. loan (see CBE, *Credit & Banking Development in 1960*, pp. 4–6).

[3] NBE, *Econ. B.*, no. 2, 1950.

[4] Thus during the 1959–60 season loans to commercial banks rose from zero in August to a peak of £E31·1 m. in December; the corresponding figures for 1960–1 were £E5·1 m. and 31·3 m. Since 1947 'direct borrowing from abroad has taken place on a comparatively small scale, if at all' (ibid. no. 1, 1953).

[5] At the end of both 1959 and 1960 total rediscounts granted to commercial banks amounted to £E6·1 m.; rediscounts show the same rise as advances by the CBE to the commercial banks, from a minimum in August to a peak at the end of the year.          [6] See, e.g., NBE, *Econ. B.*, no. 3, 1952.

It will thus be seen that the major means of control still denied to the National Bank was open-market operations, and this was granted to it by Law No. 163 of 1957;[1] the practical importance of the change was however not great, in view of the narrowness of the Egyptian stock exchanges, which severely limits the scope of such operations. The law also granted the Bank the right to fix interest and discount rates and, in emergencies, to advance the commercial banks exceptional loans, without demanding the usual security. The Bank was put in charge of the registration of all firms undertaking banking operations; and its authorization was also required for mergers and the opening of new branches. The Bank's authority over the other banks was confirmed and extended in matters of reserve and liquidity ratios (the latter being fixed in 1959 at 30 per cent of deposits), and it was given very extensive powers in the determination of the nature and evaluation of different assets held by banks and in the maximum amount of the facilities they were authorized to extend to the various sectors of the economy.[2] For the first time the Bank was also given a certain measure of control over the Agricultural, Mortgage, and Industrial Banks.

The law introduced three major changes in the structure of the National Bank. First, distributed profits were not to exceed 20 per cent of the nominal value of its shares. Secondly, the Supreme Monetary Committee was abolished and full authority was restored to the Board of Directors. Thirdly, government control over the Board was greatly increased, and in addition the government was henceforth directly to appoint the Governor and Deputy Governor as well as two members of the Board.

It remains to add that in February 1960 the Bank was nationalized

---

[1] See NBE, *Econ. B.*, no. 3, 1957.

[2] It was calculated that the ratio of currency to money – c – in Egypt in 1951–58 averaged 0·69, a very high figure compared with those of both developed and underdeveloped countries; the ratio of bank reserves to total deposits – r – averaged 0·283, also a very high figure; and consequently the monetary multiplier, which relates changes in money to changes in central bank monetary liabilities and is defined as $\dfrac{1}{c + r\,(1 - c)}$, is 1·291, a very low figure. Moreover the average deviation in those ratios was low. This would seem to imply that action by the central bank in Egypt was likely to have less effect during the period studied, on the total volume of credit than in most other countries (Joachim Ahrensdorf & S. Kanesathan, 'Variations in the Money Multiplier and their Implications for Central Banking', IMF, *Staff Papers*, Nov. 1960).

under Law No. 40 of 1960; its shares were converted into government bonds bearing 5 per cent interest and redeemable over twelve
years.[1] By another law of that year a Central Bank, which acquired
certain assets and liabilities of the National Bank, was established.[2]
The latter is now pursuing a policy 'aiming at developing its
activities as a commercial bank'[3] and for this purpose has taken over
several foreign banks (see above, p. 250).

### INFLATIONARY AND DEFLATIONARY PRESSURES

In the last fifty years Egypt has experienced three inflationary
waves, two sharp ones during the First and Second World Wars and
a gentler one starting in 1948.[4] Between 1914 and 1939 Egyptian
prices showed the same trend as those in the main world markets
and in particular the United Kingdom: a sharp rise in 1914–18; a
decline in 1919 followed by a rise in 1920; a decline until 1934,
accelerated during the depression, and a slow recovery until 1939,
interrupted by a brief setback in 1938. The link between the Egyptian
and the world economy was provided by cotton, the major and
most fluctuating element in both the country's national income and
its balance of payments.[5] The holding of large foreign reserves by
the National Bank and other banks and the transfer of funds by
foreign banks with branches in Egypt facilitated the transfer of
capital between Egypt and London and ensured that the necessary
price adjustments could be carried out without affecting the pegged
rate of exchange with sterling.

During the war several factors combined to generate a powerful
inflationary pressure. The most important was Allied military
expenditures in the country, which totalled £E314 million for the

---

[1] Foreign ownership of the Bank's shares had slowly fallen to nearly 60 per cent
by 1953; thereafter both private capital and public bodies such as the Economic
Development Organization and the Government Insurance and Provident Funds
increasingly acquired stock and by 1960 the foreign share had fallen to less than
20 per cent (NBE, *Econ. B.*, no. 1, 1960).

[2] See balance sheets in CBE, *Econ. R.*, no. 1, 1961.

[3] NBE, *Econ. B.*, no. 1, 1961.

[4] For a more elaborate treatment see Samir Amin, 'Forces inflationistes et forces
déflationistes dans l'économie ég.', *Ég. contemp.*, Oct. 1958.

[5] Between 1919 and 1938, in sixteen years out of twenty, an export surplus was
followed by a rise in the wholesale price index and an import surplus by a decline.
For the rise in prices during the nineteenth century and the sharp jump in 1903–7
see Yacoub Artin Pasha, 'Essai sur les causes du renchérissement de la vie matérielle
au Caire dans le courant du XIXe siècle', in *Mémoires présentés à l'Inst. Ég.* (Cairo,
1907), vol. v.

period 1940–5.[1] The effect of this great increase in Egypt's national income was accentuated by the bad harvests in 1941; the shortage of imported goods; and smuggling to Palestine and Syria, where inflation was even more severe. The index of wholesale prices (June–August 1939=100) rose to 143 at the end of 1940, 251 at the end of 1942, and 330 at the end of 1944. By that time wartime inflation had passed its peak, owing to the withdrawal of Allied troops and the reopening of sea routes, and the index stood at 333 at the end of 1945.[2]

During the first few post-war years there was little change in the price-level. The increase in the value of cotton exports raised incomes, as did the expansion in internal investment and budget deficits, but this was offset by the heavy import surplus. However, after the devaluation of the pound in 1949, together with sterling, the rise in import prices and, to a more marked degree, the sharp increase in the value of cotton exports, raised the price-level. The index, which had fallen to 311 at the end of 1947, advanced to 386 by the end of 1951. During the next three years there was a sharp fall in the value of cotton exports, together with a reduction of government expenditure, and various measures were taken to reduce the cost of living, and by December 1954 the index had fallen back to 342. But new inflationary pressures were soon generated by the vastly increased scale of government expenditure for defence, administration, social services, and investment as well as by the continued rise in import prices until 1957. Although the series of deficits on current account slowed down the pace of inflation, the rise in prices continued almost uninterruptedly. By December 1957 the wholesale price index stood at 419. After that it showed little change, but there seems hardly any doubt that this stability is fictitious, being due to the fact that the index is based on controlled prices which are by no means always observed in the market.

More light can be shed on this subject, as well as on the prospects of future trends, by examining the growth and composition of the money supply. Between 1950 and 1959 the income velocity of money appears to have remained fairly stable at about 2·2,[3] a level

---

[1] These rose from £E4·9 m. in 1939 to 14·8 in 1940, 46·5 in 1941, 73·7 in 1942, 75·6 in 1943, 57·5 in 1944, and about 46 m. in 1945.

[2] The measures taken by the government to check inflation are discussed in A. R. Prest, *War Economics of Primary Producing Countries* (Cambridge, 1948), ch. 4.

[3] A. R. Abdel Meguid, 'Monetary Management', *Ég. contemp.*, Apr. 1961.

which also seems to have prevailed in 1939. This figure is much lower than that in most underdeveloped countries, where ratios of 3 to 5 are more common. During that period the money supply (defined as the sum of currency, private demand deposits, private time and savings deposits, Post Office savings deposits and government deposits) fell from £E483·1 million in 1950 to 416·6 million in 1954, or by 14 per cent, and then rose to 606·2 million in 1959, or by 45 per cent. In 1960 there was a further rise to about £E660 million, or 9 per cent.[1] As for the counterpart of the money supply, in 1951 it consisted of 69 per cent of foreign assets, 1 per cent of claims on the government (in the form of Egyptian treasury bills, government or government-guaranteed securities), and 29 per cent of claims on the private sector (loans and advances, securities, and other).[2] But by 1959 the proportions were 18, 41, and 51 per cent respectively. This shift was caused by the great increase in government borrowing and also by the fact that the government extended its guarantee to an increasing number of private and mixed enterprises. In 1960 and 1961 there was a further massive shift, foreign assets falling to 11 per cent and claims on the private sector to 45 per cent while claims on the government rose to 53 per cent. In other words, until recently the expansion of the money supply had been slowed down by the liquidation of foreign assets and its inflationary effect had been checked by the large import surpluses made possible by drawing on foreign assets. But this countervailing force is no longer available. It is true that in its place there are the large foreign credits granted to Egypt (see Table 32, p. 240), but as these are to be used for importing capital and not consumer goods their anti-inflationary effect will be very slight, at least until the investments mature. Hence unless the government takes measures to cut down private and public consumption drastically there is every reason to fear that its intensified investment programme may lead to severe inflation. And at least until the end of 1961 there were no signs that the government was trying to reduce popular consumption, as distinct from consumption by the richer groups. On the contrary, many of the measures it was taking or planning, such as the reduction of house rents (see below, p. 281), bus and train fares, and electricity rates

[1] Definitions of the money supply vary considerably; for a discussion and fuller details see NBE, *Econ. B.*, no. 1, 1961 and IMF, *Internat. Financ. Statist.*

[2] The totals add up to over 100 per cent because of the presence of balancing items. For a fuller treatment see Edith Penrose, 'Money, Prices, and Economic Expansion in the Middle East, 1952–60', *Revista Internazionale di scienze economiche e commerciali* (Padua), no. 5, 1962.

and the prices of many foodstuffs and manufactured goods could only lead to greater consumption.[1]

### THE FUTURE OF CREDIT INSTITUTIONS

This chapter may be concluded with a few questions and speculations regarding the future of the institutions described above. What are the functions of the various financial organisms in a society where the greater part of the means of production is either owned or closely controlled by the government, where output is subjected to an overall plan and yet where a large sector still remains in private hands, and where foreign trade plays a vital role in the economy?

The first function described in this chapter, the custody and transference of savings, is as essential as ever. So far the government has laid little stress on the need for greater saving, and has done little to stimulate individual abstinence by either offering greater material rewards, or conducting a propaganda campaign, or enforcing compulsory saving; indeed, as noted above, the tendency has been rather to stimulate consumption. This may have been owing to purely political considerations, such as the desire to give some immediate benefit to the poorer classes; to the lack of appreciation of the extent of Egypt's needs for investment; to an overestimate of the amount of capital accumulation which can be undertaken by the organized sector, whose profits are now accruing to the government; and, not least, to the very considerable aid being received from abroad, which is covering a large part of Egypt's total investment. It is to be expected that in future the government will try to increase the volume of savings very greatly. Clearly, then, the commercial and savings banks will have an important part to play though they may have to undergo a process of amalgamation, reorganization, and differentiation.

The future of insurance companies is more uncertain and some Egyptian economists have called for their suppression and the transference of their work to the Institute for Social Insurance. The two main functions of these companies should be distinguished,

[1] An interesting new development may however be noted. It is being proposed to deduct, compulsorily, half of the amounts distributed to employees and workmen under Law No. 111 of 19 July 1961 (see above, p. 194); these deductions are estimated at £E10 m. a year and will earn 3 per cent interest (*al-Ahram*, 21 Apr. 1962). In so far as such a measure will increase the amount available for investment it is to be welcomed, but it should be noted as an example of the method, increasingly being used by communist and socialist-nationalist governments, of granting the masses benefits with one hand and taking back the greater part with the other.

namely, the provision of insurance against risks arising from fires, accidents, and other hazards and the stimulation of savings through life assurance. To put both, or even one, of these functions in the hands of the Institute would be to burden it with a task beyond its capacities. Here too it is probable that the near future will see the nationalized companies continuing to operate as at present but with much amalgamation and specialization of functions among them.

Some economists have also judged the stock exchanges superfluous, and have advocated their suppression. But as long as the present form of company organization is retained, i.e. as long as the capital of the partly nationalized and private companies continues to consist of shares, there will clearly be a need for a market where buyers and sellers can exchange securities. And as long as the private sector is expected to supply any new capital and to undertake any risks, there will be a need for the kind of indicator provided by stock-exchange quotations. To this should be added the fact that the existence of a stock exchange may somewhat facilitate the flotation of government bonds.

The second function, the provision of short-term credit by means of advances and discounts, will also remain essential. To begin with, there is the vast volume of credit required for the moving of the cotton and other crops produced by the private farmers and co-operatives. Whether part of the work now done in this field by the commercial banks can be transferred with advantage to the Agricultural Credit Bank is a moot point which may be taken up in the future.

Secondly, there is the need of the remaining part of the private sector—internal trade and small-scale industry, construction, and transport—for short-term credit. This too is a field in which much work remains for the commercial banks.

Thirdly, there are the short-term credit needs of the public sector. Here the presence of the banks can give a greatly needed flexibility to enterprises working within the general framework of the Five-Year Plan. Moreover, as the experience of the Soviet Union and the Eastern European countries shows, the banks may be used by the government for checking the expenditures and performance of the nationalized enterprises.

These general remarks also apply to the specialized banks—the Agricultural, Industrial, and Mortgage Banks—which may have to perform the dual function of meeting the medium and long-term credit needs of both the private and, possibly, the public sector. The need for the latter function is not, however, self-evident and it may well be that the government will prefer to finance the nationalized enterprises by direct budgetary allocations.

Lastly, there is the Central Bank. It goes without saying that the tasks of this institution are as vital as ever. Inflation is a threat facing socialist and mixed economies as well as private-enterprise economies and the need to regulate overall credit and purchasing power has lost none of its urgency. The coexistence of a private and a public sector raises particularly difficult problems in this connexion. So does the fact that the largest single productive sector is still agriculture, whose output is liable to fluctuate violently and greatly upset the calculations of planners, as it did in 1961. Furthermore an economy as dependent on foreign trade and outside assistance as that of Egypt is subject to severe shocks arising from crop failures, shifts in markets, changes in terms of trade, and sudden cessation of foreign aid. The adverse effects of such shocks may, to a certain extent, be mitigated by an appropriate credit policy carried out by the Central Bank. For this the latter must have control over the other credit institutions, but whether this control is exercised through the mechanisms discussed above, or whether it requires new mechanisms, is a matter that cannot be decided at this stage.

To sum up, it may be expected that existing credit institutions will continue to function for a considerable time to come, but that both their structure and their functions may undergo important modifications.

# XII

# Public Finance

*In our time, when faith in the manipulative omnipotence of the State has all but displaced analysis of its social structure and understanding of its political and economic function.*
PAUL BARAN.

*In much of Southern Asia and the Middle East governments are impelled by forces largely outside their control to undertake tasks beyond their competence.* EDWARD S. MASON.

*Experience has shown that a large proportion of the results of labour and abstinence may be taken away by fixed taxation, without impairing, and sometimes even with the effect of stimulating, the qualities from which a great production and an abundant capital take their rise. But those qualities are not proof against a high degree of uncertainty. The government may carry off a part; but there must be assurance that it will not interfere, nor suffer anyone to interfere, with the remainder.* J. S. MILL.

## STRUCTURE AND SIZE OF BUDGET

Until quite recently the structure of the Egyptian budget was very simple: practically all revenue and expenditure was included in a single budget.[1] But since May 1953 there has been a separate Development Budget, and the 1950's witnessed a number of Annexed Budgets for such activities as the railways, Petroleum Authority, agrarian reform, universities, &c. During the union with Syria, another budget was introduced, covering matters of common concern such as defence, foreign affairs, the presidency, and the National Assembly; about 75 per cent of the total revenue of this budget came from Egypt and 25 from Syria; the budgets of the various central ministries were annexed to the unified Budget.

---

[1] The years 1905–14 carried Extraordinary Budgets and 1937/8 had an Anglo-Egyptian Treaty Expenditure Budget. For a detailed account of the development of the budget see Muh. Tawfiq Yunis, 'al-Mizania al-misriya fi'l-khamsin sana'l-akhira', in *Buhuth*, pp. 303–416.

Thus in 1961/2 there were no less than 56 budgets, some of which overlapped.[1]

The 1962/3 budget, drafted after the break-up of the union with Syria and the nationalizations, showed further changes.[2] The budgets of all the departments and organizations in the public sector aggregated £E2,351·8 million. Of this £E889 million represented the budgets of the companies included in the public sector. The balance, both gross and net (i.e. deducting items appearing under more than one heading, such as subsidies to local authorities), was as follows (in £E million):

|                                        | Gross   | Net     |
|----------------------------------------|---------|---------|
| General services budget                | 471·8   | 471·8   |
| Budgets annexed to general services    | 31·4    | 2·6     |
| Budgets of local authorities           | 138·7   | 44·9    |
| Budgets of productive sectors          | 820·9   | 493·4   |
|                                        | 1,462·8 | 1,012·7 |

The size of the budget has greatly increased, both in absolute terms and relatively to national income and population. Just before the First World War expenditure totalled £E17 million but by 1919 it had doubled, owing to wartime inflation. By 1929 the figure had risen to £E41·1 million, during the Depression it dropped to 31·6 million and then rose again to 40·4 million in 1938/9. Dividing by the cost-of-living index shows a rise in real terms of 80 per cent between 1913 and 1938; as a percentage of national income government expenditure doubled, rising from a little over 10 in 1913 to over 20 in 1938. The increase was accounted for mainly by expenditure on defence, education, and health, as well as administration.

During the Second World War government expenditure more than doubled, but expressed in both real terms and as a percentage of national income it fell below the 1938/9 level. However, by

[1] These were: the Unified Budget with an expenditure of £E141·1 m., of which 109·7 for Egypt; 14 Budgets annexed to the Unified Budget, £E112·8, of which 100·2 for Egypt; ordinary budget for the Southern Region, £E335 m.; production budget for the Southern Region, £E315 m.; 29 budgets annexed to the Southern Region's budget, £E97·2; ordinary budget for the Northern Region, £S552·4 m.; development budget for the Northern Region, £S428·3 m.; and 8 budgets annexed to the Northern Region budget, £S162·4 m. (see *Exposé on Budget Project for FY July 1961–June 1962*, pp. 2–37). It may be added that the beginning of the fiscal year was shifted in 1914 from 1 January to 1 April, in 1927 to 1 May, in 1948 to 1 March, and in 1951 to 1 July.

[2] See *al-Ahram*, 30 June–8 July 1962 and NBE, *Econ. B.*, nos. 2 and 3, 1962.

1950/1 expenditure totalled £E190·6 million, or a little over 20 per cent of national income; in real terms the increase over 1938/9 was nearly 60 per cent. With a brief interruption in 1952/3, when the revolutionary government tried to restore order to Egypt's disturbed finances, expenditure shot up rapidly and uninterruptedly throughout the 1950's, to £E484·8 million in 1959/60; this represented an increase of 114 per cent in real terms.[1] By the latter date public expenditure represented about 40 per cent of national income. The increase represented greater expenditure on defence and economic and social development. After 1954 expenditure consistently outran revenue and the internal and foreign debt grew accordingly.

The next three years saw a vast increase in the budget owing to the various development and nationalization measures, and once more expenditures considerably exceeded revenues. By 1960/1 expenditure had risen to £E700 million and by 1961/2 to 779 million, representing some 60 per cent of national income.[2] The 1962/3 estimates put total expenditure at £E1,012·6 million, or some 63 per cent of estimated national income.

### GOVERNMENT EXPENDITURES

The evolution of government expenditure since 1950 is shown in Table 35 (p. 278); earlier developments have been discussed on p. 42 above. The most noteworthy feature is the twelvefold increase in expenditure between 1950 and 1961 on directly productive sectors, because of the nationalization of existing enterprises and, to a greater extent, the allocation of considerable funds for development; within that group industry and electricity show by far the greatest increase.

Social services have little more than doubled, with most going to education and research, expenditure on research of all kinds having risen from £E200,000 in 1950/1 to 5·6 million in 1961/2. Organizing services have tripled. Here the largest item is defence; the budget of the Ministry of War amounted in 1961/2 to £E88·6 million, to which should be added a considerable part of the expenditure of the Organization for Military Factories, £E22·7 million, and possibly a few small items; in all, defence expenditure in 1961/2 was probably distinctly over £E100 million, or at least 7 per cent of GNP, a figure which may be compared with the following for NATO

---

[1] NBE, *Econ. B.*, no. 4, 1961; this issue contains a valuable study of public finance during the 1950's.      [2] CBE, *Econ. R.*, no. 2, 1961.

TABLE 35

## Government Expenditure, 1950–62

(£E million)

|  | 1950/1 | 1955/6 | 1959/60 | 1961/2[1] | 1962/3[1] |
|---|---|---|---|---|---|
| *Directly productive sectors* | | | | | |
| Agriculture, irriga., drainage | 13·0 | 31·0 | 46·5 | 112·4 | 147·7 |
| Industry & electricity | 14·3 | 32·4 | 137·2 | 174·2 | 243·1 |
| Transport, commns., storage | 22·7 | 38·8 | 54·6 | 99·5 | 102·9 |
| Housing & utilities | 5·5 | 24·4 | 13·0 | 32·9 | 86·1 |
| Total | 55·5 | 126·6 | 251·3 | 418·9 | 579·8 |
| *Social services* | | | | | |
| Education & research | 22·2 | 35·3 | 51·4 | 78·9 | 96·1 |
| Health | 7·3 | 10·9 | 9·0 | 20·9 | 28·8 |
| Social, religious, cultural | 38·0 | 52·6 | 44·9 | 26·1 | 32·5 |
| Supply | 12·4 | 6·7 | 9·5 | 19·7 | 47·8 |
| Total | 79·9 | 105·5 | 114·8 | 145·5 | 205·2 |
| *Organizing services* | | | | | |
| Presidential & supervision | 4·7 | 5·0 | 8·1 | 15·2 | 13·5 |
| Commercial & financial | 10·8 | 17·1 | 18·3 | 69·4 | 75·8 |
| Defence, security, justice | 39·7 | 88·8 | 92·3 | 118·4 | 138·2 |
| Total | 55·2 | 110·9 | 118·7 | 203·0 | 227·5 |
| Grand total | 190·6 | 343·0 | 484·8 | 778·9[2] | 1,012·6 |

[1] Estimated.
[2] Incl. £E11·6 m. (reserve for other projects).

*Sources:* NBE, *Econ. B.* no. 4, 1961; *Exposé on Budget Project for Fiscal Year July 1961–June 1962*; *al-Ahram*, 30 June 1962.

countries: Denmark 2·7, Belgium 3·2, Norway 3·3, Italy 3·6, Netherlands 4·1, West Germany 4·3, Turkey 4·3, Greece 5·3, United Kingdom 6·5, France 6·7, and United States 9·2.[1] The servicing of the public debt rose from £E6·1 million in 1950/1 to 17·0 million in 1961/2.

A breakdown between current and development expenditure

[1] *The Economist*, 20 Jan. 1962; the Indian figure is 2 per cent.

shows a large increase in the share of the latter, from 16 per cent of the total in 1950/1 to 26 per cent in 1955/6 and 1959/60 and 41 per cent in 1961/2. A more difficult figure to determine is the proportion absorbed by salaries and pensions; in 1950 the Financial Committee of the Senate[1] estimated that these two items actually accounted for 40 per cent of total expenditure and although the figure must have declined since then (owing to the sharp rise in expenditure on construction and equipment), it is probably still high. There is no doubt that the Egyptian civil service is greatly overstaffed; in 1952–6, at a time when the government ran practically no economic enterprises except for the railways, the number of cadred officials was over 200,000, excluding both military personnel and workmen.[2] In 1959/60 the number of officials was put at 397,000 and their salaries at £E63·7 million; these figures include both temporary officials and workmen but exclude certain branches; moreover the salary figure excludes all salary and wage elements outside the First Title (salaries and wages) of the budget, which are considerable, as well as cost-of-living allowance and social-security payments.[3]

REVENUE

As noted earlier (p. 42, above), the freeing of the Egyptian government from various international controls in the 1930's was followed by the imposition of a protective tariff, the raising of land-tax and the introduction of an income-tax and, later, of death duties. Since the Revolution further important changes have occurred. In the first place the tax burden has slightly increased. The total of taxes and fees rose from £E131·6 million in 1950/1 to 190 million in 1959/60, both figures representing some 15 per cent of national income; for 1961/2 the estimate was £E232·1 million, or perhaps 17 per cent of national income.[4]

Secondly, the share of total revenue contributed by government-owned establishments has risen sharply, with the extension of the public sector through new investment and nationalization; income accruing under this heading, which now appears in the various Annexed Budgets, rose from £E39 million, or 18·2 per cent of total government revenue, in 1951/2 to 154·4 million, or 27·3 per cent, in 1961/2.[5] In the next few years the absolute figure is likely to rise

[1] *al-Ahram*, 16 Dec. 1950.   [2] *Coll. Basic Statist. Data*, p. 43.
[3] NPC, Memo. no. 406.
[4] Total ordinary government revenue rose from £E184·7 m. in 1950/1 to 294·5 m. in 1959/60 and was estimated at 420·8 m. in 1961/2.   [5] *Exposé*, p. 9.

further and the percentage still more since tax revenues cannot increase correspondingly.

Thirdly, there has been an appreciable shift from indirect to direct taxes. In 1951/2 income taxes and fees accounted for 28·6 per cent and customs and excise duties for 49·2 per cent of total government revenue from all sources but by 1961/2 the figures were 24·1 and 30·8 respectively; this reflects a small increase in customs duties combined with a doubling of direct tax receipts. However, a movement in the other direction may now be expected, in conformity 'with the socialist policy which requires a reliance on indirect taxes and custom duties without resorting to direct taxes now that large differences between individual incomes have been diminished',[1] and the 1962/3 budget provides for higher excise duties, on alcoholic drinks, cigarettes, woollen textiles and the finer qualities of cotton textiles, petrol, and motor car batteries and tyres.[2]

It is now possible to review briefly the main taxes and duties. Customs and excise duties are still by far the most important single item of revenue but they have shown little increase in the last dozen years, the yield rising from £E93·3 million in 1951/2 to 103·9 million in 1959/60 and an estimated 130·2 million in 1961/2. This total increase is the resultant of five separate trends: the sharp reduction in the yield of export duties, owing to the cancellation of the tax on cotton; the drastic decrease in imports of luxury goods, owing to very high duties or outright prohibitions; the decline in imports of manufactured consumer goods, against which Egyptian industry has been protected; the exemption of capital goods and most producers goods and foodstuffs from duty; and the sharp rise in yields of tobacco duties owing to much higher duties and somewhat greater total consumption. Recently a tariff reform has been introduced, with effect from 1 January 1962. It replaces the previous system of four superimposed duties by a single *ad valorem* duty, reduces rates on certain producers and capital goods and raises them on some consumer goods such as coffee, tea, tobacco, and beverages, the net result being a small anticipated rise in import duties from £E73·6 to 76·5 million.[3]

Among direct taxes[4] the oldest is land-tax, levied on the assessed

[1] *Exposé*. The same idea is echoed in an interesting article by Abdel Razak Hassan, 'The Future of Taxes in our Society', *al-Ahram*, 8 Feb. 1962.

[2] Ibid. 30 June 1962.   [3] NBE., *Econ. B.*, no. 4, 1961.

[4] For a brief summary see Abdel Razek Hassan & Nasouh el Dakkak, *United Arab Republic: some economic features* (n.d.), pp. 80–83.

rental value of agricultural land. In 1939, following a revaluation of land by the Cadastral Commission, the rate was fixed at 16 per cent with a maximum of PT164 per feddan. Between 1942 and 1945 small landowners were granted considerable remission and in 1949 the rate was reduced to 14 per cent and the maximum was abolished. Landowners assessed at up to £E4 per annum are exempt and those assessed up to £E20 are exempted from £E4 of the assessment. Under the Agrarian Reform Law of 1952 land in excess of the permitted maximum was subjected to an additional tax equal to five times the land-tax until the time when it was actually taken over by the government.

The second oldest tax, dating from 1884, is that on built property; since 1954 it has been assessed at 10 per cent of the rental value, after deduction of 20 per cent of the latter to cover all the landlord's expenses; buildings with a yearly rental of up to £E18 are exempt. In July 1961 Law No. 129 replaced this flat rate by a progressive one, rising from 10 per cent where the average annual rental per room does not exceed £E3 to 40 per cent where it is above £E10; the 20 per cent deduction was maintained. In November 1961 Laws No. 168 and 169 effected a reduction in rents wherever the yearly rental per room does not exceed £E5; this ranges from 20 per cent for the lowest groups to 15 for the highest; reductions are to be recouped by the landlord from the buildings tax due by him. It has been estimated that the consequent loss to the state will be some £E7 million.[1] Between them, land-tax and buildings tax were estimated to bring in £E20·2 million in 1961/2, compared with 16 million in 1951/2.

The first income-taxes were imposed in 1939.[2] Incomes were divided into four categories: dividends and interest; profits of financial, commercial, and industrial enterprises; incomes of liberal professions; salaries and wages. Dividends, interest, and profits were taxed at a flat rate of 7 per cent, raised in 1942 to 12 per cent, in 1950 to 14 per cent, in 1951 to 16 per cent, and in 1952 to 17 per cent. Until 1950 agricultural profits were exempt except when made by joint-stock companies—one more manifestation of the power which the landed interest then enjoyed. Members of the liberal professions, who also exercised great political influence, paid a tax equal to 7·5

[1] *al-Ahram*, 3 Nov. 1961 & 9 Feb. 1962.
[2] For a useful annotated compendium of legislation concerning income taxes and death duties, up to the end of July 1961, see Hasan Said Salim, *al-Marja al-daribi* (1961).

per cent of the rental value of their offices, but in 1950 this was replaced by a progressive tax on income rising from 1 to 7 per cent and in 1951 by a flat rate of 10 per cent which was raised in 1952 to 11 per cent. Wages and salaries were taxed at 2–7 per cent, with an exemption of £E60; this very low limit was raised in 1950 to £E100 with a maximum of £E150 for married persons. When the rise in the cost of living is taken into account, it will be seen that the limit was actually reduced. In 1952 rates for the higher income groups were raised to a maximum of 9 per cent.

Comparing the Egyptian and British tax systems in 1948, a British expert made the following comments:

> The existing systems of direct taxation in Egypt and Great Britain are based on widely opposed theories, those in Egypt on the *Nature of the source*, those in Great Britain mainly on *ability to pay*. In each case equality of sacrifice is attempted, but the result is that where in Egypt some individuals pay far more tax than others enjoying similar amounts of income . . . in Great Britain all incomes are treated alike, the reliefs granted being common to all.[1]

In order to remedy this deficiency, a general income-tax on aggregate income from all sources, including land rent not subject to the income-tax levied on other sources, was introduced in 1950, with rates rising from 5 per cent on incomes of less than £E1,500 to 50 per cent on incomes over £E100,000; an exemption limit of £E1,000 was allowed. In 1951 rates were raised to a minimum of 8 and maximum of 70 per cent on incomes above £E50,000 and in 1952 the rates on the higher incomes were raised again, increasing the maximum to 80 per cent. There is no doubt that these measures greatly improved the fiscal system of Egypt.

No further changes took place until July 1961, when Law No. 115 raised the rates again. As before, incomes up to £E1,000 are exempt, after which the rate rises sharply, from 8 per cent on the £E1,000–1,500 group to 25 per cent on the £E4,000–5,000 group, 55 per cent on the £E7,000–8,000 group, and a maximum of 90 per cent on incomes above £E10,000. These changes have suddenly converted Egypt into one of the countries with the most progressive rates of taxation; relatively to the per-capita income, the amount exempted from general income-tax, or hit lightly, is quite high, but it must not

[1] Min. of Fin., *Rep. on the Eg. Taxation Dept.*, quoted by Rashed Barawi, 'The Taxation System in Egypt', in *M.E. Affairs*, Dec. 1951.

be forgotten that all incomes remain subject to the schedular taxes, whose exemption limits are low.[1]

The number of persons assessed for the schedular taxes in 1960 was 457,000 and of those for the general income-tax 42,000 (see breakdown above, p. 118). Evasion has been widespread and it has been roughly estimated that receipts in 1956/7 should have been nearly twice as high as actual collections; among the causes given for this were: the fact that income-taxes are relatively recent; the constant rise in rates; the introduction of several new laws and modification of existing ones, with loose phrasing and conflicting provisions; the small number of officials charged with collection and their inadequate training; and poor organization, resulting in failure to spread the work load over the year[2] to which should be added a certain amount of corruption. It will thus be seen that there was considerable leeway for increasing government revenues by more efficient administration, rather than by the imposition of new taxes or nationalization of enterprises, if this had been desired.

The yield of the schedular taxes rose from £E16·3 million in 1951/2 to 26·3 million in 1959/60 and was estimated at 28·1 million in 1961/2; the corresponding figures for the general income-tax were 5·6, 5·2, and 5·7 million.

A bill levying death duties was introduced in 1939, but it was blocked by the Senate until 1944 when the net share of each beneficiary was taxed at a rate varying according to the degree of kinship and the size of the inheritance. In 1950 and 1952 (Law No. 159) the rates were raised and now range from 5 per cent on the first £E5,000 to 12 per cent on sums above £E50,000 for parents, children, and spouses; for more distant relatives the rates are increased and are four times as high for heirs of the fourth degree. Law No. 159 of 1952 also levied a tax on the net value of the whole estate; an exemption of £E5,000 is granted and the rate rises from 5 per cent on the £E5,000–10,000 group to 40 per cent on sums above £E100,000. The yield of these taxes rose from £E800,000 in 1951/2 to 3 million in 1959/60 and was estimated at 3·5 million in 1961/2.

[1] A few recent changes may be noted. The exemption limit for daily workers has been raised from PT30 to 50 and it is proposed to allow greater deductions from the general income-tax for those paying the tax on wages and salaries (*al-Ahram*, 15 & 27 Feb. 1962). It has also been ruled that government Organizations engaged in economic activities are subject to the tax on profits, an indispensable provision if their performance relatively to the private sector is to be judged correctly (see article by the Under Secretary of the Min. of the Treasury in *al-Ahram al-iqtisadi*, 15 Aug. 1961).   [2] NPC, Memo. no. 31A.

## PUBLIC DEBT

In the 1880's Egypt's public debt of over £E100 million was some ten times as high as annual government revenue and must have been considerably higher than the national income, but the rapid expansion of the latter brought down the ratios to six times and about two-thirds in 1913. During the inter-war period the debt was steadily reduced, as well as partly repatriated, and by April 1940 the total outstanding, including the non-consolidated debt, was £E93·2 million, of which 15·3 million was held by the government; the amount held by the public was therefore equal to only twice the government revenue and some 40 per cent of national income. The conversion of 1943 changed the debt from a sterling to an Egyptian one without increasing its amount but post-war loans (see above, p. 42) raised the total to £E175 million by June 1951, or the equivalent of one year's revenue and about a fifth of national income.[1]

During the 1950's the debt mounted rapidly and by November 1961 stood at £E579·3 million, or the equivalent of one and a third times the government's ordinary revenue and over two-fifths of national income. At that date the public debt was as follows:[2]

TABLE 36

### Public Debt, 30 November 1961

(*£E million*)

| | |
|---|---|
| Palestine loan, 3 per cent, 1969/79 . . . | 15·0 |
| Development loans, 2½–3½ per cent, 1964/5–1973/5 . | 217·0 |
| Loans for external financing,[1] 3 per cent 1970/5–1973/6 . | 57·0 |
| Nationalized institutions bonds,[2] 5 per cent 1970/2 . | 22·2 |
| Treasury bills . . . . . . | 198·0 |
| Total | 509·2 |
| Agrarian reform bonds, 1½ per cent . . . | 42·1 |
| Government-guaranteed bonds,[3] 3 per cent 1962/7–1966/71 | 28·0 |
| Grand total | 579·3 |

[1] Held by Central Bank.
[2] National Bank, Misr Bank, & Port Said Bank.
[3] Agricultural Credit Bank & Industrial Bank.

*Source:* CBE, *Econ. R.*, no. 4, 1961.

[1] For further details see NBE, *Econ. B.*, no. 2, 1953.
[2] In recent years most new loans have had maturities of 11–15 years and carried 3 per cent interest; at the end of 1961 government bonds were quoted at prices ranging from 87·9 to 99·9; for further details see ibid., no. 4, 1961.

To this figure should be added two further large sums. First, there is the value of the shares acquired by the government by the nationalizations of 1961: £E124 million (see above, p. 60); compensation is to be made to expropriated owners in 4 per cent fifteen-year bonds. Secondly, there is a large and rapidly mounting foreign debt, owed to the United States, the Soviet Union, the International Bank, and others (see above, p. 239). Altogether, it is quite likely that Egypt's public debt will in the near future, once more equal its national income.[1] The servicing of the debt was estimated at £E17 million in 1961/2 and will no doubt considerably increase in the next few years.

[1] Prof. Ragnar Frisch has hazarded the guess that the foreign indebtedness may rise to a total of £E1,000–1,500 m. ('Why National Planning?', NPC, *Current Notes*, no. 17).

# XIII

# Problems, Projects, and Policy

---

*Die Höhe reizt uns nicht die Stufen, den Gipfel im Auge wandeln wir gerne auf der Ebene.*
WILHELM MEISTER.

*Eppur si muove.*
GALILEO.

*Africa makes an almost unlimited demand for help upon the rest of the world and yet at the same time makes any response to that demand supremely difficult.* MARGERY PERHAM.

*There are always several ways out of every crisis, the only way that is utterly Utopian in such situations being a return to the status quo.* IGNAZIO SILONE.

## PROBLEMS OF DEVELOPMENT

Like other backward countries trying to carry out, in a twentieth-century political and social context, what is essentially a nineteenth-century economic revolution, Egypt faces several great obstacles. But, also like them, it is offered many opportunities which were denied to the forerunners.

The first difficulty is the low per-capita income. The leading authority on this subject has stated: 'it would seem that the per-capita income levels in Western Europe before industrialization must have been significantly higher than in the underdeveloped countries of Africa and Asia today',[1] and there is no doubt that the present level of living of the Egyptian peasants is much lower than that of seventeenth-century English peasants. This fact correspondingly reduces the capacity to carry out the large-scale saving required for development. It also means that the bulk of national expenditure goes to food and that the income elasticity of demand for food is high; yet it is far less easy to expand the output of food in response to a rise in demand than that of manufactured goods for which, at a higher income level, the elasticity of demand is greater.

[1] Simon Kuznets, 'Quantitative Aspects of the Economic Growth of Nations', *Econ. Dev. & Cult. Change*, Oct. 1956.

There is, secondly though by no means always, the high population level and the consequently high man-land ratio. Other things being equal, this means that the economy is operating in the region of lower returns of the production function and has less slack on which to draw in the form of unused land and other resources.

Thirdly, there is the high rate of population growth, in most underdeveloped countries 2–3 per cent per annum and probably due to rise to 3–4, compared with about 0·5 per cent in European countries during the early stages of the Industrial Revolution. This demands a correspondingly high rate of investment; even assuming that the capital-output ratio is as low as 3, a population growth of 3 per cent requires the investment of 9 per cent of the GNP just to maintain per-capita income. A secondary problem is the difficulty of increasing food and agricultural production in the same proportion. But of course population increase does not represent a pure loss, since it provides manpower and, by making possible a fuller utilization of overheads, may reduce the capital output ratio.

Another set of difficulties is posed by the fact that whereas the Industrial Revolution sprang up spontaneously on western soil it is being implanted full grown in other cultures. One consequence is the ever-widening gap between the techniques used in everyday life and those of contemporary industry and transport. This means that developing countries cannot draw, as the Europeans and Americans did, on their craftsmen for the skills needed to run modern machines, especially in view of the stagnation, and indeed retrogression, of the crafts caused in many countries by the replacement of old domestic products by machine-made imports. It is true that, at the lower levels, less skill is needed than fifty or eighty years ago. But the fact that, in contemporary industry, the skill has been 'put into the machine' only means that there is a correspondingly greater need for highly qualified managers, engineers, and technicians. And the fact that the backward countries have not gone through the same slow development as the west means that they have failed to acquire certain attitudes and habits which account for much of western economic and industrial achievement. Among these may be mentioned aptitude and respect for mechanical and other manual work, the absence of the fear of soiling one's hands, the habit of caring for and maintaining equipment and a much more diffused sense of responsibility and leadership, which supplies not only managers but the no less important supervisors and foremen. The lack of these elements, and the consequent deleterious effects, have been commented on by almost every technical or economic mission that has visited such countries.

Another consequence is the ever-growing scale of contemporary industry and the ever-greater volume of resources required. This may be illustrated by contrasting nineteenth-century iron works with the huge integrated steel mills that have to be set up today if the industry is to be at all competitive.

Thirdly, there is the fact that the developing countries have to depend on the advanced ones for their machinery and research, and that these are designed primarily to meet the needs of the latter, with their very different 'factor mix'. More specifically, they are designed primarily to save labour, of which the advanced countries are short, and not land or capital, which are scarce in other countries. In addition there is the growing tendency among western and western-trained engineers and architects 'to minimize the local factors of construction and production' in favour of more convenient imported ones; yet greater use of local factors is essential if the economic and technical benefits of a project are to be widely diffused in a given society.[1]

Lastly, there is the intangible but none the less important question of social attitudes. The processes summed up under the general heading of economic development—the replacement of subsistence by cash crops, the introduction of modern transport, the spread of a financial network, and the beginnings of industrialization—are bound to have a disruptive effect and to generate resentment among large sections of the population. Where, however, these processes have come about as part of an alien domination and have yielded a large share of their fruits to foreigners, the hostility they evoke must be much greater. This cannot but affect adversely the willingness and ability of a people to operate the technological and financial mechanism required by contemporary society. And even after foreign political and economic domination is over, the country will continue to suffer from the fact that it has developed into what has been called a 'dual economy' and may more properly be termed a 'dual society', with the contrast between 'the few highly westernized, trousered natives, educated in western universities, speaking western languages, and glorying in Beethoven, Mill, Marx or Einstein,

---

[1] Michael Ionides, *Divide and Lose* (1960), p. 209.

and the great mass of their countrymen who live in quite other worlds.'[1]

The prevailing economic ideology also creates many problems. In the west development came mainly through private enterprise but in the backward countries it is axiomatic that the greater part, if not the whole, is to be carried out by the state: 'We are all socialists now'. The reasons for this attitude, centring in the alleged failure of business men in backward countries to show enough enterprise and to invest sufficiently in sectors which serve vital national needs, have often been given.[2] And it is evident that state enterprise can secure great results, as is shown by the achievements of Russia and China, which were able fully to draw on the technology evolved by the west and to exploit the advantages open to late-comers. Indeed its total *effectiveness*, in the sense of the average annual rate of growth, may well be greater than that of free enterprise, among other reasons because it can usually squeeze more savings out of the people. But *efficiency*, i.e. the output-input ratio, is another matter; the efficiency of socialist enterprises, with their cumbrous bureaucracies and irrational systems of pricing and allocation of factors of production, is undoubtedly lower than that of firms subject to the discipline of the market and paying by bankruptcy the penalty for continued losses—even where new sanctions are introduced, in the form of concentration camps and firing squads.[3] Again, generally speaking, socialism, or at least a planned equalitarian society, offers fewer positive incentives than private enterprise, though it may overcome this shortcoming too by imposing still greater penalties. Lastly, its

[1] W. A. Lewis, 'Economic Development with Unlimited Supplies of Labour', *Manchester School of Econ. & Soc. Studies*, May 1955. The gap between the two segments is, however, narrowing. On the one hand, in many countries, the truly westernized group has been drastically reduced by emigration, exile, and imprisonment. And on the other the outlook of the mass of the population is being if not westernized at least rapidly modernized.

Two other social handicaps may be noted. First, illiteracy is higher in backward countries today than it was in eighteenth- or nineteenth-century Europe or America, but it is likely to be reduced more rapidly; secondly, these countries are much less likely to benefit from the spontaneous immigration of entrepreneurs and skilled workmen who, in Europe and America, not only contributed to economic development but merged completely with the native population.

[2] For a recent discussion in the Middle Eastern context see Yusif A. Sayigh, 'The Visible or the Invisible Hand?', *World Politics*, July 1961.

[3] For a vivid picture of the inefficiencies of a planned economy see Nove, chs. 6–8; of course a market economy has its own inefficiencies, but their overall impact is smaller.

responsiveness to the needs of the people is much lower and therefore there is a much greater chance of its misallocating resources. And, as a Yugoslav economist pointed out recently, 'the maximum increase in national income is not achieved by mere increases in quantity of production but by the actual satisfaction of demand'.[1]

Another set of difficulties arises from the foreign economic relations of developing countries. In international trade there is the increasing imbalance between imports and exports. On the one hand import needs grow because of rising consumption due to the population growth, to the conspicuous consumption fostered by a traditional agrarian society,[2] and to the 'demonstration effect' stimulated by western salesmanship and media of communication; and 'it is always easier to adopt superior consumption habits than improved production methods'.[3] To this should be added the still greater, and far less easily compressible, needs for imports of capital goods, fuels, spare parts, raw materials, and technical services created by economic development and magnified by the inflation which accompanies development in most countries.

But the prospects of increasing exports correspondingly are poor. Exports of primary products are clearly not growing at the rate which could have been anticipated by extrapolating nineteenth-century trends and are not likely to do so in the near future. This means that, except for certain articles like petroleum, exports of primary products are not likely to repeat today the part played by silk in the economic development of Japan, timber in that of Sweden, or wheat in that of Russia or Canada. This slackening is not caused by the failure of the main markets, Western Europe and the United States, to grow—indeed their GNP is increasing at an unprecedented rate. But, first, a large part of the increment is being spent on services—a phenomenon natural at their present level of

[1] Janez Stanovnik, 'Planning through the Market: the Jugoslav Experience', *Foreign Affairs*, Jan. 1962. For a good summary of the 'socialism capitalism' economic arguments see Balassa, pp. 1–25. Edward S. Mason, *Economic Planning in Underdeveloped Areas* (NY, 1958), contains many interesting ideas on the subject indicated by its title.

[2] In the Arab world perhaps the most widely admired legendary hero is Hatim al-Tai, who slaughtered his only remaining camel to provide a guest with a suitable meal.

[3] Ragnar Nurkse, 'Some International Aspects of the Problem of Economic Development', *Am. Econ. R.*, May 1952. It has, however, been rightly pointed out that advanced countries also exercise on the backward ones an 'investment demonstration effect', which helps their development (see Albert O. Hirschman in Mass. Inst. of Technology, *Investment Criteria*, p. 48).

affluence—and thus does not directly increase the demand for primary products. Secondly, their increasing efficiency is leading to much greater economy in the use of raw materials; for example, whereas in 1920 3 lb of coal were required to generate 1 kwh of electricity in the United States, by 1955 the figure had fallen to 0·95 lb.[1] Thirdly, there is the growing use of home-made synthetics; a dramatic example is the United States, formerly the main market for rubber, now almost self-sufficient. Together with this slackening in demand has gone an increase in the supply of primary products from the advanced countries, whose agricultural progress has been amazing: the United States, Canada, Australia, and now France and other West European countries. This has completely refuted the predictions of nineteenth-century economists who foresaw a great rise in the relative prices of raw materials owing to diminishing returns in agriculture and mining. Lastly, there is the failure of the primary producers to increase their exports owing to a slow rise in output coupled with greater consumption at home caused by population growth and industrialization—one need only mention wheat and cotton in India and Egypt.

This raises the question, which has perplexed so many international organizations, of whether the terms of trade for primary products are deteriorating. The evidence is not conclusive, especially if the improvement in the quality of manufactured goods be taken into account, as it clearly should be.[2] But it would seem that, taking primary producers as a whole, the sharp improvement in their terms of trade up to 1870 has been followed by a deterioration since that date, interrupted only by the two world wars and the Korean war. And it is unlikely that the coming years will witness a reversal of that trend.

A separate question, though one often connected with the previous one in popular literature, is the variation in the export price of primary products. A United Nations study claimed that in 1901–51 the price variability of raw materials was more than twice that of manufactured goods.[3] These fluctuations are certainly unfortunate,

[1] A similar process is of course taking place in the Soviet Union: 'For example, the norms of expenditure of hot-rolled ferrous metals in production were cut by more than 25 per cent between 1948 and 1956' (Yevenko, p. 189).

[2] Thus an American car buys more bags of Brazilian coffee or Argentinian wheat today than it did in the early 1920's. But whereas at that time a car was scrapped after running some 25,000 miles, its life today is nearly 100,000 miles, a fact which is not taken into account in indices of terms of trade.

[3] UN, Dept. of Econ. Aff., *Instability in Export Markets of Underdeveloped Countries* (1952); these findings have, however, been contested.

though there are many fiscal and financial devices for softening their impact on the domestic economy,[1] and the underdeveloped countries can learn to live with them as did the now advanced countries in their time; besides, their amplitude seems to be decreasing.

In view of the not too favourable prospects for primary products, many developing countries are building extravagant hopes on exports of manufactured goods. Here too they, or at least the smaller ones, face handicaps from which the early comers—the United Kingdom, France, Belgium, Germany, Italy, and even Japan until the 1930's were exempt. The latter had the whole world to which to export, and moreover a world characterized in the main by low tariffs and the absence of quotas or exchange controls. Today's prospective exporters are, however, caught in a threefold squeeze. First, there is the competition of the advanced countries, established in many markets and using the most up-to-date methods. Secondly, there are the Soviet bloc countries, for whom costs are a secondary consideration and who are prepared to undercut whenever they can get an immediate economic advantage, such as access to a market or the securing of a needed raw material, or a short or long-term political advantage. Lastly, there are the Asian giants, China, India, and Pakistan, with very low wages and an internal market sufficiently developed to permit large-scale operations and low-cost exportation. To which should be added the fact that many would-be markets are themselves making every effort to industrialize and following a highly protectionist policy.

But, when all is said, there still remain great opportunities for exports of both primary produce and manufactured goods by countries with sufficient enterprise and flexibility; this is shown, for example, by the success of Lebanon, which lacks any natural advantages for either agriculture or industry, in penetrating the most distant and unlikely markets.

Another aspect of international economic relations is that of foreign private investment. This has supplied both capital and entrepreneurial and technical skills, playing a crucial role in the growth of many countries where a national bourgeoisie failed to develop, and supplementing the efforts of that bourgeoisie at a subsequent stage. Today, however, it is clear that private capital is not going to flow in large amounts to backward countries, with their very narrow markets. For one thing its experience in recent years has been one of discriminatory taxation, regulation, nationalization, ex-

[1] See the symposia in *Kyklos*, 1958 & 1959.

propriation, sequestration, and 'intervention', to use the latest Cuban addition to the vocabulary of confiscation and spoliation. For another, the opportunities offered to private capital by the rapidly expanding economies of the United States, Western Europe, and other advanced countries such as Canada and Japan are immense. The situation today is radically different from that of the nineteenth century, which continues to dominate the thinking of people in backward countries. For at that time by far the most important lender was the United Kingdom, which had very limited opportunities at home, needed to develop overseas the raw materials and markets it required, and was therefore under great pressure to invest abroad. It is not accidental that, in the post-war years, very little private investment has gone to underdeveloped countries except in search of oil.

To these economic difficulties are added political ones, which may be briefly dealt with. There is first the fact that whereas in most parts of the western world, internal political upheavals succeeded the Industrial Revolution, in Asia and Africa they are preceding, or at best accompanying it. In the greater part of Europe and in the United States the traditional social structure stood firm and gave way only when undermined by the changes caused by industrialization and modern warfare. Even in Russia a great part of the Industrial Revolution was achieved within the framework of the old régime, which might have carried out the whole but for the shattering effects of the First World War.[1] In Asia and Africa, however, the old order has been disrupted or deeply undermined by two factors. First, there was the impact of the west in the political, economic, social, and cultural fields, carried out by the implantation of western businessmen, administrators, institutions, means of communication and ideas. And secondly, there was the nationalist struggle against foreign domination or influence, a struggle perforce drawing on the lower strata of society, appealing to new loyalties, and employing hitherto unknown techniques of political agitation and social organization. In an increasing number of countries the old political order has broken down and the ensuing upheavals have been succeeded by dictatorships based on either the army or a single party. Such systems present obvious advantages, such as greater

---

[1] It is often forgotten that between 1880 and 1913 the rate of industrial growth in Russia was appreciably higher than that of any major country in the world, including the USA and Germany (see S. J. Patel, 'Rates of Industrial Growth in the Last Century', *Econ. Dev. & Cult. Change*, Apr. 1961).

driving power and unity of purpose; moreover it is vain to deplore the disappearance of constitutional government in countries that lack the economic and social preconditions of democracy.[1] But it is relevant to point out that it is much more difficult for dictatorial governments to be properly informed of the economic needs and performance of their country and that moreover a great proportion of their energy has to be diverted into the sheer repression, espionage, and domestic propaganda required for the survival of the régime.

There is, secondly, the internal balance of the classes; urbanization and centralization have transferred much power to the urban working class, which can provoke riots and unseat governments. This fact, together with the awakening social conscience, the 'revolution of rising expectations' provoked by the example of the more advanced countries and the pressure exerted by communist agitation, means that a greater proportion of the national product has to be devoted to urban working-class consumption, in the form of private consumption or social services and protective legislation, than in the corresponding stages of industrialization in the west, Russia (both Tsarist and Soviet), and Japan. It is probable that the resources so used will pay for themselves in the long run, especially if they are concentrated on points where they can promote economic development: education, especially technical, health of workers, &c. But the immediate effect of such a policy is to decrease the funds available for investment, though in view of the vast amounts of foreign aid which most of these countries are getting this is not a major consideration. And it is certain that protective legislation can be misapplied. One example is the difficulty of dismissing redundant labour in private or state enterprises, which has drawn fire from United Nations experts in Iran, Turkey, and many other countries; another is prohibition of overtime and the forcing of employers to hire additional workers provided for by the Egyptian Law of 28 July 1961.

A much more serious factor is the vast expenditure on armaments. In several countries defence is absorbing 8–10 per cent of the gross national product, a figure much higher than that spent by even the Great Powers until very recently (see above, p. 278). And whereas in the past a country's expenditure on armaments gave a great stimulus to the development of its heavy industry, today's jets,

[1] See Issawi, 'Economic and Social Foundations of Democracy in the Middle East', *Int. Aff.*, Jan. 1956.

tanks, heavy guns, and other weapons have to be imported by under-developed countries, exerting no beneficial effect on the internal economy but only a heavy strain on the balance of payments. With the increasing complexity of warfare and the growing desire of even small countries to have missiles and other modern weapons, the situation will become still worse. To all of this should be added the overweening ambition of some states and the consequent expenditure on propaganda and agitation which they feel they have to carry on outside their borders.

Another important factor is the condition of the civil service. In the west economic development preceded, and paved the way for, the reform of the corrupt and nepotic civil service. But this was possible only because the prevailing political climate was one of *laissez-faire*, in which state interference was reduced to the minimum. In the backward countries today, economic development is being carried out largely by the state. To be effective, this necessitates an efficient and honest civil service and not the bureaucratic monstrosities characteristic of most developing countries. But the reform of the civil service at a time when it plays such an overwhelmingly important part in the life of the country, is surrounded by so many temptations, and exerts so much power, is a much more formidable task than was the reform of the British civil service in the Victorian era.

Lastly, there is an intangible but none the less real factor, the growing tension between underdeveloped and developed countries. It is true that the past actions of the latter were originally to blame for this hostility, but there is no doubt that it is being pursued today with great zest and zeal by the former colonies, generally long after the need for it has passed away. This tension is preventing the emergence of what could have been a mutually advantageous system of interdependence. For the small countries resent being dependent on the great and the latter in turn are being forced to develop substitutes for commodities which may suddenly be cut off, for purely political reasons, as was Middle East oil in 1956.

These handicaps are truly impressive. But, in the opinion of the present writer, they are outweighed by the advantages open to late-comers who can profit from the experience of their forerunners; adopt the latest techniques; avoid many technical, organizational, and social mistakes; and who do not have to bear the huge costs of experimentation and development but can pick the fruit without having to grow the tree or indeed who are often offered the fruit, in a gift wrapping, in the form of foreign aid.[1] It is not fortuitous that the rate of economic growth has risen steadily as development spread from its original home in Britain first to Western Europe and the United States, and then to Japan, Russia, and China.

There is, first, the tremendous advance of modern technology which opens horizons undreamt of in the past. This takes many forms such as the implantation of new processes in previously unsuitable places; the discovery of hitherto unsuspected or unutilizable resources by new techniques; the replacement of unavailable or expensive raw materials by substitutes such as hydro-electricity, plastics, and other synthetics; the great increase in productivity thanks to such innovations as hybrid maize or automatic looms; and the possibility of economizing scarce factors of production, for example capital, by such inventions as the radio and motor car, or skilled labour and management by certain forms of automation and automatic controls.

Secondly, there is the much wider range of countries on which developing countries can draw today for capital goods and technical aid; these include not only the United States and the numerous Western European states but the Soviet bloc and Japan, and may soon include India and others. This makes it much easier for a country to find an article or a process suited to its particular conditions.

Another factor is the small but significant financial and technical aid furnished by such international organizations as the International Bank and Fund, the United Nations and the Specialized Agencies. Such aid is a new phenomenon in human history and one which may be expected to gain in importance.

Last, and most important, comes the enormous flow of government grants and loans, running into several billions of dollars a year, from the developed to the backward countries. Such funds have gone both to those who have unequivocally taken sides, such as Greece, Turkey, and Pakistan, and to those who have played off one side against the other, such as India, Indonesia, Yugoslavia, and Egypt. This too is a completely new phenomenon; in the past the rich and powerful exploited the poor and weak; now the roles are reversed and there is no doubt that the change is for the better.

[1] Of course the latter involves certain drawbacks, e.g. the products may have been designed for the needs of advanced countries. And even the adaptation of foreign processes presupposes a certain internal development of science and technology. But the advantages remain immense.

In conclusion, a question may be briefly discussed which has exercised many people in the Middle East and elsewhere: whether the adoption of a modern economic structure is possible without a great degree of westernization, and whether the assimilation of western culture, with all the incompatibilities and contradictions between its successive phases and its various exponents, including the Soviet Union, is possible within a reasonably short period of time. The events of the last fifteen years have made it possible to define this problem more clearly. What the non-western civilizations are aiming at is not westernization but modernization. They accept western industrialization, technology, and science without reservations and indeed with greater enthusiasm than westerners themselves, many of whom are somewhat disillusioned with the results achieved. They also accept the principle of an egalitarian society, though the implications of that principle are not always fully grasped and its application often leaves much to be desired. Equally clearly they reject what many would regard as the core of western civilization: respect for the individual, based on the Christian doctrine of the supreme value of each human soul, and his protection by constitutional and legal safeguards; hence the toleration of political and other forms of opposition. It is also clear that these countries are willing to take what they need from any source: the United States, the various Western European countries, the Soviet bloc, and even Japan which, paradoxical as it may seem, has become an important channel for the diffusion of certain aspects of western culture.

One last point may be made. Of all the oriental civilizations, the Islamic is, intrinsically, one of the best equipped to cope with both economic development and cultural modernization. Islam is basically a rational, positive, equalitarian, and non-ritualistic religion. It does not impose upon its followers such formidable handicaps as does Hinduism with its caste system and rigid diet. In certain ways, such as its attitude towards birth-control and its respect for commercial activity,[1] it is particularly conducive to economic development. It is at least possible that Islam, or Arab nationalism, or a combination of both, will succeed in evolving a spirit which will furnish the driving force required for the great transformations lying ahead.

[1] It has been remarked that Islam is the only world religion to have been founded by a successful business man. This may partly account for the respect for commerce prevalent in medieval Islam. For example, the ninth-century writer al-Jahiz reminds his readers that the Prophet and his three immediate successors engaged in trade.

POPULATION

Egypt's economic problems can be summed up in two words: poverty and overpopulation. Although inextricably bound up, the two questions are distinct and it is advisable to begin with the second. Before doing so, however, it is necessary to define the limits of this analysis. The present author is convinced that Egypt's long-term prospects are good because it should, eventually, be able to make much fuller use of its deserts (see above, p. 132). But this is unlikely to occur before a few decades have elapsed and in the meantime the country will continue to face great economic difficulties.

Egypt's density of population is one of the very highest in the world. The inhabited part, which is the only one that should be considered at the present time, carries over 650 persons per square km., of whom nearly 60 per cent depend on agriculture. This compares with an overall density of 298 in Belgium, 214 in the United Kingdom, and 213 in West Germany, in which countries the percentage engaged in agriculture is only 5–15. Except for Japan and small portions of eastern and southern Asia, no agricultural region is as thickly populated as Egypt.[1]

The question of over-population may also be approached from the angle of underemployment. In the Egyptian cities there are many forms of disguised unemployment and also some overt unemployment. In agriculture there is the threefold phenomenon of seasonal unemployment, underemployment due to the small size of farms, and disguised unemployment owing to the fragmentation of farms and the consequent increase in work, e.g. walking from one plot to the other. Almost all observers agree that there is a large surplus rural population, i.e. that the same volume of agricultural production could be produced, with present techniques and only minor changes in

[1] Thus in 1949–50 the rural population density per sq. km. of cultivated land in Egypt was put at 542, which may be compared with 327 for Puerto Rico, 238 for India, 181 for Belgium, 164 for Mexico, 97 for Germany, 85 for the UK, and 18 for the USA, and which was exceeded only by the Japanese figure of 698. Another comparison puts the number of males engaged in Egyptian agriculture at 73 per standardized sq. km.; the next closest figures were Korea 36, India and Pakistan 31, China and S.W. Asia 25, and Japan 24; for Europe the figures were: Belgium 13, W. Germany 10, France 8, and UK 5; for the Soviet Union and the USA they were 3·1 and 1·2. But the latter estimate is open to a serious objection: it is based solely on climate and does not take into account topography and the nature of the soil. These are particularly favourable in Egypt, a fact which would appreciably reduce its relative density of rural population (El Sherbini & Sherif in *Ég. contemp.*, 1956; Colin Clark, *The Conditions of Economic Progress*, 3rd ed. (1957), p. 309).

organization, by a much smaller number of people.[1] Thus the former Minister of Agrarian Reform put the labour needs of agriculture at only 1·8 million men and 1·7 million women and children,[2] out of a rural population now standing at 17 million. Assuming an average of 280 working days a year for men and 200 for women, Saab calculated the available labour power of those engaged in agriculture in 1947 at 1,023 million man-days and 780 million woman-days. But with present crops, rotations, and techniques, a feddan required only 50–60 man-days and 60 woman- or child-days, or a total of some 360 million of each category.[3] Naturally account must be taken of seasonal peaks and of the considerable work that has to be done outside the fields such as the clearing of canals and drains, the construction of farm buildings, and the reclamation of marginal land. But when allowance has been made for all these requirements, it remains true that perhaps as much as a third of the rural population is surplus. This figure tallies with an estimate based on the conclusion of L. Dudley Stamp that, at a Western European standard of productivity per acre (and Egypt has reached such a standard), an acre will support one inhabitant. This would allow Egypt a *total* population of a little under 10 million. When adjustment is made for a lower standard of living, a rural population of 10 million seems ample.[4]

This already very serious situation is of course being aggravated by the rapid population growth. It is sufficient to quote the official extrapolations showing a total of 31·9–34·8 million by 1972 and 38·5–44·7 by 1982 compared with the 1960 figure of 26·1 (see above, p. 77). The improvement in hygiene and consequent reduction in

[1] The implication is that the marginal productivity of labour in Egyptian agriculture must be very close to zero. This is suggested, though of course not proved, by the fact that although the rural population increased by over 70 per cent between 1913 and 1950–4, as against an increase in cultivated area of under 8 per cent and in cropped area of about 25 per cent, and although the use of fertilizers, better seed, pesticides, and machinery has multiplied severalfold, average yields per feddan rose by only some 10 per cent. Considering that in 1913 the average productivity of Egyptian agricultural labour was already very low and therefore the marginal productivity presumably still lower, its present marginal productivity must be very close to zero (see figures given by Tanamly, in *Buhuth*, pp. 99–95).

[2] Sayyed Mari, in *Al-Majalla al-ziraia*, July 1959.

[3] *Motorisation*, pp. 6–7 and 327–8.

[4] *Land for Tomorrow*, p. 217. Three more supporting opinions may be quoted: Gamal al-Din Said estimated the surplus in 1937 at 5·6 m. persons (cited in Saab, *Motorisation*, p. 7); Sherbini & Sherif put it at 50 per cent for the same year (*Ég. contemp.* 1956); the Five-Year Plan (p. 112) puts actual employment in agriculture in 1959/60 at 4,220,000 and the number required to do the work at 3,245,000.

death-rates makes even the upper limits distinctly too low. The mere absorption of this increase, not to mention the diminution of the present surplus, presents a formidable challenge.

To meet this challenge, the Five-Year Plan envisages an increase in the number employed from 5,975,000 in 1959/60 to 7,001,000 in 1964/5 and 8,938,000 in 1969/70.[1] But even the planned increase of 1,026,000 jobs by 1965 would absorb little more than the anticipated population growth of 3·5 million during the same period. And the possibility of achieving the planned increase may be seriously doubted. Thus by 1965 employment in agriculture is expected to rise by 550,000, or 17 per cent, a figure which is far higher than the anticipated increase in the cultivated area and is hardly accounted for by any intensification which could be achieved during this period. Similarly employment in industry is expected to rise by 215,000, or 34 per cent. This may seem reasonable in view of the planned increase of 98 per cent in the net output of industry and electricity; however, it should be remembered that the increase in industrial output of about 73 per cent between 1947 and 1958 was achieved with a practically constant labour force (see above, p. 181). And the anticipated rise of 97,000, or 16 per cent, in commerce and finance is quite uncalled for, unless its purpose be to build up a huge bureaucratic apparatus in a sector so far happily free from it.

This means that other solutions must be sought for the population pressure. Emigration must be excluded, since the only Arab countries which could take in significant numbers, Sudan, Iraq, and to a lesser extent Syria, have made it clear that they have no intention of allowing any immigration. Hence excess labour will have to be absorbed at home. This can be done, to a limited extent, by community development projects, rural housing, cottage industries, and other similar projects which provide much productive employment and require little capital but do presuppose much organizational and other skills of which Egypt is short.

Still another field for constructive endeavour is that of social services, especially education. A nation-wide campaign against adult illiteracy—so far conspicuous by its absence from the many plans being implemented—need not cost very much money, if the necessary enthusiasm can be generated. Accompanying this, there could be simple agricultural and technical instruction, to develop badly needed skills, and other means of awakening the minds of the villagers. For 'the key to an accelerated growth of the under-

[1] *Cadre du Plan*, pp. 21 & 109–15.

developed areas of the world lies in bringing about fundamental changes in both the mental outlook and the technical knowledge and skill of their peasant populations'.[1]

The use of unemployed labour does not, however, end with community development or welfare schemes. Labour can and should be used to create capital. 'By far the greater part of a country's real capital structure consists of objects that require local labour and local materials for their production or construction.'[2] Many difficulties must naturally be faced in any attempt to use unemployed or underemployed labour for capital formation, but these difficulties are not insuperable and there is scope for an expanded scheme of small-scale public works.

But all this does not in any way diminish the imperative need to slow down the population growth by introducing birth-control, although—or perhaps precisely because—such measures can make their effect felt only in the long run.[3] The efforts being made in this field by the government of India seem to have achieved worthwhile results and the research now under way in advanced countries may make it possible to accelerate the diffusion of birth-control. As regards Egypt, matters have been made easier by several pronouncements by *ulama* since 1937, including one by the Mufti of Egypt, which leave no doubt that Islam has no theological objections to birth-control; this does not, however, mean that the sociological attitude or role of the mass of the *ulama* has changed significantly.[4]

[1] Nicholas Kaldor, *Essays on Economic Stability and Growth* (1960), p. 242. Japan may be quoted as an example of how much can be done with limited means. With a farming population of 38 m. cultivating 12½ m. acres, only one-third of which were double-cropped, its per-capita agricultural income around 1950 was probably no higher than that of Egypt, although in other sectors it was, of course, higher. Yet 97 per cent of farmers had electricity, more than 95 per cent could read and write, and more than 50 per cent had radios (see Keiki Owada, 'Land Reform in Japan', *Conference on World Land Tenure Problems*, Madison, Wis., 1951).

[2] Ragnar Nurkse, *Some Aspects of Capital Accumulation in Underdeveloped Countries* (Cairo, 1952).

[3] As was pointed out by Jan Tinbergen in his *Draft Report on Planning in Egypt* (Nov. 1957): 'In the short run nothing much can be done about it, but the overwhelming importance of the population problem and the desirability of family planning are brought out by these figures.'

[4] For an interesting account of the attitude of the medieval Moslem theologians towards birth-control see G. H. Bousquet, 'L'Islam et la limitation volontaire des naissances', *Ann. de l'Inst. des ét. orientales* (Algiers, 1948), and the article 'azl' in *Encyc. Islam* (2nd ed.). Extracts from the *fatwa* of 1937 are given in *News of Population and Birth Control*, May 1952, published by the Internat. Planned Parenthood, NY & London.

Nor has the attitude of the rural masses changed; a doctor in charge of one of the rural social centres told the present author that the number of peasants who consulted him on means of having more children was if anything larger than that of those who wished to limit their number. As for the government, its attitude and policy have passed through three phases. During the early years of the Revolution it showed interest in birth-control and took some tentative steps such as opening clinics.[1] Then it changed its mind, probably because of the rising nationalism and the quite mistaken belief that manpower is a source of military strength—as though it were not obvious that Sweden or Switzerland or Finland are much stronger Powers than Indonesia or Brazil, with more than ten times their number![2] An illustration is provided by a recent official pamphlet advocating a larger population and by the following quotation: 'The large size of population is preferable in a world governed by the law of the forest [*sic*]. . . . Our plan is not to interfere in fertility.'[3] But this attitude is in turn changing; very recently it was announced that the setting up of forty rural centres for family planning was under study; in the *Draft of the Charter* of 21 May 1962 President Abdel Nasser stated that 'the problem of population increase is the most serious obstacle facing the efforts of the Egyptian people in their drive to raise the level of production' and advocated family planning; and the first congress on family planning was held in Cairo in 1962.[4]

[1] The following official pronouncement is also significant: 'Under present circumstances, it is possible to state that the rapid growth in population is in itself an obstacle to economic development and the spread of public services in Egypt; it also prevents the great majority of the people from getting an income which would ensure a standard of living compatible with the hopes that they had fostered with the coming of the new régime' (Perm. Council of Public Services, *The Population Problem in Egypt* (Cairo, 1955), p. 23).

[2] It is possible that this change in attitude also owes something to the influence of the official communist view that there is no such thing as over-population but only under-production, and that birth-control is an imperialist device designed to impede the growth of underdeveloped countries. This approach certainly helps Soviet foreign policy, since the swifter the population increase of these countries the more intractable their problems become and the readier they are to accept communism as the only working alternative.

[3] El Daly in *Ég. contemp.*, 1953.

[4] *al-Ahram*, 8 Apr., 22 & 24 May 1962. It is perhaps not just a coincidence that similar shifts have occurred in China, where the government first advocated birth-control, in 1957, and then came out strongly against it; now, however, it has gone so far as to urge that 'no man should be a father until he is 26 and no woman a mother until 23' (*The Economist*, 25 Aug. 1962).

## PRODUCTION AND PROJECTS

The above analysis has shown that there are no short cuts which Egypt can take to improve its level of living. This can come about only by increasing production, a process which raises three questions: the rate of growth, the pattern of growth, and the nature and direction of foreign economic relations.

### Rate of Growth

The anticipated rate of growth has been established by the Five-Year Plan, which provides for an increase in GNP ('value added') from £E1,282 million in 1959/60 to 1,795 million in 1964/5 and 2,564 million in 1969/70, an increase of 40 and 100 per cent respectively. This is to be achieved by investing £E1,577 million during the first and 1,717 million during the second five-year period. Without repeating detailed criticisms of the Plan (see above, p. 69), the following main points may be made. First, as has been seen, the Plan proposes an annual compound rate of growth of GNP of 7·2 per cent, compared with about 4–4·5 in recent years; this, though not impossible, is certainly a very ambitious target for a country with as few untapped resources as Egypt, and the objectives set for certain sectors, notably agriculture, seem quite unrealistic. Secondly, the Plan is based on the rather low capital-output ratio of 3·1 and the high savings ratio of 14 per cent in 1959/60, rising to 20 per cent by 1964/5; for the various reasons given earlier, both ratios may be challenged. A third criticism concerns inter-sectoral relations, which do not seem to have been thought out sufficiently. In the same way the relations between the market mechanism, acting through prices, and the planning mechanism, aiming at targets, is by no means clear. Two further criticisms relate to foreign exchange. First, requirements of foreign exchange during the first five-year period are put at £E646 million or 38 per cent of total investments, a figure which far exceeds all the credits opened to Egypt.[1] Secondly, as a result of the first Plan, imports are expected to drop by 6 per cent and exports to rise by 36 per cent, which seems highly optimistic. Again, serious doubts may be expressed regarding the capacity of the Egyptian bureaucracy to carry the heavy burden thrown on its shoulders, which consists of nothing less than the management of the country's agriculture, industry, transport, media of communication, finance, and foreign trade, heaped on top of the more usual

[1] The last statement, which was true at the time of writing, may cease to be so by the time this book is published.

government functions. Lastly, population growth has been under- and that of per-capita income over-estimated.

It would, of course, be premature to say that the targets set by the Plan will not be attained, but scepticism seems justified. And it is a fact that the Plan has got off to a bad start, owing to the disastrous crop failures of 1961 and the considerable disruption caused in certain sectors by the nationalizations and sequestrations.

### Pattern of Growth

The pattern of growth is also set by the Plan, but there is no need to repeat here the objections regarding the lack of inter-sectoral consistency and balance. Instead the question will be approached from the angle of economic strategy: what are the products and services on which Egypt should concentrate if it is to get the most out of its resources?

As regards services the situation is clear. There is first and foremost the Suez Canal which, as has been seen, Egypt has been operating with great efficiency. Traffic has been steadily growing, owing to the rising flow of oil and with it receipts, and work is under way to increase the capacity of the Canal. Barring a political catastrophe, such as occurred in 1956, or a policy which will drive oil to other routes, the future of the Canal seems assured.

The second service Egypt can offer is its location on air routes from Europe to Africa and Asia. Here, however, the position is much less favourable. For one thing the revenue that can be earned is much smaller than that accruing from the Canal. And for another Egypt faces intense competition from Lebanon, Israel, Turkey, Syria, Iran, and Iraq. However, given a moderately hospitable and equitable attitude towards foreign businesses, and some restraining of the propensity to confiscate them or tie them up in red tape, Egypt may hope to increase its share of the ever-growing air traffic.

The same considerations apply still more forcefully to tourism, where Egypt enjoys great advantages of climate, location, historical, and artistic interest. It often seems to be forgotten that tourists visit a country for pleasure and are not likely to come in large numbers to a place where they are subjected to numerous formalities, or from which they are scared off, by xenophobic pronouncements. And in this field, in particular, Egypt faces formidable competition from other Mediterranean lands, whose attractions are at least as great.

As for agricultural production, Egypt's policy is clearly indicated by its location, its climate, the scarcity of its land and water, and the abundance of its labour. All of these point to the need to concentrate on valuable, labour-intensive crops. In the past Egypt followed such a policy by developing cotton, onions, and rice at the expense of wheat and barley but now it is due for another shift to even more valuable and labour-absorptive products such as fruit, vegetables, flowers, and dairy produce. There are a few signs that the government has realized the possibilities open in this direction, but none that it has understood the nature of the means required. It is not merely that such products demand large capital investments in processing plants, refrigeration, and transport, and far-reaching organizational changes in marketing. It is above all that they are essentially of the type that can be best grown and sold under private enterprise, in contrast with more standardized and tougher crops, such as grains, which demand less attention and can more easily survive the heavy hand of public ownership. The care and attention needed by such products can be given only by an owner-farmer and, so far at least, the government is accepting the principle of private ownership in land, within quite reasonable limits. But even more important is marketing, which has been nationalized. And it is difficult to imagine the cumbrous, inefficient, and fairly corrupt Egyptian bureaucracy following the needs of various foreign markets, adapting products and packaging them to suit their tastes, and getting the highly perishable goods there on time. Indeed, even before nationalization, the experience of the few enterprising land-owners and merchants who tried to develop new markets or to export new goods was most discouraging; often by the time they had filled in the manifold forms and obtained the innumerable signatures required, either the merchandise was unfit to be shipped or the season of scarcity in the foreign market was over (see above, p. 244).

To this should be added one more consideration. The bulk of such exports would normally be directed towards the countries of Western Europe. But, given Egypt's attitude towards these countries in the last few years, it is difficult to imagine any great eagerness on their part to take Egyptian goods if alternatives are available, as they are in Spain, the Eastern Mediterranean, and North Africa, many countries of which may soon be associated with the European Common Market.

Passing on to industrial production, it may be noted that in Egypt this has so far proceeded on the basis of import substitution. This is nearly complete for most kinds of consumer goods, including many durables, and will doubtless continue until imports have been reduced to an incompressible minimum.[1] Efforts are also being made to manufacture more and more producer and capital goods, but the narrowness of the Egyptian market means that production of such goods would have to be restricted and costs would be correspondingly high, unless outlets are found abroad; and Egypt is now seeking to break into foreign markets. Similarly, exports of various consumer goods are to be greatly expanded.

Given its low wages—which however do not always imply correspondingly low labour costs (see above, p. 191), Egypt stands a good chance of competing in those goods for which low-cost raw materials are available locally. Among these are cement, phosphates, canned fruits and vegetables and, if the quality of skins is improved, leather goods. Still greater possibilities are open for cotton textiles but only if Egypt follows the policy advocated by some economists, including this author, for over twenty years—and apparently adopted by the government at the end of 1961—namely importing short-staple cotton for the manufacture of cheap textiles consumed internally and using Egyptian cotton mainly for high-class goods for export. As for other industries, Egypt has little chance of competing in ordinary circumstances—which raises the question of the nature and direction of foreign economic relations.

## Nature and Direction of Foreign Economic Relations

These may be considered under three headings: the developed countries, Africa, and the Arab countries. Egypt's relations with the developed countries—Western Europe, the United States, the Soviet bloc, and Japan—admit of little variation. Exports to them will continue to consist mainly of primary produce—cotton,[2] rice,

[1] See *Cadre du Plan*, p. 86–88.

[2] The following general remarks may be made regarding the prospects for Egyptian cotton. First, world cotton prices have been holding well in the last few years, after the 'Korean boom' and the subsequent collapse, and may be expected to continue doing so in the immediate future. World consumption of cotton rose from 6,190,000 tons in 1947, or almost exactly the 1934–8 level, to 9,800,000 in 1959, i.e. by over 4 per cent a year. Naturally, man-made fibres have been advancing much more rapidly, and in 1959 their consumption was 2,968,000 tons, or 21 per cent of total fibre consumption, compared with 11 per cent in 1934–8. Moreover their price has risen much less than that of cotton—between 1934–8 and 1956–7 United States cotton prices rose by 153 per cent and Egyptian by 284 but rayon by only 20 per cent, standing at a level distinctly below that of cotton, while nylon declined by over one-third from its 1941 price. Man-made fibres have taken over the automobile tyre market from cotton and invaded many of its apparel

vegetables, and petroleum—with perhaps an increasing amount of labour-intensive consumer goods such as cotton textiles. In return Egypt will import capital goods and large amounts of capital.

Many Egyptians are building great hopes on sub-Saharan Africa as a market for their manufactured goods. Trade missions have been sent to various countries and agreements have been concluded with several of them, export-promotion loans have been granted to Mali, Guinea, and Somalia, every effort has been made to turn anti-imperialist, neutralist and pan-African sentiments to economic advantage, and Egypt has played a leading part in sponsoring an African Common Market and Development Bank. But the possibilities of sending considerable exports to these countries do not seem to be great. First there are difficulties of the distances involved, compounded by lack of direct transport lines or financial links. Secondly, Egypt cannot take much in return, since its consumption of the products which constitute the bulk of the exports of tropical Africa—cocoa, groundnuts, palm oil, cotton, rubber, diamonds, copper, &c.—is strictly limited. Thirdly, there is intense competition not only from the western countries, the Soviet bloc, and Japan but also from India in East Africa, Morocco in West Africa, and Israel, which has extended financial and technical assistance to several countries, in both regions. Even Brazil has designs on the African market, to be furthered by its new anti-colonial policy.[1] Lastly, there is rising protectionism, designed to develop many industries producing precisely the goods Egypt is able to export; this process is most advanced in those countries with which Egypt has the friendliest relations, such as Ghana and Guinea, as well as in Nigeria, which hopes to become the industrial centre of West and Central Africa.

This leaves the Arab countries, which in many ways form Egypt's natural market. Egypt contains by far the greatest concentration of industrial capital and skills of any Arab country and should be able to meet the needs of its neighbours for many manufactured goods.

markets. But cotton has adapted itself to the situation and has found many new uses, e.g. non-ironing clothing.

As for Egyptian cotton, it is increasingly suffering from the competition of other long-staples, notably Peruvian, Sudanese and more recently American, which have invaded many of its traditional markets in the UK and USA. But new markets have been opened and Egyptian cotton will continue to command a premium over others because of its quality (see NPC, Memo. no. 32 & FAO, *Per Caput Consumption*).

[1] See the article by ex-President Janio Quadros, 'Brazil's New Foreign Policy', *Foreign Affairs*, Oct. 1961.

In return, it could draw on oil and foreign exchange from the Persian Gulf and Libya, grains and livestock from Iraq, Syria, and the Sudan, and various kinds of fruit and vegetables from Lebanon and Jordan. The realization of this complementarity, and of the great benefits to be derived by Egypt from such a division of labour, partly explain the change in Egyptian policy from isolationism to the championing of Arab unity. In the economic field two instruments have been used: bilateral agreements, such as the ones with Syria in 1956 and Saudi Arabia and Iraq in 1958; and the two multilateral agreements for the encouragement of trade and transit and the facilitation of payments and capital movements, which were signed on 7 September 1953, subsequently ratified by Egypt, Iraq, Jordan, Lebanon, Saudi Arabia, and Syria, and amended on 15 December 1954 and 25 January 1956. While the second multilateral agreement has remained inoperative, the one on trade and transit, which exempts agricultural produce from customs duties and reduces those on manufactured goods by 25–50 per cent, succeeded in appreciably raising intra-Arab trade between 1954 and 1958.[1] In particular, Egypt's exports to Saudi Arabia, Lebanon, Syria, and Jordan increased several-fold. Since 1957, however, tensions between the Arab governments, and more particularly Egypt's quarrels first with Iraq and Jordan, then with Lebanon, then with Saudi Arabia, again with Iraq, and most recently with Syria and Yemen, and its strained relations with Tunisia and Libya have led to a decline in inter-Arab commerce and a marked drop in Egypt's trade with its neighbours. A further difficulty has been created by the nationalization of Egyptian foreign trade. Already at the beginning of 1960 the Sudanese government was complaining that the channelling of Egyptian exports and imports through one company was hurting Sudanese traders by confronting them with a monopoly and monopsony,[2] and since then this process has gone much farther. However, although such measures may complicate they obviously do not prevent trade with the Arab countries, since the latter continue to carry on active relations with the Soviet bloc, which also operates through state monopolies.

The nationalization of foreign, including much Arab, property and Egypt's new socialist policy—so far unaccompanied by any similar policy in other Arab countries—are, however, a much more serious obstacle to Arab economic integration, which seeks to go

---

[1] See Gen. Union of Chrs. of Comm., Ind. & Agric. of Arab Countries, *al-Taqrir al-iqtisadi al-arabi*, Dec. 1961.   [2] *Ég. indust.*, Mar. 1960.

beyond a mere increase of trade and aims at a greater flow of capital from the oil-rich to the other Arab countries, the establishment of a Development Bank, the co-ordination of investment and production plans, regional co-operation in irrigation and transport, the exchange of experts, and other similar measures. Hopes of such an integration received a serious setback from Syria's break-away from the union with Egypt. Among the reasons for this—in addition to Syrian resentment of alleged domination, the friction provoked by the presence in Syria of several thousand Egyptian soldiers and civilians, and the resistance offered by the vigorous native bourgeoisie to the nationalization measures of July 1961—was the realization of the economic role reserved for Syria in the union. Syria was made to buy certain industrial products exclusively from Egypt. And an examination of the Syrian Five-Year Plan[1] shows that no less than 40·0 per cent of total investment was allocated to agriculture and irrigation, against 18·7 per cent for manufacturing, mining, and electricity, and of the latter figure three-fifths was devoted to petroleum and petro-chemicals; this compares with 23·5 and 33·7 per cent respectively in Egypt. Although concentration on agriculture and petroleum was justified, in view of Syria's factor endowments as well as the scarcity of well-thought-out industrial projects, it caused resentment among Syrians, who believe as firmly as any other people that industry is the golden road to progress and who objected to seeing their country become an agricultural appendage of Egypt.

In other words, until recently the quarrels that divided the Arabs were mainly on the governmental level and were based on dynastic or personal rivalries or, at most, on differing foreign policies. The second Egyptian revolution, of 1960–1, has, however, introduced a far deeper cleavage between different economic and social systems and ideologies. Egypt's experiment in socialism is naturally dreaded by the upper and much of the middle classes of the other Arab countries, over whose heads President Abdel Nasser is openly appealing to the masses. Egyptian leadership is also meeting a broad-based resistance in several countries, such as Iraq, Lebanon, Sudan, and Syria, which have developed a strong local nationalism that clearly manifested itself in the crises of 1958–61. Although eventually unity under or around Egypt is probable, the struggle of rival ideologies and systems is bound to be bitter and prolonged, and in

[1] *Mashru khitat al-tanmia al-iqtisadia wa'l-ijtimaia li'l-sanawat al-khams* (Damascus, July 1960).

the meanwhile co-operation between the Arab countries, both political and economic, is sure to suffer.

### WESTERN DILEMMAS

The question of inter-Arab relations naturally leads to that of the relations between the Arabs and the outside world. In 1953 the present writer stated:

It is highly probable that unless the West can establish a new relationship with the Middle East, which will both restore its self-respect and start it on the road of economic and social progress, the whole region will, after an interval of violence and chaos, end up by going Communist. This argument, of course, implicitly assumes not only that the Middle East is worth saving, but also that the West thinks it is worth saving and that the Middle Easterners themselves want to be saved; but, judging from the actions of both sides during the last few years, the two latter assumptions are by no means self-evident.[1]

The events that have occurred since that time have brought about only one change: today the region is much closer to communism than it was then and there is much less elbow room left to either the west or the Arabs.[2] It would be futile to seek to assess responsibility for this drift, which is shared by both sides—the west because of such policies as the staunch support for Israel until 1956, the Baghdad Pact, the withdrawal of the offer to finance the High Dam, the disastrous and lamentably executed Suez invasion and the Eisenhower doctrine, and the Arabs—and more particularly the Egyptians —because of their utter ignorance of the nature of Soviet imperialism,[3] their continuous and quite unnecessary provocation, since

---

[1] *EMC*, p. 275.

[2] It is true that, in certain respects, the foreign policy of Egypt and that of some other Arab countries is less closely aligned on that of the Soviet Union than in 1956 to 1960. It is also true that there is more awareness than previously of the internal danger posed by Soviet communist infiltration. But it is no less true that the economic, social, political, and cultural changes of the last few years have brought these countries much closer in structure, behaviour, attitudes, and feelings to communism, albeit so far a nationalist communism and not one subservient to the Soviet Union. In other words the immediate danger of absorption by the Soviet bloc is smaller than it was a few years ago; but at the same time there has been a great alienation from the western way of thought and life and a drawing closer to the Soviet way, and this change may considerably facilitate eventual absorption.

[3] It would be interesting to know, for instance, how many of those in charge of Arab economic life have taken the trouble to study the methods of pressure used by the Soviets in their economic relations with weaker countries such as Finland

1953, of the west in Africa, Asia, and now even in Latin America, their enthusiastic opening of the gates to communist propaganda and influence and, most recently, because their leaders have initiated social revolutions whose dynamics they are far from understanding and which will take them—or more probably their successors—to destinations whose existence they do not even suspect.

No study of contemporary Egypt can avoid raising the question of whither? This author's belief is that it is moving towards at best a Titoist system and at worst to what may be called the economics of neo-barbarism or the 'Chinese way'. The reason for this is that the recent measures have broken the spring which made the old order work, however imperfectly—that of private enterprise supplemented by government control of certain leading sectors; no adequate motive power has, however, been put in its place, and the resulting decline in efficiency might have already led to very serious consequences but for the resilience possessed by every social as well as physical organism, which enables it to stand much abuse before collapsing. But a more important sustaining factor has been the vast amount of aid extended by the United States—which has averaged nearly $130 million a year and by the beginning of 1962 was approaching $200 million. This has supplied, in addition to many capital goods, the grains and other foodstuffs without which Egypt would either have faced starvation or been forced to give up its development plans.[1]

The relief of human hunger is the first, and perhaps most cogent, argument for continued aid to Egypt. The second is that, in Egypt as in other underdeveloped countries, industrialization and economic development deserve full support. Again, such aid can, by reducing Egypt's great economic dependence on the Soviet bloc, help it to preserve its freedom of action and pursue a neutralist foreign policy. Lastly, help to the present government may moderate the pace of its drift towards complete totalitarian socialism, or else prevent its collapse and replacement by something less acceptable to the west. In Egypt the eggs have been broken and they cannot be unscrambled,

and Yugoslavia—for a succinct analysis of these methods see Milton Kovner, *The Challenge of Coexistence* (Wash., 1961). Another massive sphere of ignorance is the nature of Soviet rule in Moslem Central Asia and the Caucasus.

[1] Soviet aid has also been considerable, though up to now well below American, but it has taken exclusively the form of armaments, capital goods, and technical assistance. While such aid is of great importance for the country's future, it does not in any way help it to acquire the goods it needs for sheer daily consumption and survival. By mid-1962 about half of the wheat eaten in Egypt was American.

but the omelette is not yet fried and the danger is that the government may have to turn on even more heat to cook it. Here too
foreign aid can play a vital role. And the wisdom of such aid is in no
way diminished by the very ungracious, to say the least, behaviour
which Egypt displays in return: the constant stream of abuse and
attack on the west in radio and press, the automatic equation of
imperialism with the west, the opposition to the west on almost
every international issue, however remote from Arab concern, from
the Congo to Cuba and China.[1]

If Egypt were a country living in isolation, the case for continued,
or even increased, aid would be conclusive. But the Egyptian
government has loudly and repeatedly proclaimed its intention of
extending its revolution, which implies its control, to the other Arab
countries. In so far as western aid releases Egyptian resources, and in
particular foreign exchange, it is directly helping Egypt to spread its
influence abroad and indirectly promoting the spread of the political,
social, and economic pattern which Egypt represents. This raises the
whole question of western policy in the Middle East, a matter far
beyond the scope of this book. All that can be stated here is that the
prime western interest in the region is first to keep it from being
absorbed in the Soviet bloc and secondly to safeguard the continued
flow of its oil. Would the extension of Egyptian control to the
Persian Gulf, fulfilling the dream of Arab unity, give more stability
to the region? And would it jeopardize western access to, or only
ownership of, the oil?[2] What are the chances of the emergence of a
secure and effective government in Iraq which can develop its huge
resources and play a more active part in Arab politics? How far off
is the revolution in Saudi Arabia? Can the oil shaikhdoms make a
greater contribution to the economy of the region—as they clearly
should—without being absorbed politically? Will Syria succeed in
composing its internal tensions and can it recapture the very rapid
rate of growth it achieved in 1945–57 while keeping some of the
more beneficial measures introduced during the period of union, such
as agrarian reform and participation of workmen in profits? Can
Jordan, which has made considerable progress in the last few years,
become a viable country? Will Lebanon continue in its present

[1] One cannot, however, avoid asking whether the Soviet Union, which pro-
claims so loudly that 'no strings are attached' to its aid, would have continued to
help a country which subjected it to similar treatment.

[2] Needless to say, western oil interests in the Persian Gulf are menaced by other
local nationalist and communist forces; indeed some of these may present a greater
and more immediate threat than the one posed by eventual Egyptian control.

euphoria? Is it possible to maintain Arab-Israeli tensions at a relatively moderate level? And, looking beyond the Arab countries, can Iran be helped to weather the present storm and steered to the immense opportunities that lie before it? Can Turkey restore the golden days of the early 1950's, when rapid economic growth went hand in hand with political liberty and stability? And, more generally, can economic progress and social justice be achieved in the Middle East within a political framework which ensures a modicum of liberty—if not, they will be sought outside that framework. These are some of the questions that have to be answered before a suitable policy is evolved. Given the balance of social and political forces in the region and the widespread revolutionary drive to overthrow old régimes and reshape the economic and social order, and given the very limited choice open to the west and its very restricted means of action, the present policy of increased aid to Egypt, together with continued assistance to other Middle Eastern governments, may well be the best in the circumstances.[1] But whatever the answer to these questions may be, and whatever the consequent policy, one thing is certain: the west will have to pay for its past mistakes by heavy political and economic losses in the Middle East, probably including the oil. And similarly the Arabs will pay dearly for their mistakes—indeed they are already paying.

There are two points that the author wishes to make in conclusion. First, the west must make every effort to reduce its dependence on Middle Eastern oil; for this dependence has produced a profoundly unhealthy relationship between the two sides and one which can lead either one to repeat the kind of behaviour that caused the conflict of 1956. Secondly, the west must co-ordinate and unify its policy in the region to a much greater degree than it has done in the past. At present there is nothing but confusion and disarray. To take only Egypt, at the beginning of 1962, political

[1] It may be argued that the results of United States aid to Spain and Yugoslavia show that help to a totalitarian government does the donor more harm than good, but the conclusion seems unwarranted to the present writer as regards both countries. Additional arguments against helping Egypt are the nationalizations and sequestrations of 1961, the harmful effects of which have by no means yet made themselves fully felt. But such reasoning ignores the irrational but apparently irresistible urge towards totalitarian socialism prevalent in underdeveloped countries; it may well be that, by taking these measures, Egypt has gained a chance to escape a still worse fate; in this connexion one should recall Lincoln's wise words: 'a universal feeling, whether well or ill-founded, cannot be safely disregarded'.

relations with France were frankly hostile, with Britain frigid, with the United States cool, and with Germany and Italy cordial.[1] In the economic field, western governments and businessmen are tripping over each other, and some times tripping up each other, in their efforts to extend credits and capture contracts. One is reminded of Lenin's saying: 'The capitalists will sell us anything, even the rope to hang them with.' Clearly the time has come for a co-ordination of both political and economic policy. And this is perhaps easier to achieve than at any time since the end of the war. For one thing the Common Market has bound up the Continental countries and made it both more feasible and more urgent for them to pursue compatible policies. For another, the wholesale liquidation of British, French, Dutch, and Belgian colonies—soon to be followed by the Portuguese—has both removed many particular interests which caused divergence between the metropolitan countries and eliminated certain moral liabilities which made it difficult for some western governments to associate themselves too closely with the policy being pursued at any given moment by one or other of their allies. As regards the Arab world, now that the Algerian war is at last over, there is hardly a single question on which any western country need hesitate to support its allies. In the Middle East, as elsewhere, the west is fighting for its very existence and its peoples must either stand together or perish separately.

Since the above was written, revolutions have broken out in three Arab countries, Yemen, Iraq, and Syria. The first, which led to a civil war that is still not over, has shown how fierce is the struggle between the forces of revolution and conservatism in the Arab world, how widespread are the repercussions of any change in the *status quo*, and how acute are the consequent dilemmas posed for western policy. The implications of the Iraqi revolution are more far-reaching, though less evident. By replacing a cruel, capricious, and incompetent government by one that seems abler and more reasonable it has removed an important obstacle to the realization of the economic and political potentialities of Iraq. The new régime seems more likely to achieve friendlier relations with other Arab countries and end Iraq's isolation, a fact that can only be welcomed. As regards relations with Egypt, they may be expected to be closer and more harmonious than under Kassem, but how much is a matter for

[1] Now that the war in Algeria has ended, it is probable that Britain will replace France as the main object of Egyptian and Arab hostility. Unless, of course, that role devolves on the United States.

speculation. The Syrian coup, the latest in a series of power struggles in the year and a half since the dissolution of the union with Egypt, has once more shown both the political instability of the country and the strength of the more radical elements. Here too closer relations with Egypt seem likely.

Two recently published studies may be noted:

Anouar Abdel Malek, *L'Égypte, société militaire* (Paris, 1963)—an interesting Communist account of the pre-revolutionary and revolutionary periods.

Dieter Weiss, 'Die aegyptische Wirtschaftsplanung', *Schmollers Jahrbuch* (Berlin, 1963)—a critical study of investment and planning, based on an as yet unpublished thesis.

# Appendix I

## GROUPING OF PUBLIC ORGANIZATIONS UNDER MINISTRIES, 1961

The number after each Organization is that of the companies it supervises.

*Ministry of Industry:* Mining 12; Foodstuffs 28; Weaving and Spinning 38; Chemical 41; Building Materials and Ceramics 10; Metallic Industry 8; Engineering 23; Petroleum 8; Co-operative Organization and Small Industries.

*Ministry of War:* Military Factories (includes United Arab Airlines).

*Ministry of Agriculture:* Agricultural Co-operative Organization 11.

*Ministry of Communications:* Internal Transport 20; Maritime Transport.

*Ministry of Housing & Public Utilities:* Housing Co-operative; Contracts and Construction 16; Public Buildings; Housing and Rehabilitation 4.

*Ministry of Agrarian Reform:* Desert Reclamation; Rehabilitation; Land Reclamation 4.

*Ministry of Labour:* Social Insurance.

*Ministry of State:* Broadcasting and Television (including factory for television sets); Tourism and Hotels 5; News, Publicity, Distribution and Printing.

*Ministry of Supply:* Consumer 30; Consumer Co-operatives; Silos and Storage 3; Fisheries 2.

*Ministry of Health:* Pharmaceutical Products, Chemicals and Medical Equipment 8.

*Ministry of Economy:* Trade 27; Cotton Trade 18; Banks 27; Insurance 16; Savings.

*Ministry of Culture & National Guidance:* Acting and Cinema; Film Consolidation Fund; Theatre and Music; Authorship, Translation, Printing and Publications.

*Ministry of Public Works:* Electricity.

# Appendix II

## ESTIMATES OF INVESTMENTS, 1946–61

AN official series puts gross investment in 1946 at £E64 m. (of which private was 55 m., public 11 m., and stocks −2 m.) and shows a steady rise to £E149 m. in 1951 (115 m., 26 m., and 8 m. respectively); there was a drop to £E115 m. in 1952 and 111 m. in 1953 after which the upward trend was resumed with 128 m. in 1954 and 160 m. in 1955, followed by a drop to 130 m. in 1956 (72, 49, and 9 m. respectively).[1] These figures, if correct, would indicate that gross investment accounted for some 15 per cent of national income in 1946–56, and a somewhat smaller percentage of GNP. On the other hand the National Production Council estimated the gross rate of capital formation in 1953 at only £E69 m. (imports of machinery and equipment 18·3 m., buildings 40·6, other 10·1) or 8 per cent of the national income, and the National Bank put the net value of capital formation at £E37 m. in 1953 and 65 m. in 1954.[2]

Another series puts average gross investments in 1945–52 at £E100 m., or 13 per cent of GNP and in 1958 at 171 m., or 17 per cent; the figures for 1953–7 were: £E117 m., 131 m., 159 m., 163 m. and 143 m.[3] The components of the 1958 total were: dwellings £E48 m., basic equipment 56 m., and direct investment (industry, commerce, and private transport sector) 67 m.; it was covered as follows: savings of households 49 m., surplus of government receipts over expenditure 37 m., self-financing of private sector 52 m., and deficit in the balance of payment 33 m. The last figure was about equal to those for 1955–7 and represented an average of 21 per cent of gross investment.[4]

These figures may be supplemented by data from other sources. Gross investment in private buildings in 1949–54 averaged about £E33 m. a year (NPC, Memo no. 30A). The number of joint-stock companies rose from 297 in 1946 to 422 in 1953 and their paid-up capital from £E88·6 to 186·8 m., or an average increase of 14 m. a year (ibdi. no. 30); the figures for 1934 were 188 companies and 67·6 m. and for 1939 225 and 55·6 m. In 1945–50 government expenditure on 'new works' averaged £E25·6 m. a year, and in subsequent years this figure rose very considerably (NBE, *Econ. B.*, no. 1, 1952). To this should be added investment in agriculture, industry, and stocks by unincorporated business.

---

[1] NPC, Memo. no. 40A. The figures for 1947–50 were: £E88, 121, 130, and 137 m. respectively.      [2] NBE, *Econ. B.*, no. 1, 195C.

[3] Samir Amin, 'Le Financement des investissements dans la province ég. de la RAU', *Ég. contemp.*, July 1959; this article contains much valuable information.

[4] NPC, Memo. no. 128.

Fixed capital formation in all forms of transport in 1948–54 averaged
£E14·5 m. a year, but the bulk of this was carried out by the government
or by joint-stock companies and is therefore accounted for in the above
figures.

Another estimate for 1958, based on a study of financial flows, put total
gross investment in the private sector at £E105·8 m., of which private
business accounted for 90 m. and households for 15·8 m. Private savings
were put at £E71·5 m., of which households contributed 12·5 m., self-
financing by the unorganized sector 27 m., and the retained earnings of the
organized sector 32 m. The gap between savings and investments was met
by loans from other sectors, of which the most important were £E7·8 m.
from the government Pensions and Insurance Fund and 20·5 m. from the
Rest of the World.[1]

For 1959/60 total gross investment was estimated at £E203·9 m. or
16·5 per cent of GNP;[2] this was subdivided into: fixed capital formation
in government administration 80·1 m., fixed capital formation in business
sector 103·7 m., increase in stocks 11·1 m., and investment in household
sector 9·0 m. Investment was financed as follows: savings of business
sector £E111·1 m., savings of family sector 23·6 m., savings of government administration 42·3 m., and external financing (equal to the deficit
in the balance of payments) 22·9 m. or 11·4 per cent of the total[3]. The
1960/1 estimate puts total gross investment at £E305·4 m., or 20·3 per
cent of GNP; external financing was 58·5 m.[4]

[1] NPC, Memo. no. 451.

[2] The balance consisted of: family consumption £E975 m. and consumption in
government administration 57·9 m.

[3] *Cadre du Plan*, pp. 169–70. The last figure seems difficult to accept. The deficit
in current transactions was £E36·0 m. in 1959 and 23·6 m. in 1960 (see Table 31,
p. 232) or an average of 29·8 m. It also underestimates the foreign contribution in
another important way. In 1959–60 US aid alone was running at about $120 m.
a year, or some £E40 m., and the resale by the Egyptian government of the grains
and other goods provided by the USA generated large counterpart funds which
have been re-lent for development. To this should be added the considerable Soviet
and other aid (see Table 32, p. 240). Other figures which may be questioned are
those on savings; the 1962/3 budget estimates put total savings in 1959/60 at only
£E132·5 m. (see *al-Ahram*, 30 June 1962).

[4] *Detailed Plan*, p. 244.

# Appendix III

## DATA ON MAIN BRANCHES OF EGYPTIAN INDUSTRY

THE following pages list the main facts regarding capital, employment, equipment, and output in the principal industries, as well as plans for expansion. They are based mainly on the Egyptian Federation of Industries *Yearbook 1961* (in Ar.) and their monthly review *L'Égypte industrielle*, on the Five-Year Plan, and on press items.

### Fuel and Power

*Coal.* Very recently coal deposits, estimated at 80 million tons, were discovered at a depth of 500 metres at Uyun Musa, close to Suez. The coal has a low heat and high gas content, but is judged to be suitable for steam engines, for reduction, and for the generation of various gases and chemicals. It has been decided to invest £E4·7 million in developing the fields and to start production soon.[1]

*Petroleum.* Egyptian oilfields do not form part of the Persian Gulf deposits and proven reserves are only 50 million tons, or about 0·2 per cent of the world total. Although Egypt was the first Middle Eastern country to start extracting oil, in 1911, it is still a minor producer and its cumulative output, some 45 million tons up to 1961, is below one year's production in Kuwait, Saudi Arabia, Iran, or Iraq.[2] Output was for long concentrated on Gemsa and Ghardaqa, on the Red Sea coast, but in 1938 Ras Gharib, on the Gulf of Suez, was tapped and made it possible to raise production from 380,000 tons in 1937 to 1,282,000 in 1946. In the post-war period attention shifted to the west coast of Sinai, where the fields of Sudr, Asl, Wadi al-Firan and Balaim were discovered; this made it possible to raise output to 2,434,000 tons in 1950 and, after a drop in the middle 1950's, to 3,800,000 in 1961. In all, fifteen fields have so far been discovered of which two are exhausted and two others have not yet been brought into production.

Until very recently, production was carried out exclusively, and refining and marketing mainly, by foreign companies; of these the oldest and most important was Anglo-Egyptian Oilfields, an affiliate of Shell, which in 1944 concluded an agreement with Socony for joint operations.[3] In 1948 Law No. 136, on Mining and Quarrying, was

---

[1] *al-Ahram*, 4 & 9 Nov. 1961.

[2] For more details see S. H. Longrigg, *Oil in the Middle East* (1961); *al-Betrol fi'l-gumhuria al-arabia al-muttahida*, 1960; *al-Ahram al-iqtisadi*, spec. issue on petroleum, 15 Oct. 1961, & *Petroleum Press Service*, Jan. 1962.

[3] Anglo-Egyptian Oilfields was sequestrated in 1956 but subsequently released. In 1961, under Law No. 118, the government acquired half of the privately owned shares, raising its own share to 55 per cent of the capital of £E5,523,000. The company's name was changed to Nasr Company for Exploitation of Oilfields.

enacted which, among other inconveniences, refused to guarantee subsequent development rights to companies which had been granted
prospecting permits. As a result Standard Oil (New Jersey) relinquished
its concession, after having spent $12·3 million between 1937 and 1949[1]
and discovered Wadi al-Firan. The law was amended in 1953. Another
concession, acquired by Conorada in the Western Desert, was abandoned
in 1958 after an expenditure of $35 m. had led to no results. On the other
hand the concession taken over in 1957 by the Compagnie Orientale des
Pétroles d'Égypte is still in effect; by July 1961 the government had
acquired a 50 per cent interest in the company under Law No. 118
and the balance belonged to AGIP, an affiliate of the Italian Ente Nazionale
Idrocarburi (ENI); the total capital is £E6 m., and profits are shared with
the government under a complicated formula.[2] The company discovered
both Balaim and Rudais fields and a formation offshore Balaim. It remains
to add that, recently, bids have been put by American firms for concessions in the Western Desert and that an agreement was signed under
which ENI acquired concessions in the northern Delta and along the Red
Sea coast and will in return extend a credit for up to $50 m., for drilling
equipment and petrochemical plants, to be repaid by Egypt in $6\frac{1}{2}$ years
at 4 per cent interest. All exploration expenses will be met by ENI;
development costs will presumably be shared by the government
which will take 75 per cent of profits, a pattern set by ENI in Iran and
elsewhere.[3]

As regards Egyptian organizations engaged in petroleum, there is the
General Petroleum Organization, founded in 1956, which supervises the
industry and operates the government refinery and the pipelines (see
above, p. 206), and the General Petroleum Company, which was founded
by the Economic Development Organization in 1957 with a capital raised
to £E6 m. by 1961; the latter has discovered two fields, at Bakr and
Karim, and has started production.

The Petroleum Co-operative Society, founded in 1934, and whose
capital has been raised to £E8·1 m., now accounts for over a third of
total marketing of products, the balance being carried out by Shell,
Mobil Oil (capital 3 m.) and, for certain products, Caltex.

Refining is undertaken in three plants: the government refinery in
Suez, founded in 1921 and expanded by successive steps to 1·2 m. tons a year;
the Nasr (formerly Anglo-Egyptian Oilfields) refinery in Suez, founded
in 1912 and successively raised to 3·5 m. tons; and that of the Société
Égyptienne pour le Raffinage et le Commerce du Pétrole in Alexandria
(whose capital of £E1·5 m. is 73 per cent government owned with the
balance belonging mainly to Texas Oil), founded in 1955 with a capacity
of 250,000 tons which is being raised to 1,250,000. The nature of Egyptian
crude makes it necessary to import over 2 m. tons, to produce the required

[1] Leonard M. Fanning, *Foreign Oil and the Free World* (NY, 1954), p. 15.
[2] See *al-Ahram al-iqtisadi*, 15 Oct. 1961.          [3] *al-Ahram*, 15 Nov. 1961.

lighter and middle products, leaving nearly a million tons of crude for export. Output of refined products, 4·47 m. tons in 1960, almost covered local consumption of 4·75 m.[1] The range of products has been extended and a contract was signed in 1961, with an Italian firm, for the erection of a delayed coker for extracting middle distillates, a catalytic reformer, a sulphur recovery unit, and a dodecylbenzine unit for producing detergents at a total cost of £E9 m.

Petroleum now plays a significant part in the Egyptian economy. Its contribution to GNP has been estimated at £E24 m. and it employs 19,000 persons in its various stages. The Five-Year Plan provides for an expenditure of £E126 m.,[2] to increase production to nearly 7 m. tons and refining to 6·5 m., to extend pipelines and storage, and to develop the petrochemical industry.

*Electricity*. Until very recently practically all Egypt's electricity was thermic. Output rose rapidly from 288 m. kwh. in 1938 to 992 in 1952 and 2,125 in 1959. In 1960 the generation of hydro-electricity from the Aswan dam, which has a capacity of 345,000 kw. and cost about £E28 m., started and by 1961 total production had risen to an estimated 4,800 m. kwh., of which industry absorbed 64 per cent. Egypt's per-capita annual consumption has thus risen to about 180 kwh, compared with 50 as late as 1951. This increase has come about, in addition to the Aswan scheme, by a rise in thermic capacity from 325,000 h.p. in 1948 (of which the government owned 75,000, industrial companies 90,000, and public utilities 160,000) to 1,060,000 in 1959 (government 640,000, industry 213,000, and utilities 207,000); investments in 1954–9 totalled £E40 m., of which the government contributed 38 m.[3]

Consumption in 1964 is estimated at 7,400 m. kwh., of which presently existing industries will absorb 1,400 m., future industries 4,000, irrigation and drainage 230 m., water and sewerage 220 m., and lighting and household 700 m. The estimated output of Aswan dam is put at 2,300 m. kwh., and its unit cost at 0·7 m/m; the balance will come from thermic plants at an estimated unit cost of 4·6 m/m.[4] The High Dam, with an installed capacity of 2·1 m. kw. costing some £E100 m., will start generating electricity in 1967 and by 1972 it is hoped to produce 10,000 m. kwh.; judging from the anticipated revenue, it is planned to sell the current at 10 m/m per kwh. (see above, p. 130).

The electricity generated at Aswan is being used to make fertilizers and part of that of the High Dam will also be absorbed locally but the bulk is to be transmitted to the Delta over lines more than 1,000 km. long and estimated to cost some £E50 m.[5] In the meantime, the needs of northern Egypt are to be met by expanding thermic capacity, including a station

[1] Net foreign exchange disbursements on petroleum in 1960 were almost £E17 m.; by 1964, however, it is hoped that needs and availabilities will be nearly in balance (*Petroleum Press Service*, Jan. 1962).     [2] *al-Betrol*, p. 7.
[3] NPC, Memo. no. 475.     [4] Ibid. Memo. no. 416.     [5] *al-Ahram*, 9 Mar. 1962.

west of Cairo with a capacity of 240,000 kw., the largest in Egypt.[1] An atomic power station is also to be built at a cost of £E20 m.[2] A more important scheme, which has been under study for over thirty years and is likely to be implemented in the near future is that of the Qattara depression, 200 km. west of the Delta and 50 metres below sea level. Hydro-electricity could be generated by drawing in sea-water, across 70 km. Various schemes envisage a capacity ranging from 64,000 to 200,000 kw. at costs of £E45–210 m.; the most recent one estimates that electricity can be delivered in the Delta at 1·7 m/m per kwh., compared with present thermic costs of 6–9 m/m.[3]

## Mining and Quarrying [4]

Egypt does not seem to be particularly rich in minerals, but it should be remembered that only a small fraction of the country has been adequately surveyed. In the post-war period development was held up by the 1948 Mining Law, by political uncertainty and administrative red tape and by lack of water and inadequate transport. Some of these handicaps still exist, but in recent years the government has intensified prospecting, including aeromagnetic and photomapping surveys with Soviet help, and worth-while results have been achieved. The Five-Year Plan provides for an expenditure of £E4·3 m. for exploration and 34·4 m. for expansion of output. Total production of mining in 1960 was £E6·1 m. and of quarrying 1·7 m., or almost double the 1951 total; by 1964 a rise to £E16·1 and 3·0 m. respectively is planned. At present 40 enterprises employing 6,700 persons are engaged in mining and quarrying.

Deposits of iron ore were discovered in the 1930's some 50 km. from the Nile near Aswan. They lie close to the surface but consist of thin, separated layers. The iron-ore content averages 40 per cent iron and contains almost no sulphur and little silica and phosphorous oxide. The deposits have been estimated at nearly 200 million tons. Production, which is entirely for local use, started in 1955, rose to 240,000 tons in 1960 and was expected to reach 420,000 in 1961. More recently attention has turned to the deposits, consisting mainly of hematite and limonite, of Bahria oasis, which have been known since before the First World War; reserves are estimated at 150 m. tons of which 50 m. are superior to those of Aswan[5] and it is planned to connect the oasis to Qus, by a railway costing £E8 m., to invest a further 7 m. for developing the fields, and to start exploitation in the near future.[6] Substantial deposits have also been located in the

[1] *al-Ahram*, 8 Mar. 1962. A grid is also planned to cover the Delta and Canal Zone, which consume the bulk of Egypt's electricity (NPC, Memo. no. 475).

[2] *L'Orient*, 20 Jan. 1962.

[3] Muh. Kamal Gawhar, *Tariqa jadida li tawlid al-kahraba min munkhafad Qattara* (Dec. 1959).

[4] For a useful though slightly out of date account, with good maps, see Platt & Hefny, pp. 261–85.     [5] *al-Ahram*, 5 Feb. 1962.     [6] Ibid. 4 Nov. 1961.

Eastern Desert, in the regions of Qusair, Safaga, and other places, but their iron content seems to be low. The Plan provides for further exploration, for an increase in the annual output of the Aswan mines to 550,000 tons, for the concentration of Aswan ore from 42 to 49 per cent, and for the extraction of iron in the Eastern Desert.

Two major phosphate deposits, with a tricalcic content of 60–70 per cent, one near Isna and the other near Safaga, have been worked since before the First World War; in the early 1950's they were estimated at 180 m. tons. Further deposits of 150 m. tons have been discovered between Dakhla and Kharga oases,[1] but their content is only 45–50 per cent, and other reserves have been found in Sinai. Since about half the total output is exported, the balance being converted into superphosphates, production fluctuates; the 1960 figure was 570,000 tons, compared with 629,000 in 1959, but the trend is upward. Further expansion is planned.

Manganese is mined in Sinai and in the Eastern Desert; total deposits were estimated at 12 m. tons in the early 1950's but since then the figure has been raised, to perhaps as much as 20 m. tons; the deposits contain both high-grade (42 per cent) and low-grade (22–24 per cent) ores. The damage caused to the mines during the Sinai campaign has been repaired and output rose to 276,000 tons in 1960, a figure slightly below the 1953 peak. Much development is being undertaken and it is planned both to increase total output and to concentrate some of the ore for use in local industry; at present all output is exported.

Salt is produced from Mediterranean salines. Formerly over half the output was exported to the Far East but this has greatly declined and as a result production fell from a peak of 607,000 tons in 1951 to about 500,000 in 1960.

Other minerals produced on a significant scale, with the latest production figure, in tons, are: sulphur 18,000; ilmenite 12,000, to be raised to 40,000 in the near future; kaolin 20,000; asbestos 450; and natron 1,500. Production of gold has greatly fallen off, from 17,000 troy oz. in 1952 to 1,000 in 1960. Plans are under way to exploit copper, zinc and the uranium recently discovered in Fayyum.[2] Quarrying is carried out on a large scale.[3]

*Textiles*

As in other newly industrialized countries textiles, and in particular cotton textiles, are the most important branch of industry. Also as in other countries, weaving was developed before spinning and for quite a long time Egypt had to import a large part of its yarn, but now it is

---

[1] Ibid. 23 Nov. 1961.    [2] Ibid. 22 Mar. 1962.
[3] The latest production figures, in cubic metres are: limestone, used for cement and fertilizers, 3,010,000; sand, for bricks, 1,200,000; basalt, for road construction, 320,000; gypsum 400,000; and glass sand 31,000.

self-sufficient in all stages of production. The Five-Year Plan provides for a total investment of £E48·6 m. in the industry.

*Cotton.* The spinning industry consists of 1,300,000 spindles,[1] against 500,000 in 1950 and 250,000 before the war, and output has risen correspondingly. The fact that local firms were compelled to use high-quality and expensive Egyptian cotton forced them to shift to finer counts, and the proportion of low counts (below 24) fell from 79 per cent in 1954 to 67 per cent in 1960;[2] the largest firm is actually producing counts of up to 190 and is aiming at 240.[3] Helped by a government subsidy, export of yarn has increased considerably and in 1960 stood at 21,000 tons, Western Europe being the main customer.

The weaving industry had 22,000 looms in 1960, representing a 50 per cent increase over 1950, and here too output has increased correspondingly. Two-thirds of production is accounted for by large and well equipped firms and one-third by medium and small factories as well as by handlooms, of which there may still be some 50,000. All the finishing processes are carried out in Egypt and in recent years dyeing and designing greatly improved and have reached a very high standard. Exports of fabrics, which also receive a subsidy, rose to 14,000 tons, worth £E7·9 m. in 1960; by far the leading buyer was the United States.

The Five-Year Plan provides for an investment of £E23·2 m. in spinning, to raise capacity by 330,000 spindles, and 3·6 m. in weaving; output of fabrics is to rise to 79,000 tons by 1965.

*Man-made fibres.* In 1960 output of all kinds of artificial silk yarns and staples aggregated 13,500 tons, while nylon yarn and thread amounted to 240 tons; production is based on imported pulp. The number of reels in the industry is 56,000. The Plan envisages an investment of some £E2·5 m. in the various branches of reeling.

The weaving of rayon is carried out on some 12,000 looms. Output in 1960 amounted to 8,700 tons and exports, again helped by a subsidy, to 1,300 tons, worth £E1·1 m.; the main customers were the Sudan and Saudi Arabia. Employment in all branches was over 15,000.

*Wool.* The government has gradually shut out all imports of woollens and in 1960 the industry met the whole of domestic consumption. Output amounted to 4,000 tons of yarn and 2,750 tons of cloth; all of this was based on imported wool.[4] The quality of woollens has greatly improved

---

[1] *Akher Saa*, spec. issue on industry, 1961.

[2] At the end of 1961, however, the government decided to import American cotton to meet the bulk of domestic consumption, reserving Egyptian cotton for finer products and releasing £E10 m. of Ashmuni for export. There is no doubt that this decision, which has been greatly overdue, is a wise one.

[3] *al-Ahram*, 3 Dec. 1961.

[4] In addition domestic wool was used to produce 2,500 tons of blankets and a substantial number of rugs. In the early 1950's there were 1,000 looms for carpets and 2,000 for cheap rugs, with a capacity of 60,000 and 450,000 sq. metres respectively.

during the last twenty years but they are still distinctly inferior to, as well as more expensive than, imported cloth.

*Other textile products.* The hosiery and knitwear industry has a capital of some £E3 m., a labour force of nearly 6,000, and an equipment of some 900 machines for hosiery and 1,200 for underwear, with a total capacity of some 15,000 tons; output in 1960 amounted to 4·8 m. dozen, weighing 8,100 tons, and met the bulk of domestic consumption. Linen is made from local flax; output in 1960 amounted to 1,300 tons of yarn and 1,250,000 metres of cloth. The jute industry, which relies entirely on imported jute, has made very rapid progress and in 1960 turned out 11,300 tons of gunnies, hessians, and other products. The ready-made clothing industry, which consists of a few dozen large factories and over 100 small ones, meets the bulk of local demand.

## Food, Beverages, & Tobacco

Only a brief survey of the leading branches of this industry, the second most important in Egypt, will be attempted; under the Plan a total of £E31·7 m. is to be invested in it.

The oldest and largest branch is the crushing and refining of sugar-cane, with a capital of £E11 m. and a labour force of 11,000–16,000 workers. Until recently, a private monopoly operated four mills and one refinery, the third largest in the world. Since the sugar content of Egyptian raw sugar is higher than that of some other varieties, some 20,000 tons are imported and used to meet part of local needs, leaving some Egyptian raw sugar available for refining and export.[1] Domestic sales have risen very rapidly, owing to both population growth and higher per-capita consumption, and it is planned to set up a new crushing mill with an annual capacity of 40,000 tons—to be increased eventually to 80,000—at a cost of £E8·1 m., and to raise the daily capacity of the refinery by 1,200 tons. Longer-term plans envisage a tripling of total output, to 1 m. tons a year, with a corresponding increase in sugar plantations.[2] It may be added that the industry is efficient, although costs are raised by the high price of sugar-cane. Confectionery and chocolate production was carried on in 1960 by 60 firms, with a combined capital of £E5 m.; output amounted to 57,000 tons, showing no increase in the course of the 1950's.

Cereals milling and rice bleaching are carried on in both modern factories and, to a decreasing extent, in primitive handmills; the whole industry was nationalized early in 1962. Output of macaroni, biscuits and similar products nearly doubled during the last decade, reaching 33,000 tons in 1960 and meeting the whole of local demand; however, production is still far below capacity. Production of starch, from maize and rice, has considerably expanded and amounted to 9,000 tons in 1960; that of glucose has increased several-fold, to 26,000 tons.

[1] Exports amounted to 7,000 tons in 1959 and 48,000 in 1960, almost wholly to the Sudan.                                    [2] *al-Ahram*, 2 Mar. 1962.

The canning, freezing, and dehydrating food industry consisted in 1960 of 74 establishments with a capital of £E6·1 m. and a labour force of 8,600. This industry had expanded greatly during the Second World War and suffered badly from outside competition in the late 1940's. In recent years, however, it has both widened its range, to include fruits, fish and shrimps, and increased its output; in 1960 production of all kinds amounted to over 9,000 tons. Nearly half of this consisted of dehydrated onions and garlic, which are produced entirely for export. The capacity of refrigerators was 98,000 cubic metres in 1960, or twice the 1950 figure.

Vegetable oils are produced by over 30 factories employing some 8,000 workers; in some equipment is very modern and efficient. Cotton-seed oil production is now a little over 100,000 tons while linseed and other oils provide another 5,000 tons. The oil is used partly for cooking and partly for soap-making and the seed-cake for fodder.

The milk-products industry still leaves much to be desired in the way of purity and cleanliness, but good progress has been made in certain branches. Of the total milk output of a little over 1 m. tons, 10 per cent is consumed in liquid form and 50 per cent is converted into butter and 40 per cent into cheese. Only 8,500 tons of milk were pasteurized in 1960, but under the Plan £E4·2 m. are to be spent on milk-processing and pasteurization plants.

Beer is produced in two breweries, with a capital of £E500,000 and a labour force of 500. Output reached a peak of 39 m. litres in 1945, owing to the presence of the Allied troops in Egypt, but thereafter dropped to about a quarter of this figure and in 1960 stood at 11 m. Local barley is used, but part of the malt and all the hops are imported. Output of wine was 3·5 m. litres in 1960 and quality has greatly improved. Other alcoholic drinks amounted to 1·8 m. litres. Soft drinks are produced by 28 factories, with a capital of £E3·9 m., 2,800 workers, and an output of 400 m. bottles.

The tobacco industry consists of 19 firms, of which one accounts for nearly three-quarters of output. All the raw tobacco is imported, mainly from the Near East and Africa but to an increasing degree from the United States. Output in 1960 was 13,000 tons, which covered local consumption and, helped by a subsidy, made it possible to export a very small amount.

## Building Materials and Construction

The cement industry is favoured by the proximity of its basic raw materials, limestone and clay, to its main market, Cairo. It also has relatively cheap petroleum. Capacity has doubled since 1951, standing at 2·4 m. tons in 1960, and although consumption has also risen rapidly, to 1·4 m. tons in 1960, output has increased still more; consequently exports grew from 5,000 tons in 1952 to 650,000 in 1960, the main markets being the Persian Gulf, Saudi Arabia, Pakistan, and Burma. The range of products has also widened and now includes superconcrete, sulphate-resisting cement, white Portland cement, and iron cement, the last drawing on by-products of the steel mill at Helwan. The industry, which consists of four firms, has some of the largest machinery in the world and its costs are relatively low; thus it has been stated that local white cement is being sold at £E18 per ton, compared to import prices of £35–40.[1]

There is also a large output of cement products, such as pipes, electric transmission posts, telegraph and telephone standards, and cement bricks and tiles.

Output of gypsum has risen to 170,000 tons while that of bricks has remained for several years at 800 m. units and that of sand bricks has declined to 11 m. Refractory bricks are produced, for use in the steel, glass, cement, and other industries, but their quality is below that of imported products. The ceramics industry has also developed appreciably.

The glass industry, which contains both well-equipped and obsolete factories, produced 37,000 tons in 1960; of this 15,000 consisted of sheet glass and the balance of bottles, tumblers, and lamp glass. Costs are high, owing among other reasons to the fact that many raw materials are imported,[2] and imports of glassware still amount to 4,000 tons.

The wood-using industry, which consists of many small firms, has made some progress in recent years and, although all the raw material is imported, not only meets the bulk of local demand but exports a small amount of furniture to neighbouring countries.

The construction industry employs some 170,000 workers. Residential building was adversely affected by Law No. 344 of 1956, requiring permission for new building or repairs costing over £E5,000. In 1959 140,000 rooms were built, at an estimated cost of £E52 m. The Plan provides for the building of 100,000 popular houses, costing £E35 m., 50,000 middle-class houses, costing 40 m., and 17,500 high-income houses, costing 25 m.

### Chemicals

This is one of the most rapidly growing branches and the one which perhaps offers the greatest hopes for Egypt since most basic raw materials are available locally, the necessary skills are being acquired, and the demand for chemicals from industry, agriculture, and consumers is swiftly expanding. The Five-Year Plan provides for an investment of £E57·8 m. in the industries covered in this sub-section.

Production of basic chemicals has increased several-fold. Sulphuric acid is produced by three firms; output passed the 100,000-ton mark in 1960 and capacity is to be expanded by two-thirds, but consumption is rising and imports are still substantial, amounting to 45,000 tons in 1960. The capacity of the caustic-soda industry has been increased several-fold

---

[1] *al-Ahram al-iqtisadi*, 1 Aug. 1961.      [2] *Ég. indust.*, May 1958.

by the opening, in 1961, of a 20,000-ton plant; consumption is estimated at 40,000 tons; much chlorine is generated as a by-product and is being exported or absorbed by several industries.[1] Other basic chemicals include sodium and calcium hypochlorite, carbon dioxide, and sodium silicate, while gases produced include acetylene, oxygen, nitrogen, and carbon dioxide. Alcohol is manufactured from molasses; capacity is 22 m. litres and output in 1960 was 11 m.; a small amount is exported. The most ambitious project, scheduled to start production in 1962, is a £E5 m. plant at Helwan which will produce 350,000 tons of metallurgical coke, 13,000 tons of tar, 5,000 tons of ammonium sulphate, and other chemicals; the plant is to be expanded further in the future.[2]

Output of fertilizers has also risen several-fold and now meets half of consumption.[3] Superphosphates are produced by two firms, with a capital of £E2·1 m. and a labour force of 1,300; expansion of present plant and the establishment of a third firm is to raise capacity to 410,000 tons. Thomas phosphate is produced as a by-product of steel; output in 1960 was 21,000 tons and is due to rise to 50,000. Calcium nitrate, based on oil refinery gases, has been produced since 1951 in a factory in Suez with a capital of £E7 m. and a labour force of 1,700; output in 1960 was 255,000 tons. A plant with a capacity of 100,000 tons of ammonium sulphate is to be established near-by, with United States aid. An ammonium nitrate factory, with a capital of £E16 m. and a capacity of 370,000 tons of 20·5 per cent nitrogen, has started production at Aswan, using the electricity generated from the dam; costs are estimated at £E24 per ton, compared with import prices of £E28–36.[4]

The paper industry, which has been greatly expanded to meet the rapidly growing demand, consists of three large and five small plants; its capital is £E8 m. and its labour force 3,400. Capacity is 56,000 tons and in 1960 output was 49,000 and imports 100,000 tons. The types produced include cardboard, writing and printing paper, and cellophane; most of the pulp is imported and much use is also made of waste paper.[5]

Soap is manufactured by some 20 large and nearly 300 small firms with a combined capital of £E3 m. and a labour force of 4,000. Capacity is put at 200,000 tons but output, which meets local demand, has levelled off at 80,000. The bulk of the oil, as well as the other raw materials, is imported.

The most important firm in the rubber industry is a tyre-manufacturing plant, with a capital of £E2·5 m., established in 1954; output in 1960 was 280,000 outer and 200,000 inner tubes. The factory meets the greater part of local demand and has exported small quantities. Other firms produce pipes and various industrial and household articles. All the rubber is imported.

The leather industry consists of 170 tanneries, 130 shoe factories, 20

[1] *al-Ahram al-iqtisadi*, 1 Sept. 1961.    [2] Ibid. 15 Nov. 1961.
[3] For further details see NBE, *Econ. B.*, no. 4, 1961.    [4] Ibid.
[5] For further details see Little, *Opportunities for Ind. Dev.*, pp. 42–50.

factories for other leather goods, and a very large number of small work-shops. Output of tanned leather in 1960 was 9,000 tons and of shoes 10 m. pairs, to which should be added 4 m. pairs of rubber and canvas shoes.[1] The quality of many leather products is excellent but the industry continues to be handicapped by the poor quality of both local hides and those imported from the Sudan.

There are five match factories, with a capital of £E750,000 and a labour force of 1,100; output in 1960 was 25,000 m. units. The wood, phosphorus and potassium chlorate are imported.

The pharmaceuticals and cosmetics industry has made rapid progress, helped by strict control of imports and by the fact that packaging, which accounts for a large proportion of total cost, can be done more cheaply in Egypt. However, a study made in 1959 drew attention to the following factors which made for high costs: low utilization of capacity; excessive administrative, marketing, and advertising costs; and the presence of too many intermediaries between producers and consumers. It also stated that consumers had a marked preference for foreign pharmaceuticals.[2] The industry consists of 43 firms with 4,300 workers. So far, the bulk of materials used has been imported but the Plan provides for the setting up of a plant, with a capital of £E4·2 m., to produce penicillin, streptomycin, dextrane, sulfas, and salicylates and other products. In 1960, sales of local pharmaceuticals amounted to £E2·3 m. and imports to 3·9 m. Cosmetics meet the bulk of local consumption.

*Basic Metals*

The basic metals, metal-using, and equipment-making industries have developed very swiftly in the last fifteen, and more particularly in the last five, years. In 1960 the number of firms affiliated with the Chamber of Metal and Mechanical Industries was 275, their paid-up capital £E36 m., and their labour force 25,000. These figures exclude many small firms, as well as the Military Factories, which produce a wide range of goods for civilian consumption and whose sales amounted to £E7 m. in 1961.

Egypt started producing steel, from scrap, in 1949 and by 1956 output, from three firms, had risen to over 100,000 tons a year, at a cost competitive with imports. In 1958 the first integrated plant, set up by the government with the participation of Egyptian and German private capital, started production and in 1960 a second blast furnace went into operation. The capital of the company has been raised to £E19 m. and it employs 4,600 workers. Coke is imported, through Alexandria, and iron ore is carried from Aswan, nearly 1,000 km. away; owing to these high transport costs, to the relatively small scale of the plant, to operation below capacity (in 1960/1 the blast furnaces worked at 66 per cent of capacity), to the inexperience of management and workers, and to

---

[1] Some 80–90 per cent of the shoes were produced mechanically and the rest by hand (Min. of Ind., *al-Nahda al-Sinaia*, May 1959).     [2] Ibid.

inadequate use of by-products, costs of production are twice as high as those of imported goods and quality is inferior.[1] But it is planned to expand the capacity of the blast furnaces from 800 to 1,500 tons a day, to increase that of the rolling mills and install a stripmill, and to reduce costs by concentrating iron ore at Aswan, matting granulated ore, producing coke from imported coal, and substituting oil for some of the coal used in the furnaces.[2] In all, the Plan provides for an expenditure of £E46·9 m. on basic metals by 1965, by which time Egypt should be self-sufficient in steel products.

Output in 1960 was as follows: blast furnaces 140,000 tons, Thomas converters 92,000, and electric furnaces 24,000; in the rolling mills it was 123,000 for beams, 35,000 for sections, 26,000 for steel plates, and 9,000 for sheet steel. Imports of steel products amounted to 120,000 tons.

Output of ironware, mainly pipes, amounted to 50,000 tons in 1960. As for products made of non-ferrous metals, output was as follows: copper and brass 7,000 tons, lead 1,600 tons, and aluminium 700 tons.

*Mechanical Industries*

Several kinds of transport equipment are now being manufactured or assembled in Egypt. A Ford assembly plant has been operating since 1950, but its output declined from a few thousand units in the 1950's to only 730 in 1960. The manufacturing of the Egyptian Ramses car started in 1960 with 240 units and an output of 600 was scheduled for 1961; a Fiat plant is also due to start operations soon. Similarly 614 lorries and 253 buses were assembled in 1960, with 800 and 700 respectively anticipated for 1961, and 195 diesel engines were manufactured, with 1,200 scheduled for 1961. Other transport equipment included 500 railway freight wagons of 10–20 tons, with production of 30–40 ton wagons and passenger coaches scheduled to start in 1961; 4,000 bicycles, with 36,000 anticipated in 1961; and 2,000 tons of river craft. A tractor plant is under construction and the production of motor cycles is also envisaged. (For shipyards see above, p. 211.)

A wide variety of other metal products is also being produced. In 1960 15,000 refrigerators, 4,700 washing machines, 1,700 air-conditioners, and 3,000 sewing machines were made, the motors and some other components being imported. Other articles, with the 1960 output, were: metal furniture, 6,500 tons, with a small export surplus; 1,500 butagaz geysers, with 6,000 anticipated in 1961; 46,500 butagaz stoves; 22,500 butagaz cylinders; 138,000 metal barrels; tinplate boxes 10,000 tons; metal building materials such as locks and hinges 1,600 tons; springs 800 tons; spare parts for cars 600 tons; cutlery 80 tons; fire-extinguishers 155 tons; 1,250 pumps; and 150,000 kerosene stoves. The Plan provides

---

[1] *al-Ahram al-iqtisadi*, 15 Nov. 1961.

[2] *Akher Saa*, spec. issue on industries. For further details see Chbr. of Metallurg. & Mechan. Ind., *Iron & Steel Industries Fair* (in Ar. & Engl., 1961).

for the investment of £E52·9 m. in metal-using industries and those making machinery, transport, and other equipment.

## Electrical Equipment

With the spread of electrification, there has been an expansion of industries making electrical equipment.[1] In 1960 the following were produced: 5·6 m. bulbs, 50,000 electric meters, 1,500 tons of electric cables, 78,000 storage batteries, 3·4 m. dry batteries for torches, 20,000 dry batteries for transistors, 95,000 dry batteries for radios, 40,000 radio sets, and 24,000 transistors assembled from imported components, 2,700 electric heaters, 78 transformers with a capacity of 34,000 kva., and the above-mentioned refrigerators, washing machines, and air-conditioners. The Plan provides for the investment of £E4·5 m. in industries making or repairing electrical equipment.

## Cottage Industries

An attempt is being made to develop cottage industries by grouping farmers in producers' co-operatives, under the supervision of the General Producers' Co-operative Organization, but the Plan envisages a total expenditure of only £E1·9 m. for this purpose. By the end of 1961 the number of such co-operatives was 109, and it was planned to raise this figure to 130, with 13,000 members, by 1962.[2] Among the activities to be encouraged and supervised are handloom weaving, the dyeing of cloth, rugmaking, mats, various products made from palm-leaves, leather work, sewing and embroidery, and honey and milk products. Assistance in maintaining and improving tools is to be given to handicraftsmen in both towns and countryside. There is no doubt that a large export market for certain kinds of Egyptian handicrafts could be developed but several attempts to do so in the past have been defeated by administrative red tape.

[1] For further details see *Ég. indust.*, Mar. 1961.
[2] *al-Ahram*, 29 Oct. 1961.

# Select UAR Official Periodical Publications

*Note: Unless otherwise specified, the language is Arabic and the work is an annual publication.*

## GENERAL

*Official Journal* (daily).
*United Arab Republic Yearbook* (Ar., Eng.).
*United Arab Republic Pocket Yearbook* (Ar., Eng.).
*Draft of the Charter*, 21 May 1962 (Ar., Eng., Fr.).
Ministry of Treasury. *Exposé on the Budget* (Ar., Eng.).
Statistical Dept. *Annuaire statistique* (Ar., Fr.).
— *Pocket Statistical Yearbook* (Ar., Eng.).
— *Industrial and Commercial Census.*
National Planning Committee. *General Five-Year Plan* (Ar., Eng., Fr.).
— *Detailed Plan for 1960/1.*
Economic Organization. *Yearbook.*
Ministry of Public Works. *Technical Bulletin* (monthly).
— *Departmental Monthly Bulletin.*
Ministry of Supply. *Monthly Bulletin.*
Ministry of Economics. *Journal of Companies* (monthly).
Central Bank of Egypt. *Economic Review* (Ar., Eng., quarterly).
National Bank of Egypt. *Economic Bulletin* (Ar., Eng., quarterly).
Misr Bank. *Economic Review* (quarterly).
Bank of Alexandria. *Bulletin* (quarterly).
*The General Directory.*
*The Egyptian Directory.*

## POPULATION AND SOCIAL AFFAIRS

Dept. of Statistics. *Population Census.*
— *Health Statistics.*
— *Quarterly Bulletin of Births, Deaths, Infectious Diseases, Marriages and Divorces.*
— *General Statistics on Educational Institutions.*
Ministry of Health. *General Annual Report.*
Ministry of Education. *Statistics on Education.*
— *Administrative Statistics.*
— *Cultural Register.*
— *Results of Examinations and Fields Subsequently Entered by Graduates.*
— *Egyptian Cultural Bulletin.*

Ministry of Culture and Guidance. *Monthly Cultural Bulletin.*
— *The Arts.*
Higher Council for Sciences. *Report.*
Higher Council for Arts and Literature. *Annual Report.*
Higher Council for Youth Guidance. *Report of Council's Activities.*
*The Message of Science* (quarterly).
Ministry of Municipal and Rural Affairs. *Council of Municipal and Rural Affairs.*
Cairo University. *Yearly Almanac.*
Alexandria University. *University Publications* (monthly).
Ain Shams University. *Yearly Almanac.*
Fellah Dept. *Annual Report.*


## AGRICULTURE

Ministry of Agriculture. *Agricultural Census.*
— *Agricultural Yearbook.*
— *Agricultural Income.*
— *Production and Consumption of Foodstuffs.*
— *Agricultural Research* (6-monthly).
— *Agricultural Scientific Abstracts* (quarterly).
— *The Agricultural Review* (monthly).
— *Agricultural Guidance Bulletin* (monthly).
— *Monthly Bulletin of Agricultural Economics and Statistics.*
Ministry of Economics. *Cotton Bulletin* (fortnightly).
Ministry of Agrarian Reform. *The Agrarian Reform in /years/.*
Dept. of Statistics. *Monthly Bulletin of Agricultural and Economic Statistics.*
Crédit Foncier Égyptien. *Annual Report* (Ar., Fr.).
Egyptian Land Bank. *Annual Report* (Ar., Fr.).
Agricultural and Co-operative Credit Bank. *Annual Report* (Ar., Fr.).
— *Bulletin* (quarterly).
*Agricultural Science* (quarterly).
*Yearbook of Agricultural Science.*


## INDUSTRY

Ministry of Industry. *Monthly Bulletin.*
— *Industrial Renaissance* (quarterly).
— *Journal of Industrial Productivity* (quarterly).
Ministry of Economics. *Annual Report of Department of Industrial Property.*
Department of Statistics. *Census of Industrial Production* (quarterly).
— *Statistics of Employment, Wages and Working Hours.*
General Petroleum Organization. *Petroleum Bulletin* (monthly).
Survey Dept. *Report of Activities of Department.*

Industrial Bank. *Annual Report.*
— *Bulletin* (quarterly).
Federation of Industries. *Annual Report.*
— *Yearbook* (Ar., Fr.).
— *L'Égypte industrielle* (Ar., Fr., monthly).
Inst. of Building Research. *Annual Report.*
*Petroleum Journal* (monthly).
*Middle East Petroleum* (bi-monthly).


## TRANSPORT

Ministry of Communications. *Financial Report on State Railways.*
Egyptian State Railways. *Annual Report.*
Dept. of Roads and Land Transport. *Annual Report.*
Post Office Administration. *Report of Activities.*
Dept. of Statistics. *Annual Statistics on Movement of Shipping and Foreign Trade.*
Suez Canal Organization. *Suez Canal Report* (Ar., Eng.).
— *Monthly Bulletin* (Ar., Eng.).
Administration of Mixed Transport in Alexandria. *General Annual Statistics.*
*Arab Roads* (monthly).


## COMMERCE AND BALANCE OF PAYMENTS

Dept. of Statistics. *Yearbook of Foreign Trade* (Ar., Eng.).
— *Monthly Bulletin of Foreign Trade* (Ar., Eng.).
— *Monthly Abstract of Foreign Trade.*
Ministry of Economics. *Report on Egypt's Foreign Trade.*
— *Monthly Bulletin of Internal Trade.*
— *Journal of Commercial Names* (monthly).
Dept. of Customs. *Report on Foreign Trade.*
Dept. of Tourism. *Tourism Statistics.*
— *Information on Tourist Movements.*
— *Tourist Movements.*
— *Encouragement of Tourism in Egypt.*
Alexandria Chamber of Commerce. *Review of Alexandria Chamber* (monthly).
Cairo Chamber of Commerce. *Commercial Regulations* (fortnightly).


## FINANCE

Dept. of Insurance. *Annual Report on Insurance Activity in Egypt.*
Dept. of Insurance and Savings Funds. *Final Accounts and Annual Report.*
Post Office Administration. *Report on Post Office Savings Banks.*

Dept. of Statistics. *Statistics of Joint-Stock Companies.*
Central Bank of Egypt. *Annual Report* (Ar., Eng.).
National Bank of Egypt. *Annual Report* (Ar., Eng.).
Misr Bank. *Annual Report.*
Bank of Alexandria. *Annual Report.*
Bank of Cairo. *Annual Report.*
Inst. of Banking Studies. *Lectures* (Ar., Eng., Fr.).
*Egyptian Stock Exchange Yearbook* (Ar., Eng.).
*Stockholders' Yearbook: Egyptian Stock Exchange and Shares of Egyptian Companies.*
*Economics and Accountancy* (monthly).

## PUBLIC FINANCE

Ministry of Treasury. *National Budget.*
— *Budget of Unified Departments.*
— *Final Accounts.*
Audit Bureau. *Report of Bureau on Final Accounts.*
Dept. of Statistics. *Statistics of Officials and Employees in the Government and Public Organizations.*
Personnel Bureau. *Annual Report.*
— *Journal of Government Officials* (quarterly).
Alexandria Municipality. *Budget.*
Cairo Municipality. *Budget.*
*Customs and Economic Affairs.*
*Financial and Fiscal Legislation* (monthly).

# Index

*Printed by
Jarrold & Sons Ltd.,
Norwich, England*